Birgit Beumers is Reader in the Russian Department at Bristol University. Her publications include *Burnt by the Sun* (I.B.Tauris, 2000) and *Nikita Mikhalkov* (I.B.Tauris, 2004), *Pop Culture Russia!* and *A History of Russian Cinema*. She is editor of *Russia on Reels: The Russian Idea in Post-Soviet Cinema* (I.B.Tauris, 1999) and *The Cinema of Russia and the Former Soviet Union (24 Frames)*. She is also editor of the online journal *KinoKultura* and of *Studies in Russian and Soviet Cinema* and a member of the Editorial Advisory Board for the Tauris KINO Series.

Nancy Condee is Professor of Slavic Studies and member of the Film Studies Program at the University of Pittsburgh. Her publications include *The Imperial Trace: Recent Russian Cinema* as well as the edited and co-edited volumes *Soviet Hieroglyphics: Visual Culture in Late Twentieth-Century Russia*, and *Antinomies of Art and Culture: Modernity, Postmodernity, Contemporaneity*. She is Executive Producer for the CD-Rom database on Russian cinema, *Thaw Cinema*.

Published and forthcoming in KINO: The Russian and Soviet Cinema Series

Series Editor: Richard Taylor

Advisory Board: Birgit Beumers, Julian Graffy, Denise Youngblood

Alexander Medvedkin: kinofile Filmmakers' Companion
Emma Widdis

Central Asian Cinema: A Complete Companion
Edited by Michael Rouland and Gulnara Abikeyeva

Cinema and Soviet Society: From the Revolution to the Death of Stalin
Peter Kenez

The Cinema of Alexander Sokurov
Edited by Birgit Beumers and Nancy Condee

The Cinema of Tarkovsky: Labyrinths of Space and Time
Nariman Skakov

The Cinema of the New Russia
Birgit Beumers

Dziga Vertov: Defining Documentary Film
Jeremy Hicks

Eisenstein on the Audiovisual: The Montage of Music, Image
Robert Robertson

Film Propaganda: Soviet Russia and Nazi Germany (second, revised edition)
Richard Taylor

Forward Soviet!: History and Non-Fiction Film in the USSR
Graham Roberts

Real Images: Soviet Cinema and the Thaw
Josephine Woll

Russia on Reels: The Russian Idea in Post-Soviet Cinema
Edited by Birgit Beumers

Savage Junctures: Sergei Eisenstein and the Shape of Thinking
Anne Nesbet

Soviet Cinema: Politics and Persuasion under Stalin
Jamie Miller

The Stalinist Musical: Mass Entertainment and Soviet Cinema
Richard Taylor

Vsevolod Pudovkin: Classic Films of the Soviet Avant-Garde
Amy Sargeant

The Cinema of Alexander Sokurov

Edited by Birgit Beumers
and Nancy Condee

Published in 2011 by I.B.Tauris & Co Ltd
6 Salem Road, London W2 4BU
175 Fifth Avenue, New York NY 10010
www.ibtauris.com

Copyright Editorial Selection and Introduction © 2011 Birgit Beumers and Nancy Condee

Copyright Individual Chapters © 2011 José Alaniz, Birgit Beumers, Eva Binder, Robert Bird, Nancy Condee, Julian Graffy, Sabine Hänsgen, Jeremy Hicks, Stephen Hutchings, Mikhail Iampolski, Nariman Skakov, Denise J. Youngblood

The right of Birgit Beumers and Nancy Condee to be identified as the editors of this work has been asserted by them in accordance with the Copyright, Designs and Patent Act 1988.

All rights reserved. Except for brief quotations in a review, this book, or any part thereof, may not be reproduced, stored in or introduced into a retrieval system, or transmitted, in any form or by any means, electronic, mechanical, photocopying, recording or otherwise, without the prior written permission of the publisher.

ISBN 978 1 84885 343 0 (pb)
ISBN 978 1 84885 906 7 (hb)
eISBN 978 0 75569 803 5
ePDF 978 0 85772 073 3

A full CIP record for this book is available from the British Library
A full CIP record is available from the Library of Congress

Library of Congress catalog card Number: available

KINO: THE RUSSIAN CINEMA SERIES

GENERAL EDITOR'S PREFACE

Cinema has been the predominant art form of the first half of the twentieth century, at least in Europe and North America. Nowhere was this more apparent than in the former Soviet Union, where Lenin's remark that 'of all the arts, cinema is the most important' became a cliché and where cinema attendances were until recently still among the highest in the world. In the age of mass politics Soviet cinema developed from a fragile but effective tool to gain support among the overwhelmingly illiterate peasant masses in the civil war that followed the October 1917 Revolution, through a welter of experimentation, into a mass weapon of propaganda through the entertainment that shaped the public image of the Soviet Union – both at home and abroad for both elite and mass audiences – and latterly into an instrument to expose the weaknesses of the past and present in the twin process of *glasnost* and *perestroika*. Now the national cinemas of the successor republics to the old USSR are encountering the same bewildering array of problems, from the trivial to the terminal, as are all the other ex-Soviet institutions.

Cinema's central position in Russian and Soviet cultural history and its unique combination of mass medium, art form and entertainment industry, have made it a continuing battlefield for conflicts of broader ideological and artistic significance, not only for Russia and the Soviet Union, but also for the world outside. The debates that raged in the 1920s about the relative merits of documentary as opposed to fiction film, of cinema as opposed to theatre or painting, or of the proper role of cinema in the forging of post-Revolutionary Soviet culture and the shaping of the new Soviet man, have their echoes in current discussions about the role of cinema *vis-à-vis* other art forms in effecting the cultural and psychological revolution in human consciousness necessitated by the processes of economic and political transformation of the former Soviet Union into modern democratic and industrial societies and states governed by the rule of law. Cinema's central position has also made it a vital instrument for scrutinising the blank pages of Russian and Soviet history and enabling the present generation to come to terms with its own past.

This series of books intends to examine Russian, Soviet and ex-Soviet films in the context of Russian, Soviet and ex-Soviet cinemas, and Russian, Soviet and ex-Soviet cinemas in the context of the political history of Russia, the Soviet Union, the post-Soviet 'space' and the world at large. Within that framework the series, drawing its authors from both East and West, aims to cover a wide variety of topics and to employ a broad range of methodological approaches and presentational formats. Inevitably this will involve ploughing once again over old ground in order to re-examine received opinions, but it principally means increasing the breadth and depth of our knowledge, finding new answers to old questions and, above all, raising new questions for further enquiry and new areas for further research.

The continuing aim of this series is to situate Russian, Soviet and ex-Soviet cinema in its proper historical and aesthetic context, both as a major cultural force and as a crucible for experimentation that is of central significance to the development of world cinema culture. Books in the series strive to combine the best of scholarship, past, present and future, with a style of writing that is accessible to a broad readership, whether that readership's primary interest lies in cinema or in political history.

Richard Taylor
Swansea, Wales

CONTENTS

ix	List of Illustrations
xiii	Acknowledgements
xv	Note on Transliteration
xvii	Notes on Contributors

1		Introduction *Birgit Beumers and Nancy Condee*

Part I Documentary Beginnings

13	Chapter 1	Sokurov's Documentaries *Jeremy Hicks*
28	Chapter 2	Sokurov's Film Portraits *Eva Binder*
43	Chapter 3	Sokurov's Cinematic Minimalism *Sabine Hänsgen*

Part II Borderlines: Geographical, Literary and Cinematic

59	Chapter 4	Intertextual Visions of the Potudan *Nariman Skakov*
74	Chapter 5	Living and Dying in Sokurov's Border Zones: *Days of Eclipse* *Julian Graffy*
90	Chapter 6	Medium Intimacy *Robert Bird*

Part III Intimate Encounters

109	Chapter 7	Truncated Families and Absolute Intimacy *Mikhail Iampolski*
122	Chapter 8	A Day in the Life: Historical Representation in Sokurov's 'Power' Tetralogy *Denise J. Youngblood*

138	Chapter 9	History, Alienation and the (Failed) Cinema of Embodiment: Sokurov's Tetralogy *Stephen Hutchings*

Part IV Remapping the Empire

155	Chapter 10	Crowd Control: Anxiety of Effluence in Sokurov's *Russian Ark* *José Alaniz*
176	Chapter 11	And the Ark Sails on... *Birgit Beumers*
188	Chapter 12	Endstate and Allegory *Nancy Condee*

Part V Russian Responses

203   Script-Sound-Editing

203   1. Yuri Arabov: The Director Becomes the Author
206   2. Vladimir Persov: This is a Process
212   3. Leda Semenova: Montage is the Final Approximation to the Idea

216   Film Reviews

216   4. Oleg Kovalov: We in *The Lonely Voice*
220   5. Maya Turovskaya: 'How is it with me when every noise appals me? What hands are here?'
223   6. Petr Bagrov: On Music – However Strange

226   The Oeuvre

226   7. Sergei Dobrotvorsky: The City and the House
233   8. Mikhail Trofimenkov: Sokurov in the Struggle with Reality
237   9. Andrei Plakhov: Rulers and Tyrants

245   Filmography

253   Bibliography

257   Index

ILLUSTRATIONS

The editors would like to thank Liubov Arkus and Vasili Stepanov of the journal and publishing house *Seans*, St Petersburg for their generosity and support throughout this project, and for making available numerous stills for this publication: unless otherwise indicated, images are from the *Seans* collection.

Page　　　　　　　　**Introduction**

3　　Alexander Sokurov and the actress Cécile Zervudacki during the filming of *Save and Protect*, 1988
4　　Alexander Sokurov and Alexei Ananishnov during the filming of *Days of Eclipse*
7　　Alexander Sokurov during the filming of *The Sun*

Page　　　　　　　　**Chapter 1**

17　　Still from *Maria*
22　　Still from *Spiritual Voices*

Page　　　　　　　　**Chapter 2**

29　　Still from *Maria*
34　　Still from *Soviet Elegy*: Yeltsin
38　　Still from *A Humble Life*

Page　　　　　　　　**Chapter 3**

45　　Still from *Spiritual Voices*
47　　Still from *Evening Sacrifice*
51　　Still from *Mother and Son*

Page　　　　　　　　**Chapter 4**

63　　Still from *Lonely Voice of Man*. The Chronicle. From the author's collection
67　　Still from *Lonely Voice of Man*. Liuba and the Photographs. From the author's collection
69　　Still from *Lonely Voice of Man*. The Wood. From the author's collection

Page　　　　　　　　**Chapter 5**

76　　Still from *Days of Eclipse*
79　　Still from *Days of Eclipse*
84　　Still from *Days of Eclipse*

Page	Chapter 6
93	Still from *The Lonely Voice of Man*
97	Still from *The Lonely Voice of Man*

Page	Chapter 7
110	Still from *Alexandra*. Courtesy of ProLine Production
113	Still from *Second Circle*
115	Still from *Save and Protect*
118	Still from *Father and Son*

Page	Chapter 8
124	Still from *Moloch*: The dinner scene
128	Still from *Taurus*: Lenin and Krupskaya. Courtesy of *Iskusstvo kino*
130	Still from *The Sun*: Hirohito with one of his objects of study. Courtesy of Artificial Eye
132	Still from *The Sun*: Hirohito during the dinner with MacArthur. Courtesy of Artificial Eye

Page	Chapter 9
141	Still from *Moloch*: Hitler in the car
143	Still from *Moloch*: Eva Braun and Hitler *en plein air*
146	Still from *Taurus*: Lenin
150	Still from *The Sun*: Hirohito and MacArthur. Courtesy of Artificial Eye

Page	Chapter 10
159	Still from *Evening Sacrifice*: The crowd
161	Still from *Russian Ark*: Gerghiev conducting the orchestra
165	Still from *Russian Ark*: The Ball
170	Still from *Russian Ark*: The Guests leaving the Ball

Page	Chapter 11
178	Still from *Russian Ark*: Custine enters the Raphael Loggias
182	Still from *Russian Ark*: Custine with Khmelnitsky and Yeliseev before the Tintoretto painting
186	Still from *Russian Ark*: The view onto the Neva at the film's end

Page	Chapter 12
190	Still from *Alexandra*: Alexandra Nikolaevna. Courtesy of ProLine Production

193   Still from *Alexandra*: Alexandra Nikolaevna and Denis. Courtesy of ProLine Production
195   Still from *Alexandra*: Malika. Courtesy of ProLine Production

Page	Part V
204	Still from *Second Circle*
221	Still from *Sonata for Hitler*
222	Still from *Sonata for Hitler*
227	Still from *Moscow Elegy*
231	Still from *Save and Protect*

ACKNOWLEDGEMENTS

We would like to thank first and foremost Liubov Arkus and her team at *Seans* for their unwavering support, for granting permission to translate the texts in Section five and for assisting us with illustrations: without them, much would be missing in this volume. We also thank Liudmila Mishunina at *Iskusstvo kino* for supplying images. We are indebted to Richard Taylor, who is not only a generous and talented translator, but also a series editor whom one just has to look up to. Philippa Brewster at I.B.Tauris is the most patient and understanding editor one could wish for. Our institutions should also be thanked: the Arts Faculty Research Fund at Bristol University has supported Birgit Beumers by funding research in Moscow and St Petersburg; Nancy Condee would like to thank the Russian and East European Studies Center at the University of Pittsburgh, the British Academy, and St Antony's at Oxford for support and work conditions that contributed to the research. Both editors thank Kinotavr Film Festival for their generosity in providing us with the opportunity to realise this project.

NOTE ON TRANSLITERATION

Transliteration from the Cyrillic to the Latin alphabet is a perennial problem for writers on Russian subjects. We have opted for a dual system: in the text we use the Library of Congress system (without diacritics), but we have broken from this system (a) when a Russian name has a clear English version (e.g. Maria instead of Mariia, Alexander instead of Aleksandr); (b) when a Russian name has an accepted English spelling, or when Russian names are of Germanic origin (e.g. Yeltsin instead of Eltsin; Eisenstein instead of Eizenshtein); (c) when a Russian surname ends in -ii or -yi this is replaced by a single -y (e.g. Dostoevsky instead of Dostoevskii), and all Christian names end in a single -i; (d) when 'ia' or 'iu' are voiced (at the beginning of a word and when preceded by a vowel) they are rendered as 'ya' or 'yu' (e.g. Daneliya, Yuri, Ilya) – with the exception of the name Asya to avoid confusion with the continent, Asia. The name Iampolski is preserved in the way the author spells his name in English-language publications, but for Russian publications we use, of course, the transliterated version; and we differentiate between the Soviet name of the town Nizhny Novgorod, Gorki, and the writer Maxim Gorky. In the scholarly apparatus we have adhered to the Library of Congress system (with diacritics) for the specialist.

NOTES ON CONTRIBUTORS

José Alaniz is Associate Professor in the Departments of Slavic Languages and Literatures and Comparative Literature at the University of Washington, Seattle. His research interests include post-Soviet Russian culture, death and dying, disability, cinema, eco-criticism and comics. His work has appeared in scholarly journals; his first book, *Komiks: Comic Art in Russia* was published in 2010. His current projects include a history of Czech comics and a study of disability, death and dying in the American superhero comics genre.

Birgit Beumers is Reader in the Russian Department at Bristol University. She specialises on contemporary Russian culture, and has published widely on cinema and theatre. Her most recent publications include *A History of Russian Cinema* (2009) and, with Mark Lipovetsky, *Performing Violence* (2009), and she has compiled the *Directory of World Cinema: Russia* (2010). She is editor of the online quarterly *KinoKultura* and of the scholarly journal *Studies in Russian and Soviet Cinema*.

Eva Binder has taught at the Department of Slavonic Studies at the University of Innsbruck since 1999, having completed her studies in English and Russian philology in Innsbruck and Moscow. Her current field of research is twentieth-century Russian culture, with a focus on film, media and cultural studies. She has published widely on various aspects of Soviet and Russian cinema and visual culture.

Robert Bird is Associate Professor in the Department of Slavic Languages and Literatures, Cinema and Media Studies at the University of Chicago. His main area of interest is the aesthetic practice and theory of Russian modernism. He is also the author of two books on Andrei Tarkovsky: *Andrei Rublev* (2004) and *Andrei Tarkovsky: Elements of Cinema* (2008). His works in progress include a biography of Dostoevsky.

Nancy Condee is Professor of Slavic Studies and member of the Film Studies Program at the University of Pittsburgh. Her publications include *Imperial Trace: Recent Russian Cinema* (2009) as well as the edited volumes *Soviet Hieroglyphics: Visual Culture in Late 20c. Russia* (1995); *Endquote: Sots-Art Literature and Soviet Grand Style* (with M. Balina and E. Dobrenko, 2000); and *Antinomies of Art and Culture: Modernity, Postmodernity, Contemporaneity* (with T. Smith and O. Enwezor, 2008).

Julian Graffy is Professor of Russian Literature and Cinema at the School of Slavonic and East European Studies, University College London, where he has worked since 1976. He is the author of *Gogol's The Overcoat*, 2000, *Bed and Sofa: The Film Companion*, 2001, *Chapaev: The Film Companion*, 2010, and several articles on Russian literature and film. He is currently researching a study of the representation of foreign characters in Russian film.

Sabine Hänsgen studied Slavic literature, history and art history at the University of Bochum. She is currently a researcher at the Freie Universität Berlin. Among her publications are: *Moskau, Moskau: Videostücke* (1987); *Präprintium. Moskauer Bücher aus dem Samizdat* (1998, as Sascha Wonders); *Sovetskaia vlast' i media* (2006, edited with Hans Günther); *Der gewöhnliche Faschismus. Ein Werkbuch zum Film von Michail Romm* (2009, edited with Wolfgang Beilenhoff and Maja Turowskaja).

Jeremy Hicks is a Senior Lecturer in Russian at Queen Mary University of London (UK) where he has taught courses on Russian film and literature since 1998. Russian and Soviet documentary film is his prime area of interest and expertise, and he is the author of *Dziga Vertov: Defining Documentary Film* (2007), and various articles on Russian and Soviet film, literature and journalism published in scholarly journals. He is presently completing a book about Soviet wartime film representations of Nazi genocide, entitled *Cinema's Black Book: Soviet Film and the Holocaust, 1938–46*.

Stephen Hutchings is Professor of Russian Studies at the University of Manchester. He is Director of Research at the School of Languages, Linguistics and Cultures, and is currently President of the British Association for Slavonic and East European Studies. His major publications include *Russian Modernism: The Transfiguration of the Everyday* (1997), *Russian Literary Culture in the Camera Age: The Word as Image* (2004), *Television and Culture under Putin: Remote Control* (with Natalya Rulyova; 2009), and *Russia and its Other(s) on Film: Screening Intercultural Dialogue* (2008).

Mikhail Iampolski is Professor of Comparative Literature and Russian Studies at New York University. Before moving to the USA in 1991 he has worked at the Institute of Film Studies and at the Institute of Philosophy of the Russian Academy of Science in Moscow. He has authored many books on film and history, and on the theory of representation.

Nariman Skakov is Assistant Professor of Slavic Languages and Literatures at Stanford University. His research interests include Andrei Platonov, literary theory, cinema and contemporary post-Soviet art. He has published an article in *Studies in Russian and Soviet Cinema*, and is currently completing a book-length study of the cinema of Andrei Tarkovsky.

Richard Taylor is Emeritus Professor of Politics at Swansea University in Wales. He is the author of numerous articles and books on Soviet cinema, including *The Politics of the Soviet Cinema, 1917–1929* (1979), *Film Propaganda: Soviet Russia & Nazi Germany* (1998) and studies of Eisenstein's films. He has also co-edited *The Film Factory: Russian & Soviet Cinema in Documents, 1896–1939* (1988, 1994), *Inside the Film Factory: New Approaches to Russian & Soviet Cinema* (1991, 1994) and *Eisenstein Rediscovered* (1993) with Ian Christie, and *Stalinism and Soviet Cinema* (1993) with Derek Spring. He has edited and part-translated the British Film Institute edition of Eisenstein's writings in English, re-published by I.B.Tauris in 2010, and is General Editor of the *KINO* series of studies of Russian and Soviet Cinema for I.B.Tauris. He is currently working on a monograph on *The Stalinist Musical*.

Denise J. Youngblood is Professor of History at the University of Vermont and has written extensively on Russian and Soviet cinema. Her most recent books are *Russian War Films: On the Cinema Front, 1914–2005* (2007) and *Cinematic Cold War: The American and Soviet Struggle for Hearts and Minds* (2010, with Tony Shaw).

INTRODUCTION

Birgit Beumers and Nancy Condee

Whilst Alexander Sokurov is one of the most widely distributed Russian *auteurs* of the post-Soviet era – certainly occupying a prominent place since *Russian Ark* (2002) – no full-length English-language study has been devoted to his oeuvre.[1] The reasons for this lacuna would appear to lie, on the one hand, in the disparate nature of his work, veering between documentary and fiction film. On the other hand, the lacuna could be explained by a certain stubborn consistency: in neither documentary nor fiction film could Sokurov's cinema be described as 'user-friendly'. Instead, his work is often a non-narrative visual experiment, somewhere between photography and painting, rather than film in the traditional sense of the term. Basically, we would suggest, Sokurov challenges that cinema conceived as a method either to capture or narrate reality.

At the same time, the literary and historical dimensions that have informed most of his fiction films allow some recognition of a 'plot': many of his early films were adaptations of Russian and world classics – Andrei Platonov, nineteenth-century Russian classics, the Strugatsky Brothers, George Bernard Shaw, Gustave Flaubert – while later films focused on historical figures, such as Hitler, Lenin and Hirohito. In the documentaries, too, the viewer encounters a whole host of well-known figures, from Vytautas Landsbergis to Boris Yeltsin, from Alexander Solzhenitsyn to Galina Vishnevskaya and Mstislav Rostropovich. Yet the visual representation Sokurov finds for these literary works and historical figures substantially undermines the viewer's expectations of conventional literary adaptation or historical documentary, by focussing on the 'other', shadow side of canonical literature and history in Soviet culture and official media discourses generally. Thus Sokurov's films caused intense controversy during the late Soviet years when he began his career in documentary cinema. His work not only undermined Soviet values, but also subverted the camera's use as a means to render comprehensible, audible and visible that which is hidden in everyday reality, whether official, public or private.

Sokurov's choices might well suggest a creative credo that challenges and ultimately annuls the role of cinema. In that sense, the title of this volume should perhaps be seen ironically, as a cinema that challenges its own status.

Yet as long as Sokurov is recording on a medium that captures image and sound – one that anticipates distribution through television or projection – we are dealing with cinema, for want of another word. And when Sokurov's recent project involved a non-changing set (a radio studio), a static camera, and a collection of people (some known, others not) reading texts recorded by studio microphone, then one might wonder whether this is indeed cinema (in the sense of 'moving' images), or whether it is a creative reversal of such work as that by Etienne-Jules Marey (1830–1904) and Eadweard Muybridge (1830–1904), whose efforts to set into motion still photographs gave rise to chrono-photography.[2]

Despite these reservations, we proceed in a broadly chronological order for this volume, which comprises five sections. Section One contains three essays on the documentaries; Section Two deals with the early feature films (*Lonely Voice of Man*; *Days of Eclipse*; *Whispering Pages*). Section Three is devoted to the 'family-films' (*Mother and Son*; *Father and Son*) and the tetralogy of leaders (*Moloch*; *Taurus*; *The Sun* – at the time that this volume is going to print in 2010, the fourth film, *Faust*, is in post-production). Section Four is concerned with *Russian Ark* and *Alexandra*. The final Section Five contains texts from Russian sources hitherto unavailable in English: these are interviews by three permanent collaborators on script, sound and editing; reviews of three of Sokurov's films; and general thematic essays, written by eminent Russian scholars and critics.

In the first section, therefore, writing about the documentaries, Jeremy Hicks makes a cogent argument for the value of examining these works as both distinct from the feature films, and also as inflecting the feature films with its own dominant practices. Exploring the ways in which the documentaries, which comprise nearly twice as many works as Sokurov's feature films, make a contribution in their own right, Hicks moves chronologically through them to situate Sokurov's contribution in the Russo-Soviet documentary tradition. Hicks pays particular attention to the technique that Viktor Listov has dubbed 'double vision', requiring us to look again and to change that way we look. This technique reverses the process of distancing the viewer, common in conventional documentaries. Among the practices that Hicks explores in greater detail is Sokurov's long take (made famous in *Russian Ark*).

The film portrait – a sub-genre of the documentary – is the theme of Eva Binder's essay. She reviews the traditional signature of the journalistic portrait – its focus on the subject's individual character, embedded in contemporary events and discursive practices of the age – so as to ask how Sokurov's documentary portraits redefine those conventions. With particular attention to Sokurov's elegies, Binder interrogates the structural principle of the elegy and explores the unconventional relation of Sokurov's narrator to the substance of narration: that which requires no mention is said; that which (in a more conventional rendition) should be narrated is omitted. Sokurov's unique fusion of technological experimentalism with deeply traditional views is situated in a larger discussion of cinema time and its relation to the static shot. Sound editing also falls within this field of inquiry, which examines the frequent recombinant mix of ambient sound with contemporary musical composition.

Alexander Sokurov and the actress Cécile Zervudacki during the filming of *Save and Protect*, 1988.

Sabine Hänsgen returns to the historical minimalism originating in the years immediately following the Second World War as the basis for a discussion of features of reduction in Sokurov's cinema. Tracing Sokurov's minimalism in his long, continuous shots, his deceleration of film time, his reduction of movement by both camera and actors, and his eventlessness, Hänsgen ascribes Sokurov's practices to a renewed commitment to enchantment, a restoration of the aura whose diminution Walter Benjamin had addressed in his *The Work of Art in the Age of Mechanical Reproduction*.[3] In radical contrast to the tempo of mass media, Sokurov demands of the viewer a different relation to the image, renewing its potential connections – on the one hand, to still photography and, on the other, to the enduring traditions of oil painting. The ensuing rendition, for example, of military life – now no longer as action, violence, blood, and chaos, but rather as that space where nothing happens – resituates the viewer *vis-à-vis* cinema's function of rendering legible the quotidian matter of social life. In Section One, these three essays share a single concern: the revisions that Sokurov applies to the conventions of the documentary. Whether they address the intersection of cinematic with literary (elegy) or musical (sonata) forms; whether they concern the reduction of cinematic devices; or whether they investigate the experimentation with mechanical and optical devices, Sokurov innovates the documentary genre and turns it into one in which the medium ultimately reflects upon itself.

The second section explores in depth some of the early fiction films. Nariman Skakov discusses intertextuality in *Lonely Voice of Man*, making connections between Andrei Tarkovsky and Sokurov on the one hand – in the understanding of time – and between Andrei Platonov and Sokurov on the other – a classical literary source that is 'reduced' (as discussed later in this volume in an essay by Yuri Arabov) to suit Sokurov's purposes. Skakov analyses the rejection of linear time, a principle Sokurov shared with Tarkovsky, but a sacred, discontinuous time that lies outside the concept of historical progression: it is, as Skakov argues, a 'non-time'. Similarly, the spaces occupied in Sokurov's films lie somewhere 'beyond', apparently without a beginning and an end. Skakov's analysis of time and space in *Lonely Voice of Man*, based on Platonov's story 'Potudan', dwells on the concept of spatial and temporal liminality, which is central also to Julian Graffy's discussion of *Days of Eclipse*. Graffy offers a detailed reading of the film, highlighting its associations and references to other texts, cinematic and other, which position the work 'in between' genres and media. Similarly, the characters exist on the borderline of the Soviet empire (in Turkmenia), and in a borderline state between life and death – at a time when the empire crumbles to give way, soon, to a new order. Graffy thus connects the historical and political significance with that of the state of limbo in which the characters exist, offering a coherent reading of this complex film.

Robert Bird likewise starts his discussion with the *Lonely Voice of Man*. Studying those features in the film that suggest the 'rejection of cinema art' and dwelling on the collapse of time and of documentary/fictional genre, Bird illuminates new aspects of Sokurov's affinity to Tarkovsky. Bird continues by exploring Sokurov's work in opera, using the example

Alexander Sokurov and Alexei Ananishnov during the filming of *Days of Eclipse.*

of *Boris Godunov* (staged 2007), and pointing out the cinematic techniques that Sokurov takes with him onto the opera stage, such as the use of sets that allow the montage of scenes and a dimly-lit tapestry backdrop blurring the scene changes (akin to cinematic cuts). Bird emphasises the intimacy to the spectator sought by Sokurov in both the cinematic and performance media, suggesting that intimate perspectives serve the mediation of life, historical or public, where the act of viewing becomes an absorption in vision itself. The essays in this second section share an emphasis on spatial and temporal liminality. They point at the director's preoccupation with the medium – whether through intertextual references, or through changing artistic form (film, opera) – in order to draw attention to the device of the camera lens. With its option to zoom in, bringing life so close as to be nearly unrecognisable – a feature most stunning in the opening scene of *Mother and Son* – Sokurov's work can hover between still painting and a cinematic/moving images, a dyad in some respects homologous to that between death and life.

In the third section, Mikhail Iampolski connects the family films with Sokurov's films about the leaders. He begins with a research puzzle: what sense do we make of the fact that Sokurov's families construct themselves as a truncated unit, with a missing family member? The family is a topic that has preoccupied the director certainly from *Second Circle* onward, in such works as *Mother and Son*, *Father and Son*, and *Alexandra*. The perpetually absent member of the classic nuclear family, Iampolski suggests, produces the reduced, dyadic structure. He further discusses the availability of this dyad to an interpretation of the father-son, mother-son, or (in the case of *Alexandra*) grandmother-grandson as a pre-Oedipal construct, before the imposition of the incest taboo – that is to say, not the degradation of the Oedipal triangle, but rather its pre-history. This 'pure undifferentiation of simple dual structures' facilitates an understanding of the apparent eroticism (variously perceived by critics as homoeroticism or incest) that has aroused such controversy in Sokurov's work. Sokurov's posited world of pre-Oedipal intimacy comes within cinematic reach through the removal of the third member and (with that absented figure) the removal of the progression toward law, power, and separation. Taking this early, polymorphous state as a basis for examining other forms of intimacy, Iampolski turns his attention to Sokurov's portraits of the semi-infantilized figures of Hitler, Lenin, and Hirohito.

In a very different methodological vein, historian Denise Youngblood offers a reading of the leader-trilogy through the works of Robert Rosenstone and Hayden White, thus bringing a new set of research questions to bear on the embedding of postmodern history in the historical film. Sokurov's power tetralogy engages elements the Rosenstone has identified as central to the postmodern historical film, including an irreverent and self-reflexive approach to historical 'truth'; a tolerance of contradictory or uninhibitedly partisan viewpoints; and the inclusion of evidently fragmentary or poetic knowledge.[4] Youngblood examines the tension between a system of interpretation that would take historical truth as an empirical reality and a system of interpretation that would integrate multiple, partial, or unverifiable evidence into its notion of the historical film. Moving through the tetralogy in the chronological order of the films' production, she demonstrates an increasing degree of complexity and deviation from conventional notions of historical truth and evidential representation.

Stephen Hutchings provides another, distinctive incursion into the power tetralogy. Surveying the range of apparently incompatible assessments that Sokurov's work has received from critics, Hutchings sees an analogous, 'incompatible' range with the director's work itself, from his intimate portraits of family relations to the ambitious tetralogy of twentieth-century dictators. Within the latter subset of Sokurov's work, a critical tension is sustained between the global military and political consequences of these leaders and their infantile incompetence, as sketched out in Sokurov's work. Our estrangement from history – did Hitler know about Auschwitz? Did Hirohito order the strike at Pearl Harbor? – exists as a corollary to our estrangement from the intimate, even (at times) nauseatingly close-up portraits of the leaders themselves. Crosscutting a set of recurrent oppositions, the films are united in a kind of de-eroticized bodily intimacy that functions alternately as repulsion and obsession.

Sokurov's more recent films are explored in Section Four, which focuses on *Russian Ark* and *Alexandra*. We begin with a study by José Alaniz of the crowd manipulation in *Russian Ark*. Managing a cast and crew of over 5,000 for the 90-minute one-take digital shot on location at the Hermitage Museum, Sokurov worked with a German cinematographer through a translator; he had to foresee and defuse countless technical issues; he had to keep himself and seven other staff carefully out of frame for the entire single take; and most importantly, he had to herd hundreds of actors, extras and technicians through complicated, clockwork-like movements which had to be precise down to the second and centimetre, with any visible error spelling disaster. Alaniz examines the phenomenon of Sokurov as traffic cop, at the centre of a remarkable, real-time filmic event, and its resonance with issues of aesthetic authority; nationalist ideology; 'film flubs' and cinematic excess; and the fraught meaning of the 'masses' in post-Soviet Russian culture.

Taking another angle, Birgit Beumers explores *Russian Ark* in terms of the historical and artistic context. She analyses the parallels between Sergei Dreiden's character of de Custine and the views the Marquis had expressed in his infamous (and banned in Russia) travelogue *Russia in 1839*, establishing the apparent historical accuracy established through a real historical figure, contradicted and juxtaposed through the staged scenes that perform history for the camera – and for the Marquis himself. Similarly, the camera's selection of paintings is viewed in the context of its focus on frames and doorways that form openings and obstacles for the (spectator's and camera's) gaze. The meanings of paintings and artwork remain obscure to Custine, but accessible to Russian visitors to the museum. Ultimately, the camera fails where art succeeds. The only image the camera is left is a grey, murky fog: cinema's ultimate *reductio* lies in this digitally created (artificial) shot of the void.

In this section's final chapter, Nancy Condee takes Sokurov's *Alexandra* as the central focus for a broader discussion of the concluding moments in Sokurov's work, and their relation to allegorical meaning. In an argument

Alexander Sokurov during the filming of *The Sun*.

that references several other feature films (*Second Circle, Moloch, Taurus, Russian Ark, The Sun*), the chapter sees in *Alexandra* a moment where Sokurov's preoccupation with allegory engages a more explicit geo-political project. A key question posed by the film (in its structure as well as its narrative) is whether the work's maturation tale is a potential resource for questions of sovereign self-determination. Operationally useful to this argument are contemporary discussions of allegory as the projection of metaphor across the metonymic axis of film narrative. Sokurov's increasing preference for minimal plot (and a related affinity for the still image) lends weight to the allegorical possibilities of the film as an idealised political tableau.

The final, fifth section comprises a choice of texts by Russian collaborators and critics. Sokurov's (almost) constant scriptwriter for the fiction films, Yuri Arabov, discusses the shift in their working relations in the late 1980s and early 1990s. As the scripts underwent a rigorous editing process and were considerably reduced in size, an insistent minimalism is discerned not only by Arabov, but also by editor Leda Semenova in her essay. Vladimir Persov, Sokurov's sound editor, describes the artistic decisions associated with the filming of *Mournful Unconcern* as a directly recorded speech soundtrack rather than a studio soundtrack, added at a later stage. Persov's description highlights Sokurov's preoccupation with real-time virtuosity that anticipates the one-take virtuosity of *Russian Ark*. As ever in Sokurov's filming practices, the method is overlaid with a philosophical quest that imbues this experiment with metaphysical significance. Editor Leda Semenova provides a description of the working conditions and shared decisions that inform the editing process. Her account lends concrete information about the ways in which each stage of the production process is philosophically informed, and how the limits of visibility (or audibility, for her professional counterpart in sound editing) are conceptually-driven decisions intimately linked to, for example, human relations with nature. Her account of editing decisions that support the global authorial conceptions confirms the general characterisation of shifts toward a greater laconism in Sokurov's later work.

Some of the early film reviews by Russian critics reflect the Russian reception of his work at home. Oleg Kovalov speculates as to why Sokurov's early film, shot while he was still a student at the Film Institute VGIK, encountered such resistance, while other controversial works of the period, including Andrei Tarkovsky's *Mirror* [Zerkalo, 1975] were released, albeit in limited distribution. Linking Sokurov's filmic language to Andrei Platonov's capacity to conjure up a first-person-plural narrator – a plural self at a time when any 'we' was indistinct from its corrupt state embodiment – Kovalov describes the ways in which the film circulated among VGIK students in unofficial and late-night club screenings. The film is embedded in the milieu of mid-Stagnation cultural politics, and managed to rise above publicistic clamour to preserve a distance from everyday life that the author would see as characteristic of Russian culture more broadly.

Maya Turovskaya situates Sokurov's *Sonata for Hitler* against its original source material. Much of *Sonata*'s German wartime newsreel and other documentary footage had been earlier selected by Soviet director Mikhail Romm, together with writers Maya Turovskaya and Yuri Khaniutin, for their Thaw documentary *Ordinary Fascism* [Obyknovennyi fashizm, 1965]. Turovskaya's astute observation ('Sokurov is not offering novelty at all') suggests a link to Sabine Hänsgen's essay on Sokurov's affinities with the early postmodernist figure of Andy Warhol. Sokurov is engaged in an act of selection that would later come to be understood as cinematic recycling. *Sonata* is, in this respect, a compilation film that draws on Romm's already-existing compilation of 4,000 metres of material selected from newsreels and documentary footage in Soviet archival possession. Turovskaya's remark that the film contains an imaginary viewer supports Jeremy Hicks's argument that the film-maker's refraction of the documentary image often passes through a perceiving subject. Sokurov draws upon the Romm montage for his own ends: he recasts the Soviet master's accumulation of images (principally organised around Hitler's hand-washing gestures and their Shakespearian reverberations), and subverts them to serve a new end, transforming the comic tonality of the older sequence into one of fear and self-defence.

Petr Bagrov writes about the strategic non-correspondence between the compositional soundtrack and the montage of images in *Sonata for Viola. Dmitri Shostakovich*. In the documentary's intentional cross-editing of sound and image, he sees an odd entry point into the fraught question of Shostakovich as Hero of Socialist Labour and winner of five Stalin Prizes on the one hand, and the 'artist condemned to create within the paralysing confines of Stalinist ideology', on the other. The documentary's kaleidoscopic principles of composition disperse the viewer's attention away from the conventional focus on politics (and even away from the cinematic image itself) to a more contemplative consideration of the music and its cultural context.

The final batch of Russian criticism contains three pieces by eminent Russian critics on themes of Sokurov's films. Sergei Dobrotvorsky examines the image of the house as a rich, multivalent source of meaning. Juxtaposed to the image of the cemetery, the tombstone, and the coffin, the house/home emerges as a dominant figure in numerous documentaries – as Eva Binder's article also maintains. In *Moscow Elegy*, for example, Sokurov juxtaposes the welcoming and warm exile of Italy – that which is not home – to the dreary wasteland of Tarkovsky's own native country. Tarkovsky's homelessness is taken not merely as biographical fact, but as a philosophical assertion about life as a transitional stage to eternity. The illusions of life and the inevitability of death are two interrelated poles that Dobrotvorsky sees as intimately intertwined with Sokurov's feature films as well, most compatibly with his *The Lonely Voice of Man* and *Mournful Unconcern*, in which Shaw's original historical cataclysm is transformed into a state of apocalypse and the end of days. This apocalyptic vision is structured into the very architecture of Sokurov's houses and urban landscapes. In this regard, Dobrotvorsky would like to situate Sokurov's work more ambitiously in a broader range of architectural visions that would include such masterpieces as Fritz Lang's *Metropolis* [1927] and Alexander Medvedkin's *New Moscow* [Novaia Moskva, 1938].

Mikhail Trofimenkov takes as his starting point the tendency, shared by such luminous predecessors as surrealist Luis Buñuel in *Land without Bread* [Las Hurdes, tierra sin pan, 1933], to fuse documentary and feature cinema as a conceptual unity. Shifting the director's task away from a narrative account of the life and works of the documentary subject, Sokurov instead works from a series of signature devices – the static shot, the old photograph – to invoke a human commonality to his documentary subjects, whether they be the obscure peasant woman Maria Voinova of *Maria*, or the (then) political outcast Boris Yeltsin of *Soviet Elegy*. Trofimenkov sees in Sokurov's work a scriptural dimension to this passage of humanity from one generation to the next and suggests that Sokurov's apparent neglect of the documentary subject's contribution serves as a means to shift our attention to more abstract questions of generational succession and enduring cultural values.

Finally, Andrei Plakhov traces the development of Sokurov over the last twenty-odd years and distinguishes three phases in his development. Above all, though, he positions Sokurov as a film-maker devoted to the epic mode (after all, the historian's training shows) rather than a poetic mode (more compatible with Tarkovsky's work). For Plakhov, the initial phase of Sokurov's work is characterised by a concern for the relationship of the artist and the regime and the relationship of the people (or the little man) and power. Both in his films and in his career of this early period, the film-maker challenges the authorities to grant creative freedom to the artist/individual. The film characters of this early period – fictional and documentary – accomplish its mission against the backdrop of fate. The second phase that Plakhov discerns is one of 'hermetical esotericism', culminating in *Mother and Son*. In the final phase, Sokurov is preoccupied with the individual secluded from the world and living instead in a virtual world, having lost contact with reality. Only the fear of death draws out his similarities to the 'little man' out in the real world, leading to a (comic) incongruence. Plakhov argues that the apparent shift 'from the intimate to the epic' is in fact the opposite. It is in Sokurov's later work that the isolation of the lone figure, celebrated though he might be, becomes the core concern.

It is, of course, a daunting task for the contributors in this volume collectively to account for a film-maker whose work is as wide-ranging and substantial as that of Alexander Sokurov. The effort here is itself a tribute to the international attention his work has generated from scholars and critics, journalists and archivists, as well as from members of his working crew, represented here by three figures: a long-time sound editor, scriptwriter, and film editor. In its own way, the volume is conceived as a kind of time capsule. By this we mean not only that the scholarly chapters trace his work from the early documentaries to contemporary work. We also intend by this image that, in retrospect, the three professional clusters – an international cohort of scholars, our Russian colleagues, and Sokurov's crew – mutually illuminate elements of his work that we would not notice, working in isolation. Film editor Leda Semenova's description of montage, for example, reverberates in unintentional ways with several scholars' comments here on Sokurov's *Russian Ark*, filmed without a single cut. Sabine Hänsgen's argument on Sokurov's cinematic minimalism, for example, has new implications when it is juxtaposed to scriptwriter Yuri Arabov's account of his shifting participation in the writing process.

Alexander Sokurov's cinema is famously one that elicits extreme responses – from cultish devotion to extreme irritation. We do not aspire to shape that critical process, which will follow its own dynamic, independent of this contribution. Instead, this volume offers twenty-one essays from a range of professional perspectives that attempt to respond to the complex and idiosyncratic diversity of this major figure in world cinema.

Notes

1   The situation is different in France, where Diane Arnaud has published *Le Cinéma de Sokourov. Figures d'enfermement*, Paris: L'Harmattan, 2005.
2   See Marta Braun, *Picturing Time: The Work of Etienne-Jules Marey*, Chicago and London: University of Chicago Press, 1992; Anson Rabinbach, *Energy, Fatigue, and the Origins of Modernity*, Berkeley: University of California Press, 1992; Phillip Brookman (ed.), *Eadweard Muybridge*, London: Tate Publishing, 2010.
3   Walter Benjamin, 'The Work of Art in the Age of Mechanical Reproduction' (1935), in his *The Work of Art in the Age of Mechanical Reproduction*, London: Penguin Books, 2008, pp. 1–50.
4   Robert Rosenstone, 'The Future of the Past: Film and the Beginnings of Postmodern History', in Vivian Sobchack (ed.), *The Persistence of History: Cinema, Television, and the Modern Event*, New York and London: Routledge, 1996, pp. 201–18 (p. 206).

Part I

DOCUMENTARY BEGINNINGS

Chapter 1

SOKUROV'S DOCUMENTARIES
Jeremy Hicks

While Alexander Sokurov's most celebrated films have used actors, he is on record saying that he sees documentary and fiction film-making as two alternative methods within art:

> The only difference I see between fiction and documentary is that the artist uses different tools to create a picture, or let's say to build a house. In fiction, the director uses much larger-scaled blocks of the actual building, large sized-stones. In documentaries, the house is usually a more fragile, transparent, glasslike structure.[1]

Since these two modes of film-making are ostensibly of similar importance to the director, and he has in fact made more documentary films (28) as opposed to fictional ones (16),[2] it seems strange and unbalanced that so much attention has been accorded the director's fictional films, and so little to his documentaries.

Yet, with few exceptions, when Sokurov's documentary films are discussed, they are seldom treated in their own right, but rather as juvenilia, an apprenticeship, or a testing ground for techniques fully deployed only in fictional films using actors (referred to hereafter as 'feature films').[3] While it is true that Sokurov's career began in TV documentaries, developing elements of a style and vision explored more extensively in the more critically acclaimed features, Sokurov has continued to make documentary films throughout his career, despite long having access to the kinds of funds that would keep him making features exclusively for some time, if that were his sole aim. Clearly then, documentary film remains important to Sokurov. Yet, if we persist in viewing the documentary films exclusively through the prism of the features, then we risk missing certain important aspects of Sokurov's practice as a documentarian, elements of his style, such as the use of archive footage, the manipulation of sound and the deployment of the long take that function differently in the documentary films. What is more, such a perspective obscures a sense of Sokurov's unique position within and contribution to the art of documentary both in Russia and more broadly.

Having examined Sokurov's documentaries in their own right, it may then be possible to reassess and reconsider their relation to Sokurov's wider work as a director. Indeed, a further clear benefit of looking at Sokurov's *oeuvre* through the prism of his documentaries is that it might liberate us from the more obvious approach to Sokurov whereby we slavishly follow Sokurov's own self-view and place his films in the context of Russian (and to a lesser extent Western, and Japanese) literature of the nineteenth century, and classical music and painting. But while these are influences and inspirations for the film-maker, we can gain a different and equally illuminating kind of insight by placing his work in contexts he himself mentions seldom if at all. The context of Soviet and Russian documentary film, as well as documentary film more widely is a particularly rewarding context.

Sokurov and Russian Documentary Tradition: Evolution

While there have been many attempts to define documentary, the easiest to defend is what Bill Nichols calls the institutional definitions that documentary is what is held to be documentary by documentary production companies or documentary film-makers.[4] Thus, any understanding of a given documentary implies a sense as to its place within a specific institutional tradition. While, since the mid-1990s, Sokurov has been partly financed by foreign production companies, and has found his most appreciative audiences at film festivals and with TV stations outside Russia, the origins of his film-making art nevertheless need to be traced to his interaction with the Soviet documentary film industry, and its generic conventions.

If we briefly consider Sokurov's work for Gorki regional television, through to his first documentaries made for Leningrad Documentary Film Studios (LSDF), the films polemicise with the established genres and themes of Soviet documentary film, and the core subject matter and techniques, ones that run through most of the director's work, may be said to be largely determined by this polemic, whereby Sokurov attempts to define himself in opposition to and to free himself and his art from a traditional Soviet perspective. However, while he is broadly successful in creating a distinctly un-Soviet identity as a film-maker, this intertext still informs his documentaries as a whole: the centrality of biography and portraiture in his films, the approach to death, the refocusing on unrecordable inner states and subjectivity rather than a recordable objective world, and a privileging of ambiguity and structures that only make sense when the whole is seen from the perspective of the end (itself analogous to death). All of these positions may be said to be elaborated in dialogue with Soviet documentary film.

The works for Gorki TV which Sokurov made in the early part of his career are generally undistinguished in visual style. A 1974 film *The Earthliest of Concerns* is an unremarkable film showing how advances in irrigation are transforming Soviet agriculture. Sokurov is credited as director here, but this is very much a film made to a template in which problems are described before their solution is shown. Nevertheless, as with all of these early works, the location recorded synch-sound interview is the central technique, one that remains important for Sokurov throughout his subsequent career as a documentary film-maker. Indeed, indicative of Sokurov's profound interest in sound, is his claim to have wanted to make radio plays in the early part of his career.[5]

In *Call Sign R1NN* (1975), about the exploits of pioneers of Soviet radio, the interview is similarly central, but the greater scope of the historical subject matter enables Sokurov to insert still photographs, and get his interviewees to respond to such images. The interviews, some of which are with a couple of people, are also combined with archive footage, in a manner that it is not unlike that of the author of the treatment for this film, veteran Gorki TV director, Yuri Bespalov, whom Sokurov has cited as a pivotal influence.[6] Neither this film, nor *The Earthliest of Concerns* appears on Sokurov's website filmography: an indication, presumably, that the director regards these as lacking any distinct authorial voice. Indeed, in both of these films there is a voice-over commentary, but it is not the voice of Sokurov himself, as it is in so many of his mature films, but that of a standard 'voice-of-God' figure.

For *The Last Day of a Rainy Summer* (1978), which chronicles the decline of a rural community, Sokurov is credited as one of a team of eight film-makers, which may explain why this film too does not appear on the official Sokurov website filmography, although it has been released on DVD under his name.[7] Nevertheless it has more of the feel of a Sokurov film than the two films already discussed, for its use of interviews with the subjects responding to photographs, for its use of sound bridges to link sequences evocatively, for its theme of a community in decline and for its imagery of wistful decay.

The final film relating to this period, *Maria*, is the first example of the use of a personalised voice-over and is without doubt the most significant work of this early part of Sokurov's career. This film comprises footage taken during his time in Gorki, but finished off with a much more distinctive second half made ten years later and released together in 1988. With this film, and *Sonata for Hitler*, made in 1979 but only released in 1989, Sokurov established key elements of his technique as a documentary film-maker.

However, after leaving Gorki TV in 1980 Sokurov made a number of films for Leningrad Documentary Film Studios that demonstrate his need to polemicise with the hallowed traditions of Soviet documentary, and begin to use observational filming techniques overlaid with carefully calibrated sound which at times almost imperceptibly colours and interprets the image. The two key films here are the 1985 *Patience. Labour. Studies about the Leningrad School of Figure Skating*, and the more ambitious 1987 *Evening Sacrifice*.

The first overturns the familiar Soviet narrative about the triumph and nobility of work and art by emphasising the suffering and sacrifice, the set-backs and falls in the life of would-be figure skaters. There is in *Patience. Labour* no edifying narrative and no pompous voice-over to underpin it. Similarly *Evening Sacrifice* takes the theme of the May Day parade, a stock Soviet documentary genre since the 1920s and, instead of the rousing revolutionary music and columns of tanks, presents largely disorganised milling crowds, dispersing after the official parade, and a rich, but broad montage of sounds comprising Russian folk music, Orthodox choirs, pop music both Russian and Western including the Beatles' *Can't Buy Me Love*, as well as ambulance sirens and the constant hum of conversation. These sounds and images prevail over that of the traditional artillery salute, also shown here, but the viewer's attention is drawn to images of smoking, spent howitzer shells and funeral bells and choirs, suggesting the moribund nature of this regime and its May Day ritual.

This contesting in *Evening Sacrifice* of the optimistic ideology of the Soviet regime is an important context for Sokurov, and informs the widely identified basic theme of his films: that of death.[8] Another significant early example of Sokurov's elaboration of his own distinct approach to this theme through a polemic with the traditions of Soviet documentary film comes in *Moscow Elegy*, his film about Andrei Tarkovsky, where Sokurov intercuts archive footage of Tarkovsky with scenes from his films. Above all the purpose here is to show Tarkovsky's presence as an artist, characteristically pensive, and brooding on his separation from Russia. Russia itself is shown particularly in images of the documentary films made of the funerals of dead premiers: first of Leonid Brezhnev and then of Yuri Andropov. In hackneyed tones, the voice over declares that 'Brezhnev will always remain an example of service to the Communist Party'. While this archive footage serves to anchor the narrative in time, it is also made emblematic of a false, Soviet attitude to death in which the ongoing Communist political cause recuperates and triumphs over death. The implication seems to be that, just as the death of Tarkovsky is an unredeemable loss, so is his art truly meaningful and a legacy that will outlive him in a way that contrasts with the doomed Communist regime. To choose the funeral genre, one of the foundational tropes of Soviet documentary film-making since Vertov's film of Lenin's funeral (*Kinopravda 21: Leninist kinopravda*, 1925) made it a powerful image of the transcendence of the Communist ideal, is a significant gesture that contrasts Sokurov's view of art and death with that purveyed by Soviet film, and the newsreel and documentary in particular.

Sokurov's Documentary Art

While, as we have seen, Sokurov's evolution as a documentary film-maker can be productively traced as a relationship with the traditions of Soviet documentary film-making, we can gain a better sense of his contribution to documentary film more widely from a consideration of the stylistic and compositional elements that characterise his films.

Double Vision or the Benefits of Boredom

Sokurov's emergence as a documentary film-maker with a distinct and original style is associated with the ways in which his mature films make the viewer see in a different manner. One aspect of this may be described through the notion of 'double vision' as proposed by Viktor Listov. Listov commented fascinatingly upon *Maria* that it demands from viewers a kind of 'double vision':[9] although we have a sense that something was missing from, or that we had missed something in, the first part, it is in fact only when we see the second part, that we realise we must look at the first again. What we had missed (because we were not told) was the fact that Maria was someone defined by grief for her son killed by a drunken driver. The fact that it is death that was obscured by the focus of the first part of the film is of course far from incidental, as this is Sokurov's primary theme throughout all forms: Sokurov seems to be suggesting that death more broadly, and this kind of everyday tragedy in particular, are somehow overlooked by our habitual view. As Listov puts it:

> Sokurov's great merit is that he tries to reconfigure our vision, teach us to see the sprinkling of a terrible truth among the familiar fabric of the everyday.[10]

This attempt to make us look again, to literally change how we look and what we see is fundamental to Sokurov's approach to documentary, and is used

Still from *Maria*.

repeatedly in later films. What is particularly unusual about it is the attempt to trick us into bored, inattentive viewing, only later to show us that we have missed something. Oleg Aronson has argued that a boring film is the truly authentic documentary film, in that it has succeeded in becoming everyday, getting us to take it for granted as part of life rather than a reflection upon it.[11] Emerging with *Maria*, this proves to be one of Sokurov's essential strategies as a documentary film-maker: Sokurov manipulates boredom, daring us to get bored, only to show afterwards, that we were in fact missing something important during our bored, inattentive spectatorship.

The Long Take

A crucial element of this approach is Sokurov's extensive use of the long take. This technique has been widely discussed, starting with the work of Bazin; and, in the Russian context, Tarkovsky's use of the device has attracted a great deal of attention too.[12] However, its use in documentary fulfils a slightly different function than in features, as has been explored by David McDougall. McDougall argues that film typically forecloses meaning by inserting it into a narrative system or 'chain of signification', whereby the meaning is grasped in the first seconds of a shot. With the long take we are forced to stay with an image after we think we have grasped its initial sense and invited to demonstrate a 'coasting perusal' or observe something occurring.[13] In consequence, there is a far greater ambiguity, and sense of process.

McDougall sees this potential as being used with particular effect in observational documentaries, and argues that at their best, such films use the long take to retain the unfinished, developmental quality of the rushes, which tend to include irrelevant, marginal and background material permitting alternative interpretations, all of which are typically eradicated in finished films.

Sokurov's documentaries make extensive use of the long take inviting us to reassess, to take a second look at what we thought we understood, or to make us wait, bored or observantly for something to happen, and suddenly realise that something is happening, that what we thought insignificant or inanimate is alive and relevant. The long take is central to this aesthetic strategy.

Refracting Images through a Perceiving Subject

Another sense in which Sokurov's documentaries invite us to reconsider what we see is through their use of images of someone looking, a 'subject of vision,' through whose eyes we are invited to see the subsequent sequence, which is often archive footage in the early films. Sokurov's first film to employ this technique extensively was *Sonata for Hitler*.

The status of the war in official Soviet discourse was sacrosanct, and this was especially the case after the twentieth anniversary of victory, in 1965, since victory over fascism has been an event almost everyone in Soviet, and then post-Soviet Russian, society agreed was a positive achievement.[14] The war had a particular impact upon documentary film, as the 257 Red Army cameramen took some of the most exhilarating combat footage of the war in the battles for Moscow and Stalingrad, with 33 of them dying in the process.[15] They also recorded the most appalling atrocities of the war as they liberated the death camps of Majdanek and Auschwitz. Yet, of all documentary films made about the war, the most influential and significant Soviet film by far, was Mikhail Romm's *Ordinary Fascism*. This was an analysis of the reasons for the rise of fascism mostly compiled from archive footage and still photographs. It argued that Nazism is a kind of abdication of individual moral responsibility in favour of the collective, a message widely and controversially seen as having ramifications for the Soviet experience too.

While its political effect was explosive, it was also a landmark in Russian documentary film, achieving its most striking effects through its discordant editing, juxtaposing sharply contrasting footage and through Romm's own very sardonic, highly personalised voice-over commentary.

Sokurov's film uses a great deal of the same footage as Romm's film; indeed, Maya Turovskaya, who co-wrote the treatment for *Ordinary Fascism* has said that all of the footage was from that collected for the earlier film.[16] Yet, despite the similarity of the imagery, the fact that it also highlights the performed nature of Nazism and even the way in which the film also juxtaposes contrasting images of Nazi pomp and Nazi atrocity, Sokurov's ultimate purpose and effect are completely different from that of Romm's film.

One of the ways in which Romm's film attempted to shock the spectator was through the novel nature of its archive materials, such as the still photographs of atrocities kept as mementos by Wehrmacht soldiers. By contrast, Sokurov's film shows us no new or surprising images: this revelatory power of documentary is of little interest to him. What is more, whereas Romm's commentary is able to contextualise and invite the spectator to look at a certain aspect of the image, Sokurov uses no voice over in this film, and so emphasis is made through the editing and structure, the music, and the use of close-ups of still images. Indeed, the lack of context is not an obstacle in *Sonata for Hitler*; rather, it is a given: the film assumes that we will recognise the broad connotational meaning of most of the images. They are then reworked so as to suggest that what we see is a kind of final reflection upon his fate by Hitler himself. Instead of an external, analytical view of history, we see the history of the Reich through Hitler's own mind's eye.

This notion is established by the first post-title shot, the image of Hitler seated, eyes down-cast, wringing his hands. This same image is repeated many times over the course of the film, often on a loop, and extended through slow-motion so as to suggest that it is of longer duration than it actually is, with the longest use coming in the last shot of the film. The effect is to define everything we see in this short film as filtered through Hitler's consciousness, as the Third Reich nears collapse. Thus the sound of the Bach flute sonata can be seen as an attempt on Hitler's part to see Nazism as coherent and glorious. This attempt, doomed through the images depicting the rapacious acts of the Nazis and punishment by SS guards, belies this would-be coherence, as does the discordant music of

Krzysztof Penderecki. The repeated image of Hitler suggests guilt, and the many images of hands emphasise the guilty associations of wringing one's hands, as well as the idea that the scenes of war and devastation are all, ultimately, like the 'Heil!' salute, Hitler's handiwork.

Sonata for Hitler stands out for its use of the medium of documentary film not to actually record or document an empirical reality, and not to mobilise any such evidential power for the purposes of persuasion, but instead to grant insight into the individual psychology. This emphasis is that of Sokurov's approach to the documentary form as a whole. The device of cueing what we see through a particular perceiving or observing subject is very widely used in Sokurov's documentaries, including *Sonata for Viola*. *Dmitri Shostakovich*, *Moscow Elegy*, *Petersburg Elegy*, *Soviet Elegy* and many more. It is also employed in a number of his feature films, notably *Russian Ark*.

Sokurov's use of music in *Sonata for Hitler* is also significant and indicative of its importance in his oeuvre. Music often functions in Sokurov's films as a symbol of greater coherence, sense, as emblematic of art as something of lasting value. In his many biographical films, musicians such as Shostakovich, Chaliapin, Rostropovich and Vishnevskaya feature largely, and here the sonata of the title seems to represent a coherence and sense that Hitler strives towards without achieving, as the discordant sound and images suggest: he achieves something like the opposite of music and its harmonious order. Sokurov's most famous use of these associations of music comes in his best-known feature, where the final concert in *Russian Ark* symbolises the impending tragic loss of what is shown to be pre-Revolutionary Russia's harmonious grandeur.

Yet this form of the 'Sonata', if it is intended to be a film genre, is not a productive one for Sokurov, who does not attempt any more such works. One reason is that its vaguely musical structure, based upon the repetition of the key image and the reworking of motifs, such as that of hands, is one that depends primarily upon editing. As Sokurov developed his distinctive style as a documentary film-maker, editing came to play a less important role. Far more significant is the long take, here approximated in the looped shot of Hitler. Moreover, as he was soon to discover, it is possible to direct the spectator to scrutinise the image and reflect upon the subject's inner life more effectively through the voice-over commentary, than through editing structures, themselves rendered less significant through the director's increasing reliance on the long take.

With this emphasis in his use of the documentary form, Sokurov cuts a strange figure in the world of documentary, in that he is rarely really interested in the capacity of the medium to record any empirical reality. As he puts it: 'I'm not trying to make documentaries as a realistic type of art. I'm not interested in real truth. I don't think I could possibl[y] understand reality that well.'[17] This perspective runs against the dominant commitment of the documentary form to claim that what it depicts has occurred in the 'actual' world, and to provide not a story 'about *a* world', but evidence from '*the* world'.[18]

For the most part, as with *Sonata for Hitler*, Sokurov uses documentary to get at the inner lives of his subjects. In this he seems to be taking his cue from portraiture, which he has repeatedly praised, stressing his preference for pre-Modernist, figurative painting and stressing the importance of the eyes in particular.[19] While this aim is not unusual in the observational traditions of direct cinema, it is this commitment to psychology which sets Sokurov apart from the dominant traditions of Soviet documentary film-making, the great strengths of which have been characterised as essay-like genres of propaganda and persuasion on the one hand, and dense poetic imagery on the other.[20]

These two defining works: *Maria* and *Sonata for Hitler*, ultimately saw light in the late 1980s when the new leadership of the Soviet Film-makers' Union finally enabled Sokurov to exhibit his films. This was a period in which documentary went through the roller-coaster ride of initially being, in the 1980s, at the centre of public attention, to effectively being ignored in the 1990s and beyond.[21] Even if taken from the shelf, Sokurov's documentaries never enjoyed popularity, as he is a documentary maker who almost completely avoided the contemporary social themes dominant in the Perestroika era, expressing a total opposition to topicality.[22] Having earlier made films for the shelf – the enlightened future viewer – as is the case with *Sonata for Viola. Dmitri Shostakovich*, and with *And Nothing More* – he then continued to make films with almost no commercial appeal, destined for the film festival, and the professional critic.[23] In this he is not unlike the majority of significant directors working in the documentary form in Russia at the present.[24] Indeed, probably the most noteworthy of Sokurov's achievements in forms of documentary virtually ignored by the wider Russian public came with his turn to digital technologies in the 1990s.

The Coming of Digital and the Lengthening Long Take

The advent of digital technologies in the mid 1990s enabled features of Sokurov's style already evident in the early work to dominate in an entirely new way. Although the other features of Sokurov's documentary style appeared here too, in particular Sokurov is able to use the long take much more extensively, taking it almost to the limits of its possibilities in the films *Spiritual Voices* and *Confession*, which run to a colossal length of 327 minutes (*Spiritual Voices*) and 225 (*Confession*).[25] These kinds of lengths would have been far harder to make and distribute in the analogue age.

Spiritual Voices took the long take to an almost Andy Warhol-like extreme in its 30-minute-long opening shot of a landscape on which very little happens. The shot is accompanied by the voice of Sokurov discussing issues around the lives and deaths of composers Mozart and Messiaen. Visually, the spectator's attention is drawn to the shifting light and the greater detail it reveals. It is only later in this first part of the film, that we realise that what we are seeing, and possibly what we are hearing, is probably inside the head of a soldier serving with Russian border troops in Tajikistan. This characteristic refracting of what we see through the mind's eye of a character, as already noted, is one of Sokurov's key representational strategies, and here too it is pivotal to this scene, combining with the 'double-vision' approach to showing us the apparently insignificant before slowly enabling the spectator to re-attune, and notice significant things that had previously been ignored by the spectator. In this case, the strange mismatch between what we see and what we hear is something that confuses us utterly, until we realise firstly that this landscape stands in contrast to the landscape in which the dreamer in fact finds himself, in Tajikistan, and secondly, that this contrast appears to illustrate the voice-over commentary's reflections upon the incongruity between appearances and deeper realities, illustrated in the assertion of the incompatibility of great people (such as the physically unprepossessing Mozart) with life on Earth: 'The more remarkable and outstanding a person is the more difficult and contradictory their relationship with life – this life on earth. These beings stand little chance of being reconciled with life.'

It is hard here to be sure exactly through whose mind's eye we are seeing these images: although we see unnamed soldiers later on, it may be Sokurov's eye that guides us. Yet the title asserts that this is a 'war diary', but it is really only in Sokurov's later, and more accomplished *Confession* where the diary is identified and the perspective is that of an unnamed officer.

In any case, the film's opening seems an extended attempt to reflect upon the central problem in the film: we are asked to look at a landscape that does not seem interesting, not entirely sure what to look for, but ultimately we realise that the landscape and looking at it were significant. This is the situation too of the Russian border guards uprooted from the familiar Russian environment of the first part, and posted to the Tajik–Afghan border. Their routine, day-to-day activities occupy the central space of the film, and their boredom is interrupted in part four of the film by a firefight, and the very real fear of a violent death.

Still from *Spiritual Voices*.

The inner lives of these guards and their thoughts about their situation are intimated primarily by the observational portraiture and dialogue, but also through extra-diegetic music and sound effects, such as the whistle of trains, the wind, the barking of dogs and the twitter of un-Tajik birdsong.

In this rather prolix way, Sokurov is attempting to create a war film that incorporates the very real sense of boredom experienced for most of their service by soldiers, and the fact that war is, as the commentary puts it 'unaesthetic'. At the same time, the film attempts to make the soldiers' predicament a metaphoric state of uneasy waiting and to comment on the problematic experience of viewing as such and the misleading nature of appearances. Characteristically, the sound is the sphere where the directorial hand intervenes to clarify and interpret most, whether this be through voice over or the addition of extra-diegetic noises and music. While the film's immense length makes it demanding to watch, it is ultimately a thought-provoking work with a subtle technique.

The experience of *Spiritual Voices* is built upon successfully in *Confession*, which is similar in length, theme and technique to the earlier film, but ultimately a richer and more rewarding viewing experience, due primarily to the more clearly thought-through character of the diarist's voice-over. Yet, before considering this film in the context of documentary, it should be noted here that the film is prefaced by a short note saying that 'The plot and characters of this film are no more than the author's fantasy.' This curious disclaimer may be seen as signalling the fictional nature of the figure of the ship's commander, through whose consciousness everything we see is filtered, although the actual voice-over is spoken by Sokurov who refers to him in the third person, and we see images of the commander as we hear the words. However, this refracting consciousness is in large part only a more explicit formulation of the core Sokurov documentary device of undermining the documentary status of what is recorded and shown by implying that we are seeing it as if in someone else's mind's eye. While there is a scripted, invented element to what we see, and to a degree the commander is playing a part, all of which might be seen as effectively placing the work outside of the conventional understanding of the documentary tradition. Yet this fiction is itself something of a fiction, as the commander's various flashbacks appear not to have been reconstructed, but in fact to have been photographed in a broadly observational manner, with the commentary then added subsequently to shape the material according to Sokurov's conception. The film is largely documentary despite its claims to be a diary being played back inside the commander's head.

While the character of the commander remains largely a mouthpiece for familiar Sokurov thoughts and concerns, the fact that he is not Sokurov, and therefore not an artist, enables Sokurov to approach a number of his philosophical concerns from the perspective of a military man. Thus the commander's reflection upon military service becomes one about time, process and work. A conscript who is said to simply want to speed up time and get out of military service as soon as possible is described as a 'slave' for trying to cheat time. The sounds of a chicken clucking, and other birdsong comment upon his desire for freedom, and suggests the hollowness of this striving.

Similarly, the Commander is unable to remember any particular events of his first day in service, and says that sense that his life has lacked events. This lack of events is at the heart of the film's conception, since it too lacks them, and gives us nothing but endless process.[26] The sequences following the induction of new recruits trace their false expectations that their first or subsequent days in the navy would be memorable, and that something would happen, but in fact there is only routine, the need to work conscientiously and the constant effort of keeping body and clothes clean. These unjustified expectations of something momentous or dramatic are those implicitly too of the first time viewer of the film, and Sokurov grinds down all hope of action and excitement, refocusing attention on the minutiae of the diurnal, suggesting this is the true nature of military service, and, implicitly, of life more broadly. Sokurov's use of observational techniques and the long take are perfectly suited to his emphasis upon process.

However, the film also seems to become frustrated with this vision of endurance, so that by the end of the film, the commander increasingly perceives this absence of event as an absence of change, a sense of stasis. He comes to see his attachment to the sailors for their endurance and patience as stopping him from taking an unnamed important decision, although ultimately he decides to stop writing a diary, a decision that implicitly enables there to be an end to the narrative.

These frustrations seem to be linked to a sense that the commander and the military more generally are not really capable of educating, and scepticism as to the edifying value of work is heightened by the mention, at the beginning and end of the film, of the GULag labour that built the jetty they are now using. Indeed, at one point, the commander, seeing soldiers loading coal, thinks he is back in the Stalin era. Such parallels broaden the commander's reflections to take in Russia more generally, and subtly suggest deep anxieties over the direction of Russian society.

One of the great strengths of *Confession* is its use of sound, probably Sokurov's most varied and imaginative in the documentary form. While the film is not unusual in its use of classical musical motifs, its great strength is the deployment of a panoply of sounds such as the whistling of the wind, the creaking of ship, and the faint sound of orders being shouted in background to underline the atmosphere of the ship, and the consuming nature of the routines aboard it. At the same time Sokurov counterposes the various sounds of the inner lives of the sailors: from birdsong, to women's voices to gunshots. These inner-diegetic sounds are a parallel to the occasional images that show the conscripts' thoughts drifting back to home life. Here once more, we see Sokurov's documentary technique of conveying inner lives through ostensibly documentary technique.

By using the extensive possibilities of the digital form, Sokurov has created in *Confession* a mammoth work, and one that is highly dependent upon the observational traditions of documentary. So distinct a film cannot plausibly be treated as merely an attempt to try out techniques perfected in feature films.

Conclusion: Sokurov's Documentary Features

All of which brings us back to the question posed at the start of this chapter as to the nature of the relationship between Sokurov's documentaries and his feature films. In part, no doubt through a desire to stress his role as an artist, Sokurov has repeatedly rejected the notion that he makes truly documentary films, partly because he is not interested in recording as such, but rather in conveying a subjective vision, and exploring psychology in depth.[27] While the documentary might seem to provide a less obvious vehicle for this kind of agenda than the feature, as we have seen, Sokurov has been successful in bending the form to his design.

Yet there is another dimension to this relationship: as Diane Arnaud has noted, there is an interplay between Sokurov's features and documentaries, and Sokurov's features employ a number of stylistic devices commonly associated with documentary.[28] Most saliently, many of Sokurov's films, especially his early features, employ a great deal of archive footage. What is particularly interesting is the way in which this documentary material is incorporated in the features: in *Lonely Voice of Man*, for example, it serves the conventional purpose of anchoring the acted sequences in the recognisable historical time of the Civil War, but at the same time the footage is sutured into the diegesis through the use of the eye-line match, suggesting that one of the characters sees the images of a 1920s workshop. Moreover, it is manipulated for expressive ends, with slow motion emphasising the back-breaking effort of the labour portrayed, as Sokurov's own diaries indicate.[29]

The documentary approach informs other elements of Sokurov's features, most notably *Russian Ark*, which, as noted above, shares a number of characteristics with Sokurov's documentary films: it is shot on location and not in a studio, it uses the long take and personalised voice-over. But more importantly, *Russian Ark* uses the structural device of filtering what is seen through a given consciousness so central to Sokurov's documentaries. We see what someone else sees in a kind of inner point-of-view shot whereby what we see is some kind of memory, rather than an immediate perception.[30]

On this reading, then, Sokurov's documentaries, rather than being a laboratory or form of apprenticeship, are an important and influential strand within Sokurov's cinematography. Considered in their own right, they demonstrate a distinct and noteworthy style and set of themes that deserve to be seen within the broader context of documentary. At the same time, Sokurov's achievements in documentary film inform his features, suggesting that a deeper understanding of the better-known works can be productively anchored in the documentaries.

Notes

1 Alexander Sokurov interviewed by Paul Schrader, 'The History of an Artist's Soul is a Very Sad History', *Film Comment* 33.6 (Nov.–Dec. 1997), pp. 20–25 (p. 25). Sokurov has repeated this opinion elsewhere, such as 'Stenogramma vstrechi s A. N. Sokurovym, (Sankt-Peterburg, Filosofskii fakul'tet, 20 aprelia 1998 goda)', in E. Ustiugova (ed.), *Aleksandr Sokurov na filosofskom fakul'tete,*

St Petersburg: Izdatel'stvo Sankt-Peterburgskogo filosofskogo obshchestva, 2001, p. 22.
2 *Island of Sokurov*, http://sokurov.spb.ru/isle_ru/isle_flm.html (accessed 1 Sept. 2009).
3 Tatiana Egorova, 'Effekt disgarmonii', *Iskusstvo kino* 5 (1989), pp. 82–84 (p. 82). A significant exception to this is Arnaud, who stresses the interplay and interdependence between Sokurov's use of the two modes: Arnaud, *Le Cinéma de Sokourov*, p. 109.
4 Bill Nichols, *Introduction to Documentary*, Bloomington: Indiana University Press, 2001, p. 22.
5 Alexander Sokurov, Interview with Vladimir Pozner, 'Pozner', First Channel, 22 December 2008.
6 Aleksandr Sokurov, 'Izobrazhenie i montazh', Interview with Dmitrii Savel'ev, *Iskusstvo kino* 12 (1997), p. 111.
7 Filmography on *Island of Sokurov* at http://sokurov.spb.ru/isle_ru/isle_doc.html (accessed 22 July 2009); DVD release: Ideal Audience International and Facets Video, 2006.
8 Oleg Aronson, 'Giperdokument, ili svidetel'stvo o zhizni. Lenin po Aleksandru Sokurovu', *Metakino*, Moscow: Ad Marginem, 2003, pp. 173–83 (p. 174).
9 Viktor Listov, 'Konets idilii', in Liubov' Arkus, (ed.), *Sokurov. Chasti rechi. Kniga 2*, St Petersburg: Seans, 2006 (henceforth referred to as *Sokurov 2*), pp. 25–31 (p. 28).
10 Listov, 'Konets idilii', p. 29.
11 Aronson, *Metakino*, p. 134.
12 See for example: Fredric Jameson, *The Geopolitical Aesthetic: Cinema and Space in the World System*, Bloomington and Indianapolis: Indiana University Press and London: BFI, 1992, p. 98.
13 David McDougall, 'When Less is Less: The Long Take in Documentary', *Film Quarterly*, 46.2 (Winter 1992–3), pp. 36–46 (p. 37).
14 See Nina Tumarkin, *The Living and the Dead: The Rise and Fall of the Cult of World War II in Russia*, New York: Basic Books, 1994, p. 136.
15 Konstantin Simonov, 'Zrimye dokumenty istorii', in *Iz kinoletopisi Velikoi Otechestvennoi 1941–1945*, Moscow: Iskusstvo, 1975, pp. 6–8 (p. 6).
16 Maiia Turovskaia, 'Sonata dlia Gitlera,' *Sokurov 2*, p. 147.
17 Alexander Sokurov interviewed by Paul Schrader, p. 25. There are exceptions to the bias against recording in Sokurov's work, notably in the *St. Petersburg Diary* films, where, as the generic marker might suggest, the director's touch is light, and the films record significant events or places in the city's cultural life in an almost protocol style.
18 Carl Plantinga, 'Moving Pictures and the Rhetoric of Non-Fiction: Two Approaches', in David Bordwell and Noël Carroll (eds), *Post-Theory: Reconstructing Film Studies*, Madison: University of Wisconsin Press, 1996, pp. 307–24 (p. 310); Bill Nichols, *Representing Reality: Issues and Concepts in Documentary*, Bloomington and Indianapolis: Indiana University Press, 1991, p. 115.
19 Aleksandr Sokurov, ' "Glavnym iskusstvom po-prezhnemu ostaetsia literatura…" Obsuzhdenie fil'ma "Kamen'", organizovannoe redaktsiei zhurnala "Seans" (25 iiunia 1991 goda, Sankt-Peterburg)', *Kinovedcheskie zapiski* 23 (1994), pp. 65–75 (p. 66).
20 G. S. Prozhiko, *Zhanry v sovetskom dokumental'nom kino 60–70-kh godov*, Moscow, 1980, quoted in Anastasiia Sukhikh, ' "Distantsionnyi montazh" v poetiko-filosofskom dokumental'nom kinematografe', G. E. Dolmatovskaia, G. I. Kopalina (eds), *Posle vzryva: Dokumental'noe kino 1990-kh*, Moscow: Andreevskii flag, 1995, pp. 126–32 (p. 127).

21 'Ot sostavitelei', *Posle vzryva*, p. 3.
22 'Stenogramma vstrechi s A. N. Sokurovym', p. 23.
23 Galina Pozniakova explains the method by which Sokurov made films for 'better times'; *Sokurov 2*, p. 72.
24 Prominent Russian documentary maker Vitalii Manskii has highlighted the marginal position of contemporary Russian documentary. See 'Neigrovoe kino ≈ resurs igrovogo. Kruglyi stol', *Iskusstvo kino* 10 (2008), pp. 5–23 (p. 7).
25 The release title *Confession* represents a mistranslation of the original title *Povinnost'*, which would be better rendered as *Service*. However, the volume follows the title of the DVD release.
26 Sokurov himself comments upon this 'event-less' aspect of the film: 'Stenogramma vstrechi s A. N. Sokurovym', p. 23.
27 See Schrader, p. 25. Oleg Kovalov has called this emphasis spiritual rather than psychological: 'He is the first to have endowed the document with a spiritual dimension', *Noveishaia istoriia otechestvennogo kino. 1986–2000. Kino i kontekst*, vol. 4, St Petersburg: Seans, 2002. http://www.russiancinema.ru/template.php?dept_id=15&e_dept_id=6&text_element_id=35 (accessed 2 September 2009).
28 Arnaud, *Le Cinéma de Sokourov*, p. 109.
29 *Sokurov 2*, p. 35.
30 It is interesting to note, in this context, that Sokurov considered using an authorial, observational figure in *Lonely Voice of Man*. *Sokurov 2*, p. 35.

CHAPTER 2

SOKUROV'S FILM PORTRAITS
Eva Binder

A significant proportion of Alexander Sokurov's documentary work explores the lives of individuals. These works are film portraits in the general sense of the genre.[1] Film portraits explore the individual through the lens of the encounter between the director and the subject. Grounded in the here-and-now, film portraits capture a moment in time and often refer to contemporary events and broader social discourses. Portraits seek both to depict and to meditate on the subject's life by exploring his or her distinctive character, whilst simultaneously formulating more universal statements. Film portraits treat their subjects with respect rather than unmasking or exposing them.

These characteristics of journalistic film portraits are evident in Sokurov's film portraits, but his works are further marked by an artistic tension that stems from Sokurov's departure from the genre's conventions. Sokurov's documentary works break with the traditions of the documentary genre, which employs facts and objective information to make statements about concrete phenomena. The contrast between Sokurov's portraits and conventional television journalism, with its predilection for closed narratives and conflict resolution, is even more conspicuous. With their conservative and occasionally anachronistic political attitude, his portraits seem at times lop-sided, discordant and provocative. Sokurov's films break with the conventions of journalistic film portraits, which invite viewers to explore broader social issues through the experience of the individual. Instead, his portraits explore the fate and suffering of individual figures. The films are meditations on the themes of transience and death, and it would seem that Sokurov is ultimately concerned with the preservation of the spiritual dimension of human existence in the age of media.

The Sub-Genre of the Film Portrait
Sokurov's official website currently classifies twenty-eight of his films as documentaries. I shall focus here on Sokurov's film portraits in the strict

sense of the term, viz *Maria (Peasant Elegy)*, Sokurov's first documentary film about the Russian kolkhoz worker Maria Semenovna Voinova; *Elegy* and *Petersburg Elegy*, two portraits of Fedor Chaliapin; *Moscow Elegy*, a portrait of Sokurov's colleague Andrei Tarkovsky; *Soviet Elegy*, a portrait of Boris Yeltsin; *A Simple Elegy*, a portrait of Lithuanian politician Vytautas Landsbergis;[2] *A Humble Life*, a portrait focussing on Sokurov's encounter with a Japanese kimono maker; *Elegy of Life*, a portrait of opera singer Galina Vishnevskaya and cellist Mstislav Rostropovich.[3] I shall explore these portraits in the light of their underlying elegiac mood through an analysis of the formal characteristics, themes and leitmotifs that distinguish them, whilst also paying attention to the continuities and shifts in the artistic techniques that Sokurov has developed in the course of almost thirty years.

The elegy is, of course, above all a literary form, which relies on the juxtaposition of two worlds – transience and permanence, loss and its contemplation, (remembered) past and (lived-in) present. This is best illustrated through *Maria*, which in its two parts establishes a structuring principle that is closely linked to the elegy. If in literary terms the elegy juxtaposes internal and external structures, then Sokurov's documentaries translate this principle into cinematography through a range of approaches: first, the role of the narrator, who is at times subjective and domineering, at times elusive and confusing. Second, internal and external structures can conflict on the private and public levels, as I demonstrate on the basis of the elegiac portrait of Yeltsin. Third, the experimentation with media serves to slow down motion, thus contributing to the elegiac mood of the picture. Finally, the house features in Sokurov's film as a recurrent leitmotif for loss – of a home, of the native land, of the private space – and

Still from *Maria*.

stands at the heart of the documentaries as the image for the elegiac mood of loss.

The elegy as Structural Principle

A central quality of Sokurov's films is their implication in broader cultural and artistic traditions. Sokurov's film portraits draw significantly on the European tradition of elegiac poetry. The term 'elegy' generally refers to an ancient lyrical genre characterised by a sorrowful tone of resignation and the use of the elegiac distich, or couplet. Two closely related genres, the epigram and the epitaph, frequently employ the elegiac distich. Sokurov's reference to the elegiac genre in the titles of several film portraits is indicative of both the mood and the concerns underlying these films.

In his study of German elegiac poetry, Klaus Weissenberger[4] attempted to establish criteria for the genre and identified antithesis or, to be more precise, the 'antithetical tension' inherent in the internal and external structure of such works, as an underlying principle of elegiac poetry. Elegiac poetry is distinguished not by a lyrical eruption of sorrow and melancholy, but by a haunting, yet distinctly attenuated sense of sorrow and loss. The genre's contemplative quality creates a sense of distance that takes the edge off the immediate lyrical experience. Elegiac poetry is thus characterised by two specific modes of expression: the genre is self-centred and personal, while simultaneously diminishing the sense of loss and pain through the act of contemplation.

The antithetic tension underlying elegiac poetry stems from the integration of different moments in time within a single lyrical space. When the past and the present meet, as they often do in elegiac poetry, the past is retrieved and situated within the present context. Elegiac poetry relates the past and the present to one another in a manner that strips them of their individual functions: 'The past is drawn into the present time in order for it to form the antithesis to our momentary experience. The description of the present moment loses its experiential character and becomes something more universal.'[5] This integration of two disparate time frames – the past and the present – contributes to the elegy's effect of alleviating the anguish that loss and death inflict upon us. The elegy achieves this by juxtaposing anguish and joy. Elegies contrast the end of life with the memories of earlier joys, and – in the face of imminent pain – bring more idyllic moments to mind.

The documentary film *Maria* illustrates well Sokurov's use of the elegiac mode. Made for Gorki television in 1978, the first part of Sokurov's film portrait of a simple kolkhoz worker is a sensitive exploration of rural culture that contrasts starkly with the media representations and narratives of heroic kolkhoz workers that Soviet ideology demanded. In a lyrical montage, footage of labourers and machines harvesting flax is interwoven with panoramic shots of the Russian countryside. The images are accompanied by a sound montage that includes synchronous voices, machines and ambient environmental sounds. Sokurov's sound and film montage speaks to the viewer's emotional-sensory awareness, inviting him to partake in a more holistic way of life. *Maria* subscribes to a more poetic style of documentary film-making: the images, voices and sounds are self-explanatory; the images are consistent and demonstrate a sympathetic and respectful approach to the subject.

The second part of *Maria* was made nine years later, in 1987, when Sokurov returned to the original locations with his camera team. The mood now is marked by sorrow and loss, contrasting sharply with the idyllic overtone of the earlier film. The elegiac principle of exploring the antithetic tension comes to the fore in the film's external and internal structures. While the first film consists of largely homogenous visual material, the second film draws on a diverse range of visual and audio materials including photographs, original sound recordings, voice-overs, shaky handheld recordings, black-and-white panorama shots of the village's cemetery and wintry streets, colour footage from the first film, a modern composition by Alfred Schnittke and Glinka's lullaby. The film is fragmentary, incongruous and disturbing; it accentuates the film-maker's subjective point of view: footage shot during a journey by car through a rainy autumnal landscape is followed by a scene which documents the screening of the first part of the film in the village club. The emphatic tone of the voice-over, which dominates the second half of the film, undercuts the visions of a simpler and harmonious way of life that emerged in the first part. Maria, the subject of the film's first part, is not among the audience: she died in 1982, and the film hints that she may have killed herself. Maria's widowed husband has since remarried, causing a rift between father and daughter. The narrator outlines the story of a woman who 'barely had the strength to live for 45 years'. Her story is typical of the experiences of many Soviet women who belonged to a generation which 'literally worked itself to the bone' before being ground under by the demands of the kolkhoz economy.

The more disjointed editing in the second part reflects Maria's increasingly unstable world rather than technical experimentation, and assists the building of tension that is crucial for Sokurov's elegiac mode. The film's antithetic tension stems from the bucolic idyll of the first part and the lamentation at its passing in the second. But parallel to the film's elegiac poetics, Sokurov also seeks to reconcile these two poles. The anguish of loss is alleviated, at least partially, by the memory of the past. On a formal level Sokurov seeks to transcend the gulf between the past and the present through his treatment of the visual material. Rather than merely presenting the photographs in sequence, Sokurov explores each image with the camera, zooming in on particular details. Thus Sokurov instils the images with presence, motion and time. Likewise, the static shots of Maria's daughter's family sitting before the camera are robbed of their natural motion. The film's final scenes show Maria's daughter breastfeeding her child, an image that is followed by a sweeping pan across a lonely cemetery and a shot of Maria Voinova mourning at her son's grave. The sequence creates a web of connections between the various narrative moments and transcends their singularity. A moment in time transcends its temporal limits and is elevated to a universal level. The eternal cycle of life transcends death and alleviates the suffering of the individual as narrative strands that are connected on an abstract, non-representational level.

The Subjective and the Elusive Narrator

The role of the narrator who sympathises with the subject whilst not being involved in the action is typical of Sokurov's elegies. Indeed, most of Sokurov's documentaries are accompanied by a narrator who comments on the filmic images. This narration provides the kind of explanatory commentary that is typical of the genre, but Sokurov further accentuates the narrator's subjective point of view in his commentary. His insistence on the subjective nature of artistic endeavour – a point which he has expressed in numerous interviews – contradicts the conventional notions of documentary filming.

> I would like to emphasise again that I do not make documentary films. It seems to me that my films do not contain a single word of truth. Unfortunately, that's just something that I cannot do. I am a very subjective person and apart from the fact that my films are the result of a real process, there is no other connection between my films and real events, processes or situations. They are much more concerned with my thoughts and feelings about a particular topic.[6]

The dominant role of the narrator and Sokurov's insistence on a subjective point of view make his documentaries veritable monologues and leave the films' subjects few opportunities to express themselves. Sokurov narrates his films in a grave and plaintive tone. But the narrator's ultimate identity and the question of whether narrator and director are identical is only resolved in the few films that show Sokurov interviewing his subjects, i.e. where there is a visual presence. These films tend to be more dialogical, and this approach remains largely limited to his interview films.

The role of the narrator in Sokurov's portraits is to recount his subjects' biographies. Sokurov's portraits often begin with a condensed version of his subjects' life stories – a raw list of biographical details, including place of birth, family and descendents. These sequences are clearly modelled on the genre of the epigraph (related to the elegy), which details an individual's identity, lifespan and origins in the briefest possible manner. In the first part of *Maria*, Sokurov refrained from using a voice-over and allowed his protagonist to introduce herself and briefly recount her story in her local dialect:

> I was born in the village of Vedeneno, where I still live today, on 16 August 1936. My family consisted of my sister, my brother, myself... and my grandmother who is sitting here beside me now. I grew up and married my beloved husband Voinov, Ivan Klementevich at the age of twenty. We had a son, and then a daughter.

Similarly, Sokurov provides few details about Tarkovsky. The little information that he does offer is contained in a few standard phrases and includes such seemingly insignificant details as his place of birth and family history.

In most of his portraits Sokurov's commentary reaches back at least one generation; in his portrait of Tarkovsky it spans centuries:

> The family of Maria Ivanovna Vishniakova insisted that she give birth to her child in their village. She gave birth to a son who was named Andrei. This took place in the village of Zavrazhe in the district of Yurevetsk, Ivanovo region, on 4 April 1932. Andrei was soon joined by a sister named Marina. The children's father was the great Soviet-Russian poet Arseni Alexandrovich Tarkovsky. The Tarkovsky family originally came from Daghestan and their family history spans no less than seven centuries. The Principality of Tarkovsky was the oldest state in the Caucasus region and existed until the mid-nineteenth century.

An equally condensed life story is provided in *Soviet Elegy*, which is composed of a number of recordings of the politician Boris Yeltsin that were made in January 1989. Sokurov's portrait of Yeltsin is one of his most condensed biographical studies and is, from a formal perspective, maybe his most fascinating portrait. Made at a time when Yeltsin had reached a low point in his political career, the film minutely details his origins and his parents' lives. Sokurov's narrative scope emphasises a continuity that extends across the generations – in spite of the social upheavals of the Soviet regime. His use of phrases such as 'God's earth' (*svet bozhii*) and '23 years after the birth' (*v 23-kh let ot rodu*) draws on colloquial and rural modes of speech:

> In 1906 a boy was born to a peasant family and named Nikolai: Nikolai Ignatich. This took place in the village of Butka in the Talitsk district, Sverdlovsk; these are, of course, the contemporary place names. In 1929, at the age of 23, Nikolai proposed to a young woman called Klavdiia, two years his junior. They had a classical village wedding. [...] Early in the famine-plagued 1930s Nikolai was forced to leave the village with his family. They settled in the city of Berezniki near Perm, where Nikolai found work at a potash processing plant. Their son Boris was born in 1931. [...] At university Boris met his future wife, who was studying at the same faculty. They had a classic student wedding. Boris' father Nikolai Ignatich passed away at the age of 69 years in 1975.

In spite of its subjective style, Sokurov's commentary fulfils an explanatory function; yet it is also marred by significant omissions and his failure to comment on numerous associative chains. Sokurov's portraits frequently include sequences that remain unexplained and open to interpretation. The narrator disappears at the moment where the viewer actually needs guidance or an explanation: he is an elusive figure. The final scene in *Soviet Elegy* is a graphic example of Sokurov's practice of eschewing to comment on constellations of figures and events: it shows Boris Yeltsin sitting in the kitchen of his apartment together with another person. Yeltsin remains in a contemplative pose at the table, while the unknown figure leaves the room. The figure returns after several minutes of real film time have passed, by which time the film is finished. Sokurov explained the story behind this scene in an interview: after asking Yeltsin a question, Sokurov left the room for five minutes, and Yeltsin answered his query on his return. Yeltsin's answer was not meant for the public, however, and Sokurov then switched off the camera.[7]

Sokurov's narrative monologues are thus characterised by the omission of information on the one hand, and their often redundant character on the other, when he recounts what viewers can clearly see for themselves. This redundancy heightens the meditative character of Sokurov's visual and audio montages. *Soviet Elegy*, for example, opens with a self-explanatory announcement: 'You are now watching the documentary film *Soviet Elegy*.' Sokurov's portrait of Andrei Tarkovsky also includes a number of meta-comments that begin with the phrase 'You are now watching...'.

The apparently contradictory roles of the narrator, guiding the viewer and stating the obvious in the voice-over commentary on the one hand, whilst on the other hand confusing the viewer by omitting essential information, run through Sokurov's documentaries (and indeed culminate in *Russian Ark*, where the narrator claims to have lost his memory whilst knowing both past and future history of his country better than his counterpart, de Custine). More importantly for this chapter, the narrator positions himself both within the world of his subject (an answer not meant for the public is not publicised) and outside (as a competent historian who guides us through time).

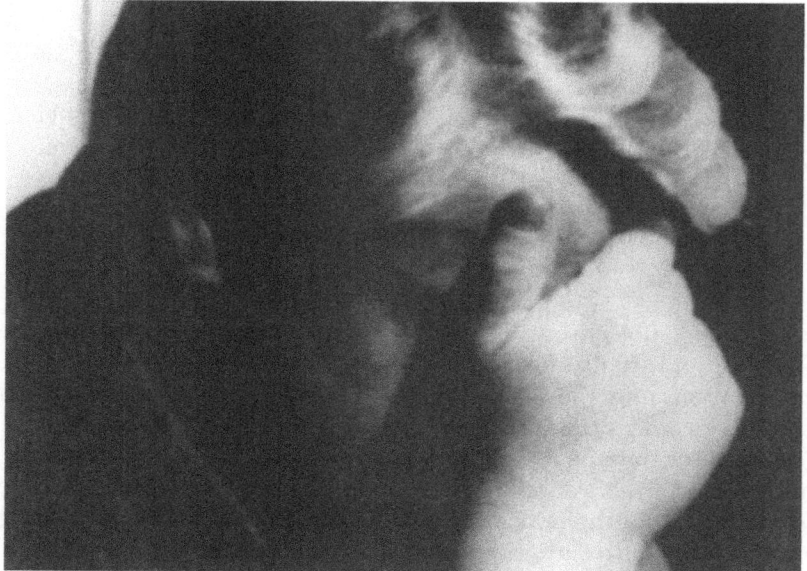

Still from *Soviet Elegy*: Yeltsin.

Techniques of Reduction

Just over half an hour long, *Soviet Elegy* is both a minimalist portrait of a politician and an elegy to seventy years of Soviet history. Two series of photographs form the centrepiece of *Soviet Elegy*. The first series of images depicts the Yeltsin family and is accompanied by the brief summary of the family history (as discussed above). The second series presents a montage featuring photographic portraits of over one hundred high-ranking Soviet politicians. This gallery of images encompasses almost all of the Politburo's full members since 1919, along with a number of non-voting candidates – a function which Yeltsin held from 1986 to 1988. The gallery begins and ends with an image of Lenin, and a few Politburo members – including Mikhail Suslov, Leonid Brezhnev and Eduard Shevardnadze – appear twice. Some of the recurring images are enlarged; for instance the camera zooms in on Mikhail Gorbachev's lips. The monotonous series of images and the accompanying name recital are reminiscent of an ecclesiastical litany for the deceased. In its exhaustive thoroughness this sequence represents the apparatus of the Soviet regime. The sequence seems like a farewell to the Soviet era – and Sokurov's premonition (the film was made in 1989) was soon confirmed by history.

Sokurov constructs his portrait of Yeltsin around the two series of photographs – family and politics, private and public – and other juxtapositions. His use of audio material is limited and similarly reductive, echoing flatly the changes of perspective performed by the camera: Sokurov foregoes the use of music and restricts the soundtrack to a sampling of repetitive notes and ambient sounds. *Soviet Elegy* begins with a black-and-white series of shots that express a mood of elegiac sorrow and invite the viewer to contemplate the transient nature of human life. As the camera pans across a landscape of autumnal leaves, it captures the image of an old gravestone inscribed with the words 'Your will be done, Lord' and reveals a peaceful graveyard planted with tall leafy trees. The camera moves along the vertical axis from the sky to the ground and vice versa. The sound sequence opens with a tolling bell, which gradually fades into the buzzing whir of insects that is then overlaid with birdsong and cries of a cuckoo. At first these ambient sounds are disturbed only by the squeaking of a playground swing, but eventually they are drowned out by the noise of traffic. Parallel to this shift in the soundtrack, the camera leaves the vertical axis to move along the horizontal plane. The visual focus shifts accordingly, with a prefabricated apartment block coming into view beyond the gravestone, before the scene shifts to reveal rows of freshly filled graves in the otherwise empty grounds of a new graveyard. Finally, a new apartment building blocks our view to the horizon in the background.

This sequence is followed by documentary footage with glimpses of an impoverished way of life that is neither rural nor urban: children playing on a swing outside their barrack-like home, laundry hanging on a line to dry, a woman with a bucket of water, a wooden house and a tin shack.[8] Together with the image of the new graveyard, with its associations with a serial production line, Sokurov's sequence of minimalist black-and-white images laments the loss of individuality and suggests that to live in the Soviet Union was to live on a construction site that was never to be completed. At the same time, he juxtaposes – and links – the permanence of nature (the autumnal trees, the birds) with the passing of life (the cemetery) and the transience of everyday life (washing, playing, working).

The film reaches its climax just as the tension is reduced to a bare minimum in the final (colour) scenes, showing Yeltsin in his apartment. In the first scene he is standing in front of his television, clad in a jacket, fur hat and sweatpants. His political opponent Mikhail Gorbachev is speaking on television, but the sound is muted and Gorbachev's voice cannot be heard. The second scene shows a silent Yeltsin sitting in his kitchen, deep in thought. The antithetical tension of these two scenes results from their stark contrast to more familiar media representations of Soviet politicians. Sokurov's film portrayal of Yeltsin is focused on the silence and a sense of privacy surrounding the politician. With hindsight, *Soviet Elegy* is a minimalist portrait of Soviet society in decline, as it offers a glimpse into a society undermined by the discrepancy between a utopian vision and its implementation; by the gulf that separated the rulers and the people; and by the violent modernisation it underwent. Sokurov's portrait of Yeltsin has little in common with the genre of political reportage, whilst it is prescient of the power struggle that would erupt between Mikhail Gorbachev and Boris Yeltsin.

The contrast between public and private spaces and between social roles and private lives also informs the portrait of the Lithuanian politician Vytautas Landsbergis, *A Simple Elegy*. Sokurov follows a quiet scene in Landsbergis' office with footage of a mass demonstration in front of the Lithuanian government buildings. The silence is broken by the sound of music as the scene changes to show Landsbergis outside his normal social role, playing a nocturne by the Lithuanian composer Mikalojus Čiurlionis on a piano in his government office.

The reduction of a subject's life story through a limitation of camera movements (vertical/horizontal), the condensation of history through picture-sequences, the contrast of public and private through screened/staged images and moments of privacy and intimacy (kitchen, laundry, piano) are typical of the elegiac mode as they reflect the public/external and private/internal structuring principles.

Experimenting with Media

Many critics have commented on Sokurov's idiosyncratic blend of experimental and traditional approaches to film-making. Mikhail Iampolski noted Sokurov's unique style in the late 1980s and described him as a 'moralising avant-garde artist'. Iampolski argued that Sokurov's films combined exuberantly experimental avant-garde aesthetics with a traditionalist-conservative ethical position grounded in Sokurov's deep appreciation of the cultural and moral values of nineteenth-century culture.[9]

Sokurov's 'avant-garde' position is based on his experimentation with the artistic potential of the medium and his reflection on a range of modes of expression, including literature, music, painting, photography and film.[10] Sokurov's films explore the manifold relationships between media, interrogating their technical limitations and seeking to transcend current modes of perception. Unlike fiction films, Sokurov's film portraits do not claim to create a self-contained fictional world. Instead, his portraits represent a kind of laboratory, a space for experimentation with new techniques and unconventional forms of media experience.

Sokurov's film portraits reflect the evolution of media over the last decades. He worked with traditional celluloid film until the mid-1990s and his films from this period explore the relationship between photography and moving images. Both in his documentaries and fiction films, a primary artistic technique has been to impart a temporal dimension to still photography. Sokurov complements this technique by slowing film images and reducing their most intrinsic quality – motion – to a standstill. This technique of deceleration applies equally to the movement of the camera and to the movement within and between the images. Another of Sokurov's characteristic techniques is to highlight the material nature of the respective medium. Sokurov achieves this, for example, through montage of television footage or by including within the shot the hand that holds a photograph.

Sokurov complements the technique of deceleration by reducing both the narrative complexity and the amount of information conveyed in his films. His two elegies on Fedor Chaliapin, *Elegy* (1986) and *Petersburg Elegy* (1990) are compilation films that draw on a range of sources, including archive material and clips from feature films.[11] Sokurov's first elegy to Chaliapin is marked by its balanced editing rhythm, informative style of commentary and a linear narrative that follows the stations of Chaliapin's biography from his flight and emigration through to the return to his homeland. The second film is edited in a markedly slower fashion and lacks the narrative component which characterised its predecessor. *Petersburg Elegy* is composed of clips, including an excerpt from G.W. Papst's film *Don Quichotte* with Chaliapin in the lead role. These clips are only loosely connected to the film's narrative, which overall possesses less of an informative aspect. The dominant narrative technique in *Petersburg Elegy* is the associative montage of individual fragments, which comes to a standstill on several occasions. This first occurs in the near-motionless scene when Chaliapin's daughters return to their childhood home. The narrative halts a second time in one of the film's final scenes: an eight-minute-long shot of an aged man sitting at a table – the man, we realise, is none other than Chaliapin's son.

Sokurov's formal and technical experiments are clearly linked to the messages underlying his films. In *Petersburg Elegy* Sokurov stops the movement just as his protagonists return to their childhood home. The practically motionless filmic image gains its effect from its duration in time. Sokurov's approach situates disparate narrative moments in the here-and-now. The past – the painful experience of emigration – is contained in this moment. The silence of Sokurov's figures manifests their grief at the loss of their home.

In contrast to this treatment of filmic images, which are slowed down to bring time to a standstill, Sokurov also seeks to impart a temporal dimension to photographic images. Unlike filmic images, the latter 'speak' to the future by testifying to that which will cease to be. In a study of photography's transcendent nature, Roland Barthes described this effect, which contributes significantly to the wistfully elegiac mood of Sokurov's works, as the 'punctum', or, that 'which pierces the viewer'. The 'punctum' compresses our perception of time, locating the present and the imminent future in a single moment. A photograph of a man sentenced to death, for example, locates his death in the future: 'I read at the same time: This will be and this has been; [...] By giving me the absolute past of the pose (aorist), the photograph tells me death in the future.'[12]

Since the mid-1990s Sokurov has almost exclusively worked with video for his documentary projects. This move altered the aesthetics of his films. Working with video, and later with digital recording devices, extended the available recording time, while the format's utility significantly closed the gap between the camera and the world. The ease with which digital images can be altered or manipulated also tends to facilitate more subjective approaches to film-making. In addition to Sokurov's use of special recording techniques (lenses, filters, etc.), these innovations counteract the medium's tendency for mechanical reproduction. In an interview Sokurov has defended this artistic principle of deforming film images: 'I'm not shooting a concrete picture of nature, I'm creating it. [...] I destroy real nature and create my own.'[13]

Thus, a notable aspect of *A Humble Life* is Sokurov's exploration of the video camera's aesthetic potential. The film, which focuses on an elderly Japanese kimono maker, is perhaps his most intimate and personal portrait. The camera's approach to the kimono maker and the house in which she lives and works is gentle. The camera moves carefully through this

Still from *A Humble Life*.

microcosm and explores it from a respectful distance, even during the film's more extreme close-ups. Rather than attempting to penetrate this microcosm intellectually, Sokurov's camera explores the texture of its various surfaces: the cracks in the wooden walls, the rough surface of the floor, the coarse fibre of the floor mats, the light from outside, and the play of shadows on the ground and the walls.

At the heart of the film lies the physical presence of a body. Sokurov communicates this presence in images that show the kimono maker going about her everyday life as she combs and pins up her hair, lights a fire, drinks a cup of hot tea and goes about her work with scissors, needles and thread. But her body is also present as an actual physical entity – it is an aged body, as the close-ups reveal. The quality of the colour footage is scaled back and largely restricted to brown and green hues. By reducing the intensity of the colour and cross-fading images, Sokurov blurs the border that separates background and foreground. Just as the house and its natural surroundings are one, the house and the tailor also form a harmonious whole. The inside of the house is transparent and our gaze is continually drawn outside through the open doorways. Instead of exploring the surroundings, the outdoor scenes offer us glimpses of an enchanted leafy landscape hidden in swirling mists. During these sequences it becomes apparent that these images are the narrator's inner visions. *Oriental Elegy*, also made in Japan, is composed entirely of such inner visions, necessitating an even more extensive artistic intervention in the technical process.

The sound editing in *A Humble Life* is restrained: analogous to his treatment of the images, Sokurov has not attempted to create a true-to-life reproduction. Instead, the sound montage draws on an artistic blend of ambient recordings, distorted sounds and quietly played musical compositions. The kimono maker herself does not speak until the final scene when she proudly recites some traditional *haiku* poems that she has written. This window into her soul is not opened until the final scene of the film – she offers us but a fleeting glimpse of her inner world.

Nearly ten years separate *A Humble Life* from Sokurov's most recent portrait. Sokurov's portrait of opera singer Galina Vishnevskaya and cellist Mstislav Rostropovich, *Elegy of Life*, is astonishingly conventional in comparison to his earlier works. The film includes footage from interviews with the film's two subjects and provides viewers with a wealth of biographical detail. The unmanipulated realism of the digital material is another notable quality of Sokurov's portrait. Sokurov's extensive use of photographic images, blending up to six images within a single *frame*, is reminiscent of a modern computer-assisted presentation. It is the ostentatious conventionality of the technique that Sokurov employs in this portrait, which creates an antithetic tension.

As the title hints, *Elegy of Life* is a baroque hymn celebrating both life itself and music as a pan-European cultural achievement. Sokurov substitutes the restrained style of other works with a strategy of visual saturation that is based not on manipulation, but on the actual subject at hand. The portrait is framed by the couple's 50th wedding anniversary celebrated in the opulently decorated rooms of Moscow's Metropole

Hotel. The couple's huge Moscow apartment, with its antique furniture and art objects, presents a similarly baroque vision of abundance. The film's antithetical effect is created by the couple's simple, yet vivacious character, a result of the privations that preceded their current lifestyle. Vishnevskaya's reception room, decorated with stage costumes and life-size portraits, contrasts starkly with the anecdote which she recounts: during the Leningrad siege, at the age of just 18, she gave birth to a son, who died shortly after birth.

The House as Leitmotif

The house as the epitome of belonging and rootedness constitutes a central theme in Sokurov's film portraits. Often, however, Sokurov explores this leitmotif *ex negativo*; his focus is on the dispossession and sorrow caused by emigration, war and modernisation. The essentially positive sentiment of *Elegy of Life* sets this film apart from Sokurov's previous elegies. The couple's new Moscow apartment denotes a state of satisfaction and happiness – yet their happiness is not given, but the result of painful experiences and individual effort.

By contrast, the house in *A Humble Life* is a place of yearning and a vanishing point in the narrator's imagination: it represents a world and a way of life that cannot be reconciled with the demands of modernity. The kimono maker inhabits a house bereft of any modern comforts; her door remains open even when the temperature drops below zero. The house is a microcosm, a world in itself: the kimono maker lives and works in the house, thus avoiding the alienation that characterises industrial production. The qualities that the narrator ascribes to the house might equally apply to the film's protagonist: 'In everything there is persistence, obstinacy and immutability'.

Yeltsin's home is very unlike the kimono maker's house: it is a typical product of modern attitudes to living. Yeltsin's house is defined by a number – a sign welcomes visitors to 'Building Nr. 358'. There is no trace of a harmonic unity that characterised the kimono maker's relationship to her home. The visual montage in *Soviet Elegy* reveals a vision of modern homelessness that is denoted as typically Soviet. The impersonal and industrial architecture of the prefabricated apartment blocks and the ramshackle barracks are disastrous ideological and political interventions in their inhabitants' lives. People here remain homeless even in death – the graves at the new Soviet cemetery leave hardly any room for traditional forms of sorrow and mourning.

Sokurov's earlier portraits in particular closely link the homestead with the experience of loss. The dispossession and displacement caused by emigration are a central theme in his works. Sokurov foregrounds these themes in both of his portraits of Chaliapin, while also exploring the experience of returning to one's origins in both a direct and metaphorical sense. Chaliapin died in Paris in 1938 and the return of the Russian opera singer's remains to his former homeland in 1984 forms the basis of Sokurov's portraits. Emigration is also a central theme in Sokurov's elegy to Andrei Tarkovsky: *Moscow Elegy*. The film focuses on Tarkovsky's final years, following his departure from the Soviet Union in 1982 through to his death in Paris in 1986.

Sokurov complements diverse footage with his own shots after Tarkovsky's death, visiting the various places in Russia where Tarkovsky once lived.[14] The camera slowly guides viewers through rooms and carefully explores their atmosphere, taking us to an apartment on the 13th floor of a new tenement block that is still haunted by Tarkovsky's presence. Sokurov also visits Tarkovsky's now derelict ground-floor apartment in a typical two-storey building in Moscow's old Zamoskvorechie area, where the film-maker lived as a child with his mother and sister. Finally, the camera takes us to a building 90 kilometres from the city of Riazan where the Tarkovsky family once spent their summers. Sokurov associates Tarkovsky's homes with warmth and homeliness. But the visit to the summer house is overshadowed by an intense sense of sorrow and loss at Tarkovsky's death. Sokurov finds the atmosphere in the house now cold and empty – not even the warmth of the fire can raise their spirits: 'Even after lighting the fire, we still couldn't get warm'.

Another sequence that exemplifies Sokurov's exploration of the home as a leitmotif begins with a shot of Tarkovsky on the balcony of screenwriter Tonino Guerra. In the following shot we seem to share Tarkovsky's view from the balcony – the broad horizon of a snowy Russian landscape, broken by a small country road. The camera pans to complete a full circle and reveals a row of crooked electricity pylons and a small settlement snuggled against the earth. These panoramic scenes are an integral element of Sokurov's visual repertoire. They express his desire to capture the essence of 'home' and to give expression to a particularly Russian character and a national-cultural identity in the traditional sense of the term. Sokurov remains true to this spiritual ideal in his final portrait (*Elegy of Life*), but assumes a much broader notion of 'home'. Vishnevskaya and Rostropovich did not adopt a foreign citizenship during their years in emigration and refused to accept Russian citizenship on their return to their former homeland. Instead they have equipped themselves with travel documents from the state of Monaco that do not specify their nationality. They see themselves as global citizens – conscious of the fact that Russia is a part of our global cultural heritage, and that they are intrinsically linked to Russian culture and all its traditions. Sokurov's admiration for their way of thinking is unmistakable.

Over his thirty years as documentary film-maker, Sokurov has refined the genre of the film portrait through innovative use of filming devices and narrative delusion. Most important, he has introduced conventional formal elements of the elegy which, on the one hand, have kept his films within the documentary mainstream (and made them suitable for television screenings), whilst on the other hand he has fractured the genre precisely through the translation of the elegiac conventions to cinema.

Translated by Damian Harrison

Notes

1. See Sylvia Egli von Matt, Hans-Peter von Peschke, Paul Riniker, *Das Porträt*, Konstanz: UVK Verlag, 2003, p. 43.
2. Vytautas Landsbergis (b. 1932) was the statesman who led Lithuania to independence from the USSR in 1990.

3   *Sonata for Viola. Dmitri Shostakovich*, a portrait of the composer Dmitrii Shostakovich; *Hubert Robert. A Fortunate Life*, a portrait of French painter Hubert Robert commissioned by the State Hermitage Museum in Petersburg; and *dolce…*, a portrait of Japanese writer Tosio Simao and his family remain beyond the scope of this chapter. Sokurov has also filmed portraits of Russian soldiers stationed in the country's border regions – *Spiritual Voices* and *Confession* – both films are constructed as fictional diaries. His documentary cycle *Petersburg Diary* records the cultural life of St Petersburg. Sokurov completed two of the films in this cycle in the 1990s: a report on the unveiling of the memorial statue to Fedor Dostoevsky, titled *Inauguration of a Monument to Dostoevsky*; and the documentary portrait *Kozintsev's Flat*, which surveys Sokurov's own private apartment in long, sweeping pan shots. *Elegy from Russia* is a portrait of contemporary and historical Russia based on the works of Russian photographer Maxim Dmitriev (1858–1948). Sokurov's interview films *An Example of Intonation* with Boris Yeltsin and *Dialogues with Solzhenitsyn* also draw on the portrait genre.
4   See Klaus Weissenberger, *Formen der Elegie von Goethe bis Celan*, Bern, Munich: Francke Verlag, 1969.
5   See Weissenberger, p. 51.
6   'Aleksandr Sokurov im Gespräch mit Hans-Joachim Schlegel', in Schlegel (ed.), *Die subversive Kamera*, Konstanz: UVK Medien, 1999, pp. 153–63 (p. 158).
7   'Es ist der Zuschauer, der des Films bedarf…', (Alexandr Sokurow im Gespräch mit Galina Antoschewskaja), *Katalog des Internationalen Leipziger Festivals für Dokumentar- und Animationsfilm*, Leipzig, 1997, pp. 95–101 (pp. 99–101).
8   In her review of *Soviet Elegy*, Maya Turovskaya characterises Sokurov's images as *sovetskost'*, i.e. quintessentially Soviet: Maiia Turovskaia, 'Sovetskaia elegiia', in Liubov' Arkus, (ed.), *Sokurov*, St Petersburg: Seans, 1994 (henceforth referred to as *Sokurov 1*), pp. 149–51 (p. 150).
9   Michail Jampolski, 'Sokurows Regiearbeit', *Kunst und Literatur* 3 (1990), pp. 309–15 (p. 309 f.).
10 See Sabine Hänsgen, 'Stille Bilder. Zur Minimierung des Filmischen bei Aleksandr Sokurov (Film > Photo > Malerei)', in Mirjam Goller, Georg Witte (eds), *Minimalismus*, special issue of *Wiener Slawistischer Almanach* 51 (2001), pp. 375–90.
11 The fragments which Sokurov used in *Petersburg Elegy* were taken from several sources, including a 1915 silent film featuring Fedor Chaliapin as Ivan the Terrible; *Don Quichotte* by G.W. Pabst (1932), featuring Chaliapin in the main role; and Federico Fellini's *Roma* (1972) featuring Fedor Chaliapin Jr. in a minor role.
12 Roland Barthes, *Camera Lucida, Reflections on Photography*, New York: Farrar, Straus and Giroux, 1981, p. 96.
13 Schrader, 'The History of an Artist's Soul is a Very Sad History', *Film Comment* 33.6 (1997), pp. 20–25 (p. 23).
14 The portrait includes numerous clips from Tarkovsky's final two films, *Nostalghia* (1983) and *Sacrifice* [Offret, 1986], and from his intimate work *The Mirror* [Zerkalo, 1975]. But Sokurov's portrait also features diverse documentary footage of Tarkovsky, including Chris Marker's footage of the bed-ridden director in the final months of his life. These images also formed the basis of Chris Marker's film about Andrei Tarkovsky, *Une Journée d'Andrej Arsenevitch* (2000).

Chapter 3

SOKUROV'S CINEMATIC MINIMALISM

Sabine Hänsgen

In various art forms and media, the term 'minimalism' is used to describe the transnational phenomenon of an aesthetic of reduction. The development of minimalist practices in film began after the Second World War when a modern cinema that reflects on its own temporality replaced the classic cinema of action.[1]

Of special interest to me is the question whether specific strategies of minimalism can also be found in contemporary Russian cinema. What potential could minimalist film aesthetics possibly unfold in Russian culture against the historical backdrop of revolutionary maximalism, avant-garde claims of universality and rhetorical strategies aimed at overwhelming the audience in Soviet mass culture?[2]

The starting point of my exploration of this question is Ulrich Gregor's notice of the use of the minimalist method in the films of Alexander Sokurov that display 'events of extended phenomenological observation and only minor dramatic variation'.[3] Referring to a series of examples, I will make an attempt at finding more systematic criteria to describe the forms of cinematic reduction in Sokurov's oeuvre. A tendency towards minimalism in his work will be examined in the context of the Russian-Soviet history of film, technical developments in Hollywood cinema as well as the Western avant-garde cinema of the sixties and seventies.

The Film Images Slow Down

The defining feature of the cinematic medium is movement. Contrary to the cultic origins of drama and theatre, film is the result of an advance in photographic technology to facilitate the representation of moving images. By projecting twenty-four images per second and taking advantage of the limited response time of the human eye, film is able to deliver a simulation of movement and the flow of time to its audience.

In Sokurov's work, a tendency to subvert this fundamental condition of the cinematic medium can be observed, taking the form of a minimalisation of movement, a deceleration of the film images that can eventually even have the effect of their seemingly coming to a standstill. This impression of slowness is created by an extreme limitation of cuts in favour of long, continuous shots, the restriction of camera movement as well as a restraint of character movement in a reduced dramatic composition.

Sokurov often rejects the concept of montage as a method aiming at the fragmentation of the homogeneous space of an organic work as a whole propagated by earlier revolutionary film theorists like Sergei Eisenstein, Lev Kuleshov, Dziga Vertov et al. In his later work in particular, he criticises distraction as a mode of reception and, with his aesthetics of 'still images', strives for a restoration of the aura of art that Walter Benjamin considered to have been overcome precisely by film's mechanical reproduction.[4] Meditative contemplation takes the place of shock-like dynamic and, in the course of this, the reduction of movement is compensated for by opening up a space that has to be filled by the perception, reflection and imagination of the audience. Similar to Andrei Tarkovsky's work[5] and contrary to its technical characteristic, the cinematic medium here serves the purpose of contemplative immersion. Time and movement seem suspended in a cultic space of perception. In an interview, Sokurov describes his cinematic ideal of time as a continuous duration that approaches the limits of eternity:

> There is a tense in the English language that I like very much: *present continuous* – if my intuition does not deceive me, this form exists in no other language. [...] It delineates such a broad space of time that one is forced to reflect on where everything comes from and where it is headed. Life itself is short but death lasts a long time.[6]

By presenting an event or a condition in a very long or even in its entire duration – without compressing its representation into easily consumable temporal units – Sokurov challenges his audience to experience time in a way that is very different from the rhythms of mainstream mass media. It is not the film image that changes to draw the spectators' attention but the spectators themselves who have to change to perceive the liminal variability of the images. What we are dealing with here is an appeal to reshape the perceptual apparatus beyond the comprehension of a narrative.

A rather radical example of this from Sokurov's oeuvre is *Spiritual Voices*. In this film, the distance between beginning and ending is expanded to downright monumental proportions by means of a minimalist strategy of slowing down time.

Sokurov continues Bazin's tradition of the ontological film where – owing to the great depth of field of the images – long, continuous shots can be realised in *plans-séquences*. Bazin conceptualised film as a medium of duration: Now, for the first time, the image of things is likewise the image of their duration, change mummified, as it were.'[7] To visualise even minimal nuances of change through gradual transformation of single picture

Still from *Spiritual Voices*.

elements in *Spiritual Voices*, Sokurov makes use of electronic video technology that he adopts, contrary to a televisual utilitarianism, for his film aesthetics: 'Video – that is a world of inertness and aggression. The only thing we took from the video experience is the technology of the long, continuous shots.'[8]

Spiritual Voices shows more than five hours from the lives of soldiers who lie in wait at the Tajik–Afghan border. Barely perceptibly changing shots immerse the viewer's gaze in the barren landscape of the border region: sky, mountains, earth; the shape of a human crossing the frame; the sun slowly vanishing behind the horizon, smoke rising from a fire, the face of a sleeping young man... These images are accompanied by music and the author's comments that also refer to the composers Mozart, Beethoven and Messiaen. This superimposition of visual and acoustic layers creates a cinematic space in which – by means of the interaction of seeing and hearing and corresponding to the title *Spiritual Voices* – the sense of sight that is directed at the physical world is devalued in favour of a more verbally orientated inner vision.

The duration of the shots in *Spiritual Voices* seems disproportionate to their narrative content. The plot of a war film is implied but not developed into an exciting staging of combat scenes.[9] The focus is on vacuous activity, on the breaks between military actions; almost nothing happens. Sokurov explicitly opposes the conventional representation of war in film that aims solely at spectacularity:

> In war, there are no picturesque explosions, sensational time lapses, people who grab their heads. There are no blinding flashes, no

blood that slowly runs down a finger. And actually, there is no excitement either. [...] Long breaks between the attacks, in which there is relaxation. A great amount of vacuous activity: erratic advances, long periods of looking around.[10]

The Film Images no longer Tell a Story

The process of slowing down of the film images is linked with a reduction of narrative complexity – a simplification of plot structure that borders on eventlessness. Sokurov's contemplative shots amount to a rejection of the aesthetics of identification of narrative cinema whose most developed form can be found in the techniques of Hollywood cinema.[11] By means of precisely calculated changes of framing and point of view, especially the direction of the gaze of the shot-reverse-shot-method, the audience is drawn into the action that is supposed to grip, thrill, scare or move it to tears. Sokurov's films have a distinct effect against the backdrop of the tradition of the Soviet epic film that, incidentally, was also influenced by American film techniques. The film images of Socialist Realism tell the great secularised story of salvation that forms the basis of the ideology of Marxism and Leninism; the stillness of Sokurov's images frees them from any legible sense of history.

As a minimalist reply to the festive day chronotope that is a central element of the canonical plot of Soviet film, I would like to take a closer look at Sokurov's *Evening Sacrifice*. The festive day chronotope of Socialist Realism offers the possibility of transcending a negative everyday reality by staging the dream of the communist paradise, the bright future, as an all-encompassing festival of joy in the present. The cinematic representation of this collective festival is orientated towards a maximalist effect. By means of purposeful employment of the sensual and emotional allures of movement, rhythm, music, colour, etc., the audience is infused with a 'utopian sensibility', an exceptional sensation of energy, abundance, intensity, transparency and a physically and sensually tangible community.[12]

Sokurov's *Evening Sacrifice* refrains from any such intensive treatment of the viewer's psyche. The utopian potential of transcendence is withdrawn from the film images, subtracted, and the production and emotional values of the staging of the festival are minimised in favour of an effect of contemplation. *Evening Sacrifice* is a documentary about one of the great Soviet public holidays in May, although it remains uncertain whether its images of a spring day in Leningrad were captured on the first or ninth of May. The political-ideological meaning cannot be deduced from the shots since there are no unambiguous signs or symbols referring to it. The actual events of the festive day are left aside. None of the usual joyful faces, parades and fireworks are shown; instead, the camera focuses on the happenings on the fringes of the festival.

Evening Sacrifice is divided into two parts: In the first part, the social ritual of firing a salute is sketched out in rhythmic variations of repeating shots as an elementary process of loading, command, firing of the salvos and, finally, the empty shell casings falling to the ground; the second, longer main part focuses on the depiction of the crowd – images reminiscent

Still from *Evening Sacrifice.*

of the aesthetics of film pioneers like the Lumière brothers – that, after the festival has ended, swarms past the camera across the Nevsky Prospekt in an extraordinarily slow movement of indeterminate energy. At times, the crowd seems to be approaching the audience; then again it seems to remain in one place.[13]

The isolation of the festive day chronotope from any kind of history reveals the physical dimension of actions beyond their ideological meaning in social ritual. Two different collective bodies are juxtaposed: the mechanical movements of soldiers and a crowd driven by instincts that is not – as it would be in keeping with the convention of Soviet festive day representation – arranged in synchronised movements as a decorative ornament.[14]

Long, static shots from opposed but identically high points of view dissolve into each other. By intercutting these wide shots of the crowd with shorter medium shots and close-ups that capture single persons, faces and gestures, Sokurov creates a tension between the individual and the collective and explores the relationship between the single body and the body of the crowd in a time at the end of ideology.[15]

The Film Images are Silent

In contention with a hypertrophic verbalisation of film in the Soviet Union's ideological culture – which, for example, found its expression in a much more intensive censorship of screenplays, the literary scripts, than their visual realisations –, the reduction of the text dimension in *Soviet Elegy*, a cinematic portrait of Boris Yeltsin, actually results in the obliteration of human speech in the silence of the film images. Sokurov robs the politician of his essential means of articulation, verbal rhetoric, and places him inside a zone of silence.[16]

By dispensing with language almost entirely, the extremely long, continuous shots, on the other hand, open up a space for the perception of the physical dimension of representation. The voice-over commentary is limited to very few informative sentences and contains no references to the party careers of the person portrayed in the film. The visual signs of Yeltsin's elevated status only provide a backdrop for a presentation of the most elementary situations and actions. For example, the camera accompanies him on his long way from his office through endless corridors out of the building to his car and observes the activity of walking itself. In a reversal of the ideological principle, vision replaces words: beyond the realm of signs, details, accidental and unpredictable moments come into view; beyond the realm of words, noises, sounds and tones become audible.

In his dacha, Yeltsin is shown as secluded, isolated from his political surroundings, in a way as a private citizen in front of his TV. Mikhail Gorbachev, his rival at the time, is seen on the screen at a party convention, delivering a speech that cannot be understood because the sound is subdued, the volume turned down. The political message is erased or rather displaced by the sounds of everyday life in the dacha (steps, the clinking and rattling of dishes, and the like) as well as 'empty' white noise, a sound effect created by an active receiver. In the subsequent, extremely long shot – whose view through a window from outside also lends it the appearance of a framed picture – Yeltsin sits in front of a microphone in a reflective pose, silent and motionless, conveying the impression of a pause in the flow of information. The camera slowly zooms in on his face until we see it in a close-up. This shot lingers for an almost agonisingly long time, staring at his features, freezing the pose. Beyond verbally articulated textual clichés of political speech, the reality of the body is exposed by the means of staging.

While political leaders appear as embodiments of the process of history in the historical-biographical films of the Soviet era – the cinematic portraits of Lenin and Stalin immediately come to mind – Sokurov's silent images address this mythical fusion of the actual and the ideal, of status quo and utopian objective, and thereby reflects the relationship between ideological concepts and physical-material reality.

The 'silent' sequences can also be interpreted in the context of the long tradition of a negative semiotics, which has been of special importance for Russia since the Middle Ages with regard to the 'negative' or 'apophatic' theology that dates back to Dionysius the Areopagite and casts doubt on the ability of speech to comprehend deity.[17] Even though this thought is secularised here, the point nevertheless is to demonstrate that speech can only miss its object – in this case physical-material reality – over and over again.

And yet another interpretative tradition lends itself to an examination of this example. Yeltsin's reflective pose of the head resting on a hand, the reduced movement and the freezing of the images refer to the iconography of the 'Saturnine' melancholy that developed with Albrecht Dürer's copper engraving 'Melencolia I' from 1514. Erwin Panofsky and Fritz Saxl have fundamentally described the semantic field of the melancholic gesture:

> We are here dealing with an ancient gesture, which essentially – as a gesture of mourning – has its origin in Egyptian reliefs. Besides, it expresses fatigue and creative thinking. Because of this triple meaning it was predestined for the representation of Saturnine melancholy, which unites in itself gloom, exhaustion and thinking.[18]

This mood of grief, gloom and lamentation is not only predetermined by the title *Soviet Elegy*. The final, freezing shot of a sitting Yeltsin[19] mirrors the gravestone sculpture of an angel – its head also lowered onto its hand in a melancholic pose – from the first sequence of the film, in which the camera slowly pans across an old, overgrown cemetery. This angel from pre-Revolutionary times resides in close proximity to the five-pointed Soviet star. A cuckoo's call serves as a reminder of the eternal cycle of life and death. This 'memento mori' is a leitmotif for a cinematic meditation on the transience and finiteness of physical existence as well as the futility of any human pursuit of perfection. The melancholic view on history, which also appears as a process of decay, is a pessimistic one.

The Film Images Stand Still

Along with the reduction of the text dimension in the silence of the film images, there is also a reduction of movement in Sokurov's work that takes the form of the images coming to standstill whereby the potential capabilities of the cinematic medium as a movement-image – described by Gilles Deleuze – are counteracted:

> In short, film does not give us an image to which movement is added; it immediately gives us a movement-image. It does give us a section, but a section which is mobile, not an immobile section + abstract movement.[20]

In the process of projection, the figurative differences between film's rapidly sequential photographs create an impression of movement, a kind of virtual intermediate image between two phase-delayed static ones.[21]

Whereas Sergei Eisenstein actually made use of this effect in his early experiments to create the illusion of a stone lion awakening and rising by assembling three still images of differently shaped statues,[22] there are sequences in Sokurov's oeuvre that eliminate this cinematic movement effect from the intermediate images in favour of a display of the frozen moment of photography.[23] This is achieved by erasing the differences between the repeating images and thus letting the 'empty intermediate images' become frames that isolate the photographs from their surroundings and give them an auratic dimension, even though the images cannot deny their technical character.[24]

In a series of dissolves between images of similar shape whose juxtaposition produces no kinetic energy resulting from figurative tensions,

Soviet Elegy unfolds a portrait gallery of people who played different roles in Soviet political history. The series begins and ends with Lenin; in between, 120 portraits are arranged, only partly in chronological order. Revolutionaries stand next to bureaucrats, perpetrators next to victims, famous faces next to ones that remain obscure.[25] The formation of an impression of timelessness is even further reinforced by a voice-over reading out the names of those portrayed like in a liturgy of a secular commemoration ceremony.

The 'mortifying' image form of photography enters into a paradoxical relationship with the cinematic medium that first made the representation of movement and of the passage of time possible. In the context of film, the use of the older photographic medium results in a special intensity of the imagination of death:

> I read at the same time: This will be and this has been; I observe with horror an anterior future of which death is the stake. By giving me the absolute past of the pose (aorist), the photograph tells me death in the future.[26]

The Film Images Become Painting

In the cinematic medium, Sokurov continues his attempts at subverting the technical quality of his own images and circumventing the processes developed in the machine age. By creating special optical conditions for capturing an object, even technical media can be used to produce a painterly effect. To achieve this goal, various choices such as the position of the camera, lighting, depth of field, processing of the filmstrip's photosensitive layer, manipulations of the camera's optics with special lenses and filters, the relationship between surface and space as well as format play a crucial role.[27]

Most notably in his film *Mother and Son*, which premiered at the 'documenta' in Kassel in 1997 – i.e. at an art venue and not a cinema – Sokurov reflects on the relationship between film and painting. The austere story of *Mother and Son* – a young man cares for his dying mother in a country house – is condensed to a few shots like cinematic paintings[28] whose atmosphere is characterised by an intricately produced but minimalist Dolby stereo soundtrack consisting of wind noise, chirping birds, soft music and whispered scraps of conversations.[29]

The manipulative treatments of the sick body, the physical contact during care (combing, feeding, a consoling embrace) define the relationship of the son to his mother. Fatigue, sleep, absorption and approaching death are in turn elements of Sokurov's melancholic depiction of man. The last traces of movement point to total motionlessness: the torpor of death.

In his analysis of the film, Ian Christie discovers the iconography of an 'inverted pietà' – when the son carries his mother through the garden in his arms – or implies an interpretation of the last communion with nature – when the son leans his mother against a birch trunk – as an allegory of 'Mother Russia.'[30] Such single-frame references become exceptionally apparent because shot length dominates over the power of montage to create meaning. To Sokurov, the traditional medium of the fine arts serves as an inspirational reservoir of image motifs, shot compositions as well as perspective, light and colour arrangements. To prepare for the shoot of *Mother and Son*, he visited several museums together with his director of photography, Alexei Fedorov, to study the traditions of Russian and European landscape painting. Sokurov himself most notably cites Caspar David Friedrich's *The Monk by the Sea* (1808/10) as a source of inspiration, a Romantic painting that, in the vein of a metaphysics of absence, effectively lets man in his insignificance vanish in front of the grandness and immeasurability of nature: 'The dramaturgical context of the painting corresponds completely with that of my film.'[31]

Of particular media theoretical interest, however, is Sokurov's development of film techniques that suggest an approximation of painterly practices. Just as in traditional painting, he accentuates the artist's subjective signature, his transforming intervention in the process of painterly or graphical shaping. Sokurov converts the camera's technical images, products of a mechanical device, to approximate the pre-technical, manual, handcrafted images of painting[32] by working on the camera lens with brushes, paint and other tools of painting as he himself describes in his comments on *Mother and Son*:

> I employed very simple technical means. We used special optics but also worked on the lens itself with very simple tools like brushes, paint and the like – artistic methods originating from painting. This is also the source of the special demands placed on composition. A lot of very precise, very careful work went into the composition of every single image – just as one would work on a precious stone, by the millimetre, gently and affectionately.[33]

Still from *Mother and Son*.

The technical aspect of the cinematic medium is suspended by the imitation of human perception. Sokurov does not see the camera as an instrument of mechanical reproduction that records quasi-physical imprints of material reality, but rather uses it with the perceptual perspective of the subject as a point of reference. The probing exploration of reality is abandoned in favour of the traditional artistic ideal of a contemplative vision.

In this transitional condition between painting and film, Sokurov particularly reflects on the relationship between surface and space:

> It was simply the first film [*Mother and Son*], in which I exerted influence on the development of colour as well as on the development of space. I did not want to create three-dimensional spaces but a surface, a picture. In the end, I wanted to be honest for once and say: the art of film lies when it claims to be able to create a three-dimensional space, a volume. A three-dimensional space on the screen is simply unachievable.[34]

This theoretical understanding has its consequences in artistic practice. By using a special lens, the volume of space is compressed, creating the simulative effect of a painterly surface structure within the film image. In *Mother and Son*, shots often appear curiously flat. The unusual, extremely distorting perspectivity that comes with this results in dissolution of the contours separating the human body from its surroundings. In the process of dying, the body becomes an organic part of nature. The wrinkled skin of the mother is interwoven with the furrowed surface of a tree trunk in close-up. The problem of death is reflected upon in the additional dimension of representation as a transition from a state of physical objectivity into a sphere of optical illusion. With death, the human figure merges with its surrounding landscape and becomes a speck of colour in a pattern of light and shadow. Mortal reality thereby seems transformed into an aesthetic value of eternity.[35] *Mother and Son* emerges from the tension between the tactile quality of simulated painterly surface structure and the abstraction of visual representation, from the tension between tactile image and visual image that Heinrich Wölfflin described in his definition of the painterly:

> Unified seeing, of course, involves a certain distance. But distance involves a progressive flattening of the appearance of the solid body. Where tactile sensations vanish, where only light and dark tones lying side by side are perceived, the way is paved for painterly presentment'.[36]

In Sokurov's work, painting is not simply appropriated by film; instead, the old medium is reflected upon with the means of the new medium. This can also be observed in the short film *Robert. A Fortunate Life* (1996), a commissioned work for the Hermitage about Hubert Robert, the eighteenth-century artist of ruins and master of dreamy elegies. Sokurov not only shows Robert's paintings in their frames and thereby brings their status as paintings into focus. By scanning their surface structure with the camera, he also imbues them with a physical presence of their own. In the end, their architectural subject is, in a sense, turned outwards as Sokurov cinematically establishes a relationship between them and the surrounding architectural space of the Hermitage.

Similar to Sokurov's film images, Robert's renderings of ruins convey a melancholic insight into the transience of the world. Everything is directed towards death and 'in the natural death of a work of architecture there is no awakeness, only melancholy.'[37] In a way, the architecture of the ruins melts into nature, becomes a *nature morte*.

The desire for something long past that is no more within reach gives rise to a reflection on temporality. The idea of progress is challenged just as much as any linear model of artistic evolution. The ruin appears as a materialised symbol of failure; it mirrors a fundamental experience of modernity right up to the catastrophes of the twentieth century.[38]

From a film-historical perspective, however, Sokurov's work can also be examined against the backdrop of international avant-garde cinema of the 1960s and 1970s. One possible context here would be the structuralist film tradition that reflected on the possibilities of its medium with extremely reduced cinematic forms of expression. Michael Snow's *Wavelength* (1967), for example, consists of a single, forty-five minute shot showing a mostly empty room, accompanied by a rising sinusoidal tone. The camera slowly zooms in until a photo of sea waves on the opposite wall finally fills the entire frame.[39] Similarly, Andy Warhol's single-shot-films like the famous *Empire* (1964), which shows the Empire State Building in New York for a full eight hours,[40] can also be seen as distant relatives of Sokurov's works. However, whereas the structuralists tried to eliminate the subjective aspect of authorship in their films and the pop artists employed mass culture's reproductive and serial techniques not only in film but also in the fine arts, Sokurov, by contrast, uses the ideals of traditional painting, the aura of the artwork and the master's signature as points of reference even within the reproductive film medium. He strongly rejects avant-garde art as totalitarian design:

> This century is, after all, a time when people where convinced and capable of subordinating art to pragmatic, trivial goals. That was the first step away from classical, academic art. Modernism, the avant-garde, different forms of this direction – they are all art that requires no intellectual work. This is ultimately the path that brings art down to the level of design. That is, after all, the new ideology: design. One might also say that it is a certain kind of Stalinism, a totalitarian form of art that we see here *(he points at an immense number of reproductions – two walls filled with Marilyn Monroes by Andy Warhol)*. That is a different form of totalitarianism, a form that runs much deeper, is a lot more forceful, richer, but one hundred per cent totalitarian and at the same time a terror of mediocrity.[41]

In his essays and interviews, Sokurov emphatically recommends using the old media as a point of reference as a remedy against the negative effects of an aggressive contemporary visual culture of accelerated, immaterial images. Nevertheless, his attitude cannot be defined as unambiguously traditionalist. In Sokurov's aesthetics, we encounter a very distinct mixture of traditionalism and experiment; following Hans-Joachim Schlegel's paradoxical phrasing for the characterisation of Tarkovsky's position, he could be described as an 'anti-avant-garde avant-gardist.'[42]

Sokurov reacts to the cult of speed from the beginning of the twentieth century and to the effects of acceleration in the evolution of the media[43] with the demonstrative media anachronism of his still images, to an inflationary flood of images in the age of mechanical reproduction with the offer of a meditative, relaxed image reception, to the computer-generated visual effects of New Hollywood's aesthetics of simulation with an almost physical treatment of film images. Within a tension between film, photography and new media, the strategies of minimalism at work in his films create a zone of interference, of interaction between old and new media that challenges us to reflect on the status of images in our contemporary media society.

Translated by Sebastian Moretto

Notes

1 See the two-volume edition by Gilles Deleuze, *Cinema 1: The Movement-Image*, London: Athlone Press, 1992; and *Cinema 2: The Time-Image*, London: Athlone Press, 1989.
2 On the aesthetics of minimalism in Russian culture see Goller and Witte (eds.), *Minimalisms*, which contains an earlier version of this chapter in German.
3 Ulrich Gregor, 'Minimalismus im Film', in Sabine Sanio, Nina Möntmann, Christoph Metzger (eds.), *minimalismus. Rezeptionsformen der 90er Jahre*, Ostfildern: Cantz Verlag 1998, pp. 51–54 (p. 53).
4 Benjamin, 'The Work of Art in the Age of Mechanical Reproduction' (1935).
5 See Andrei Tarkovsky, *Sculpting in Time*, Austin: University of Texas Press, 1986.
6 Nikolaj Nikitin and Norbert M. Schmitz, 'Ich lese lieber! Eine kritische Befragung der Moderne mit Aleksandr Sokurov' (Interview), *Schnitt* 3 (1997), pp. 14–15 (p. 14).
7 André Bazin, 'The Ontology of the Photographic Image', *Film Quarterly* 13.4 (1960), pp. 4–9 (p. 8).
8 'Ob izobrazitel'nom reshenii fil'ma. Zapis' Dmitriia Savel'eva 1995 g', in *Sokurov 2*, pp. 506–11 (p. 509).
9 See Petr Shepotinnik, 'Kamni', *Iskusstvo kino* 3 (1996), pp. 4–11.
10 'Voina v ob"ektive kamery. Zapis' Dmitriia Savel'eva', *Sokurov 2*, pp. 512–16 (p. 514).
11 On the narrative techniques of Hollywood cinema see David Bordwell, Janet Staiger, and Kristin Thompson, *Classical Hollywood Cinema*, London: Routledge & Kegan Paul, 1985.
12 On the term 'utopian sensibility', see the study on the relationship between entertainment and utopia in popular film genres: Richard Dyer, 'Entertainment and Utopia', in Rick Altman (ed.), *Genre: The Musical*, London, 1981, pp. 175–89, esp. p. 177.
13 See Dmitrii Popov, 'Kosmicheskii rakurs', *Sokurov 1*, pp. 125–28, esp. p. 127; originally published in *Iskusstvo kino* 5 (1989), pp. 75–81. Popov points to a tradition among film pioneers regarding the representation of the crowd that, according to Siegfried Kracauer, is a self-sufficient entity.

14 See Mikhail Iampol'skii, 'Istina tela', *Sokurov 1*, pp. 165–67. Following in the footsteps of Michel Foucault, Iampol'skii examines power relations in the dimension of physical relations in everyday life using examples from Sokurov's oeuvre.
15 On the relationship between individual and crowd see Dmitrii Savel'ev, 'Saliut' – 'Zhertva vecherniaia', *Sokurov 1*, pp. 97–98.
16 Also see Sokurov's cinematic portrait of Vytautas Landsbergis in *A Simple Elegy*. Landsbergis remains silent as well, playing a prelude by Mikalojus Čiurlionis in his office.
17 For a reference to this tradition of negative theology in Sokurov's work see Viktor Listov, 'Dokumental'nyi Sokurov', *Iskusstvo kino* 9 (1991), pp. 66–74 (p. 74).
18 Erwin Panofsky and Fritz Saxl, *Dürers 'Melencolia I'. Eine quellen- und typengeschichtliche Untersuchung*, Leipzig und Berlin: B.G. Teubner, 1923, p. 57.
19 See Mikhail Iampol'skii, 'Travma molchaniia', *Sokurov 1*, pp. 153–54. Iampol'skii interprets these extremely long, freezing shots that bear a certain resemblance to statues psychoanalytically as signs of traumatic scenes and sees them as a hysterical symptom of late Soviet society.
20 Deleuze, *Cinema 1: The Movement-Image*, p. 2.
21 See Joachim Paech, 'Das Bild zwischen den Bildern', in his *Film, Fernsehen, Video und die Künste. Strategien der Intermedialität*, Stuttgart and Weimar: Metzler, 1994, pp. 163–78.
22 Sergei Eisenstein, 'Dramaturgy of Film Form' (1929), in Richard Taylor (ed.), *The Eisenstein Reader*, London: BFI, 1998, pp. 93–110.
23 On the cinematic use of photography in Sokurov's work see Oleg Kovalov, 'Elegiia iz Rossii', *Sokurov 1*, pp. 295–97. Photographic material generally takes up a lot of space in Sokurov's cycle of elegies. In *Elegy from Russia*, for example, an image of past Russia is composed from the vast legacy of the photographic classic of Maxim Dmitriev: 'the screening starts to resemble a slide show from the 'laterna magica' (p. 296).
24 On auratisation by means of framing see the interpretation of André Bazin's differentiation between 'cache' and 'cadre' by Deleuze, *Cinema 1: The Movement-Image*, 'If we return to Bazin's alternative of mask or frame, we see that sometimes the frame works like a mobile mask according to which ever set is extended into a larger homogeneous set with which it communicates, and sometimes it works as a pictorial frame which isolates a system and neutralises its environment' (p. 16).
25 See the insightful analysis in Maiia Turovskaia, 'Sovetskaia elegiia', *Sokurov 1*, pp. 149–51, particularly p. 150.
26 Barthes, *Camera Lucida*, p. 96.
27 On the relationship between painting and film see Jan Marie Peters, 'Die malerische und die erzählerische Komponente in der bildlichen Formgebung der Fotografie und des Films', in Paech, *Film, Fernsehen*... pp. 40–49.
28 See Anna Bohn, 'Pinsel und Leinwand. Aleksandr Sokurovs gemalte Landschaften in *Mutter und Sohn*', *Schnitt* 3 (1997), p. 16.
29 On this subject see Sokurov's statement: 'On "Mother and Son" I was using Dolby sound, but I don't like it because it's commercial. We had to fight the technicians because they always wanted the sound to be louder. I told them, no, it must be softer, softer. Sound is a very important part of my work. I try to arrange my work so the film is a work on two levels. So "Mother and Son" is two different pictures – one a visual film, the other a sound film. They ought to be able to exist apart from each other. If you listen to the sound on the film, it should be enough on its own'. Quoted in Ian Christie, 'Returning to zero', *Sight and Sound* 4 (1998), pp. 14–17 (p. 16).

30 Christie, p. 17.
31 *Mutter und Sohn. Ein Film von Aleksandr Sokurov* (Press booklet), For a detailed survey of the reflection on the tradition of landscape painting in Sokurov, see José Alaniz, ' "Nature", illusion and excess in Sokurov's *Mother and Son*', *Studies in Russian and Soviet Cinema* 2.2 (2008), pp. 183–204.
32 On the relationship between painting and film in Sokurov's work see Norbert M. Schmitz, 'Die Ruinen der Moderne', *Schnitt* 3 (1997), pp. 12–13: 'The really interesting feature of the encounter of painting and film here is not the leap across technical boundaries but the simultaneous confrontation of aesthetic dis-simultaneities' (p. 12).
33 *Mutter und Sohn*. Press booklet.
34 Press booklet. For a further discussion of this topic see Sokurov, 'Izobrazhenie i montazh', Interview with Dmitrii Savel'ev, *Iskusstvo kino* 12 (1997), pp. 110–123 (p. 113): 'What I think about first is: how can I transform a space that is limited by four corners into a surface. I am interested in the two-dimensionality and not the volume of space. But if I am someone who never ceases to study artistic methods of representation and eagerly observes how the professional awareness of painters develops, then I have to direct my attention above all at the "depth of the surface". Essentially, I have to transform everything into a surface, and it is this surface I already work with as with an artistic foundation.'
35 See Mikhail Iampolski, 'Representation – Mimicry – Death: The Latest Films of Alexander Sokurov', in Birgit Beumers (ed.), *Russia on Reels. The Russian Idea in Post-Soviet Cinema*, London: I.B.Tauris, 1999, pp. 127–43.
36 Wölfflin, Heinrich, *Principles of Art History*, Mineola, NY: Courier Dover, 1950, p. 23.
37 Quoted from the subtitles of the film print screened at the International Short Film Festival Oberhausen in 1997.
38 On this topic also see Hartmut Böhme, 'Ruinen-Landschaften. Zum Verhältnis von Naturgeschichte und Allegorie in den späten Filmen von Andrej Tarkowskij', *Konkursbuch* 14: Natur und Wissenschaft (1985), pp. 117–57. Also available at http://people.ucalgary.ca/~tstronds/nostalghia.com/TheBibliography/Articles/HarmutBohme_Ruinen.pdf (accessed 8 August 2010).
39 On this topic see Hans Scheugl, Ernst Schmidt Jr (eds.), *Eine Subgeschichte des Films. Lexikon des Avantgarde-, Experimental- und Undergroundfilms*, 2 vols., Frankfurt a.M.: Suhrkamp, 1974, p. 851 ff.
40 See Scheugl and Schmidt, p. 1062, as well as Michael O'Pray (ed.), *Andy Warhol. Film Factory*, London: BFI, 1989.
41 *Mutter und Sohn*. Press booklet.
42 Hans-Joachim Schlegel, 'Der antiavantgardistische Avantgardist, in Peter Jansen, Wolfram Schütte (eds.), *Andrej Tarkowskij*, Reihe Film 39, Wien, München: Carl Hanser Verlag, 1987, pp. 23–42.
43 On the aesthetics of acceleration see Paul Virilio, *Negative Horizon: An Essay on Dromoscopy*, New York: Contiuum, 2006. See especially the chapter on 'Dromoscopy' (pp. 101–14).

PART II

BORDERLINES: GEOGRAPHICAL, LITERARY AND CINEMATIC

CHAPTER 4

INTERTEXTUAL VISIONS OF THE POTUDAN

Nariman Skakov

'Intertextuality necessarily complements our experience of textuality. It is the perception that our reading of the text cannot be complete or satisfactory without going through the intertext, that the text does not signify unless as a function of a complementary or contradictory intertextual homologue', writes Michael Riffaterre.[1] The given inherent tension of Riffaterre's intertextual homologue, for it can be both complementary and contradictory, is clearly at play in Alexander Sokurov's debut feature film. Intertextual voices permeate *The Lonely Voice of Man* and create a remarkably complex polyphony of a literary-cinematic kind. Intertext for Sokurov is a crucial means by which he realises a filmic vision and all of his subsequent projects continue to apply this approach with 'borrowed' artefacts coming from all domains of art: cinema itself, literature, music, architecture, theatre and painting.

One can discern two dominant intertextual threads in the film: the obvious textual one is Andrei Platonov's 'The River Potudan' ('Reka Potudan'), the second is Andrei Tarkovsky's *Mirror* [Zerkalo, 1975] which functions as a more concealed but equally essential intertext of a visual kind. Sokurov engages with the two in a sophisticated manner – he complements and contradicts his predecessors. While the intertextual tension is almost unavoidable in the case of Platonov, for transference of material from one medium to another is never a straightforward process, the influence of Tarkovsky is more problematic. Indeed, the 'anxiety of influence' is already evident in Sokurov's following words: '[Tarkovsky] used to say that there is some kind of continuity between us. I'm not sure about this; in human terms he was very close to me, he was more important to me as a man than as a director'.[2] However, the fact that Sokurov stresses gratitude rather than influence is consistent with the complementary and contradictory nature of intertextual homologue. As a result of this tension, the director creates a highly original amalgam, which emerges as a self-sufficient discourse. A theme of spiritual search in spatio-temporal mazes, which is prominent both in Platonov's short story and Tarkovsky's 1975 feature, is unequivocally advanced by Sokurov.

Liviya Zvonnikova – a Platonov specialist and one of the director's consultants on *The Lonely Voice of Man* – recollects: 'From the first conversation with Sasha [Sokurov] it became clear to me that the film's conception had taken shape and its visual strategy has been thought through. The time and space of the Platonovian universe were the points of concern'.[3] It is remarkable that neither the plot of 'The River Potudan' nor its protagonists are mentioned. Instead, Zvonnikova emphasises the more abstract spatio-temporal categories of the Platonovian universe. The scriptwriter of the film, Yuri Arabov, also employs a lexicon charged with references to space and time and highlights that the adaptation was developed through its spatio-temporal coordinates:

> I began to reflect and speculate about how to make a screen adaptation. I decided that the most elementary metaphor of time can resolve the problem of cinematic dramaturgy, which demands at least linear structure and clarity of plot. I imagined that the action takes place in a very small place, on islands of a river in flood. Perhaps the Potudan river. The river, the islands, wandering through streets, which suddenly terminate, submerge into the water and reappear from the water – this, in my opinion, resolved the issue of entering Platonov's rhythm, his prose.[4]

Time, according to Arabov, regains its conventional Heraclitian metaphorical manifestation – its flow becomes the flow of the Potudan. Moreover, this reservoir of time is clearly spatialised – the narrative leaps of Platonov's prose are handled through mazes of streets, which, in addition, were supposed to disappear from time to time in the river's waters. The text of the short story is thus conceptualised and turned into a certain spatio-temporal model, which subsequently defines the overall representational strategy of the film.

It is no coincidence that Platonov's short story itself yields to an interpretation preoccupied with the categories of space and time. The diegetic role of the four seasons, as a calendar time manifesting itself through space, and the persistent presence of the river Potudan itself, as a spatialised flow of water-time, are poetic markers with transparent spatio-temporal intentions. These already innate textual features reverberate in the film with a new force – Sokurov advances them by means of a slight distortion and re-interpretation.

The visual plane of *The Lonely Voice of Man*, on the other hand, is inspired by Tarkovsky's most experimental project – *Mirror*, completed three years before Sokurov started conceiving the idea of 'adapting' Platonov for the screen.[5] Tarkovskian visual echoes are scattered throughout the film.[6] This becomes evident from Sokurov's use of the documentary material and his visual interplay with reflecting surfaces. However, the most striking connection between the films is the role of literary quotations in the process of spatio-temporal 'displacement'.

The four poems by Arseni Tarkovsky and the opening lines of Dante's *The Divine Comedy* contribute to the highly unstable narrative of *Mirror*. The spatio-temporal models elaborated in the poems' texts allow Tarkovsky to rupture the traditional preoccupation with linearity that characterises mainstream narrative cinema. The themes of immortality (as opposed to human finitude) and of miraculous other space (as opposed to the space of the everyday) pervade the recited poetic lines and shape the film's semantic plane. Moreover, all the visual sequences which accompany the texts contain the same motif – human movement. The protagonists 'aimlessly' traverse various topoi and these advances in space also allow them to cross the temporal flow. The five episodes which accommodate Arseni Tarkovsky's and Dante's words are all either historical or individual memories and they do not coincide with the narrative 'present', situated in Moscow of the 1970s. The visualised poems constitute a spatio-temporal displacement in terms of their semantic input and formal artistic function.

In a similar manner, Platonov's text provides themes of spatio-temporal displacement which are cinematically enhanced. The notion of memory and consciousness, so persistent in the story, finds its place in the dialogue of the film and is also advanced by means of documentary footage, which opens and concludes *The Lonely Voice of Man*. Furthermore, photographs combined with mirrors and other reflecting surfaces turn a seemingly unremarkable passage from 'The River Potudan' into a highly sophisticated *mise-en-scène* – one of Sokurov's most accomplished cinematic moments. Other themes and motifs, such as alternative states of consciousness (Nikita's delirium) or alternative topoi (Nikita's trip to the liminal space of the marketplace), also receive a congenial visual treatment. The director's screening of Platonov's text easily transcends simple adaptation – the literary predecessor becomes a 'mere' intertextual source.

I

How would the Heraclitian river, into which one cannot step twice without it changing its state, look in a typical Russian landscape? Its waters would certainly freeze in winter and this would make the river's surface appear more stable. However, spring flow of ice or 'opening' of rivers would intensify a sense of flux and movement. One might argue that Platonov's Potudan is this displaced Heraclitian river – the reservoir of universal time which altered its location from the temperate Mediterranean terrain to the severe Russian landscape and which also reveals Russia's Varangian and Greek roots.

Platonov critics disagree about the semantic origin of the river's name. Vakhitova,[7] for example, claims that Potudan' derives from the Russian word *potuda* (up to that place, up to there) and this fact highlights the river's liminal nature. Another view holds that the river was used as a spatial marker, which performed certain practical role – it delimited a territory. That is, one of the river's banks functioned as a place where Mongol conquerors collected an impost (*dan'* in Russian) from their Russian subjects, hence, *potu-dan'* (whereon-impost). In both cases the river's name reflects its 'spatiality'. The Potudan, in the same fashion as its mythical Greek counterpart, the Styx, functions as a divider between two worlds: sacred vs. profane in the first case, and domestic–familiar vs. uncanny–other in the latter. These manifest spatial qualities, combined with the traditional Heraclitian metaphor of river as a flow of time, make Platonov's Potudan a prominent spatio-temporal entity within the short story.

It is difficult to overestimate the narrative function of the river. It gives the title to the text and becomes one of the main protagonists. In the following passage the river is clearly introduced in the latter role:

> And so they were friends, patiently, almost all the long winter, tormented by anticipation of their approaching future happiness. The Potudan river also hid under the ice all winter, and the winter crops slumbered beneath the snow. Nikita was calmed and even comforted by these processes of nature: it was not only his heart that lay buried until the spring.[8]

After Nikita finds himself incapable of consummating his relationship with Liuba, he decides to commit suicide by drowning himself in the river. From this point on, the Potudan regulates the narrative flow. Platonov persistently makes it present: 'The Potudan river had begun to stir. Twice Nikita went to its bank, looked at the now flowing water and decided not to die so long as Liuba could still put up with him; when she stopped putting up with him, he would have time enough to end his life – it would be a while yet before the river froze again' (236). Nikita's intentions, which are never fulfilled, are reflected in Liuba's attempts to end her life when her husband leaves her – she comes to the river every day to look for Nikita's body and then decides to drown herself. The woman enters the Potudan as if it were the mythical Lethe, whose waters deliver complete forgetfulness. However, instead of oblivion the cold waters of the river cause a death-defying illness: 'Blood often comes from her throat: she must have caught a chill when she was drowning' (243).

Sokurov reinforces the role of the Potudan and water in general. His notes contain a remarkable entry, which presents the river as an obstruction: 'A boat on the river – a man is rowing, he is tired, he lies down in exhaustion on the boat's floor, the boat drifts, it is carried together with the enervated rower. This occurs several times. Finally, the tired boat is carried ashore. Fedor (Nikita), having failed to cross the river, comes out on the bank, the boatman, irreparably tired, sits on a bench, the oars dipped in the water…'.[9] The flow of the time-river seems to be impassable, and the protagonist and his fellow traveller are bound to remain where they are, as if they have entered a world without progress or culmination, such as depicted in the Old Testament: 'All the rivers run into the sea; yet the sea is not full; unto the place from whence the rivers come, thither they return again' (Ecclesiastes 1:7). The current of the river does not function in this case as a flow of linear time since it makes any progression or movement impossible – instead a vision of time as a looped cycle is introduced.

In addition, the river appears to act as a metaphysical and omnipresent background: in several episodes of *The Lonely Voice of Man*, the Potudan functions as a reservoir of sacred knowledge. This role, however, is assigned to it by means of another intertext – a small episode from Platonov's novel *Chevengur*. The passage describes a fisherman who wants to learn 'the secret of death'[10] and decides to drown himself in a lake because he believes that fish, which stand 'between life and death',[11] already possess the sacred knowledge and he strives to reach its domain. In Platonov's own words: 'Secretly he did not believe in death at all. What he really wanted was to have a look and see what was there: it might be a great deal more interesting than life in a village or on the shore of the lake; he saw death simply as another province, situated beneath the sky, as if at the bottom of cool water, and this province attracted him'.[12] The lake in *Chevengur* becomes the river Potudan by means of a cinematic trick. A curious civil servant (or 'commissar', according to the director's notes), who registers the marriage of Liuba and Nikita, acts as a fisherman in Sokurov's adaptation of Platonov's story. He drowns himself and, crucially, comes to the surface of the water unlike the man in *Chevengur* who is found dead.[13] The disappearance in the water and the consequent re-emergence are separated in the film's narrative[14] – the dive to gain the sacred knowledge takes place in the middle of the film (in the course of Nikita's escape to the market) while the return from the domain of death takes place at the end (after Nikita's return). This narrative 'loop' is not coincidental and reflects the general cyclicity which the director seems to advance.

The film opens with a documentary image of a river (probably the Neva) followed by images of a dockyard with peasants performing a repetitive task of moving a wooden wheel while standing on barges – 'haulers,

Still from *Lonely Voice of Man*. The Chronicle. From the author's collection.

rotating the enormous wheel of life'.[15] It closes with identical images where water, in all its photogenic glory, dominates the screen. The cyclicity of this scene is not accidental, either. The vision of time in the film is clearly cyclical. For instance, the four seasons (the definitive natural cycle) influence the narrative progression – the development of Nikita's relationship with Liuba is reflected in close-up images of earth (it is covered with first snow when the couple marries; it is buried under snow when Nikita's impotence is revealed, while the protagonist's departure is marked by receding snow).

The motif of return in general and cyclicity as its outcome are central to Platonov's poetics.[16] Departures and returns, disappearances and reappearances, partings and encounters prominently reverberate in each of Platonov's major texts. 'The River Potudan' is no exception; the short-story is replete with references to cycles in a mundane and metaphysical sense (for instance, 'The old man was seeing life come full circle for the second or third time'; 231). The very first passage describes the return of Red Army soldiers (and Nikita is just one of them) who have experienced some kind of transfiguration – 'They walked with faint, astonished hearts, recognizing again the fields and villages along their path' (213). This return is also accomplished with 'the world's time' as its prevalent background: the time 'went on as usual, far in the distance and following the sun' (214). The story ends with Nikita's own return to Liuba which is vividly described in the text ('Nikita left the town and began running along the deserted highroad. When he felt exhausted, he dropped to a walking pace for a while, and then ran again in the free, weightless air over the dark fields'; 244) and which receives a congenial treatment in the film.

Sokurov depicts Nikita's return by means of a close-up of the protagonist's face. Since the camera is placed below his face and creates a sense of motion (most likely it was carried by the actor himself), the spectator co-experiences the hasty return – he or she literally faces gasping Nikita with the 'jumping' horizon in the background. The slow-motion effect makes the experience of movement even more acute: every slight spatial advance is glaringly endured since the passage of time is slowed down. Furthermore, the colours of the sequence are somewhat bleak and distorted and clearly contrast the black and white 'death' market sequence. They also herald the forthcoming reunion of the lovers which is conveyed through a series of pacifying (for the viewer) window still-lives of Liuba's home in warm natural colours. At the end the protagonists are absent from the camera's 'field of vision' but the viewer hears their voices. Thus, Nikita's 'lonely voice' finds a 'response' – he is reunited with his cherished interlocutor.

II

The flow of time, looped in historical cycles, is a predominant theme of *Mirror* and it clearly served as a reference point for some of the core artistic devices in Sokurov's debut film. Andrei Tarkovsky's feature has some claim to be called a definitive exploration of space and time – memories of childhood and historical events are presented through the spaces associated with them. Due to the constantly shifting identities of the characters, the notions of space and time as such become the main protagonists of the film.

Like *Mirror*, *The Lonely Voice of Man* explores a theme of spiritual search in spatio-temporal labyrinths. However, in contrast to *Mirror*, the film is not preoccupied with historical time and individual memories mixed with dreams. Instead, it offers a vision of time as a mythical circle and the other space it explores is not a childhood dream of Tarkovsky's project but a more general domain of death. The commissar's dive into the Potudan, Nikita's delirium and his departure for the market with the consequent re-emergence are all liminal experiences and they constitute a direct meditation on the theme of death.

The use of documentary material, photographs and manipulation of cinematic image by means of reflecting surfaces in *Mirror* and in *The Lonely Voice of Man* are among those devices which help the directors to address the themes of eternity (as opposed to human finitude) and of the mysterious other space (as opposed to the space of the everyday). Moreover, these very devices, quite experimental at the time of making of the films, make the two projects unique in terms of breaking conventional narrative techniques alongside Alain Resnais's classic *Hiroshima mon amour* (1959), which also relies on documentary chronicle in order to reveal the human devastation and disorientation after the war. Interestingly, all of these films follow Gilles Deleuze's taxonomy, which suggests that the emergence of 'false continuities' in post-war cinema makes the cinematic body not a spatial entity but 'the developer [révélateur] of time'.[17] The notions of, and the relationship between, space and time are drastically reconsidered in the three films, all of which deal in some sense with post-war shock. The documentary material they utilise is a clear and literal illustration of this traumatic experience (Hiroshima after the nuclear attack in Resnais's film, devastated Berlin in *Mirror*, and a more abstract vision of workers' hard labour in Sokurov's film). These black-and-white sheets of the past lie at the centre of the discontinuous narratives presented in the films.

The Sivash Lake sequence is the longest, and probably the most memorable documentary insertion in *Mirror* and it has clear affinities with the aesthetic strategy in *The Lonely Voice of Man*. The footage, shot by an anonymous cinematographer, depicts the inhuman efforts of Soviet troops during Second World War fording the shallow bays of the Sivash in harsh weather conditions. The slow-motion effect and the elevated tone of Arseni Tarkovsky's poem 'Life, Life', which accompanies the sequence and contains prominent 'fluid' time-metaphors (for instance, 'We are all already on the shore of the sea, / And I am one of those who pulls in nets, / When immortality swims by like a shoal'), make the lake a reservoir of time – a Heraclitian river. The soldiers are depicted here as if struggling with (historical) time – they laboriously move through it.

The fact that the ultimate goal of the soldiers – the other bank of the Sivash – is not made visible in the sequence adds further ambiguity and allows the episode to remain open-ended. The crossing of the waters by the army becomes a doomed act, which is destined to continue into eternity.

The black-and-white footage emerges as an illustration of the impossibility of reaching the desired shore, it depicts merely 'aimless' movement. The postponed resolution, due to the absence of the classic movement-image narrative linearity, presents a direct image of time. The episode does not aspire to offer narrative input since most viewers are not aware of the historical background of the chronicle and do not know why, where and when or even whether the soldiers accomplished the crossing.

The doomed boundlessness of the Sivash sequence finds its reverberation in the documentary chronicle employed in *The Lonely Voice of Man*. Sokurov makes use of several discrete pieces of footage and some of them function as recurring motifs in the film. But what is more essential is the fact that most of them depict a certain repetitive motion; for instance, workers rotating a wheel on a barge (the sequence appears three times in the course of the film), or men working at a machine unit and performing once again a circular movement, or finally loggers uprooting and rolling over trees. The modernist cyclicity of human labour is an obvious refrain in the film. The repetitiveness of the movements, which are always presented in slow-motion, makes their duration (that is, time) more manifest. The director touches upon this issue in his notes:

> CHRONICLE! A passage from the chronicle – people going around in a circle. A tone of dark blue evening. This is the continuous, endless work of tired people on the river. In fact, it can be both a morning and a day job. This is a symbol of time, not historical, but physical time. The circle can be edited with Nikita. He either passes by, or walks along the bank of the Potudan and looks at the people on barges as if from above, from a hillock.[18]

The final version of the film does not contain images of Nikita passing by the river. Thus, the presence of the documentary chronicle is not motivated by narrative developments and remains 'artificial'. The real worlds of the documentary material are fused with the fictional plot of the film adaptation of Platonov's short story. Their spatio-temporal patterns do not coincide and the resulting disjunction leads to a complex amalgam of different spaces and times.

The same effect is achieved by the presence of numerous photographs in the film. While in *Mirror* a protagonist (the narrator's wife) is depicted only once while she is looking at her own and her former mother-in-law's photographs,[19] the abundant quantity of photographic images in *The Lonely Voice of Man* is striking. They come as individual images and album sets and the camera unhurriedly lingers over them. Both Nikita and Liuba spend a substantial amount of time leafing through images of distant relatives or even complete strangers. These episodes again follow Deleuze's description of the direct time-image, which gives access 'to that Proustian dimension where people and things occupy a place in time which is incommensurable with the one they have in space'.[20] Photographs are memories in the first instance and the notion of memory, which displaces the narrative flow mostly dealing with the present, is extremely prominent in Sokurov's film.

The viewer also spends a great amount of time inspecting various vignettes and group photographs with the help of the camera's unhurried tracking of the black-and-white images. At the same time photographs are used not just as an abstract conceptual device but also as a narrative means. One of the central episodes of the film – Nikita's recollection of his first meeting with Liuba before the war – revolves around photographic images.

It is notable that Platonov's original text does not contain a single reference to photographs. In 'The River Potudan' Nikita reminisces about the image of Liuba while she is reading a book (his father comments on that with some admiration 'And as for the daughter! She'll probably go to college'; 218). In the film, Liuba leafs through a photo album – she performs an act of recognition and remembrance by examining people's faces. While she is doing so, Nikita attentively and, no doubt, lovingly looks at her. However, the most important aspect of this scene in the film is that it is itself a memory. Nikita remembers his first encounter with Liuba and a photo album prompts this act of recognition. The photographic image functions here as a temporal rolling ball – a memory within a memory, an act of remembrance within an act of remembrance.[21]

Furthermore, in addition to photographs there are mirror reflections, which also participate in the act of remembering.[22] A reflection can be considered an instantaneous, fleeting photograph, which literally takes place on a mirroring surface. Nikita's act of remembrance of his first encounter with Liuba actually happens through photographic images mixed with present and past mirror reflections. Furthermore, the semantic richness of the episode is enhanced by a deliberate confusion between real objects and their 'mere' reflections.

Still from *Lonely Voice of Man*. **Liuba and the Photographs. From the author's collection.**

In general, a mirror reflection on cinematic screen can occupy two planes: derivative, as a real object's framed reflection, or 'actual', as an object which is essentially a reflection but the viewer cannot discern this fact since the mirror's frame is 'hidden' away from the camera's field of view and reflection is taken for a real object. This feature in fact reflects cinema's general mechanism: a process of registering, animating and projecting reflections acquired with a camera on the all-pervading 'mirror' – the cinematic screen. Sokurov exploits this inherent cinematic quality by extrapolating the past onto the present or vice versa through presenting a complex interplay between the protagonists and their mirror reflections in the scene mentioned above.

The episode starts with (1) a shot of Nikita's framed reflection in a wardrobe door; (2) the camera then moves to the left and reveals the sleeping Liuba; (3) this is followed by a cut to 'real' Nikita looking at Liuba; (4) a cut to the wardrobe mirror again but this time the viewer finds there a blurred reflection of Liuba, several years younger leafing through a photo-album, and the young woman gradually comes into view in focus; (5) and, finally, a cut to young Nikita standing in a door-frame. This eloquent interplay of reflections, frames and snippets of 'real' reality leads to the memory episode – the abortive courting of Liuba's mother by Nikita's father. It concludes with a similar complex amalgam: (1) Nikita in the door-frame looking at Liuba and making eye contact with her; (2) the reflection of Liuba with the photo album in the wardrobe door which gradually blurs away; (3) then the camera explores various photographs; (4) and the sequence ends with a shot of Nikita leafing through a photo album himself in Liuba's present room where she is sleeping. The whole episode is a cinematic 'epiphany' of the notion of memory and it materialises through photographic images and mirror reflections.[23]

In spite of the absence of photographs and mirrors in 'The River Potudan', the theme of memory in Sokurov's film in general is inspired by Platonov's text and developed further by the director. The latter unambiguously makes the following entry in his notes: 'Memory is Platonov's energy, his electricity'.[24] 'The River Potudan' is permeated with memory-related imagery. The following three passages, which appear on three consecutive pages of the short story, all describe a certain progression in the relationship between Liuba and Nikita and this progression is reflected by means of nouns and verbs related to the notion of remembrance:

> Nikita went up to her and looked at her carefully, for she had been precious to him even in *memory*: Had all of her truly been preserved?

> 'You don't *remember* me?' asked Lyuba.
> 'Yes, I do,' answered Nikita. 'I *haven't forgotten* you'.
> 'One should *never forget*,' smiled Lyuba.

> 'You won't *forget* me now?' Lyuba asked as she said good-bye.
> 'No,' said Nikita, 'I've no one else to *remember*'. (220, 220, 222, emphasis added)

The bond between Nikita and Liuba certainly does not manifest itself in a passionate sexual attraction but by tender 'energies' of remembering. Nikita's final return is prompted by a sudden memory of Liuba – the brief dialogue with his father extracts him from his emotionally and physically mute state, in which he 'had forgotten how to speak' and his heart 'had grown unused to feeling' (243). Nikita runs to be reunited with his wife and obtains a 'cruel, pitiful strength' (245) which is necessary to consummate his marriage. This force is unambiguously connected with the notion of memory in Sokurov's diary: 'I remember them, you remember me, they will also remember you – this a chain of existence which preserves its matter. But this gentle innermost force is a weak force'.[25]

In addition to the general theme of memory, the recurring visual motif of a wood is another predominant theme of Sokurov's film which appears to be inspired by *Mirror*. Tarkovsky's otherworldly wood sequence appears several times in sepia with a slow speed of projection. This feature allows the director to emphasise the movement of bushes gently swaying in the wind, and to create the impression that the viewer is sleep-walking through the scene. Moreover, the opening lines of Dante's *Inferno* quoted in the film ('Midway in the journey of our life / I found myself in a dark wood') function as an allegory of spiritual confusion. The importance of the wood is further highlighted at the very end of the film. The camera follows the old Mother with her small children into the field and then gradually withdraws back to the wood. The Dantesque wood reappears for the last time though in a different light (in both a literal and metaphorical sense). The scenery is shot in twilight and presented at the normal speed of

Still from *Lonely Voice of Man*. The Wood. From the author's collection.

projection. The allegory of the wood, in some sense, becomes a reality – it materialises in its full glory.

The wood of *Mirror* is transported into Sokurov's film as a visual quotation: in addition to several recurring grove-wood sequences, a wood shot in sepia and in slow-motion, almost identical to that of *Mirror*, appears in *The Lonely Voice of Man*. In both films the topographical otherness of the wood is underlined. However, the drastic difference lies in the fact that Tarkovsky's wood delineates the space and time of childhood and the mundane world, while Sokurov's grove is a liminal life-death point. Nikita meets Liuba after his return from the war: the two are shown in flickering light of swaying branches and this creates an invigorated mood. Nikita then carries a coffin for Liuba's friend Zhenia through the grove and meets Liuba there. Immediately after that, the protagonist enters the domain of death: he becomes ill and his delirium takes him to another topos – that of death (images of a slaughter-house function as a disturbing death sequence). His recovery is accompanied by a shot of an empty alley in the grove after rain. The depiction of Nikita's fear of intimacy with his wife is interpolated by three cuts to the grove, in which Liuba seems to bid farewell and to leave Nikita. After the last cut, Nikita abandons Liuba and the camera registers his departure – the protagonist leaves the wood and enters an open field.[26]

Nikita's departure is accompanied by the soundtrack of his delirium in which he asks Liuba whether he is going to die or not. This clearly colours his departure in deathly tones. Indeed, the final destination of his escape is the market – the ultimate domain of death in *The Lonely Voice of Man*. The dead animal imagery appears twice in the film and it directly connects Nikita's delirium as a liminal death experience with the market place as a site of execution. The infernal inhabitants of the market place (a stall keeper and his wife) and their 'victims' (slaughtered animals) are all shot in black and white with slow projection and the sequence is accompanied by disturbing atonal music. The viewer is bound to have a feeling that he or she is entering another realm, which drastically differs from the everyday world. This feeling is to be overcome during Nikita's run, which, as discussed above, functions as a boundary-transcending moment. The life-asserting message is delivered in Liuba's home when Nikita finally consummates their marriage and the outside world is presented in pacifying colours.

What unites Platonov's 'The River Potudan', Tarkovsky's *Mirror* and Sokurov's film is a rejection of 'normal', profane, linear time. Instead, the artists put forward the notion of 'abnormal', sacred, discontinuous non-time, whose periods, according to Mircea Eliade, comprise 'a succession of eternities' and do not participate in a historical progression of events. This sacred non-time 'appears under the paradoxical aspect of a circular time, reversible and recoverable, a sort of eternal mythical present that is periodically reintegrated by means of rites'[27]. Space as such actively participates in the process of overcoming the linearity of ordinary time. Spatial coordinates constantly shift and do not function as a means to deliver the linear progression of time – they lie beyond the categories of beginning and end.

Sokurov's debut film can be considered as a participant in the universal artistic cycle. The presence of the mentor (Andrei Tarkovsky) and the insider-consultant (Platonov's late wife Maria Alexandrovna, who is believed to be a life-model for the character of Liuba) is well documented and was crucial in the process of the development and completion of the project. *The Lonely Voice of Man* thus becomes a relay baton in the aesthetic race. Discourses are borrowed from the predecessors and the resulting intertextual homologue with its complementary and contradictory tensions is re-enacted in another space and time.

Notes

1. M. Riffaterre, 'Intertextual Representation: On Mimesis as Interpretive Discourse', *Critical Inquiry*, 11.1 (1984), pp. 142–43.
2. Ustiugova (ed.), *Aleksandr Sokurov na filosofskom fakul'tete*, p. 40.
3. Liviya Zvonnikova in D. Savel'ev (comp.), 'Odinokii golos cheloveka. (1978–87 gg.)', *Sokurov 1*, pp. 25–32 (p. 25), emphasis added.
4. Iurii Arabov in Savel'ev, (comp.), *Sokurov 1*, p. 26, emphasis added.
5. There are also obvious correlations with Eisenstein's *Strike* (e.g. the documentary material from a slaughter-house or the general man-machine interaction). However, the aesthetic end in Sokurov's case is of a different order than in Eisenstein's classical montage of attraction film: the borrowed chronicle does not participate in a dialectical clash between shots followed by relatively stable and always politically-charged meaning. On the contrary, it disrupts the narrative flow and tends to confuse the viewer.
6. On the obvious level *The Lonely Voice of Man* contains an unambiguous dedication: 'In memory of Andrei Arsen'evich Tarkovskii with gratitude for his concern with the fate of the film.'
7. T. Vakhitova, 'Peizazh u reki Potudan'', in Natalia Kornienko (ed.), '*Strana filosofov*' *Andreia Platonova: Problemy tvorchestva*, vol. 5, Moscow: IMLI-RAN, 2003, p. 87.
8. A. Platonov, 'The River Potudan', in *Soul and Other Stories*, trans. by R. and E. Chandler, New York: New York Review Books, 2008, p. 231. Further references to this story are given in brackets in the text.
9. A. Sokurov, 'Odinokii golos cheloveka. Dnevniki 1978 goda', in *Sokurov 1*, p. 34.
10. A. Platonov, *Chevengur*, in *Portable Platonov*, trans. by R. and E. Chandler, Birmingham: Glas, 1999, p. 26.
11. Platonov, *Chevengur*, p. 26.
12. Platonov, *Chevengur*, p. 27.
13. This dive into death can be linked with a number of 'black' cut-ins (cinematic dives into nothingness – the blank screen) in the film, which actually opens with one of them. The device is employed in other films by Sokurov and most prominently in *Russian Ark* where credits are followed by almost thirty seconds of a completely black screen. This passage of darkness is accompanied by the narrator's voice over, which admits to a sense of disorientation and loss.
14. This technique is associated with Artavazd Peleshian's 'distance montage'.
15. Mikhail Iampol'skii, 'Platonov, prochitannyi Sokurovym', in *Sokurov 1*, p. 49.
16. See A. Livingstone, 'Motiv vozvrashcheniia v rasskaze Platonova "Vozvrashchenie"', in Valerii V'iugin (ed.), *Tvorchestvo Andreiia Platonova. Issledovaniia i materialy*, vol. 2, St Petersburg: Nauka, 2000, pp. 113–16; A. Vaniukov, 'Sbornik rasskazov "Reka Potudan'" kak epicheskoe tseloe', in Kornienko, pp. 572–78; N. Malygina, *Andrei Platonov: Poetika 'vozvrashcheniia'*,

Moscow: TEIS, 2005; N. Babkina, 'Problema vozvrashcheniia v khudozhestvennom mire Platonova', in E. Kolesnikova (ed.) *Tvorchestvo Andreia Platonova. Issledovaniia i materialy*, vol. 4, St Petersburg: Nauka, 2008, pp. 234–40.
17 Gilles Deleuze, *Cinema 2: The Time-Image*, London: Continuum, 2005, p. xi.
18 Sokurov, 'Odinokii golos ...', p. 35.
19 Tarkovsky, however, literally staged some photographs from his family archive in several key *mises-en-scène* of *Mirror* (see Natasha Synessios, *Mirror*, London: I.B.Tauris, 2001). Private memories are accurately 'animated' by means of cinema.
20 Deleuze, *Cinema 2*, p. 37.
21 Strikingly, when Henri Bergson (*Creative Evolution*, London: Macmillan, 1960, p. 323) describes the 'mechanism of our ordinary knowledge' he uses an analogy, which unequivocally brings together cinema, photography and memory: 'the film of the cinematograph unrolls, bringing in turn the different photographs of the scene to continue each other, that each actor of the scene recovers his mobility; he strings all his successive attitudes on the invisible movement of the film. The process then consists in extracting from all the movements peculiar to all the figures an impersonal movement abstract and simple, movement in general, so to speak: we put this into the apparatus, and we reconstitute the individuality of each particular movement by combining this nameless movement with the personal attitudes. Such is the contrivance of the cinematograph. And such is also that of our knowledge. Instead of attaching ourselves to the inner becoming of things, we place ourselves outside them in order to recompose their becoming artificially. We take snapshots, as it were, of the passing reality, and, as these are characteristic of the reality, we have only to string them on a becoming, abstract, uniform and invisible, situated at the back of the apparatus of knowledge, in order to imitate what there is that is characteristic in this becoming itself. Perception, intellection, language so proceed in general. Whether we would think becoming, or express it, or even perceive it, we hardly do anything else than set going a kind of cinematograph inside us' (Bergson, pp. 322–23).
22 This fact clearly links Sokurov's film with *Mirror* where the prominence of the mirror metaphor cannot be overestimated since it is already in the title. There are multiple mirrors in the film, which produce different types of reflections with different textures. Even the very first shot of the film presents Ignat curiously looking into the blank screen of a TV set in whose grey surface a reflection of a room setting is visible. Increasing sensitivity to the mirror as a physical object culminates in the wall of mirrors towards the end of the film in the scene where the author dies (his death symbolically signified by the gesture of freeing a bird). At least eleven mirrors of different size and design are placed on the wall purely as aesthetic objects – as elements of the room's decoration. The latter reveals the autobiographical nature of Tarkovsky's film – it can be compared to an act of contemplating one's own image in the looking glass.
23 Documentary chronicle and photographs are all faithful projections of real events and real people. Their use in cinema, one of the most mimetic arts, creates a complex effect: a staged (that is, fictional) but veracious reality is infused with a hint of a real reality – historical facts recorded on film. However, these snippets of real reality, in the cases of Tarkovsky and Sokurov, obliterate the narrative unity – their presence is not justified by linear narrative progression and they are never fully intelligible. As Žižek puts it, imposed documentary material serves 'merely' 'as the texture of multiple narrative lines'. These reflections lead the critic to embark upon fundamental questions about

art – he proposes a certain pre-mimetic condition where the artistic realm is approached not by means of imitating nature but by pointing to something which is already there and naturally creative: the viewer has to 'discern the fictional aspect of reality itself' (Slavoj Žižek, *The Fright of Real Tears: Krzysztof Kieślowski Between Theory and Post-Theory*, London: BFI, 2001, p. 77).
24 Sokurov, 'Odinokii golos...', p. 33.
25 Sokurov, 'Odinokii golos...', p. 34.
26 In addition, a shot of tree crowns appears when the commissar explains why he wants to try to 'live' in death. It is then followed by the chronicle depicting workers cutting and rolling over trees.
27 Mircea Eliade, *Sacred and Profane*, New York: Harcourt Brace, 1959, pp. 63, 70.

CHAPTER 5

LIVING AND DYING IN SOKUROV'S BORDER ZONES: *DAYS OF ECLIPSE*

Julian Graffy

In a brief article about his working practice published in the Russian film magazine *Seans* in 2007 and revealingly entitled 'Border zone', Alexander Sokurov contends that, whether it is the Boris Yeltsin of *Soviet Elegy* or the Emperor Hirohito of *The Sun*, 'the people who live in my films do not exist in reality'. He further insists, with reference to the documentary film *Confession* that 'my heroes are not the way they are in life', but 'the way I would like to see them'.[1] This mixing of examples taken from both his acted and his documentary films is underlined by the suggestion in the same article that 'the difference between a professional actor and the hero of a documentary film does not exist' and that 'you cannot define the borders of reality in my pictures. It is impossible to understand where the documentary ends and where the acted begins'.[2]

It is precisely this conscious mixing of the methods of the documentary and the acted that places so many of Sokurov's films in a formal and aesthetic 'border zone' between the two modes; and his interest in marginal spaces and liminal states stretches beyond this formal element into the geographical and historical settings, the plots and the life experiences of the protagonists of most of his films.

Thus, for example, among Sokurov's feature films, *Days of Eclipse* is set in Turkmenia, on the edge of the Soviet empire, and *Alexandra* in the contested border territory of Chechnya, while the Flaubert adaptation *Save and Protect* transports Emma Bovary to the Caucasus. The documentary *Spiritual Voices* follows the lives of Russian soldiers defending the Tajik frontier during the Tajik civil war, while *Confession* is set in the Arctic waters to the north. *Moloch* finds Hitler not in Berlin but high in his mountain retreat, the Obersalzberg, near Berchtesgaden (the original script was entitled 'Mystery of the Mountain'), while Lenin in *Taurus* has been removed from the Kremlin to the estate at Gorki.

Geographical border zones are matched by historical ones. *Russian Ark* ends with a long sequence set at a grand ball given in 1913 on the eve of the First World War, a war that is also the setting of the Shaw adaptation *Mournful Unconcern*. *The Sun* is set in the dying days of the Second World War while the recent documentary *We Read the Book of the Blockade* records the experiences of victims of the Siege of Leningrad.

Individual lives, too, are regularly captured at moments of marginalisation, crisis and change. Nikita, the protagonist of Sokurov's first feature film *The Lonely Voice of Man* is outlawed by sexual failure while the taxi-driver hero of *The Degraded* has just been removed from his job. In *Father and Son*, the eponymous protagonists are about to be parted, and the hero's concern that he will be separated from his 'only friend' runs right through *Days of Eclipse*. Emperor Hirohito, in *The Sun*, is planning the speech in which he will renounce his divine status. But the concern with liminal experience is perhaps most pronounced in the preoccupation with death that stalks so many of Sokurov's films, from his earliest documentary, *Maria* to *Mournful Unconcern*, *Days of Eclipse* and *The Second Circle*, to *Mother and Son* and *Taurus*, set during the last days of the life of Lenin.[3]

In this context, and despite the fact that in his later feature films he generally eschews literary adaptations and complex plotting, *Days of Eclipse* can be seen as a key Sokurov work, one that combines geographical, historical, existential and genre elements of liminality. The film is set on the edge of the Soviet world at the end of the Soviet era. Its protagonists are stalked by death and seduced by the siren call of parting. And in formal terms, too, the film exists in border country. It uses both professional and non-professional actors. Some sequences are filmed in colour, some in sepia, while others are shot with a pink or yellow filter. The soundtrack combines local Turkmen music with the work of Offenbach, Schumann and Schnittke, Russian popular song and a haunting 'cosmic' theme by the film's composer, Yuri Khanin. These various compositions are heard in constant struggle, as one is drowned out by another, only to reassert itself a little later. And as several critics have noted, this feature film also incorporates a number of mysterious documentary sequences, which for Vincent Ostria give the film a 'deliberately fragmentary and anti-explicatory aspect', 'the air of a poetic and almost hypnotic ritual'.[4] For Dmitri Popov, on the other hand, the documentary footage has 'the task of creating a historic space, of introducing into the Strugatsky Brothers' plot the concreteness of a period through which society is living, bringing in the realia of contemporary life'. Popov, does, however, later concede that the sequences of women lying in the beds of a psychiatric hospital at the start, of a local wedding party, a music competition and a factory conveyor belt at the end never seem motivated: they irrupt into the film and leave no thread.[5] For Fredric Jameson, who has provided the most extensive commentary on the film in English, *Days of Eclipse* 'not merely unites two distinct generic aspects [...] but also dialectically allows each one to batten off the other: the fairy tale drawing unexpectedly new strength from this *ciné-vérité* and vice versa'.[6] What unites critical opinion on the film in this context is an insistence that *Days of Eclipse* repeatedly crosses the borders between genres.

The Novella

The source novella for Sokurov's film, 'A Billion Years before the End of the World', was written by the brothers Arkadi and Boris Strugatsky in 1974.[7] They wrote a screenplay explicitly intended for Sokurov in 1981, but Goskino, the State Film Organisation, condemned it as 'a mockery of mankind' and permission was not given to make the film.[8] It was only after the legendary Fifth Congress of the Union of Film-makers of the USSR, in May 1986, that work could go ahead and at this point Sokurov turned to his regular scriptwriting collaborator, Yuri Arabov. They radically changed the Strugatskys' script, moving the story from Leningrad to Turkmenia, and greatly downplaying the role of science. (The hero, Malianov, an astrophysicist in the story, becomes a hospital doctor in the film, while his mathematician friend, Vecherovsky, becomes an angiologist, a specialist in the diseases of the circulatory and lymphatic systems.) And in the new version the end of the world is perceived as being not 'a billion years' away (an allusion to the pervasive sense of stagnation of the Brezhnev years) but something imminent.[9]

Geography

Days of Eclipse was filmed in the houses and on the streets of the small town of Krasnovodsk (a translation of the local name 'Kyzyl-Su') on the

Still from *Days of Eclipse.*

eastern shore of the Caspian Sea, in what was then the Soviet Republic of Turkmenia. Russian settlement here dates from the early eighteenth century, and in 1869 General Stoletov re-established the fort and the town begin to grow, inhabited by Russian soldiers and officials and Persian and Armenian traders. At the end of the nineteenth century, with the establishment of the railway, Krasnovodsk became a major transport centre, linked by ferry to Baku. It was occupied by the Red Army in 1920. The town's association with power was reiterated by its being renamed Turkmenbashy ('Leader of Turkmens') in 1993, in honour of the then president of Turkmenistan, Saparmurat Niyazov, who had begun to use this title.

But if the atmosphere of *Days of Eclipse* is informed by the complex history of the town in which it is set, Sokurov also draws upon personal memory. As he told M. Andreev:

> My childhood, since my father was in the army, took place in that very same southern town in which we shot the film. I wanted to express on screen all the feelings that remained with me from my encounter with that natural and social milieu. When I read the Strugatskys' tale, somewhere in my subconscious it aroused memories of that particular world where people of different nationalities lived, but where there was a complete cultural vacuum, which could reduce even the most unassuming person to despair.[10]

In another interview, at the Arsenal Film Festival in Riga he suggested:

> It's one of the most complex regions of our country in both the politico-economic and the humanitarian sense. There is no stable, established cultural situation here, everything is mixed up. The Russian does not understand that he is Russian, the Turkmen that he is Turkmen. Not a single one of the national groups has the chance of realising itself fully here in its spiritual, national substance. And everything exists in parallel, in conditions of senseless interaction and mutual pressure – we tried to convey all this in the film.[11]

The liminality of the film's setting, between the Caspian Sea and desert and mountain, on the edge of the Soviet geographical, political and cultural world and the border of Europe and Asia, is echoed in the film's story, which is poised between routine and fantasy, leaving and staying, past and future, being and non-being, life and death. But in another of the film's ambiguities, the sense of life on the edge coexists with images of the town's encirclement, by water, desert and looming mountains. In all senses this is an inhospitable place, which pits man against pitiless nature, and earthquake is followed by eclipse. The Strugatskys' novella opens with the words 'the intense, white July heat, the like of which had not happened in the last two centuries, had drowned the town',[12] but the town of *Days of Eclipse* is seared by permanent heat. Sokurov recalls its effect on the houses of Krasnovodsk:

> The houses in the town are mainly three-storied. Some of these houses are painted pale red, others pale yellow and yet others are

> 'dyed' with grey-white lime. All of them bear traces of fading caused by the sun.
>
> [...] It's a seismic zone. The houses are built to withstand a point nine quake. [...] They are slated. The slate is truly grey, bleached in the sun, broken in places.[13]

Most of the houses we see are dilapidated or half built, with bowed walls. Rubble and the bones of a dead animal lie in the streets and there are abject shacks on the edge of the town.

The town is also, emphatically, a place of sickness. The film opens with scenes of people sitting, crouching, leaning against walls in the sun, torpid, bandaged, with shaven heads. Patients lie in a hospital ward, which, for Mikhail Trofimenkov, is either a madhouse or a leper colony and for Fredric Jameson 'looks like a refugee camp'.[14] One boy swallows pins that are not visible on x rays, while another is treated by his mother in a way that the exasperated Malianov insists will kill him. One man has skin missing from his face, while another looks at the camera and opens his mouth in a smile to reveal his rotting teeth.

The sense of everything being 'mixed up' to which Sokurov referred in interview is most apparent in the jumbled ethnicities of the film's protagonists. As Malianov tells his sister, 'There is everyone here (*Kogo zdes' tol'ko net*). There are even lots of Russians.' And this is, indeed, a multi-lingual, multi-ethnic town, in which the Russians (military men and other representatives of empire) co-exist with the local Turkmens (many of whom have only recently abandoned a nomadic way of life), Azeris and Armenians, as well as exiled Crimean Tatars and Volga Germans. A Russian engineer visits an Orthodox church while local boys play outside a mosque. For Dmitri Popov this makes the town a 'Tower of Babel', while Maya Turovskaya finds in it the Soviet version of multiculturalism, the multi-nationalism of Empire and exile.[15]

Yet throughout the film, and despite the signs of cultural hybridity such as the kerchiefs from the Russian town of Pavlovsky Posad worn by the local Turkmen women,[16] the television programmes which, according to Malianov, lead the locals to desire things which are of no value to them, and the words 'break', disco' and 'rock' graffitied on to the walls at the local music competition, the Russians and the locals lead parallel lives. Malianov and Vecherovsky walk indifferently past a local wedding unfurling in the street. Snegovoy's driver watches the music competition for only a few minutes. And when, at the end, an old Turkmen woman kneels down to pray in the port 'on an ugly concrete slab of some unfinished building that is becoming a ruin before your eyes', Maya Turovskaya finds in this image 'a molecule of the meaning of this film'.[17]

And the sense of oppression engendered by heat and sickness is exacerbated by the awareness that this is a place of occupation and constant silent mutual observation. Army trucks rush through the town. Malianov's neighbour Snegovoy works as a military engineer at some secret site outside it. When he dies, his flat is meticulously searched by a small army of police and soldiers. The deserter Gubar is hunted down by a search party. When

Malianov walks Vecherovsky home he insists that they are being followed (a man is clearly stalking them, though Vecherovsky refuses to believe it). Vecherovsky's house is trashed the day after he tells Malianov about the fate of his exiled family. The Russian observe the locals, the locals observe the Russians, the Russians observe the Russians. Throughout the film the locals stand and watch. At the end of the film, on the train taking Vecherovsky to the port, Malianov finally snaps and asks an inscrutable and taciturn local 'Why are you staring at me?' Throughout *Days of Eclipse* watching signifies distrust, lack of understanding, threat and the imminence of danger.

Signs of the Time

Trofimenkov sees the desert as a metaphor of the moods of the 1970s, when the novella was written,[18] but Sokurov has shifted not only the geographical location, but also the timing of the film, clearly placing these events in the period of the film's making. When Malianov sits typing he often switches on the radio, and on one occasion he listens to a mass in Italian during which the priest refers to the recent beatification of Edith Stein, a nun who died in a Nazi Concentration Camp. Edith Stein was beatified by Pope John Paul II on 6 May 1987 in Cologne. Thus the action of *Days of Eclipse* can be dated precisely to the summer of 1987, indeed to mid-August, since a later Italian radio broadcast begins 'Oggi ferragosto...' ('Today is the start of the mid-August holiday.')

In the summer of 1987 the fate of glasnost and perestroika was as yet uncertain, and Soviet troops were still in Afghanistan. The previous year had seen an explosion at the nuclear power station in Chernobyl and the

Still from *Days of Eclipse*.

first signs of the nationalist discontent in the Soviet Republics that would soon lead to the Union's demise. And *Days of Eclipse* is full of signals of both Soviet occupation and Soviet decline. There is a large armless bust of some local bigwig in the cemetery. There is a bust of Lenin in Snegovoy's flat, a portrait of him on the wall of a house as soldiers come for Gubar and a huge Lenin statue with outstretched arm looks down on him as he runs for his life up stairs reminiscent of those in *The Battleship Potemkin*. A monstrous hammer- and-sickle sign stands by the roadway in the middle of the town and Malianov walks through the hollow concrete red star that stands beside it. For Turovskaya this 'huge concrete star, erected by some ambitious official and eroded by sand is already the past;' it resembles 'an ancient graven image, a sphinx for future generations'.[19] Another enormous but dilapidated red star profanes the desert landscape. It is shot from behind so that the words of its slogan, *Partii Lenina slava!* (Glory to the Party of Lenin) are mockingly reduced to an indecipherable hieroglyph. The Hammer and Sickle emblem appears again at the end of the film on a tattered and faded flag on the boat taking Vecherovsky away. All these signs, along with the derelict houses and a lengthy sequence set in a down-at-heel factory near the end of the film speak of the abject failure here of the Soviet project.

Alexei Balabanov would use the same ugly industrial constructions of the Soviet period as symbols of the Soviet demise in his film *Cargo 200* [Gruz 200, 2008], set in 1984. Balabanov also metaphorises Soviet senility through ubiquitous images (in portraits, busts and televised speeches) of the country's geriatric leaders. In the same way, in *Days of Eclipse*, though Mikhail Gorbachev had already been in power for two years in the summer of 1987, it is the voice of Leonid Brezhnev (ironically talking at a Congress of the Young Communist League about the education of Soviet youth) that drones from a record in Vecherovsky's house. This casting of Brezhnev in the role of the undead reminds us of what Sokurov articulated in the late 1980s: 'The Brezhnev question. I never thought that he would die soon. I was sure that he would last for the entire course of my life'.[20]

Malianov

Everything about Sokurov's hero, Dmitri Malianov, distinguishes and isolates him from the other characters in the film. He is blond, tall and athletic: he can leap on to a window ledge and somersault backwards from it, he can jump on to a moving train. Tatiana Moskvina calls him 'a Russian Soviet young man' with the face of the heroes of Soviet propaganda posters.[21] A tennis racket hangs on his wall. He wears jeans and a T-shirt with the number 9 on its back, which likens him to a centre forward and makes it easy to pick him out in a crowd. He eats different food from the others, and, unlike them, he seems to cope with the heat. His outsider status is underlined in an early sequence with a postman, who cannot even pronounce his name correctly, calling him Málianov instead of Maliánov, and later by his friend, Vecherovsky, who tells him that 'You have a mark on your forehead that says that you are not quite from here.' Originally from Nizhny Novgorod (Gorki), Malianov does not remember it, because he spent six years in Moscow before being posted to this desert town. He lives in complete disorder, which exasperates his sister, but he tells her 'you can live everywhere, and here all the more so', later adding that 'the absence of a house is a help. You can do without a house'. When Vecherovsky asks him why he came here, 'after all, you're a Russian', he replies: 'I don't see any particular difference where I live. They sent me here so I came.'

Malianov is employed as a doctor in the local hospital, but is currently on leave. His sister asks him mockingly 'You're not Doctor Chekhov, are you, by any chance?', but he is never seen at work there and he does not understand the locals when they explain their symptoms. He has no Turkmen friends and avoids all contact with them – on the one occasion when he intervenes in their lives, attempting to separate two boys who are fighting outside a mosque, they turn on him, kick him to the ground and run off. He is using his leave to make progress with his dissertation, typing obsessively, even at night, irritated by the distractions of phone call, door bell or unexpected visitor. Ironically the subject of his research is the health of children in Old Believer, Baptist and Adventist families in Gorki, the place for which he feels no nostalgia. The thesis is crucially important to him but, as he admits, 'I am writing for myself'.

Despite Malianov's self-sufficiency and obsession, *Days of Eclipse* is constructed around his encounters with others, their visits to his home and his visits to theirs. The incidence of earthquake and eclipse intimates threat and danger and the intrusion of the outside world is represented as a series of enigmatic signs. In Sokurov's words:

> Real events must be nimbly interwoven with the fantastic, that is to say, with hyper-real events. If the viewer gets 'confused' – that is not too terrible. The final episode at Vecherovsky's will put everything precisely in place.[22]

Malianov pays scant attention to some of these signs – the importunate, arthritic doorbell, the phone calls from exasperating patients, the radio jabbering in Russian, Italian or English. He is also visited by a succession of strange animals, a lobster in aspic, a monitor lizard and a large python that Turovskaya calls a 'hieroglyph of the East',[23] but though they alarm his various visitors, his own attitude to them is calmly scientific.

It is Malianov's human encounters that are more consequential, since all the people he meets are rendered uneasy by their sense of imminent crisis and catastrophe. As Sokurov told Andreev:

> It's a film about the most ordinary, simple people. They do not understand the scale of the time they are living in, which is flowing round them from all sides. Their inner development lags behind their experience, their fates are not yet proportionate to their personalities.[24]

The alarm that they feel translates into instruction – time and again they question and undermine Malianov's way of life and attempt to give him advice, to effect some change in his behaviour; most frequently they urge him to stop his writing and to leave this place.

Messengers, Parting and Death

The first of Malianov's unexpected visitors is an odd, grimacing postman, who brings him a strange parcel. He behaves with an alarming intrusiveness. He quarrels with Malianov over a signature and brazenly wanders around his flat, opening his fridge and picking up the phone. Like so many of the locals, he seems to have some sort of illness. As he stands by the fridge he crosses his legs in discomfort. Malianov does not ask him about this, but he has clearly made a diagnosis, for he later tells Vecherovsky that the 'idiot postman' suffers from enuresis, the retention of urine. When the man leaves he steals some of Malianov's papers and throws them to the winds.

The reactions of Malianov's next unexpected visitor, his sister Lida, are even more explicitly negative. She is exasperated by his domestic habits and exhausted by the heat (when we first see her, Malianov is taking her blood pressure). She asks him 'what devil' tricked him into 'coming to this hole'. She calls him a 'terrible egoist', whose devotion to his research, of which she speaks only with bitterness, has stopped her from living her own life. She is badly spooked by the earthquake that occurs when he leaves her alone in the flat. Defeated, she leaves as unexpectedly as she had arrived.

The character who most directly represents the Soviet presence in the town, and therefore the historical and political dimension of the enfolding sense of crisis, is Andrei Pavlovich Snegovoy, a military engineer at a special site (*spetsob"ekt*). The first words he says in the film, spoken to his young driver in an Orthodox Church, are 'I don't understand a thing. Maybe you'll explain to me.' In response the young man quotes him in Latin the opening of Horace's ode 'Eheu fugaces', words that warn Postumus, its addressee, that life is fleeting and death is invincible. Thus from his very first appearance, and even before he enters Malianov's flat, Snegovoy is associated with death.[25]

Snegovoy suffers from insomnia and headaches, and comes to ask Malianov to examine him. But he quickly turns the conversation to Malianov's writing, insisting: 'You think someone needs it. Who needs it?' As they talk on the older man's balcony under a heavy bloody moon they strike the same pose and have their shirts open in exactly the same way. This casting of them as doubles (or perhaps as father and son) hints at a mysterious connection between them.

In a key later scene, police and army men mill around a flat, which we suspect may be Snegovoy's, and which looks as if it has been subjected to a thorough and brutal search. Eventually we see a body in the depth of the frame, and two young nurses, also in uniform. Fredric Jameson sees this scene as:

> [...] something like a *mise en abyme* of the film itself, encapsulating as it were the very concept of the Investigation as such, under mysterious circumstances, in which the investigators cannot yet even

grasp what a clue might consist in, let alone the nature of the events to be clarified.²⁶

What is the cause of Snegovoy's death? For Popov he is a suicide, who has achieved a 'tired wisdom' and a 'sober understanding that everything is hopeless and the world is doomed.'²⁷ For the scriptwriter, Yuri Arabov he is:

> [...] extremely important for understanding the film. He is yet another splinter of that other, past world. Snegovoy looks after rockets, while he lives among people who have no need of these rockets, who live by their own traditions that are difficult for us to encroach upon. This ethnos pushes out of itself everything that is alien to it. Snegovoy cannot bear it and kills himself.²⁸

Later that hot night Malianov gets up and goes to the morgue. While he is looking at the corpse the dead man turns and speaks to him:

> Why have you come? Go away. This is not a place for the living. [...] Do not take sin on to your soul. The circle is defined, you must not go outside it even for a single moment. By losing this circle, by attempting to go outside it through reason, you do not know which sentries you have aroused, which force you have directed against yourself. When you step across the border of this circle you lose forever that which is found within its borders and there is no path back...

So Snegovoy seems to be giving Malianov even more explicit warning of the danger of his behaviour, concluding: 'I shall ruin you forever, for now your place is with me.'

The connection between Malianov and death is made even more explicit in the sequence with another military man, Gubar, the most threatening of the characters who invade the space of his flat. The young lieutenant has deserted from the army, since, like Snegovoy, he has ceased to believe in the system that he serves. Like the earlier visitors, he is vehement in his opposition to Malianov's writing:

> A writer? You write! Don't write, d'you understand! Don't write!

He asks him where he comes from, and when Malianov replies 'from here', he counters: 'You're lying, fellow. There aren't people like you here.' So Malianov says that he is from Gorki, and this time Gubar replies: 'From Nizhny? That means we are from the same parts.' He closes his eyes and 'hears' the music of home, 'Sormovskaia liricheskaia' (Lyric Song of Sormovo), which, with the refrain 'Near the town of Gorki, where the dawns are bright', cements the connection with the past for which Malianov insists he does not pine.²⁹

Perhaps it is nostalgia for home that has caused Gubar to desert. But he is doomed never to return there. Soldiers track him down and kill him. As Malianov's sister did earlier, Gubar has objected to Malianov's writing and reminded him of the pull of his home on the Volga. Like Snegovoy, he has warned Malianov of the consequences of stepping of the circle of his existence, and like Snegovoy he has ended up dead.

The one character with whom Malianov has regular contact throughout *Days of Eclipse* is his 'only friend' and fellow doctor, Sasha Vecherovsky. They meet in Malianov's flat near the start of the film, but their most significant encounter occurs in Vecherovsky's house directly after Malianov's conversation with the dead Snegovoy. They talk of Malianov's work, about which Vecherovsky is as negative as Malianov's other interlocutors, sardonically suggesting that he may receive a medal for it. Just as importantly, they discuss another of the film's preoccupations, the question of home and exile from that home, but now the conversation takes on an explicitly political tone. Vecherovsky insists that 'few people live where they should live', a proposition that reverses Malianov's earlier suggestion that it does not matter where you live and that the absence of a home is an advantage. Vecherovsky also refers to the Caspian Sea (on which this town stands) as 'almost like the Black Sea', which he has not seen for some time and to which he wants to return. He explains to Malianov that he comes from a family of Crimean Tatars, deported by Stalin in 1944 and describes their sad fates. The tragic experience of exile is brought even closer to Malianov when Vecherovsky tells him about his foster-parents, whose house this is, and who are Volga-Germans. Though Germans had lived along the Volga since the eighteenth century, 400,000 of them were deported by Stalin after the German invasion in 1941. Thus the area of land along the Volga connects several characters, Malianov and Lida, Gubar and Vecherovsky's foster-parents, and the theme of home is rendered darker

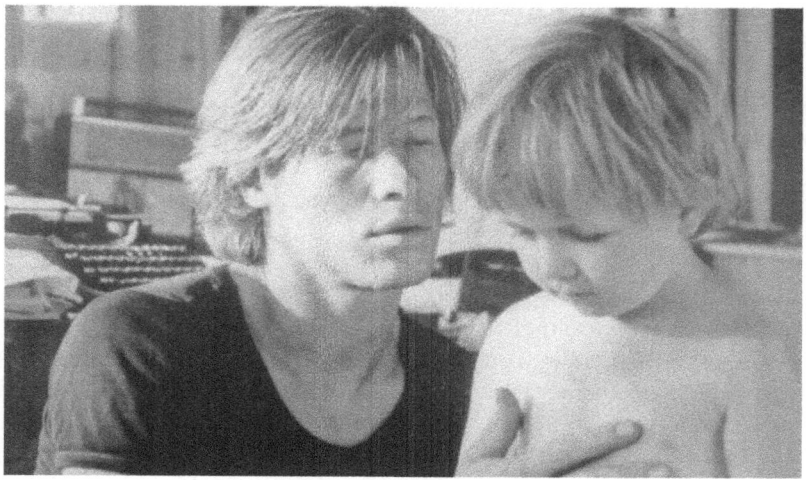

Still from *Days of Eclipse*.

and more complex. It is precisely his sense of exile that leads Vecherovsky to renounce his foster-parents' house, and their books and furniture, in the name of a world in which 'my children did not think about what nationality they were, and many other things'.[30]

When Malianov returns from visiting Vecherovsky he finds a small boy lying curled up outside his flat. The most gentle of Malianov's invaders, the boy announces: 'I am going to live with you.' Malianov washes and feeds him but the boy complains of pains: 'everything hurts', 'my head is spinning'. He has a sty in his eye and Malianov promises to cure him. But the child is unconvinced: he notices the wrinkles around Malianov's eyes and his ageing skin. In the Horace ode quoted by the soldier, wrinkles had stood for the passage of time and the inevitability of death.

Malianov promises to find the boy's parents but the boy insists that if he does so 'it'll be bad for me', adding that his parents beat him 'because of you'. This clearly alarms Malianov, for the next morning he gathers all his papers and starts to burn them. But they burn with difficulty and he thinks better of it, saving most of his notes and files from the flames. Manuscripts do not burn. He returns to his typing. He promises to take the boy to an eye doctor but the boy replies: 'You won't take me. You won't have time.' Again we hear the arthritic doorbell that represents the sounds and concerns of the outside world, the threat of disruption to his self-contained life of scholarship. An invisible man insists that he is the child's father and that his son is a fantasist. He takes the boy away with the words: 'come, my angel, spread your wings', and the boy 'flies away'. Once again, Malianov's attempts to intervene in someone's life have failed, and the cause of his failure has been his preoccupation with his own intellectual project.

When Malianov visits Vecherovsky's house for a second time he finds that, like Snegovoy's flat, the place has been ransacked and what seems like a weird dead animal has been smeared over the wall. Though the causes of this profanation are not spelled out it follows Vecherovsky's frank words about the experience of deportation. On this occasion Malianov meets the last of his interlocutors, Vecherovsky's former history teacher, Vladlen Glukhov. Both the man's profession and his given name (an abbreviation of Vladimir Lenin) bind him closely to the Soviet project and his surname, etymologically suggests that he is deaf (*glukhoi*) to the changes afoot. Glukhov tries to stop Malianov investigating the strange smearing and grabs the file that he has brought with him. When the phone rings Glukhov peremptorily tells Malianov not to answer it: 'It's not for us!' Like most of those before him, Glukhov warns him not to write, not to invent, associating his actions with biblical temptation. Malianov should stick to being a doctor. He prattles on, reducing medical practice to an amalgam of folk remedies and despair: 'gargling for angina, woollen socks and mustard for a cold, sleeping pills for insomnia'. Undeterred by Malianov's ironic reply, 'and analgesic for cancer', Glukhov tells the two young men to: 'Love life, understand the unwritten laws of life, love women, bring up children, grow trees, swim in the river'.

Suddenly there is another insistent ringing, this time of the doorbell. Again Glukhov desperately tries to stop Malianov responding. But in a rare touch of humour, it transpires that his fear of both phone and doorbell is caused not by an apprehension of mysterious forces but by a concern that his young Buriat wife will summon him back to the marital home. He asks Vecherovsky for the paper, learns that there will be an 'interesting little detective film' on the TV that evening, and wanders home in his wife's wake. Malianov's other visitors had warned him to leave. Glukhov's recipe for a happy life is a quiet evening in front of the television. This abject, petty man, as compromised and subservient in his private life as he is in his profession, is Sokurov's most transparent attack on the supine conformism of much of the Soviet intelligentsia of his generation. He offers a temptation that Malianov can easily resist.

But if Malianov's behaviour is not changed by Glukhov (a rejected father figure), then he too fails abjectly to alter the decisions of those who are near to him. In the film's extended final sequence, Malianov boards a moving train carriage, which is taking Vecherovsky (who has given him no indication of his decision) to the port, to board a steamer across the Caspian, on the first stage, we assume, of the return to his native Crimea. Unable to establish a sense of family in this place, he is still desperately searching for a home.

Malianov makes a last, failed attempt to persuade his friend to stay. The search for home and the desire to write have been explicitly contrasted since the beginning of the film, but at last Vecherovsky acknowledges the importance of his friend's actions. He hands Malianov his diaries, as if to confirm his confidence that, though he himself is not up to it, Malianov can continue to bear witness.

End of Empire

At the centre of the film lies the mysterious figure of Dmitri Malianov. In his shared personae as doctor and writer he seems to embody the intellectual hero of so many cultural products of the late Soviet period. But at the same time he is something of an abstraction, the incarnation of Sokurov's contention, quoted at the beginning of this article, that 'the people who live in my films do not exist in reality'. It is unclear whether his writing is being represented as a contribution to human knowledge and a witness to a time of change or as an escape from reality and an evasion of his human responsibilities. Some viewers will admire his determination to live his life according to his own codes while others will despise his ineffectiveness and seeming indifference. His fate and his moral and historical significance remain uncertain. The film's plot repeatedly associates him with failure. He fails to cure the postman, Snegovoy or the angel boy. He fails to stop his sister, the boy and his friend Vecherovsky from leaving. Two of his visitors, Snegovoy and Gubar end up dead. Only his writing continues to absorb his energies. At the end of the film he stands in the middle of the desert and smiles enigmatically. For Andrei Shemiakin, experience has taken him:

> [...] from an a priori and self-confident sense of his own mission to the most complete innocence, from pre-conceived knowledge to honest ignorance, more precisely to the expectation of something

new in principle that it will be his lot to understand and to tell people. Only – what?[31]

He is now 'in a border situation – between life and death, heat and cold, light and darkness'.[32] As Malianov smiles, the town, in which he has shown no interest, but which he refuses to leave, disappears before our eyes, reclaimed by the desert steppe.

What concerns lie at the heart of *Days of Eclipse*? What is it that alarms all of Malianov's interlocutors and why does he not feel it himself? It is tempting to read the film, as several critics did at the time, as a diagnosis of a doomed society, a postcard sent from the end of empire. For Irina Shilova it exudes 'guilt and misfortune', 'total indifference, lack of faith, despair, a return to the wild'.[33] For Mikhail Iampolski, it tells the story of three failed missions in this place, those of the army, the Orthodox Church and Malianov's attempts to heal the sick.[34] Several critics remark upon the 'colonial' panama worn by Snegovoy's young driver and Malianov himself is wearing such a hat at the end of the film. Natalia Sirivlia calls it 'the fullest portrait of the collapsing Soviet cosmos (including not only the social, the 'physical' but also the 'metaphysical' component of the collapse)' and describes the town in which it is set as a 'universal-town that has absorbed all the signs of the Euro-Asiatic Soviet (*sovkovyi*) socium, which is smoothly sinking into non-existence'.[35]

The trope of sending a young doctor east to assess the state of the country in a period of crisis has recently been used in Mikhail Kalatozishvili's *Wild Field* [Dikoe pole, 2008], from a script by Petr Lutsik and Alexei Samoriadov, written in response to the chaotic post-Soviet 1990s. *Wild Field* can be read as a tragic culmination of the story of *Days of Eclipse*. A decade after the events of the earlier film a doctor, once again named Dmitri, lives in isolation and without close friends somewhere in the steppe. Once again he has a brief, abortive visit from the woman closest to him. But the guardians of power are now reduced to a single policeman in a frayed uniform and supplies of medicine have run out. At the end of the film Dima too is visited by an angel, but in this case it is the angel of death.

Days of Eclipse steps into areas that will remain of central importance to Sokurov – the lives of soldiers in contested territories in the documentary *Spiritual Voices* and the feature film *Alexandra*; disquisitions about the Soviet legacy in *Taurus* and *Russian Ark*. Its inhabiting of border zones is played out across several mutually determinant registers – most evidently the geographical and historical, but also through other key elements of its production: the studied hybridity of the costumes; the mix of professional and non-professional actors; the use of documentary inserts; the intermingling of colour, black and white and sepia; the 'disharmonious counterpoint' of the music, which, like the other liminal elements, 'provides a model of the particular world' of the film as a whole.[36] Sokurov's extreme and unwavering preoccupation with this liminality is testimony to the 'border zone' of the film's very production, its situation in time and space at the very end and edge of the Soviet experience and its role as a marker of that historical moment. The film's liminality also indentifies

Days of Eclipse as typical of Sokurov's entire production, reflecting in microcosm both the formal nature of his films, on the border between fiction and documentary, and also Sokurov's chosen position on the edge of the Russian film industry, using Western co-funding to make the kind of art cinema on the kinds of subject which are increasingly unwanted and marginalised by a Russian cinema preoccupied with producing national-patriotic films for a demanding state.

And yet, for all this, like the film that Andrei Tarkovsky made from another Strugatsky Brothers' text, *Stalker* (1979), *Days of Eclipse* remains a fundamentally open poetic text, its representation of mysterious anxiety, of life and death in a border zone also available for interpretation on several other levels. It is this that gives Sokurov's film its haunting, hypnotic power.

Notes

I wish to thank Rachel Morley and the editors of this volume for their characteristically trenchant and extremely helpful comments on an earlier version of this article.

1. A. Sokurov, 'Pogranichnaia zona', *Seans* 32 (2007), p. 118.
2. Sokurov, 'Pogranichnaia zona'.
3. On the ubiquity of death in Sokurov's films, see especially Nancy Condee, *The Imperial Trace. Recent Russian Cinema*, New York: Oxford University Press, 2009, pp. 167–68.
4. V. Ostria, 'Les montagnes hallucinées', *Cahiers du cinéma* 463 (January 1993), pp. 59–60 (p. 59).
5. D. Popov, 'Kosmicheskii rakurs', *Iskusstvo kino* 5 (1989), pp. 75–81 (pp. 79, 80).
6. F. Jameson, 'On Soviet magical realism', in his *The Geopolitical Aesthetic*, Bloomington: Indiana University Press, 1992, pp. 87–113 (p. 112, note 5).
7. The novella was first published serially in the journal *Znanie – sila* 9 (1976), 12 (1976) and 1 (1977).
8. Iurii Arabov, quoted by M. Andreev in '"Dni zatmeniia" i vremia razdumii', *Nedelia* 23 (1988), p. 20. (The publication consists of Andreev's interview with Sokurov and Iurii Arabov.)
9. On the differences between novella and film see especially: Jameson, 'On Soviet magical realism'; Maiia Turovskaia, 'Dni zatmeniia, ili mertsaiushchaia aritmiia', in *Sokurov 2*, pp. 101–10; and Tat'iana Moskvina, 'Za milliard let do kontsa kinematografa', *Iskusstvo kino* 12 (1988), pp. 45–53.
10. Andreev, '"Dni zatmeniia" i vremia razdumii', p. 20.
11. Quoted by Popov in 'Kosmicheskii rakurs', p. 79.
12. A.N. and B.N. Strugatskii, *Izbrannoe v 2 tomakh*, vol. 2, Moscow: Moskovskii rabochii, 1989, p. 3.
13. '"Dni zatmeniia". Fragmenty rezhisserskikh eksplikatsii', in *Sokurov 1*, pp. 341–46 (p. 343).
14. M. Trofimenkov, 'Nigde i vsegda: Dni zatmeniia', in *Sokurov 1*, pp. 129–30 (p. 130); Jameson, 'On Soviet magical realism', p. 93.
15. Popov, 'Kosmicheskii rakurs', p. 78; Turovskaia, 'Dni zatmeniia, ili mertsaiushchaia aritmiia', p. 107.
16. Popov, 'Kosmicheskii rakurs', p. 78.
17. M. Turovskaia, 'O fil'me A. Sokurova "Dni zatmeniia"', *Sovetskaia kul'tura*, 31 January 1989 (quoted from *Sokurov 1*, p. 132).

18 Trofimenkov, 'Nigde i vsegda', p. 129.
19 Turovskaia, 'Dni zatmeniia, ili mertsaiushchaia aritmiia', p. 101.
20 'Aleksandr Sokurov, Dni zatmenija. Non sono mai stato solo. Conversazione con Aleksandr Sokurov di Ljudviga Zakrževskaja', *Quaderno Informativo XXV Mostra Internazionale del Nuovo Cinema. URSS: Dal Disgelo alla Perestrojka*, Pesaro, 1989, pp. 50–57 (p. 52. See also his reference to Brezhnev's 'immortality', p. 56).
21 Moskvina, 'Za milliard let do kontsa kinematografa', pp. 48–49.
22 ' "Dni zatmeniia". Fragmenty rezhisserskikh eksplikatsii', 1994, p. 345.
23 Turovskaia, 'Dni zatmeniia, ili mertsaiushchaia aritmiia', p. 108.
24 Andreev, ' "Dni zatmeniia" i vremia razdumii', p. 20.
25 The words the young soldier quotes from Book 2, Ode 14 of *The Odes of Horace* are as follows (they are not a complete sentence): Eheu fugaces, Postume, Postume, labuntur anni, nec pietas moram rugis et instanti senectae adferet indomitaeque morti, non si trecenis quotquot eunt dies, amice,... (Alas, Postumus, Postumus, the fleeting years are slipping by and piety will not delay wrinkles, or the advent of old age, or death, which cannot be conquered, my friend, even if you try to please dry-eyed Pluto by sacrificing three hundred bulls each day...) The original is quoted from *The Odes of Horace*, translated with an introduction by James Michie, Harmondsworth: Penguin, 1967, p. 120. The translation is my own. The learned young driver is later seen waiting in the jeep reading an issue of the London newspaper *The Guardian*, a fact that has been widely noted but never explained, except as a further (and perhaps more meretricious) sign of the strangeness inhabiting the town.
26 Jameson, 'On Soviet magical realism', p. 103.
27 Popov, 'Kosmicheskii rakurs', p. 81.
28 Arabov in Andreev, ' "Dni zatmeniia" i vremia razdumii'. p. 20.
29 T. Egorova, 'Effekt disgarmonii', *Iskusstvo kino* 5 (1989), pp. 82–84 (p. 83). See also T. Egorova, *Soviet Film Music. An Historical Survey*, Amsterdam: Harwood, 1997, p. 283. The song, with words by Evgenii Dolmatovskii and music by Boris Mokrousov, begins with the words: 'On the broad Volga, at a distant spit of land, a steamer is calling someone with its siren.' The motif of the summoning steamer will recur in the scene of Vecherovsky's departure.
30 The same pining for a world in which nationality is not a determining factor is expressed in a different way in the conversation between the Russian woman Alexandra and her Chechen friend Malika in *Alexandra*, in which they look back to a time when they were united by Russian culture and the Russian language.
31 A. Shemiakin, 'Prevrashchenie "russkoi idei"', *Iskusstvo kino* 6 (1989), pp. 40–51 (p. 50).
32 Shemiakin, 'Prevrashchenie...', p. 51.
33 Shilova's 1988 comments are quoted from *Sokurov 1*, p. 131.
34 Mikhail Iampol'skii, 'Proshche ne skazhesh'', *Moskovskie novosti*, 1988, 44, p. 15.
35 Natalia Sirivlia, 'Bez iazyka', *Iskusstvo kino* 10 (1996), pp. 38–45 (p. 39).
36 Egorova, 'Effekt disgarmonii', p. 84.

CHAPTER 6

MEDIUM INTIMACY
Robert Bird

The paradox of Alexander Sokurov is that, despite his prolific and sometimes bold experiments as a director, he has professed so little regard for cinema as a medium. Each of his films seems to pose a new task in optical and narrative form, yet Sokurov has consistently rejected the cinema's ability to be anything more than an imitation of painting in its visuality and an approximation of great Russian literature in its storytelling: 'Strictly speaking, the surface of the screen and that of the canvas are one and the same', Sokurov has said. 'The film image must be created according to the canons of painting because there are no others.'[1] This paradox is reflected in Sokurov's status in Russian aesthetic discourse as both the public face of experimental film-making and a spokesman for aesthetic traditionalism. Though film-makers' public comments are rarely the best guides to their films, Sokurov's ideology is frequently present within his films, whether explicitly, as directorial commentary, or implicitly, as a pervasive nostalgia for obsolete ways of seeing and representing the world. By linking his self-conscious aesthetic anachronism to a lament for Empire (especially in *Russian Ark*), Sokurov has gone beyond the conservative avant-gardism of an Andrei Tarkovsky or Alexei German. He hazards being regarded as a retrograde plain and simple, who uses the cinema only for reasons of expedience. Indeed, Sokurov's recent forays into theatre, public festival and the opera suggest that he might see performance as a medium more suited to his nostalgic utopia.

The paradox of Sokurov's rejection of the cinema as art is reflected differently in each of the major groupings of Sokurov's films: elegies, documentaries and feature films. Most of Sokurov's elegies commemorate individuals who stand in for broader histories, from Fedor Chaliapin to Boris Yeltsin. With his camera's attentive caress of his subjects' bodies and possessions, Sokurov seems intent on capturing their lingering traces and prolonging their physical presence in the world. Many of his documentaries chronicle and often instantiate marginal ways of life, such as the agricultural village, the ship, or the aging writer scratching out his works in long-hand. Repetitive and uneventful, more forms of service than of labour, these vocations represent threatened modes of attending closely to a specific world, a mode for which Sokurov expresses a wistful nostalgia and which he seems to imitate with his patient, almost obsessive camera-work. By contrast with the elegies and the documentaries, which have often been shot on video and shown on television, Sokurov's feature films often seem designed specifically to pose purely formal problems of optics and narrative.

Thus, *Second Circle* is a study in visual alienation, as the camera views the action as if from under a piece of furniture or from the next room, while the focus is unsteady and the colour is washed out. The most conspicuous element of *Mother and Son*, by contrast, is the use of anamorphic lenses and filters, which – by distorting the lines and exaggerating colours – bring the viewer into a wonderland of familial intimacy. Historical fictions like *Moloch* tackle explicitly political subjects in part by analyzing the ethical effects of modern optics, from the newsreel to the view-finders on weaponry and technologies of surveillance.

The mutability of these genres in Sokurov's sprawling oeuvre is illustrated especially by his literary adaptations, which combine the formal experimentation of his feature films with elements of the homage (he has mostly adapted canonical literary texts). For instance, *Whispering Pages* (1993) combines an elegiac homage to Dostoevsky and Petersburg with a rigorously experimental study of visual distortion to create a hallucinatory improvisation on 'the motifs of nineteenth-century Russian literature' (by which he primarily means *Crime and Punishment*). Rarely has a film so completely heeded the young Boris Pasternak's call to capture not the drama, but its 'surrounding plasma'. 'Let [cinema] photograph not tales, but the atmospheres of tales', Pasternak wrote in 1913; 'And, on the other hand, let its perspectives be the perspectives which are contemplated by the drama within them'.[2]

In accordance with its title, Sokurov's *Whispering Pages* also captures the mood of the nineteenth-century novel as a peculiar mode of attending to the world and as a specific material interface of experience, i.e. as a medium. Moreover, it posits the mood of literary mediation not only as a historical fact typical of nineteenth-century Russia, but as a resource for accessing and representing the subjective experience of history. Jacques Rancière has written regarding *Whispering Pages* that

> The force [...] of Sokurov's film [is] that of the characters released from the book, liberated from the author's will; of phantoms construed by our reading, by the millions of readings; of 'dream' characters, i.e. those of figures of the interface, known by their passage from one space to another, from the space of the page to the grain of the photograph or the cinematic apparition.[3]

The film is set more in the dreamscape of the printed page than in the cityscape of Petersburg.

Rarely has the problem of accessing subjective experience through technological media been such an obsessive concern as it is with Sokurov, for whom the forces of history, space, ideology and art can only be captured by localising the specific distortions they cause within the visual fields of individual subjects. Despite his sentimental rhetoric and his idylls of Empire, Sokurov is an important artist, I shall argue, because he refuses to detach his search for a lost intimacy from the specific technologies that render it available to vision. I will trace and assess Sokurov's pursuit of a new intimacy by examining three artistic encounters with Andrei Tarkovsky, a dominant force in Soviet art cinema in Sokurov's formative years.

The first of these encounters was Sokurov's debut feature *The Lonely Voice of Man* (1978/1987), which combines fictional and documentary material in a manner reminiscent of Tarkovsky's *Mirror* and set the terms for the two directors' creative relationship. The second encounter was Sokurov's *Moscow Elegy* (1988), an homage to the memory of Tarkovsky, which I shall read together with his contemporaneous memoir of Tarkovsky as articulating a moment of crisis in Sokurov's creative outlook. The third is Sokurov's production of Mussorgsky's opera *Boris Godunov* (2007), which provides the most compelling demonstration of Sokurov's distinctive engagement with the dilemmas of intimacy and mediation. The point of these analyses is not to ascertain Sokurov's indebtedness to Tarkovsky, which he has often contended, but rather to examine the cinematic documents of their relationship in order to trace the evolution of his concept of medium as a consequence of alienation and, at the same time, a site of a new intimacy.

Atmospheres of Intimacy

> *The Lonely Voice* struck us as the incarnation of our own unformed dreams of an ideal film that would liberate our consciousness from the oppressive mysteries of national history [which] are knowable not through some lofty scheme, but through a poetic image, which is always available to vision as if it has been wiped clear [*nagliaden do promytoi iasnosti*] and inexhaustible in its indistinct depths'.[4]

Thus, Oleg Kovalov has characterised Sokurov's cinematic debut *The Lonely Voice of Man*, an adaptation of Andrei Platonov's story 'The River Potudan', which made a bold declaration of intent that Sokurov has sometimes struggled to live up to. My examination of the film will focus on the linkage Kovalov makes between the film's optical qualities and its engagement with historical trauma.

Sokurov made *The Lonely Voice of Man* as his diploma project for the popular-scientific section of the directorial department of VGIK, the Film Institute in Moscow, where he had studied since 1975, after receiving a degree in history from the university in Gorki (now Nizhny Novgorod), where he had also worked at the local television studio. Originally entitled 'The Return of Platonov', Sokurov's diploma project was supposed to weave scenes from 'The River Potudan' into Platonov's biography; instead Sokurov integrated various documentary materials (including photographs from Platonov's archive) into a more or less complete adaptation of the story.

Still from *The Lonely Voice of Man.*

Choosing as his source a work by a literary master of massive authority among the Soviet intelligentsia of his day, Sokurov and his team (especially cameraman Sergei Yurizditsky and screenwriter Yuri Arabov) sought means of transposing Platonov's inimitable voice into cinema without compromising the integrity of either. In a professional milieu that was almost wholly focused on traditional narrative genres, Sokurov showed great composure in subordinating narrative and symbol to the task of capturing Platonov's very attitude of vision, his distinctive comportment before an indomitable world. After extensive manoeuvring the finished film was eventually rejected by the VGIK administration, which ordered the destruction of the negative and all positive copies. Subsequently Sokurov was allowed to receive his degree for a documentary he had made for television in Gorki, entitled *The Summer of Maria Voinova* (1978, later folded into *Maria*, 1988); sources differ on whether he was assigned the top grade or the lowest passing grade for it. He also managed to preserve *The Lonely Voice of Man*, to show it at Lenfilm studios, where he was hired as a director, and eventually to re-edit and release it in 1987 (with a dedication to Andrei Tarkovsky, who had supported Sokurov throughout his early travails).[5] The drama of these events threatens to obscure their most important lesson, namely the inseparability of the fictional and the documentary in Sokurov's cinematic images. Like Tarkovsky in *Mirror* (1975), in *The Lonely Voice of Man* Sokurov combines documentary footage with fictional and confessional registers of discourse in a way that suspends the rigid distinctions between them.[6] No less than his pure documentaries, Sokurov's fictions are always aimed at recording the intimate textures of historical forces. In this case, this means capturing the historicity of intimacy, which is such a conspicuous feature of Platonov's fiction.

Returning home from the Russian Civil War, Nikita Firsov (the protagonist of Andrei Platonov's 'The River Potudan', first published in 1937) finds his home town much changed, although strangely familiar; Platonov's narrator comments that this 'means that much life had already been lived by him, if large, mysterious objects had turned into small and boring ones'.[7] Evidently, his alienation from this world is caused by a change that has occurred deep within him. Having settled back with his father, Nikita meets his childhood sweetheart Liuba, a student of medicine, and promises not to forget her; 'I have no one else to remember', he explains. They marry after an extended and awkward courtship, during which Nikita falls ill with typhus. Nikita turns out to be impotent, and without the prospect of progeny he cannot face intimacy with his wife: 'Nikita cannot torment Liuba for the sake of his own happiness, and all of his force beats in his heart, rushing to his throat, not remaining anywhere else' (438). Unable to work, Nikita dreams of the family he cannot create, diverting his repressed desires into the fashioning of furniture and clay figurines; these latter Platonov describes as 'dead inventions like a mountain with an animal head growing out of it or a tree stump, on which the roots at first seemed normal, but were really so tangled, impassable, clutching one root with another, chewing and tormenting itself, that one felt like sleeping after observing it for a long time' (440). After contemplating suicide by drowning, he ends up leaving town to wander and work silently at an outdoor market. One day his father recognises him and tells him how Liuba's grief had driven her to attempt suicide. Nikita returns home, where he finds himself once again able to love her; in a typically Platonovian turn of phrase, Nikita tells Liuba, 'I am already used to being happy with you' (448).

While retaining the overall plot, in *The Lonely Voice of Man* Sokurov seems intent on providing an optical rendering of the distances that haunt Platonov's prose style and pervade the contemporary reader's encounter with it. He cuts the already meagre dialogue to a bare minimum, thereby rendering the characters' actions and the historical context less immediately legible (though one of Tarkovsky's major objections to Sokurov's film was that *too much* of Platonov's peculiar language had been preserved). Sokurov compensates for the loss of Platonov's dizzying verbal (il)logic with an equally dense weave of visual materials and effects. Many effects are produced in camera, including unusual lenses, filters, the alternation of black-and-white and colour stock, and rapid pulls of focus; one result is a painterly texture to many shots, even to the point of a kind of craqueleur in portraits of Liuba. Others are products of the editing, such as the use of negative exposures (to convey Nikita's typhus-riddled consciousness). Nikita's clay figurines find a cinematic equivalent in recurring sequences of grainy documentary footage from the 1920s in which workers dig up huge tree roots and toss around bovine carcasses. The story features two drastic shifts of perspective, a technique characteristic of Platonov: once the watchman at the market discovers a mute vagrant who turns out to be Nikita, and once Nikita encounters a man who turns out to be his father. Sokurov marks these sudden shifts visually, for example by shooting the scenes of the mute Nikita at the market in high-contrast black-and-white, without any dialogue, so that for a long time one is not quite sure that it is indeed him.[8] One gauzy scene features two men in a boat, neither of whom is clearly identifiable; after a philosophical conversation one of them jumps into the water.

Other optical and narrative devices produce effects not of alienation, but of intimacy. In a technique borrowed directly from Tarkovsky (especially *Andrei Rublev*), a leafy shot of Nikita's and Liuba's reunion is repeated as a leitmotif throughout the film, its vivid colours contrasting variously with the increasingly dominant tone of bleakness. Instead of medical books (as in Platonov's story), Liuba is shown leafing through photo albums; when some of the photos are shown in close-up one can recognise the young Andrei Platonov.[9] In all this (and also in the dissonant soundtrack) Sokurov draws heavily on Tarkovsky, even to the point of presenting Nikita's home village in the style of Breughel's *Hunters in the Snow* (which Tarkovsky cited in *Solaris* and *Mirror*). One also sees the influence of Larisa Shepitko's *Homeland of Electricity* [Rodina elektrichestva, 1968], also an adaptation of Platonov's prose, in which special lenses produced elongated figures reminiscent of medieval Orthodox icons. Sokurov's cameraman has recalled how he tried to reproduce the inverse perspective of Kuzma Petrov-Vodkin's painting and the Orthodox icon by constructing irregular planes in the *mise-en-scène* and creating a play of light with reflectors.[10]

The effect is that, while each character makes a reticent claim on the spectator, this multiplicity of perspectives is never resolved into a hierarchy. Mikhail Iampolski has suggested that, 'instead of accumulating perspectives identified with various points of view, the director has chosen another path: that of gradually eroding the localizability of the points of view'.[11] Within the world of the film (i.e., with respect to the characters) this de-localization of perspective could be experienced as either an unsettling disorientation or a redemptive overcoming of individual limits. It is sometimes difficult to know which effect Sokurov intends, in part because he is fascinated by the tension between these possibilities, but mostly because he is focused on activating the freedom of the viewer to negotiate them.

As in the story, Nikita is usually at the centre of the camera's attention, but he is precisely its object, not its subject. If in the story the reader is informed of Nikita's sparse memories and thoughts, the film refrains from associating the documentary footage or family snapshots directly with any character's consciousness. Memory, as in Platonov, is something impersonal, oppressive in its distance, yet the only palpable source of illumination. As Lev Anninsky has noted, '[o]ne gets the sense that things and people have become still and are listening to see whether they still exist'.[12] As Iampolski has put it, 'The film turns into a kind of gradual immersion into the vague world of a lost self'.[13] The perspectival shifts reveal less about Nikita as a character than about our evolving vision of him and his world. In a reversal of the principle of *photogénie*, the world appears not as a surface available to the gaze, but as an object sculpted by innumerable acts of seeing. Our gaze seems to oppress the actors, who behave as if their world has just been illuminated after forty years of dark hibernation. The subject of the film becomes its viewer, who is summoned into the spaces of representation as the agent of these potential memories and the animator of this history.

Kovalov has written that Sokurov is thus able to replicate Platonov's perspective from within the new collective identity, 'a world of a human plasma that is almost unsegregated into individuals'.[14] This is hardly true of Platonov's world, in which any attempt by the reader to identify with the characters or narrator is repelled by the radically alienated (and alienating) language. It is not at all accurate with respect to Sokurov's film. Encountering this alienation optically as well as verbally, Sokurov's viewer is isolated as a solitary subject, forced to hold the disintegrating world and its obsolete future in a single field of vision. The only collectivity one could hope for is that which might arise among viewers.

Since the diverse elements of the film cohere only as a material interface between the viewer and the visual field, *The Lonely Voice of Man* is as difficult to interpret as our own optical apparatus. It is only the failures of vision that render the eye visible from within. Just as death lurks close beneath the surface of Nikita and Liuba's reticent love, so also Sokurov separates sequences of flashbacks and other temporal shifts with a black screen which manifests the 'blackness' of death (to use the fisherman's phrase in the film). The result is 'a gradual liberation from the narration, the growth of a subjective vision, and at the same time an outgrowing of subjectivity (the disappearance of the protagonists) in an impersonal vision', in which 'objectivity is a profoundly lyrical picture of an individual abyss'.[15]

It is the black gaps between the shots that release the true object of Sokurov's film: time, as an unrepresentable and impenetrable medium of intimate experience, the impersonal condition of personhood, which both binds us to the world and makes it impossible for us ever to grasp ourselves fully. Sokurov's fascination with time as a medium of experience is a sign of his profound kinship to the cinema of Andrei Tarkovsky, especially those films where Tarkovsky explores the intimate sense of inhabiting a social imaginary, as in *Mirror*, which both constitutes and oppresses the freedom of the self.[16]

The effect is to create a layered, composite image out of 1920s documentary material, 1930s fictional narrative and 1970s cinematic presentation. The triadic temporality of the film is especially visible in the film's opening sequence. *The Lonely Voice* begins with a sequence of four shots of documentary footage from the 1920s played in slow motion: a river, lumber floating on water, and (twice) a huge wooden mill wheel being turned by peasants. The next shot is of a young man walking through the steppe, the camera tracking after him in conspicuous fashion. Further shots of the young man, who we later learn to be Nikita, are interspersed with the opening credits. The displacement of the utopian dreams of the 1920s can be traced to Platonov's text. Instead of viewing the Civil War as the heroic, if bloody birth of Soviet civilization, Platonov's narrative bears it as an internal wound that cuts his young characters off from any imaginable future. Barren and suicidal, Liuba ends the story as 'a wizened body [that] is frozen in the cool twilight of the late time' (448). Moreover, even in the mid-1930s, Platonov's prose seems to bear the same haemorrhage, which prevents the writer from taming the trauma of Soviet origins into a fully-formed discourse. This aspect of Platonov's prose, I would argue, is the historical mood that Sokurov sought to capture in his first experiment in the cinematic medium. As in Tarkovsky's work, Sokurov's optical and narrative displacement is a direct response to the traumas of time, i.e., to history. To a far greater degree than Tarkovsky's *Mirror*, though, Sokurov poses a specific historical condition, rooted in the impossible desires of the Revolution, manifested obliquely in Platonov's narratives, and available now as the basis of a new intimacy.

In a diary entry made during his work on *The Lonely Voice of Man*, Sokurov cites Marx's statement (from a March 1843 letter to Arnold Ruge): 'Shame is epic; it is the most revolutionary emotion'.[17] By implicating the viewer in the obscure intimacy of Nikita's shame, *The Lonely Voice* communicates the historical trauma of the 1920s and 1930s as a force still capable of wounding individual subjects in the waning years of the Soviet project. If it remains unclear to what degree this shame retains revolutionary or redemptive force, Sokurov has at least stated his case for cinema as a medium where modern history becomes a matter for intimate vision.

The Promise of Nostalgia

If Sokurov's early films were predicated on a sustaining belief in the power of film to establish intimacy, if only in a shared trauma, then *Moscow Elegy*

Still from *The Lonely Voice of Man.*

(1988) marks a moment of crisis caused by the failures of technological media to sustain and communicate spiritual value. Ostensibly, the film is an homage to Tarkovsky, who died in Paris at the age of fifty-four on 29 December 1986, having left the Soviet Union for good in 1982. Sokurov augments extensive excerpts from Tarkovsky's films *Mirror, Tempo di Viaggio* (1980) and *Nostalghia* (1983) with video footage from the shoot of *Sacrifice* [Offret, 1986] (supplied by Anna-Lena Wibum) and of Tarkovsky's hospitalization and funeral (supplied by Chris Marker). Photographs document Tarkovsky's childhood, and original footage explores Tarkovsky's abandoned homes in Russia. The soundtrack also features an audio recording of Tarkovsky reading his father's poem 'I fell ill in childhood'. The broader historical context is suggested by footage of the funerals of Leonid Brezhnev and Yuri Andropov, replete with tearful mourners. Official Soviet civilisation persists, but neither Tarkovsky in his exile nor Sokurov in his mourning show much interest in who these people are and what kind of trauma they are experiencing. The loss that Sokurov is registering is of a very different kind; it is the end of an entire dimension of spiritual existence, which media are powerless to perceive, let alone to communicate. Sokurov features French TV reports on Tarkovsky's death, highlighting the disconcerting way in which this epochal event became trivialised as breaking news communicated through modern mass media to an indifferent public, only to be forgotten on the morrow.

Though it reached its apogee only later, especially in *Russian Ark*, Sokurov's sentimentalism is on full display in *Moscow Elegy*, which focuses on three key moments of Tarkovsky's life: childhood, Italian exile and death. In Sokurov's other cinematic homages, from *Sonata for Viola* (about Dmitri Shostakovich) to *Conversations with Solzhenitsyn*, he has tended to focus his camera on the physical presence of his subject. Instead of prolonging or reproducing the effect of Tarkovsky's presence, *Moscow Elegy* seems to accentuate the irrevocability of his absence and the impotence of any technological medium to compensate. The only specific places featured are Tarkovsky's now-empty homes: in Zavrazhe, Shchipok (in Moscow), Miasnoe, Mosfilmovskii pereulok; Sokurov takes us on a posthumous tour of the last three, noting their sparse furnishings and their present state of desertion. He shows footage of Tarkovsky in Marlen Khutsiev's *Ilyich Gates* [Zastava Il'icha, 1962] and in Alexander Burimsky's *Thoughts about the Hero* [Razmyshleniia o geroe, 1974], a documentary study about protagonists in Soviet cinema, in which we recognise characteristic gestures. But these are only meagre and oblique traces of the man.

One sequence features footage of a deserted Sheremetevo airport, Tarkovsky's final port of embarkation from the USSR. Leaving the building, the camera pans left along an idle entrance ramp that seems to open onto nowhere, a rather heavy-handed allegory for Tarkovsky's exile. As the camera refocuses on the forest behind the ramp, Sokurov plays the opening of Viacheslav Ovchinnikov's soundtrack to Tarkovsky's *Ivan's Childhood*, which begins with a dreamy orchestral reverie and descends into nightmarish dissonance. On the surface Sokurov seems to be underscoring the less-than-idyllic circumstances of Tarkovsky's Italian exile (which to most

Soviets in 1987 would have seemed an enviable fate). The effect, though, is that the entire story of Tarkovsky's departure is inscribed into Tarkovsky's cinematic world. The forest is like Ivan's lost childhood; or rather it is like the alien ocean that encircles Kelvin's home at the end of Tarkovsky's *Solaris*, confusing the difference between fantasy and memory.

In effect Sokurov asserts the almost hermetic self-enclosure of Tarkovsky's life and work, which can only be replicated, but never appropriated for the needs of historical life. This is especially surprising if one considers that *Moscow Elegy* was one of the first films in which Sokurov was documenting not some more-or-less distant event in the Russian cultural memory, but rather an event of present concern and urgency. Like *Evening Sacrifice* or *On the Events in Transcaucasia*, it represents a direct contribution to the discourse of glasnost, where for the first time Sokurov was less a researcher than a witness, and where he could speak in the first-person plural on behalf of his presumed audience. At the same time the film is tantamount to a disavowal of the social power of mediation.

In a brief written testimonial from the same time, Sokurov recalls learning of Tarkovsky's death over the radio. Lying in hospital, beset by the cacophony of squeaky beds, cries of pain, 'the rattling of the syringes and needles in their metal containers' (objects that appear in Tarkovsky's *Solaris* and *Stalker*), Sokurov tunes in his short wave radio and, amidst world-wide celebrations of Christmas, hears 'a man speaking in accented Russian [...] A consciously impersonal intonation. Precise, concrete information'.

> 'Andrei Tarkovsky... has died... in Paris.' At this moment I thought I might die myself. The next morning the doctor asked me what was the matter. I told him that Andrei Tarkovsky had died. 'Really? And what has that got to do with you?' the doctor asked gently. 'Was he a relation of yours?' 'No', I replied.[18]

Sokurov recalls going out into a corridor to weep and realizing that he was weeping less for Tarkovsky than for himself. Sokurov perceives the event as Tarkovsky's desertion of his country, a perpetuation of his voluntary (almost self-indulgent, Sokurov hints) exile. Sokurov ridicules the doctor's assumption that Tarkovsky's death is of importance only to kin; however, in order to explain his distress at Tarkovsky's death Sokurov does feel obliged to detail a kind of personal bond. Sokurov recalls chaperoning Tarkovsky during the latter's visit to Leningrad.[19] He marvelled at the flocks of adoring fans who had come to hear Tarkovsky speak: 'Such people are the fulcrum and justification of Russian life. They know what it means to struggle day by day with disorderly living conditions and the difficulties of productive life. But they also know what is most important: that life is truly there to be spent in culture and faith; everything else is a miserable accessory'.[20]

Sokurov paints Tarkovsky as a link to an otherworld of cultural expressions and significations to which Tarkovsky has now made his final exit. Existence in the cultural realm is a particularly painful kind of emigration from the real world into a more-real world of culture and pure morality. In her work on emigration Julia Kristeva has described this 'weightlessness in the infinity of cultures and legacies': 'since he belongs to nothing the foreigner can feel as appertaining to everything, to the entire tradition'.[21] However, this is a world in which Tarkovsky is at home, and in relation to which Tarkovsky now extends us the possibility of a new kinship and a new collectivity. Sokurov remarks that '[the fans'] faces are enlivened by the secret hope that the gaze of the creator might rest on them for an instant, which would represent an eternity for their souls'.[22] Strangely, perhaps, Sokurov also seems to insist on the almost physical intimacy of communication in this realm. But this is an intimacy that can only be imagined, never rendered materially. This failure of mediation is illustrated by Sokurov's story of a telephone conversation that he had with Tarkovsky while the latter was in Italy: '[his] voice', Sokurov recalls, 'sounded like a dubbed cartoon character'.[23] Moreover, as his living voice becomes inaudible, Tarkovsky's films seem to be receding into invisibility. The clips in *Moscow Elegy* from Tarkovsky's films are of a very poor quality, as if taken from muddy videotapes; the extensive excerpts from *Tempo di Viaggio* are in black and white, though the film is colour, and Tarkovsky's comments are back-translated into Russian from the Italian voiceover. In his commemorations of Tarkovsky, 'culture' is strangely disassociated from the technological media by which it is communicated, i.e. from aesthetics. If to watch Tarkovsky's films is tantamount to being in the pure, unsullied presence of the master, then the master's absence makes it well-nigh impossible to watch the films without a stultifying nostalgia.

Sokurov's comparison of Tarkovsky's telephonic voice to that of 'a dubbed cartoon character' hints at his rather desultory assessment of Tarkovsky's work in emigration. It is not uncommon for Russian film-makers, critics and viewers to reject his final two films, *Nostalghia* and *Sacrifice*, as self-indulgent. It is as if, free of his native moorings, Tarkovsky lost his bearings. Perhaps Sokurov feels that Tarkovsky's art could not survive separation from his (Soviet)-Russian audience – from Russia, ultimately – because his sanctifying gaze was no longer being returned. This alienation seems irreversible; Sokurov underscores the fate in *Nostalghia* of the composer Sosnovsky, based on the real-life Berezovsky, a serf-composer who studied in the Bologna Conservatory, but returned to Russia, and to servitude, only to commit suicide. Regarding Tarkovsky's death as a consequence of his suicidal emigration, Sokurov suggests that both events are irredeemable. It is this lack of redemption, one concludes, that has made Sokurov a principal proponent of nostalgia as the appropriate attitude towards Russia's future, a future that Russia has never had.

Sokurov's grief is rooted in his inability to recover any visual trace of Tarkovsky in the abandoned spaces of his homes, his films or his friends' memories. Narrating Tarkovsky's final days, Sokurov's laments that 'We in the homeland knew next to nothing about the state of his health'. Throughout the film Sokurov eschews the words 'USSR' or 'Russia', preferring *rodina* – homeland, a concept symbolised by the birch forest that encircles the port of departure. But then, without Tarkovsky and his films, it seems that this homeland has itself receded from view. Paralysed by sentimentalism, all we survivors can do, it would seem, is to open museums at the sites of his former homes, lovingly preserving the arrangement of objects as he left them. In our world only such a museum and such a film has the power to preserve intimacy by fixing an absence and prolonging the promise of nostalgia.

Memory and Performance

In 'Death, the Banal Leveler' Alexander Sokurov recalls that at their final parting Tarkovsky took a snapshot of Sokurov in the train: 'It was half light in the compartment; only the faces showed. I have never seen those photographs, so perhaps one might assume I had imagined it all. A fine thing to imagine, though, isn't it?'[24] Sokurov's memory of these fugitive images echoes an episode from Tarkovsky's final film *Sacrifice*. The postman Otto tells the story (one of 284 such stories of the 'unexplained' that he has collected) a woman who had a portrait taken with her eighteen-year old son in 1940, days before he died in the war. She never collected the prints, but when she sits for a new portrait in 1960, the developed photograph shows her as she is in 1960 accompanied by her son as he was in 1940, as if the two photographs have bled into each other. 'We are totally blind and don't see anything', Otto exclaims before collapsing to the floor. By remaining purely imaginary, Otto and Sokurov suggest, the undeveloped photographs retain a promise of mysterious presence that protects them from the violence of history. Sokurov fears that the materialisation of the image would strip his relationship with Tarkovsky of its intimacy, by involving it in the material traffic of modern media.

These doubts concerning the material image explain in part Tarkovsky's and Sokurov's interest in performative media such as theatre and opera, which offer a completely different kind of intimacy, one that is sometimes confused with immediacy. It has historically been very difficult for cinema artists to adapt to the new conditions. Chris Marker has confessed that, after attending Tarkovsky's production of *Boris Godunov*, he stole his opera glasses 'in the hope that one day they would give me back the images they have seen'.[25] Marker seems to harbour the suspicion that, even in the opera, Tarkovsky remained oriented towards the cinematic image, a suspicion confirmed by other reviewers of Tarkovsky and echoed by reviewers of Sokurov's more recent production.[26] By examining Sokurov's production of *Boris Godunov* alongside Tarkovsky's precedent, I will trace a third moment in his complex and evolving project to reclaim the possibility of intimacy within the modern image.

At first glance Sokurov's production of Mussorgsky's *Boris Godunov* might seem to be simply his latest tribute to Tarkovsky, who staged *Boris Godunov* at Royal Opera House at Covent Garden in 1983, the same year he completed the film *Nostalghia* and the year before he commenced work on *Sacrifice*. This production was brought to the Mariinsky Theatre by Tarkovsky's assistant Irina Brown in 1993, was revived in 2003 and was restored in 2006, thus achieving a longer life-span than most opera productions by film-makers.[27] Tarkovsky's expansive design was based on a 'super-saturated' edition of the score chosen by Claudio Abbado, that 'stitches together the fullest versions of everything Mussorgsky ever wrote for the opera'.[28] It also featured a set primed for symbolism. The stage is dominated by an enormous arch that is either half-ruined or simply unfinished, and which surmounts stone ramparts on either side and looms over a ramp that leads down to the front of the stage. The main action occurs on the raised ramp, while the lower areas on either side are inhabited by faceless masses who writhe and seethe in the face of repression. At times a massive pendulum appears behind the arch, counting out the inexorable procession of fate. The set makes Tarkovsky seem to be gesturing towards a romantic vision of Russia's past, an impression strengthened by his foregrounding of Pimen, the Simpleton (i.e., holy fool [*iurodivyi*]) and the murdered tsarevich Dmitri. The overall effect is that of an operatic re-creation of *War and Peace*, less Tolstoy's experimental novel than Sergei Bondarchuk's blockbuster adaptation of 1968. Reviewing the 2003 revival, Edward Seckerson wrote that 'even 20 years ago, this show [...] looked and felt like a thing of the past. [...] This is what the Bolshoi or Kirov was doing a century ago'.[29]

Major elements of Tarkovsky's staging beg to be read as direct extensions of his film world. Tarkovsky lined the Polish court scene with statues played by stationary performers who periodically shifted position and then joined in the ball. This scene is linked to the letter of the fictionalised eighteenth-century Russian composer Pavel Sosnovsky, which is read out loud in Tarkovsky's 1983 film *Nostalghia*. An allegory for the ways in which artists can feel like puppets in a spectacle orchestrated by political forces beyond their control, this episode illustrates how Tarkovsky's production was also responding to a specific stage of the late Cold War. It was just after the debut season of *Boris Godunov*, on 10 July 1984, that Tarkovsky publicly announced his defection from the USSR. The ghostly presence of the murdered tsarevich throughout the opera underscores the links to his final film *Sacrifice*, where the protagonist is consumed by a fear of guilt for the impending nuclear apocalypse that threatens his mute son. Framed by his two final films, Tarkovsky's *Boris Godunov* seeks to capture poignant images at points where aesthetic media bend beneath the pressure of the invisible forces of history, political power and time, images that seem more at home in Tarkovsky's movies. This quest for poignantly integral moments suspended like tableaux amidst the performance threatened to make his production collapse under its own weight.

For their production of Mussorgsky's *Boris Godunov* conductor Alexander Vedernikov and artistic director Alexander Sokurov chose the 1871 redaction of the opera with nine scenes in five acts. The major differences from the more commonly performed versions, including that of Tarkovsky and Abbado, are a smaller orchestra and the omission of the Kromy scene. In an interview printed in the book-length programme Vedernikov has characterised the 1871 redaction as the earliest version to feature both the scene at the Polish court and mass scene at the Cathedral of St Basil, which punctuate the vast emotional range of the opera. In Vedernikov's view, supported by Sokurov, the chronological and musical overlaps between the scenes at St Basil and Kromy make them mutually exclusive, a fact unappreciated in previous productions, including Tarkovsky's. Instead, their version ends with the death of Tsar Boris in his private quarters, in the company of his young heir and a handful of boyars.

At first glance the 1871 version is a much more dramatic work, focused on the protagonist and his personal struggle more than on the broader historical and orchestral panoramas familiar to opera-goers, especially in Russia. It is in all respects smaller in conception and ambition and, shorn of Kromy, somewhat anticlimactic. These same qualities allow the details of the musical and dramatic design to emerge with greater relief. Instead of an epic panorama, the opera presents a clinical analysis of what Sokurov calls 'the mechanisms of power', which is a decidedly 'human creation' and is 'exercised by people'.[30]

Sokurov's comments betray some of the same contradictions as his statements on his films. Adopting the same kind of reverential attitude towards opera as he displays towards classical painting and literature, Sokurov has approached *Boris Godunov* with the overriding concern that he remain true to 'the ethical and aesthetic principles' of this conservative medium: 'Of particular importance for the Russian opera tradition, it seems to me, is an evolutionary, evolving attitude to a work. After all, the majority of Russian operas in one way or another touch upon history, the historical core, where it is very dangerous to violate ethical conventions because then the very gist of the work starts to change, and the music too – it sounds different if suddenly, via the set design or the costumes, we effect an abrupt break with a certain historical quality, essence, the correlation of events in time' (41). There is, at first glance, little hint of irony in this studied anachronism; indeed, the only challenge to traditionalist Russian tastes in his production might be a fleeting glimpse of a nude Marina Mniszech in an ornate mirror. Sokurov regards 'the entire story of the murdered tsarevich' to be 'only Boris's projection onto his own life' (41), and one could say that, by underscoring the psychological drama of Boris Godunov and his son, Sokurov has read the opera in the vein of the realist novel of Mussorgsky's day. In contrast to Tarkovsky's staging, here the viewer does not see the larger historical and metaphysical dimensions looming over the characters. One does, however, see the characters with an unusual degree of detail and texture.

One recognises several specific techniques adapted from Sokurov's cinematic practice. The sets (by Yuri Kuper, who worked with Sokurov on the 2004 film *The Sun*) are Gobelins-like fabric backdrops which can be raised and lowered in a matter of seconds, so that with careful lighting the viewer is hardly aware of the seams between scenes, an effect that reviewers have compared to montage.[31] For instance, during Pimen's aria the set changes from St Basil's Cathedral to the inside of his monastic cell. The lighting (directed by Damir Ismagilov) is supplemented by video projections (directed by Yelena Godovannaya) of clouds, sky, water, sun, and stones. Sokurov comments that 'the light flows in this production. It doesn't stand still; it flows just as time itself does' (57). This not only augments the connections between scenes, it also enriches the lush visual textures that result from the interaction between the lighting, the video projections, the hung sets and the richly embroidered costumes. The subdued colour scheme, dominated by greys and light blues, causes the entire opera to seem 'as if viewed through a haze', an effect which costume designer Pavel Kaplevich compares to 'an old black-and-white photograph with colour tinting' (51). Kuper interprets the 'monochrome colour scale' as 'a way of indicating the distance in time, our remoteness from that epoch' (57). This comment suggests that not only are the creative team aware of the obsolescence of their approach, but that they exploit it to heighten the tensions between intimacy and distance within the historical narrative itself.

Visually everything onstage seems at once materially textured and transparent, with liveable internal spaces and limitless perspectives beyond. Everything is transient, apart from Boris's internal turmoil, which, though it is never given full rein, becomes increasingly palpable as the opera proceeds. In interviews, Sokurov has repeatedly insisted that the characters in his opera are fundamentally 'happy people'; however, the peculiar nature of this happiness is evident from his qualifying statement that Boris 'is happy insofar as he has achieved his desire, but the price of the achievement poisons this happiness'. In fact, Sokurov seems to believe that opera is an inherently, almost inescapably happy medium; insofar as 'a man in song is a free man', Sokurov strove to provide the conditions for 'happy artists'.[32] Far from signalling some political lesson, then, Sokurov's utopian instinct is completely contained within the performance, as happiness and freedom result from the intimacy of the theatrical space. As in his film-meditation on Hubert Robert's 'happy life', moreover, this happiness is inseparable from the atmosphere of ruin and obsolescence. In *Boris Godunov*, Sokurov says, 'We are attempting to make a performance that is not distanced from man, but brought close to him' (43).

This intimacy is a good match for the reduced soundscape of the 1871 version, so that music and staging present a taut and disciplined unity of purpose. The staging places a great burden on the performers, who cut lonely, even forlorn figures. With the apparent emphasis on visual verisimilitude (especially in the case of Fyodor), one suspects that Sokurov chose his cast in part with an eye to being plausible in close-up,[33] which indicates the limits of Sokurov's initial engagement with the conventions of opera and, perhaps, a lingering mistrust of the voice as a medium.

Overall, however, Sokurov has successfully translated the most conspicuous qualities of his experimental traditionalism, most notably his innovative use of optical perspective, onto the opera stage, while also allowing for the specificity of the operatic medium to create a substantially different kind of access to the intimate atmospheres of history. If Tarkovsky's *Boris Godunov* dwelled on the parallel between late-medieval Rus and the late Soviet Union in order to draw a metaphysical and ethical contrast, Sokurov allows the world of the opera to be a self-contained moment of crisis that exemplifies nothing more than the fragility of motion and of vision. It is precisely because it is comfortable with its own fragility that Sokurov's production engages its viewers in the intimate textures of the history it mourns.

Conclusion

In *Tempo di viaggio* Tarkovsky speaks of his desire to see Italy as a place not of natural and manmade beauty, but as a place where a man might be unhappy, i.e., where history inhabits its individual subjects as a burden and an obligation. By contrast, Alexander Sokurov often seems intent on rediscovering within traumatic histories the conditions of happiness-in-spite-of-all, or at least of a redemptive intimacy. Although Sokurov has often claimed for his art the idyllic purpose of re-establishing conditions of prior states of intimacy, his works themselves complicate this purpose by foregrounding the material resistances within the medium and capturing the minimal distances that haunt all such artistic utopias. The act of viewing Sokurov becomes a kind of absorption in vision itself, which is positioned not as a utopian alternative to modern distraction but as a critical potentiality lurking within it, ultimately as its redemption. This potentiality has been showcased in recent films like *Father and Son* and *Alexandra*, and also in his recent forays into performance media. The fundamental anachronism of Sokurov's work is not then his stated affection for the forms of Empire, but his continuing attachment to the idea of the solitary viewer as the agent of social change; yet it is a studied and almost exuberant anachronism, which Sokurov has struggled to free from its inherent utopianism. Thus Sokurov's most profound engagement with his own time is that he (adapting Pasternak's formulation) represents the overt drama of historical life by analyzing the visual perspectives that this life contemplates, the intimate perspectives of its mediation, which in the end is tantamount to the perspective of history. Likewise, though he has been a pioneer in digital cinema, Sokurov has called digital 'a space of global irresponsibility, both moral and professional [...] a world of inertia and aggression'.[34]

Notes

1. Lauren Sedofsky, 'Plane Songs: Lauren Sedofsky talks with Alexander Sokurov', *ArtForum* 40.3 (November 2001), p. 124. Available at http://www.thefreelibrary.com/Plane+songs%3a+Lauren+Sedofsky+talks+with+Alexander+Sokurov.-a081258061 (accessed 6 January 2009).
2. Boris Pasternak, *Sobranie sochinenii v piati tomakh*, vol. 5, Moscow: Khudozhestvennaia literatura, 1992, p. 78.
3. Jacques Rancière, 'Le cinéma comme la peinture?' *Cahiers du cinéma* 531 (January 1999), pp. 30–32 (p. 32).
4. Kovalov, 'My v "Odinokom golose cheloveka"', *Sokurov 1*, p. 8.
5. On the history of the film, including Tarkovsky's role, see 'Odinokii golos cheloveka' in *Sokurov 1*, pp. 25–32.
6. Hans-Joachim Schlegel, 'Transtsendentnost' autentichnogo: O dokumental'nom u Andreia Tarkovskogo i Aleksandra Sokurova', *Kinovedcheskie zapiski* 49 (2000), pp. 180–84.
7. Platonov, *Gosudarstvennyi zhitel': Proza. Rannie sochineniia. Pis'ma*, Minsk: Mastatskaia literature, 1990, p. 425. Further references to this edition are given parenthetically in the text.
8. Tarkovsky was especially impressed by this scene; Ol'ga Surkova, 'Ital'ianskii dialog', *Iskusstvo kino* 11 (1995), pp. 197–98. Sokurov's cameraman Sergei

Yurizditsky claims that the choice of film stock was at least partially dictated by their limited resources; see 'Odinokii golos cheloveka', *Sokurov 1*, p. 26.
9 On the use of still photographs in film see: Raymond Bellour, *L'Entre-Images: Photo. Cinéma. Vidéo*, Paris: Éditions de la Différence, 2002.
10 Sergei Iurizditskii, in 'Odinokii golos cheloveka', *Sokurov 1*, p. 26. Curiously, Sokurov has stated that 'Petrov-Vodkin and the Russian icon painters were working under conditions of absolute freedom, that is, directly, without a medium'; see 'Plane Songs: Lauren Sedofsky talks with Alexander Sokurov', p. 125.
11 Mikhail Iampol'skii, 'Platonov, prochitannyi Sokurovym', *Sokurov 1*, p. 44.
12 Lev Anninskii, 'Esli budet konets sveta...', *Sovetskaia kul'tura*, 3 June 1989; quoted in *Sokurov 1*, p. 51.
13 Iampol'skii, 'Platonov...', p. 44.
14 Kovalov, 'My v "Odinokom golose cheloveka"', *Sokurov 1*, pp. 8–9.
15 Iampol'skii, 'Platonov ...', p. 49, 45.
16 See Robert Bird, *Andrei Tarkovsky: Elements of Cinema*, London: Reaktion, 2008.
17 Aleksandr Sokurov, '"Odinokii golos cheloveka": dnevniki 1979 goda', in *Sokurov 1*, p. 34.
18 Alexander Sokurow, 'Die banale Gleichmacherei des Todes', in Jansen and Schütte (eds), *Andrej Tarkowskij*, pp. 7–8.
19 Tarkovsky's diary allows us to date his visit to Leningrad as 11–16 December 1981. Sokurov's telephone conversation with Tarkovsky might have been on the latter's birthday, 4 April 1982. See Andrei Tarkovsky, *Martirolog: Dnevniki 1970–1986*, n.p.: Istituto Internazionale Andrej Tarkovskij, 2008.
20 Sokurow, 'Die banale Gleichmacherei des Todes', p. 16.
21 Julia Kristeva, *Strangers to Ourselves*, New York: Columbia University Press, 1991, p. 32.
22 Sokurow, 'Die banale Gleichmacherei des Todes', p. 16.
23 Sokurow, 'Die banale Gleichmacherei des Todes', p. 21.
24 Sokurow, 'Die banale Gleichmacherei des Todes', p. 21.
25 Chris Marker, 'Commentaire pour *Une Journée d'Andrei Arsenevitch*', *Positif*, 48 (March 2001), p.52.
26 Edward Seckerson, 'Tarkovsky's Boris Rises from the Dead', *The Independent*, 24 September 2003; Irina Murav'eva, 'Godunov po Sokurovu', *Rossiiskaia gazeta*, 28 April 2007.
27 Irina Brown's re-creation of Tarkovsky's production at the Mariinsky is available on DVD from Philips.
28 Caryl Emerson and Robert William Oldani, *Modest Musorgsky and Boris Godunov: Myths, Realities, Reconsiderations*, Cambridge: Cambridge University Press, 1994, p. 283.
29 Edward Seckerson, 'Tarkovsky's Boris Rises from the Dead', *The Independent*, 24 September 2003.
30 *Boris Godunov*, The State Academic Bolshoi Theatre of Russia, production programme (n.d.) p. 41, 43. Further citations of this bilingual source will be given in the text; here and elsewhere the English translation has been adjusted for accuracy.
31 Murav'eva, 'Godunov po Sokurovu'.
32 These comments are cited from an interview with Sokurov during the intermission of the telecast of his opera on the channel Kul'tura on 28 April 2007; accessed 12 March 2008 on http://dir4.etvnet.ca.
33 See Murav'eva, 'Godunov po Sokurovu'.
34 Aleksandr Sokurov, 'Ob izobrazitel'nom reshenii fil'ma', *Sokurov 2*, p. 509.

PART III

INTIMATE ENCOUNTERS

CHAPTER 7

TRUNCATED FAMILIES AND ABSOLUTE INTIMACY
Mikhail Iampolski

Alexander Sokurov has a special interest in family relations. Several of his films focus exclusively on relations between father and son (*Father and Son*, *The Second Circle*), mother and son (*Mother and Son*) and even grandmother and grandson (*Alexandra*). However, all of Sokurov's families have one feature in common: they are truncated, not complete. If Sokurov scrutinises father and son, the mother is never mentioned, as if she never existed. The same is true for mother and son – the father is entirely absent, and nobody ever cares about his enigmatic disappearance.

Sokurov reduces the triangular structure of a normal nuclear family to a dual structure, and this reduction is extremely significant. The triangular structure is based on Oedipal relations and the prohibition of incest. At the same time and by the same prohibition, a symbolic order of social relations is established. The father who prohibits his son's desire for his mother's body is transformed into a purely symbolic figure, an embodiment of the law, which is interiorised as a super-ego. Society emerges as a set of symbolically defined subjective positions, whose basic structure is triangular. This structure allows symbolic exchanges between positions, but keeps them separated one from another. Society is functioning as far as it prevents the collapse of the triangular structure into pure non-differentiation of simple, dual structures. An average person, who in childhood and adolescence has passed through the Oedipal transition to adulthood, finally emerges as autonomous subject no more dependent on his mother or father.

By eliminating one term from the family triangle, Sokurov creates a strange, disturbing and utopian world of a pre-Oedipal intimacy, which is not threatened by any menace of law, of power, of separation. The world of truncated families is a response to a deep visceral desire to restore the idyllic fusion between children and parents. It could also be interpreted as

Still from *Alexandra*. Courtesy of ProLine Production.

a response to a collapse of symbolic power in Russia in the late 1980s–early 2000s. This strange pre-Oedipal world is a disturbing mixture of latent sexuality and infantile innocence, because only innocence can wholly justify the troubling intimacy that Sokurov's characters develop. A kind of eroticism we can detect in these films is an attribute of early children-parents relations rather than of adult sexuality.

These relations are in Sokurov's films quite polymorphous. A mother can literally be transformed into a child, or a son into her 'father', as in a strange episode in *Mother and Son* when the son is carrying his dying mother in his arms. In *Father and Son* the father may carry his adult son on his shoulders like a little boy. These unexpected reversals of roles and of age are directly linked to the collapse of triangularity that usually maintains a relatively stable distribution of functions and roles.

The world of the licit non-sexual intimacy between adults is a utopian construction. It emerges on the ruins of society and social order seen as non-human, alienating and deeply hostile. The utopian construction of absolute intimacy is a distorted reflection of this anti-human social universe that is, for instance, visible in *Alexandra* – one of Sokurov's most ambiguous works. The film tells a story of an old woman visiting her grandson (an officer of a reconnaissance unit) in Grozny, the capital of the besieged Chechnya. It is indicative that Sokurov replaces the rather conventional figure of a soldier's mother by a grandmother. The father searching for his son on the front line had become an emblematic figure in Rezo Chkheidze's *Father of a Soldier* [*Jariskatsis mama*, 1964], and there are similar plots around mother-figures. The choice of a grandmother shows to what extent Sokurov is willing to mix up traditional roles prescribed by social order and traditional, triangular structures.

In several films Sokurov focuses on the military – the most extreme case of symbolic power that becomes a 'biopower', deciding matters of life and death. Father and son in *Father and Son* are both in the military; the main male character in *Alexandra* is a soldier, too; and Sokurov has made several documentary films about war and life in the military. He is particularly interested in situations when the dominant symbolic power collapses, which happened, for instance, in the heat of a fight in *Spiritual Voices*, where the commands are gradually separated from the symbolic power and become an expression of a simple necessity of survival. The fight is depicted by Sokurov as un-structuring of hierarchical relations, of any kind of triangulation, and the gradual emergence of an extraordinary intimacy between the soldiers. The truth of closely related bodies here replaces the falsehood of the symbolic. The military is for Sokurov an institution that, in mortal combat, destroys the symbolic and replaces it with an absolute, unquestionable proximity. The war, from this point of view, is an operation of the liberation of bodies from the oppressing domination of words and authority (a main theme also in *And Nothing More*). Proximity between bodies leaves no space for the symbolic, which requires distances. Eroticism and war, from this point of view, are very similar.

The series of 'family films' should be read against the background of Sokurov's three major films about power: *Moloch*, *Taurus* and *The Sun*. The making of these three films about Hitler, Lenin and Hirohito was surprising in the context of Sokurov's relative indifference to politics. The series looks less surprising if we see it as a reflection on the disintegration of the symbolic. On screen, the three leaders have no children; instead, they are incarnations of a father-figure for the whole nation, but Sokurov reveals that they are unable to play the symbolic part they have assigned to themselves. All three leaders are infantile; this is especially true for Lenin, who is affected by a severe illness destroying his intellect and who degrades into a speechless child (he is bathed like a child and completely dependent on his surroundings). Hirohito gradually and painfully discovers his own humanity behind the divine role that he was forced to play. His divinity disintegrates and a child emerges from the heavenly body. The Americans find him funny, reminiscent of the 'Kid', Charlie Chaplin.

In *Moloch*, Hitler is simply unable to get rid of the symbolic (he is talking endlessly while all his words are recorded), and hence is unable to establish a contact with the human. Eva Braun is not a woman in flesh for him, but an incarnation of classical beauty; he is permanently talking about a coming superman and about the approach of death, which he had hoped to overcome. He confesses that his goal is to force the evolution of German people into a superhuman race. Sokurov shows Hitler in his private residence, which resembles an old Roman church – in a parody of Wagnerian demigods. His pretension to transcend humanity, however, makes him completely grotesque. His hideous vanity paradoxically makes him human, and thus tolerable and even loveable for Eva, who is unable to love a purely symbolic figure. The film has a clear Christian background: it claims that a god can be loved and worshipped only if he has the humility to become human;¹ otherwise divinity becomes an artificial monster – Leviathan or Moloch.

Lenin's case is particularly interesting. Human beings become subjects (i.e. become humans) with the acquisition of language and the ability to speak. The symbolic, as we know from Lacan, appears simultaneously with subjectivity that deals, as soon as it is established, not with the father but with the *name of the father*. But as soon as speech is mastered, we communicate not our own experience, but its social reflection. Giorgio Agamben poses the question whether the communication of human experience (and human experience as such) is possible for a speaking person: 'A theory of experience could in this sense only be a theory of infancy, and its central question would have to be formulated thus: is there such a thing as human in-fancy? How can in-fancy be humanly possible? And if it is possible, where is it sited?'² If we communicate experience, it is already not ours; if we do not know how to speak, are we human? Is our speechless experience a human one?

For Sokurov there is no doubt that human experience is given almost exclusively outside the symbolic, which steals it and destroys. For Agamben an in-fant could be pre-human, but infancy is exactly the time when human beings have access to experience as such. Agamben believes that the specificity of a human being consists in the split between language (which is a-historical) and discourse (which is historical). This split is unknown to animals who 'are always and totally language'³ and express themselves without any split between semiotics and semantics. Lenin's regression to a stage of in-fancy is a movement that happens within this split, because Lenin is able to understand, but unable to speak. The 'historical' in him shrinks metaphorically and, like an animal,⁴ he enters the world of non-historical nature. A similarly strange relapse into infancy is seen in *Stone*, where Chekhov returns to his Yalta house and appears first of all as a child who cannot speak. Sokurov shows him in a bath, as he does with Lenin; in Sokurov's films this bathing of the naked body is a recurrent allegory of infancy, when an adult is transformed into a grown-up replica of a baby. In both cases Sokurov focuses on speakers (politicians) and writers, for whom the entire universe is exclusively symbolic.

The blockage of the symbolical is an essential feature of Sokurov's films and central for *The Second Circle*, which deals explicitly with a father's death. The father's death is a constituent event of the symbolic: a father prohibits the fusion of a son with his mother as incestuous; however, at certain moment he should himself be eliminated in order to allow to the son to occupy the father's place in his own family.⁵ A son inherits his father's name that allows him to occupy the same symbolic place that belonged to the father. The replacement of a castrating father (symbolic castration blocks the son's relation with the mother) with the *name-of-the-father* is crucial in this transition, since it requires the physical disappearance of an ancestor. In *The Second Circle*, however, this replacement is blocked by the father's body, which is oppressively present. The son cannot enter the symbolic order as the father's substitute, because the father's body is reluctant to disappear. Only the body's disappearance opens a gap that can then be filled by the *name* and that allows the replacement of a physical body with a linguistic, symbolic reality. The entire film is precisely about the inability of the son to bury his father. As long as the elimination of the body is not possible, access to the symbolic is prohibited. The film's claustrophobic space accommodates only two characters (the others are relatively insignificant): the father's corpse and the son. There is no space for anybody else – mother, sisters or brothers. *The Second Circle* establishes the duality of parent and son as a basic structure of Sokurov's universe that cannot be broken. This irremovable duality leads beyond the symbolic and into the Imaginary.

The structure of the Imaginary is provided by mirrors and doubles. A subject is unable to appropriate a symbolic place related to a linguistic signifier and created by the lack of body; he is simply forced to confront the father's body as a permanently present Other. This Other becomes an alienated image of the self, his double in a mirror. Because triangularity is prohibited, a subject is unable to change the symbolic position: he is doomed to a narcissistic reflection of the self in the visible Other that is reluctant to vanish. In the most striking episode of *The Second Circle* the son (Alexandrov) is studying the face of his dead father: both the son and the father are embodied by the same actor, thus stressing the specular similarity between the two, where circularity and specularity cannot be broken because the son's ego is completely dependent on the father's image and cannot survive without it (as if they where a body and its shadow).

The Second Circle can also be seen as an allegory of the transformation of the father into an image that is captured, frozen by death, and thus becomes inescapable. Because the subject itself is captured by this image in the mirror, he is alienated in his own double. This alienation can

Still from *Second Circle.*

liberate the subject if it is dialecticised and pushed further: the subject can open 'normal' relations with the Other. But it can easily become pathological when, instead of creating a viable figure of the Other, it only narcissistically duplicates itself. Lacan took a long time to liberate his thought from the narcissistic closure of the Imaginary.[6] In Sokurov's case, this struggle takes a particularly dramatic turn. In the adaptation of *Madame Bovary* – *Save and Protect* – made immediately before *The Second Circle*, the theme of doubling is already present. Sokurov treats Emma's search for the gratification of her desires as fundamentally narcissistic, and introduces Emma's double into the film: a really uncanny presence in a story about sexual frustration.

The situation of the Imaginary doubling re-emerges in *Mother and Son* and later in *Father and Son* – two films that desperately try to redeem doubling from its curse. *Mother and Son* was made six years after *The Second Circle*, but it very much looks like a direct response to the earlier film about a specular situation. Both films are constructed around the death of a parent. In the earlier film death is presented as the oppressive presence of a corpse. In the second film, the dying mother is in the same specular relation to her son, but specularity here is no longer treated as a nightmare, but as a utopia of absolute proximity, of absolute fusion with a sublimating and redemptive force. Six years after *The Second Circle* Sokurov comes back to the same structure but with a changed point of view.

This change partially reflects a general change in society. 1990 was the lowest point in Soviet history: the moment of complete disintegration not only of economy and ideology, but also of authority and of the law associated with it. In 1990 the Soviet Union was a 'society without the Father', to use Mitscherlich's definition,[7] on the verge of total collapse. Therefore the disappearance of the symbolic was related to the general state of society. Significantly, in 1989 Sokurov made an important documentary, *Soviet Elegy*, in which he showed Yeltsin as a big infant walled up in silence, almost completely speechless. In 1996 the fatherless society looked less dramatic. However, in Sokurov's case social readings of films could be done with caution; more general philosophical problems always prevail in his films. *Mother and Son* seems like an attempt to impose the Imaginary as a utopian alternative for a symbolic social reality that is completely eliminated from the film. The world where leaders are no longer symbolic fathers but big infants is a world of the Imaginary par excellence.

Since *Save and Protect*, Sokurov has developed a special interest in the pictorial treatment of space, which is in my opinion directly related to his fascination with the structure of the Imaginary. This special treatment of space becomes central for his poetics in *Stone*, *Whispering Pages* and particularly in *Mother and Son*. Sokurov's space is often distorted and flattened. Distortions serve to better embed figures in space; frequently they are not shown as freely moving in a neutral three-dimensional volume, but – thanks to a mutual distortion of figures and their surroundings – they are inscribed into space as if on to a surface. In this way figures lose their autonomy in relation to the space that contains them. Space and figures are amalgamated by the same energy of alteration; they are not mutually autonomous. Such treatment transforms space into a kind of womb that keeps figures wrapped in its folds. This mutual folding of space and figures accompanies the transformation of adults into infants, and occurs for the first time in *Stone*. The same special folding (or deformation) is present in *Mother and Son*, whose picturesque space has sometimes been compared to Caspar David Friedrich's paintings. I am not questioning Friedrich's influence on Sokurov,[8] but I think the most important element of Friedrich's world for Sokurov is his ability to transform openness into closure and to develop womb-like spaces, as for instance in *Chalk Cliffs on Rügen* (1818). In this view the central 'stage' is folded into something like theatrical wings. This enveloping structure can also be found in other artists who were heavily influenced by Friedrich, such as Edvard Munch. This merging of figures and space in one swathing movement is significant for the world that isolates itself from the surrounding and encapsulates, or immures the self with its double.

The structure of this imaginary 'stage' is a product of the phantasm entirely isolated from reality and with all the characteristics of hallucination.

Still from *Save and Protect*.

Oscar Mannoni has described such an imaginary space as the product of a total loss of reality.[9] As usual, such a loss is very utopian in nature: it is utopian, hallucinatory and strongly related to the collapse of the symbolic. Lacan has described the catastrophe produced by the lack of the Name-of-the-Father, i.e. by the foreclosure of the symbolic, in the following way:

> It is the lack of the Name-of-the-Father in that place which, by the hole that it opens up in the signified, sets off the cascade of reshaping of the signifier from which the increasing disaster of the imaginary proceeds, to the point at which the level is reached at which signifier and signified are stabilized in the delusional metaphor.[10]

The 'reshaping of the signifier' in Sokurov's distorted landscapes is intrinsically related to the collapse of the symbolic.

The most far-reaching recent reflection about the truncated family occurs in *Father and Son*, released seven years after *Mother and Son*. Two major new elements appear in the film: first, death is eliminated from the plot; and second, the father is unusually so young that his age almost leads to confusion: father and son look rather like brothers. In *Father and Son* the main characters are so similar that they create the effect of non-distinction, which is particularly important because the symbolic is normally based on distinction and distanciation. Many critics have read the film as a disguised homoerotic story. In spite of the vague homoerotic sensibility that is obvious in the film, I find such a reading rather misleading: even the idea of presenting lovers as father and son seems too extravagant to be true.

The film builds the image of an intimate relationship between a father and his son. The son, Alexei, is a student at a military academy; the father is a retired officer who had a traumatic experience in a recent war that still haunts him. At the beginning of the film Alexei's girlfriend announces that she will abandon him, because she cannot find a place for herself between the father and the son – a tight and mutually absorbed couple. She abandons Alexei for a man who is more mature. Alexei's obvious immaturity is imposed on him by the role of a son, a role from which he cannot escape.

This situation is vaguely reminiscent of an Oedipal triangle, but Sokurov almost immediately dismisses the Oedipal turn as irrelevant and moves into the direction of a Christian (or biblical) understanding of the father-and-son predicament. This shift involves a very unusual set that the director uses for his drama. The apartment of the protagonists is located in an old building, under the roof, and they spent a lot of time on the roof which is adorned by a rather strange structure – half-dome, half-altar. In any case, this structure indicates that father and son equally belong to a kind of heavenly kingdom. This roof structure has a certain similarity with Hitler's temple-castle in *Moloch*. Alexei even tells his father that, according to his girlfriend, 'we built a fortress and do not let anybody into it', and asks: 'Does it look like a fortress?'. 'Yes, this is our fortress', answers the father. The roof is populated by birds, and it looks quite natural that at one moment the father literally wants to fly. The *temple* metaphor is important for the plot: in Latin *templum* initially meant a figure – a circle or square – traced in the sky by an augur who observed the flight of birds in this celestial opening. It is a space of freedom, of ultimate liberation from the constraint of order and command, and a place where the Freudian/Lacanian figure of the symbolic father transcends in an openness that recognises no structural constraints.

Sokurov never really amalgamates his characters with celestial counterparts, but the analogy is vital. In Trinity God-father and God-son are not distant, but completely fused and, of course, know no trace of Oedipal distanciation; they are clearly united in a non-symbolic way. In the context of a shift from the social to the transcendent, the father significantly is a retired officer. In Sokurov's *Days of Eclipse* there is an enigmatic episode: a soldier and an officer enter an Orthodox church, and the officer asks the soldier: 'Why do you fear me and do not fear God?' The soldier does not answer, but starts to recite a prayer in Latin. His relations with God are not of command and submission, but of praying, grace and love, i.e. of an exclusive proximity that excludes fear. This relation is pre-symbolic, as it goes beyond any symbolism.

This mystical pre-symbolic union with God is paradoxical, because God incarnates the Symbolic: God-father has no *imago* and is manifested primarily by his *name*. The symbolic nature of God and the separation from him can be transcended only by love, which possesses an absolute existential dimension. The subject of divine love is introduced in a dialogue early in the film:

> *Son*: You know what the saints say? – Love your father.
> *Father*: Where did you read it?
> *Son*: A father's love crucifies. A loving son lets himself be crucified.[11] I don't even get the meaning of that.

The Oedipal motif appears when the son confesses that he has a recurrent dream in which he kills his father, but this acknowledgment is immediately dismissed by the deep anxiety that the father could die or disappear.

I do not think that the film should be interpreted as a religious parable. A Christological approach would be anti-Oedipal. The Father is the Law; and Christ, according to St Paul, 'was the end of the Law' (Romans 10:14). From this point of view Christ cancels out his Father. Christ is Love, not the Law. But the same St Paul claims that Love 'is the fulfilling of the Law' (Romans, 13:10) and not its elimination. Paul repeated this statement twice: 'Love is the sum of the commandment'(1 Timothy 1:5). Kierkegaard attempted to explain this paradox when he argues that the Law is similar to the Aristotelian *dynamis* and Love to *energeia*, the actuality of Law, which is nothing else than an indefinite, shadowlike sketch. 'Thus the Law is a sketch and love the fulfilling and the entirely definite; in Love the Law is the entirely definite. There is only one power that can carry out the work for which the Law is the sketch – namely love'.[12] The fulfilment of Law is its elimination, the negation of the father in the son. The son, being a fulfilment of Law, destroys himself in the act of Love, which is a gesture of ultimate sacrifice. Law and Love are intricately interwoven, mutual foundations.

This model of Love as a fulfilment of Law is a reversal of the Lacanian model in which the Imaginary is gradually replaced by the Symbolic. According to the psychoanalytic *doxa* the verbal, the separation, comes after the visual and the proximity. In Christology Love – the conjunction of bodies in absolute proximity – comes after the negation of the verbal, the Law. The negation of the Law (the death of the father) opens the way to the non-distinction between father and son, their total fusion. It is reversal of a process of maturation described in psychoanalysis.

Still from *Father and Son*.

In Sokurov the gradual blending of the father and the son starts when the father retires from the military and thus negates his own commanding status (his association with law) for the sake of love. This moment is so important that Arabov and Sokurov incorporated a kind of parable about this renunciation and fatherly self-negation into the film. It is a story of a young man who visits the protagonists. His father served in the army with Alexei's father, and disappeared quite recently.[13] His son comes from another city to see his dad's friend and solve the mystery of his disappearance. After his departure the father tells Alexei the story of his vanished friend: 'In 1988, my friend received some orders. A dangerous mission. All his soldiers were killed. Only he survived. He came up with the crazy idea to kill the guy who gave the orders. Actually, it's not crazy at all.'

> *Alexei*: Who was he after?
> *Father*: He didn't say. It's the man at the top, the one who decides.

In this parable the function of the military receives some clarification. The Law (in the fatherly figure of a supreme commander) orders a sacrifice (like God-Father ordered the sacrifice of Christ). The sacrifice is offered, but love is not returned to the sacrificial lamb, the son. The fulfilment of the Law is not Love. Hence the Law becomes criminal, and God – who is responsible for the deadly sacrifice – is no longer a Father, but a Moloch. The vanished father is forced to sacrifice himself in an ultimate act of love that destroys the Law by its fulfilment. Thus he abandons his fatherly role and becomes 'his own son' (Christ). All the distinctions between father and son vanish. In the symbolic triangular structure we are also dealing with the substitution of the 'dead' father by the son, who symbolically occupies his place. Sokurov opposes the symbolic because it creates distances in which love and proximity are suspended. Instead of symbolic exchanges and the permutation of roles defined by a triangular structure, Sokurov insists on sacrifice, self-annihilation, and tragic existential gesture. Humanism in society is mostly verbal and belongs to the realm of signifiers. Sokurov criticises society precisely because it is unable to overcome its purely symbolic foundation and reach to existential plenitude in human relations.

This urgency of the existential is reflected in another episode dealing with the same knot of dialectical relations. Alexei forces the visiting son of the vanished father to climb on a board suspended very high up between two houses. The guest is reluctant at first, and struck by fear. This position in the sky belongs exclusively to the father, who drives both boys off the board and fights his own son when the latter fails to get off it. The place of the Father is not a symbolic apex of an abstract triangle, but a dangerous place of an awe-inspiring experience.

Love in Sokurov is not primarily sexual, but it does not exclude corporeality. It is not a pure Platonic relation that belongs to the symbolic. A gesture of caress is always repeated in Sokurov's films, even in *Alexandra*, where the grandson gently touches the hair of his grandmother. The mutual caressing of father and son is one of the main reasons for the misreading of the film by critics. Lévinas wrote about caress that 'as a contact it is sensibility. However the caress transcends the sensual'.[14] The gesture of caress is capable of transcendence, because it does not grasp or appropriate anything. It searches, and it oriented towards the future; it has no intention of 'unveiling', but of search. 'Caress is not directed at a person or an object. It is lost in being that dissolves itself in an impersonal dream without will and even resistance, passivity, anonymity already animal or infantile, completely belonging to death.'[15]

Caress in Sokurov is a gesture of an undetermined eroticism that is always accompanied by a deep anxiety of death. The opening scene of father and son caressing each other is permeated with this anxiety. The disappearance or death of a parent explains a dissolving quality in the ultimate proximity. There is no need to show death in its merciless progress. Death emerges as a shadow of absolute proximity, of the readiness to self-sacrifice, in law (which is always death) and in love (which is law's fulfilment). An X-ray of the father's chest that father and son study can be seen as an allegory of total proximity. This image of absolute penetration, of absolute transparency, unveils the source of death lurking in a healthy and beautiful body. The same can be said about the anatomical drawing on the wall.

Caress goes far beyond representation. Representation presumes the existence of the real duality between an object and its image. But caress goes even beyond the imaginary narcissistic duality that still presumes distinction. Absolute proximity is beyond any distinction; it introduces something that can be called duality/unity,[16] or interpenetration. Eisenstein, who was fascinated by primordial unity, used a term that he borrowed from the French anthropologist Lucien Lévy-Bruhl – *participation*, when the part can stand for the whole and vice versa. The complexity of the confusing plot of *Father and Son* is partially due to the fact that the son can play the role of the father, and the father that of the son. The same is true for the vanished friend, who is father and son at the same time.

Caress triggers a regression toward an animalistic or infantile state, i.e. a being that escapes society. This regression is recurrent in different disguises in many of Sokurov's films. It is a symptom of his own personal utopia and neurosis, and a source of a highly original idea of cinema that Sokurov cherishes. This is a cinema suspicious of words and of representation; it is a cinema of generalised caress, a cinema that explores continuity, which brings together symbolically disconnected objects (an uninterrupted tracking shot in *Russian Ark*, for instance). His truncated families are his own way from a representational medium to a utopian cinema of non-representation. Representation presumes a certain stability or substantiality of the world; in *Father and Son* the world is all fluidity. The roles of the protagonists are not clearly outlined and they are not incorporated into a network of symbolic substitutions. Both are father and son at the same time. This cinema is not asked to represent reality, but to let us step in the same emotional flow of diffusion and interpenetration that Sokurov's characters experience themselves.

Notes

1. There is an important episode in the film when Eva opens a little box adorned with a swastika and finds inside a small icon of the Virgin Mary that she kisses.
2. Giorgio Agamben, *Infancy and History*, London and New York: Verso, 1993, p. 54.
3. Agamben, *Infancy and History*, p. 59.
4. Sokurov intentionally compares his inarticulate mumbling to the distant mooing of cows.
5. The phantasm of the murder of the father is a necessary condition to escape castration and its fear.
6. About this struggle, see also Mikkel Borch-Jacobsen, *Lacan: the Absolute Master*, Stanford: Stanford University Press, 1991, pp. 73–96.
7. Alexander Mitscherlich, *Society without the Father*, New York: Harcourt, Brace & World, 1969.
8. This is even more obvious in *Moloch* where some views are closely reminiscent of Caspar David Friedrich's *Wanderer above the Sea of Fog* (1818).
9. Oscar Mannoni, *Clefs pour l'Imaginaire ou L'Autre Scène*, Paris: Seuil, 1969, p. 97.
10. Jacques Lacan, *Ecrits*, New York and London: W. W. Norton, 1977, p. 217.
11. The son repeats this statement closer to the end of the film. In son's room on a wall there is an anatomical drawing of a 'crucified' man without skin.
12. Søren Kierkegaard, *Works of Love*, Princeton, Princeton University Press, 1995, p. 104.
13. In the film his disappearance has two stages. In the first he is expelled from the family by his wife because he started to drink after coming home from the front; the second is the final disappearance in his revolt against Moloch. The first stage has an obvious Oedipal dimension: a woman is responsible for his symbolic death.
14. Emmanuel Lévinas, *Totalité et infini*, Paris: Kluwer Academic, 1990, p.288.
15. Lévinas, *Totalité et infini*, p. 289.
16. The term belongs to Lévy-Bruhl: 'We picture the ghost and the corpse, and from that, for the primitive man, arises between them an intimate participation which forms a duality-unity. For the primitive man it is this duality-unity which is – not thought – but felt first...', Lucien Lévy-Bruhl, *The Notebooks on Primitive Mentality*, New York: Harper & Row, 1975, pp. 2–3.

CHAPTER 8

A DAY IN THE LIFE: HISTORICAL REPRESENTATION IN SOKUROV'S 'POWER' TETRALOGY

Denise J. Youngblood

A group of people sit down to dine. The host is elaborately courteous, especially to the two women at the table. He is the centre of attention, telling a strange story, ostensibly from his youth, about catching crabs with dead grandmothers. He gives a speech about the importance of nettles and a plan for growing nettles in Ukraine. He falls asleep in a chair – or pretends to... Does it matter that this man represents Adolf Hitler?

A decrepit invalid rides in the back seat of an automobile, an elderly woman by his side. He twice pretends to shoot the driver with his finger. This action amuses him. The car stops at a flowery meadow, a place of beauty and serenity. They have a picnic. Long stretches of silence. The woman picks at her torn stockings. Does it matter that this man represents Vladimir Lenin?

A slight, middle aged man goes over to his desk, takes the blotter from a drawer, and sets sheets of paper on the blotter. He pours water into his paint tray, finds a brush, and begins to paint a poem, a haiku. After he starts the haiku, he puts it aside for a letter to his eldest son explaining the reasons for the defeat. He writes slowly. An aide looks in on him. There are statuettes of Darwin and Napoleon on his desk.[1] Does it matter that this man represents the Shōwa Emperor, known as Hirohito?

What are these scenes supposed to convey to the viewer? The banality of evil in three leaders of world historical importance? That would be a banal observation indeed for a trio of historical films that are arguably the most important of the past decade.[2] Although Alexander Sokurov's contemplated tetralogy of power – *Moloch* (1999), *Taurus* (2001), and *The Sun* (2005) – is at present incomplete, it is not too soon to analyse the philosophy of history that he presents in these films.[3] This essay will discuss

Moloch, *Taurus*, and *The Sun* as examples of the postmodern historical film, that is, postmodern history written with images rather than words. The emphasis will be on the representation of historical figures and events and on the distortion of historical time and space.[4]

The relationship between postmodern history and the historical film has been delineated by Robert Rosenstone and Hayden White. Traditional ('modern') history *presents* historic events and people; postmodern history *represents* events and people, that is, it engages in self-conscious representation with a full awareness that history is a process of cultural construction, not the retrieval of 'reality'. Rosenstone and White believe that this type of history is told best on film, rather than in books. Indeed, White has dubbed the telling of history on film and the ideas surrounding it 'historiophoty', a play on 'historiography'. In a pathbreaking essay in the *American Historical Review*, White writes that certain types of history are told better in images than in words.[5] (Recall Walter Benjamin: 'History does not break down into stories but into images'.) Historiophoty is 'the representation of history and our thought about it in visual images and filmic discourse'.[6] According to White, postmodern history blurs the distinctions between the real and the imaginary and between fact and fiction.[7] Postmodern representation, therefore, provides 'the possibility of de-fetishizing both events and the fantasy accounts of them which deny the threat they pose, in the very process of attempting to represent them realistically'.[8]

Robert Rosenstone, who developed his theory of the relationship of the postmodern film and postmodern history parallel to White's, has done the most to flesh out these ideas, to develop an analytical paradigm, and to put them into practice in terms of his own extensive writing about the historical film.[9] Rosenstone argues that postmodern history is not History (the traditional presentation of the past) and is not for the most part practiced by Historians (credentialed practitioners in academic institutions). Postmodern history 'suspects logic, linearity, progression, and completeness as ways of rendering the past'.[10] Rosenstone has identified eleven elements that characterise the postmodern historical film. He writes that makers of these films:

> 1) tell the past self-reflexively [...]; 2) recount it from a multiplicity of viewpoints; 3) eschew traditional narrative; 4) forsake normal story development; 5) approach the past with [...] irreverent attitudes; 6) intermix contradictory elements; 7) accept selectivity, partialism, partisanship, and rhetorical character; 8) refuse to focus or sum up the meaning of past events; 9) alter and invent incident and character; 10) utilize fragmentary and/or poetic knowledge; 11) never forget that the present is the site of all past representation and knowing.[11]

Directors of postmodern historical films engage in these practices in order to interrogate traditional history as the site of objective reality. As we shall see, by Rosenstone's definition, Sokurov is a quintessential postmodern historian/director, and the films of his presently unfinished tetralogy are quintessential postmodern historical films.

I shall play Historian in deconstructing these works so that we can understand how subversive they are in traditional historical terms. The films will be discussed in the order in which they were made, not only because historians love chronology, but also because the chronology represents the films' progression away from traditional history: *Moloch* is the most conventional film (in Sokurovian terms); *Taurus* occupies a middle ground; and finally, *The Sun* is the truest example of historical postmodernism.

Moloch is constructed as 'a day' in the life of Adolf Hitler and Eva Braun, a micro-history of the couple, the focus of which is as much on the historical hanger-on, Braun, as on the leader, Hitler. Sokurov has certainly done his historical research in preparation for this film; *Moloch* was filmed on location at Kehlsteinhaus, one of Hitler's residences.[12] As we learn by inference, the film takes place in summer 1942. (Hitler, Braun, and their guests watch a newsreel in which the end of the Battle of Voronezh is reported, i.e., 6 July 1942.)[13]

Sokurov has also based his characters' personalities on the historical record. Eva is a lonely, vapid, flirtatious woman who loves gymnastics and showing off her athletic body (at the beginning of the film, she is seen doing cartwheels naked.) Hitler, an egocentric vegetarian hypochondriac, is portrayed as not so much evil as eccentric, and perhaps slightly unhinged. His mercurial temperament is quite well documented in the standard histories.[14] The trio of creepy sycophants – Joseph Goebbels, Magda Goebbels, and Martin Bormann – vie with each other to coddle Hitler. The historical rivalry between Goebbels and Bormann is made obvious.[15]

Although Hitler always has to be the centre of attention, Eva Braun is at the heart of this film. Mikhail Iampolski sees *Moloch* as an allegory,

Still from *Moloch*: The dinner scene.

with Braun as the fairy-tale princess imprisoned in the castle, representing life, and Hitler representing death.[16] (Recall that the god Moloch requires human sacrifice.) Braun is indeed a prisoner; her daily activities cannot hide the emptiness of her world. Her 'castle', the Berghof, is set high on a hill in the mountains, with fantastic views that are mostly hidden with clouds and fog (as the past is similarly shrouded). While a clock ticks loudly, a reminder of how long a day actually is when one has nothing to do, she half-heartedly practises gymnastics, takes out an enamelled box emblazoned with a swastika, puts on a record, dances a bit, examines pictures in a photo album while 'conducting' the music with her pretty legs.

When Hitler arrives at her fortress, Braun is initially tentative. The pretence is that she is Hitler's friend Fräulein Braun, not his mistress, and she must play her modest role. But her anger at this subterfuge bursts through at various points. She denounces Hitler as a hypochondriac, further insulting him by declaring 'Without an audience, you're a corpse'. She calmly leaves the dinner table after Hitler's ranting about the stupidity of women. Later on, her rage growing, she kicks him soundly in his posterior as he is raging about how disgusting children and domesticity are. But in the end, she cannot deny her aching and thoroughly irrational need for him: 'Even if you're one big zero, I love you'. She throws a hysterical fit in the elevator when she learns that Hitler and company are departing.

Even though Braun gets more camera time than Hitler, Hitler is the more fully realised character, probably because he *was* a more complex person in 'real' life. (Sokurov's portrayal of Braun as a creature of basic human needs is historically 'accurate,' conforming to the historical 'record' of reminiscences of those who knew her.) We first see Hitler engaged in an elaborate greeting ritual with the staff. He has unctuous words of wisdom for each one. After a display of petulant anger over his dog's whelping some puppies, his good will is restored by lunchtime, because his sycophantic audience (Braun, the Goebbels, Bormann, the secretary who takes down the Führer's every word) is there to fawn over him. This bevy accompanies him on a postprandial walk where he makes a great show to Braun of wanting to be alone so that he can 'etch the scenery on [his] mind'. (The mountain scenery is indeed spectacular, and Sokurov indulges in a bit of lyricism here.) Hitler enjoys a merry dance with Eva, Goebbels and Magda, Bormann clapping time like a fool.[17] Again at dinner, Hitler is at first a gracious host to his guests but then delivers the speech mentioned above on the stupidity of women.

For every sign of normality in Hitler, Sokurov shows another of irrationality. Shortly after arrival, Hitler's mood of calm and good will is abruptly interrupted by news, as noted above, that his dog has had puppies, which greatly angers him. He shrinks from Braun's touch: 'Don't touch me! I'm dying! (Recall that Hitler, like Moloch, is coded 'death'.) At lunch, he is frustrated by the failure of ordinary humans to understand the import of his anecdotes about dead grandmothers and nettles. During the nature walk, he wants to be alone for a private reason; he needs to defecate, a sight that does not go unnoticed by the snipers who guard the Berghof's inhabitants. (This is the second episode in the film in which Hitler's toilet habits come into play.) A priest comes to ask Hitler to pardon a deserter; the talk degenerates into a rambling monologue on death, maggots, and religion, but of course, not mercy. During the newsreel showing, he growls about the camera shots and the editing of the film. (Braun gaily suggests that he send the 'entire crew to Auschwitz'.)[18] Afterwards, Hitler explains why Finns are crazy. ('The snow radiates melancholy.') His lack of self confidence is noteworthy; he realises that his reputation in history will depend on whether he is victorious or defeated. ('If I lose, the lowest nobody will use me as a doormat', which would certainly be the least of his worries.) He is stone-faced as Braun rushes to his car to bid him farewell. 'Death is death', she tells him. 'It can't be conquered'. These are the last words in the film.

In the context of historiography or 'historiophoty', *Moloch* superficially presents a fairly standard, even prosaic, kind of history: a biographical examination that like much popular history focuses on personal relationships, which appeals to viewers. But its 'hyper-realism', the extreme attention to minute detail (especially painful at the beginning, as Braun moves through her morning at a glacial pace), undermines traditional modes of representation. Are *Moloch*'s details really 'important' to history? (What *is* an important historical detail?) The emphasis on voyeurism also undermines traditional historical representation, not only of the snipers, but also of Braun and Goebbels, Bormann & Co., who watch Hitler for any changing flicker in his expression. Since each witness has only one subjective view on the unfolding 'events', from whose perspective(s) is the story being told?[19] Historians must assess perspective in order to render the subjective 'objective'. Furthermore, the film's 'events' are non-events in the context of modern historiography; once again, Sokurov interrogates historical conventions by undermining them.

And what about the time frame? Like the films that follow it, *Moloch* seems to take place in one day. All the markers are there: arrival, lunch, an excursion, a film, dinner, and bedtime. Yet the viewer's certainty is shaken when Braun wakes up to find that Hitler is leaving. Given the difficulty of getting him and his entourage there, would he really leave after only one day? Sokurov seems to want to emphasise the decline of Hitler and the Reich, so why set the film before the Battle of Stalingrad (the acknowledged turning point of the war in the East), rather than *after* it? The answer is simple: Sokurov wants to disrupt old-fashioned notions of historical time and the historian's need to impose order on time. He also wants to challenge the modern historian's insistence on constructing cause and effect relationships in historical representation. (If the time sequence is 'out of order', effect may not in fact follow 'cause'.)

Taurus[20] is even more successful than *Moloch* as an example of postmodern history because of the primary importance of its visual aspects to its message. Like *Moloch*, *Taurus* has more dialogue than aficionados of Sokurov's previous work have come to expect, but the words are arguably less significant than in *Moloch*. The major exceptions are Lenin's stubborn and repeated insistence that he be allowed to do things 'by myself', and Stalin's phony obsequiousness when he visits Lenin. Here we see 'a day' in the life of a Lenin who is actually dying (unlike the hypochondriac Hitler who only thinks he is dying).

Lenin is living in a run-down mansion that 'history' tells us is his dacha in Gorki, the former Reinbot estate.[21] He is attended to by a veritable mob of mostly disrespectful soldiers and servitors, a doctor, and the two women who love him and vie for his affections, his wife Nadezhda Krupskaya and his sister Maria Ulianova. The many guards and hangers-on seem to have little or no regard for Lenin as a very sick man, not to mention a leader; he is, for example, forcefully jostled when he comes out for his excursion to the meadow noted at the beginning of this essay. A fight breaks out for control of the camera that is going to record this moment for posterity. (Ulianova wanted her brother's life documented.)

The 'events' of the day are much more limited than they were in *Moloch*, consisting of three: the picnic, Stalin's visit, and dinner. The picnic and dinner are historical non-events, but the visit by Stalin, whom Lenin cannot quite place, is obviously much more important in traditional historical terms. In their brief meeting, Stalin, who was charged by the Party's Central Committee with monitoring Lenin's health, attempts to demonstrate the close relationship he has with Lenin, by joking and playfully chasing him around. He does, however, avoid giving Lenin any useful information. (After all, knowledge is power.) And Stalin's well-known animosity to Krupskaya is clear when he roughly pinches her cheek, in a gesture of mock familiarity. After Stalin's departure, Lenin asks Krupskaya, 'Who is he? Is he a Georgian?' These questions provide Krupskaya and Ulianova their only merriment in an otherwise bleak day.

After a dinner in which Krupskaya also wants to do things 'by herself' (ladling soup), she wheels Lenin outside to rest under a magnificent tree. She abruptly leaves him alone to take a call from the Central Committee. Ironically, he feels helpless 'by himself' and cries out, but his cries go unanswered. Suddenly he relaxes in his chair with a half-smile on his weakened visage. Alone and at peace.

Sokurov rearranges historical certainties in a number of important ways, mainly having to do with time. Given that the first dictator in the tetralogy is Hitler, one would guess that the second would be Stalin, not Lenin. This clearly implies that Sokurov believes that the roots of Soviet authoritarianism lay in Lenin's rule, not Stalin's. This is in itself a bit of historical revisionism, and the subject of continued historiographical debate. If this is Sokurov's message, however, it is subverted by the fact that unlike Sokurov's Hitler, his Lenin is quite sympathetic. *Taurus* shows no misdeeds, and Lenin's ill temper is well founded.

Second, Sokurov engages in more time disruption than he did in *Moloch*. *Taurus* raises more doubts than *Moloch* that it occurs in only one day. The 'events' depicted would make a very long day for an invalid, with the photographs, the outing, the visit from Stalin, and then back out again after dinner. A more significant disruption of historical time is the chronological disjuncture, that is, the uncertainty over when the events in the film supposedly take place. Lenin did not move to Gorki until May 1923 shortly after his third stroke in March of that year, when he had a vocabulary

Still from *Taurus*: Lenin and Krupskaya. Courtesy of *Iskusstvo kino*.

of about five or six words and typically found it difficult or impossible to walk.[22] The photographs of Lenin and Krupskaya at Gorki at this time are telling; it is quite clear that he had very limited mental and physical capacity. Given that Lenin does speak and walk in this film, even though with difficulty and lapses, his condition is more consistent with that recorded after the second stroke (December 1922), when he was still living in Moscow. In the film, Lenin is too disabled for the film to have taken place after the relatively mild first stroke (May 1922), on a late summer visit to Gorki in August and September 1922.

This is available historical knowledge for anyone who has done a little research. Sokurov is clearly well versed in the history and one has to conclude that he deliberately muddled or compressed the time frame for artistic/symbolic, as well as for historical/philosophical, reasons. Gorki is a more dramatically interesting setting than Moscow because it represents Lenin's isolation from all that was important to him in Moscow.[23] Like Eva Braun, Lenin is a prisoner in a castle, far removed from 'civilisation'. As in *Moloch*, however, the deliberate manipulation of time undercuts a central tenet of historical representation, that it is essential to know exactly when events occurred in order to understand them. Sokurov asks a simple question: Why? The time frame may not be 'real', but does this manipulation render *Taurus* less *authentic*? (It does not.)

As *Moloch*, *Taurus* also plays with the definition of the historical event. Sokurov's camera recorded minute details of Braun's – and to a certain extent Hitler's – mundane daily activities that are non-events. In *Taurus*, the activities are even more mundane. Lenin cannot dress himself, so we watch him being dressed by others. His toenails must be cut by a soldier. He is read to by his timorous wife Krupskaya. He bounces in bed. He eats a candy. He sits in his wheelchair. He rests before dinner. He wants to do things 'himself', even though he accomplishes the simplest of tasks with the greatest of difficulty. He takes a bath. He is carried to bed. The pacing is languorous, again reflecting the long blank spaces of a life when one has nothing to do. For a man who had enjoyed a frenetic schedule, this is a life not worth living. Such details, however, would never find their way into the pages of a traditional history – and only possibly in a microhistory. They are plausible, but imagined.

As much loving care as Sokurov devotes to creating hyper-realistic non-events, the *mise-en-scène* in *Taurus* is highly abstracted. We see little of the detritus of an invalid. The dacha has an institutional, 'unlived-in' feeling, even though it had been Lenin's get-away since 1918. Furthermore, much more pronounced than in *Moloch,* we never understand the geography of the dacha since there are no establishing shots. We can only assume that the voyeurs who constantly appear in half-opened doorways are actually watching Lenin. What do they see?

The visual atmosphere of the film is as sombre as Lenin's life and mind: lots of fog, shadows, and darkness. The cinematography is quite different from *Moloch*'s. Unlike *Moloch*, where the images are very sharp, *Taurus* is often sepia-toned, grainy, and soft, like a fading photograph (or a dying mind). The frame is unstable; Lenin sometimes sinks almost out of it. The sound direction is also remarkable: distant thunder, loudly ticking clocks, people murmuring in half-phrases, making little sounds to themselves or the opposite, boisterous laughter and the sound of footsteps pounding the floors or the verandas. Like Lenin, the viewer strains to see, strains to hear. In sum, every aspect of *Taurus* represents a profound destabilisation of the evidentiary foundations of standard history.

The Sun destabilises these foundations even more thoroughly; Julian Graffy rightly considers it the most 'ambitious' of the three films.[24] On the surface, however, it might seem that *The Sun* deviates the least from the historical genre of biography or from the filmic genre of the bio-pic. Its reception was disappointing, which in turn disappointed Sokurov, who is accustomed to his films winning prizes. *The Sun* focuses almost completely on its central figure, Hirohito, brilliantly impersonated by Issei Ogata, and offers a micro-historical examination of the emperor at a pivotal moment in his life: the end of the war, the ignominious surrender, and the renunciation of his divinity.

We learn a great deal about Hirohito and his habits, much more than we learn about Hitler or Lenin in the two previous films. Sokurov offers a well-rounded portrait. We witness Hirohito move through his 'day', from having breakfast to getting dressed; from meeting with his military council to indulging in his hobby of marine biology[25]; from writing a haiku to meeting with the Supreme Commander General Douglas MacArthur; from being introduced to Hershey candy bars to discussing whether one can see the Northern Lights from Japan with the director of his scientific institute.

This Hirohito is mild-mannered and, like Hitler and Lenin, frail in appearance; it seems that the burdens of the Chrysanthemum Throne lie

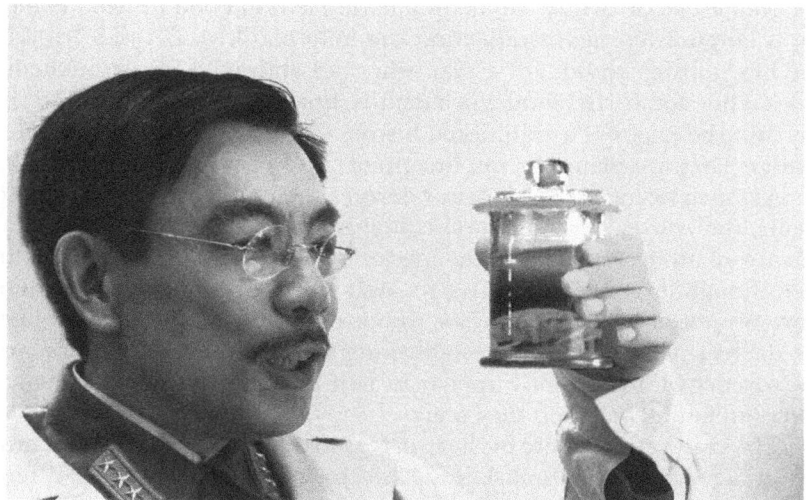

Still from *The Sun*: Hirohito with one of his objects of study. Courtesy of Artificial Eye.

heavily on his thin shoulders. The crude pack of American photographers who come to take his picture (to 'humanise' him to the American public) do not even recognise him as 'emperor'; they nickname him Charlie (Chaplin) as he smilingly poses by his pink rosebushes.[26] At their historic first meeting, MacArthur reveals his ignorance by asking why Hirohito has appeared in morning coat and top hat, rather than costumed in a kimono.[27] Hirohito complains to a disbelieving MacArthur about the difficulty of being an emperor, speaking about himself in the third person: 'of course the life of the emperor is not easy'. The emperor questions his own divinity (a reason why he gives it up with such apparent ease?). He is upset that the Pope has not answered his letters. It is a difficult time for him.

Sokurov shows us these difficulties. As he does so, Hirohito becomes more and more sympathetic and humanised. Like Eva Braun and Lenin, he is a prisoner in a palace,[28] his every move constrained, in this case by protocol and ritual. The simple act of getting dressed is an onerous procedure. He stands stock still as an elderly retainer fumbles with getting the buttons through too-small buttonholes. The old man's hands shake, and his brow glistens with sweat. The unprepossessing Hirohito looks ridiculous in his dress uniform complete with sword; surrounded by the desperate men on his military council, he seems like an imposter in the room. At his lab, he slowly takes out his dissecting tools to examine a hermit crab that has been brought to him as a specimen, so slowly and carefully that he seems frozen in time. Yet when the lab assistant falls asleep as Hirohito dictates, the emperor comes to life, responding with a furious clapping of his hands. Most painful of all the film's ritualised moments is Hirohito's reunion with his wife at the end of the film ('the empress has requested an audience'). They greet each other at a distance, with strained smiles and little murmurings and eventually an awkward embrace. The empress does not know what to do when Hirohito buries his head into her shoulder and tells her that he has given up his divinity.

Even as he seems slightly ridiculous, Sokurov's Hirohito presents true dignity and stoicism through his trials. As the emperor amiably poses for the photographers, MacArthur's Japanese-American interpreter Okumura Katsuzō is hurt by the insults the emperor receives from the mob.[29] (One can only imagine what the emperor himself is thinking.) Hirohito speaks English but in this scene pointedly pretends not to, letting the mockery roll off.

Hirohito's two trying meetings with MacArthur show the strength of his character as well as his fumbling efforts to figure out how to act like a real human, not a god. When he arrives at the American Embassy, he stands at the door silently for long moments until a contemptuous GI realises that he is waiting for the door to be opened. The audience with MacArthur goes badly. The interpreter Katsuzō is upset by the general's rude comments and refuses to interpret them.[30] Katsuzō is also upset by Hirohito's efforts to speak English, telling him that as the Japanese emperor he should speak Japanese only. MacArthur asks Hirohito odd questions – 'How are the emperor's children?', 'What have you done recently?' – with thinly suppressed anger. Hirohito tells him that the war was lost because of 'national arrogance.' At their dinner 'that evening', MacArthur lets his hostility out in the open. He is incredulous when Hirohito informs that that he has never in fact met the man that MacArthur calls his 'best friend', Hitler.[31] Hirohito incenses MacArthur when he informs the Supreme Commander that the imperial family has been moved away from Tokyo in order to avoid 'atrocities'. To MacArthur's furious retort, Hirohito denies advance knowledge of the attack at Pearl Harbor.

MacArthur is deliberately rude at the dinner, treating the emperor with even more disdain than at the earlier meeting. He leaves the table as the emperor eats, first pacing, then sitting on a divan to light a 'real Havana cigar'. MacArthur abruptly leaves on an 'urgent matter' as Hirohito is talking. The emperor at first sits stoically, then wanders about the room, doing a little dance, before snuffing out the candles as MacArthur has snuffed out any possibility for real dialogue. (MacArthur is watching through a half-open door.) When MacArthur returns, he sits *behind* the emperor, the most grievous insult of all.

Hirohito is also a man who demonstrates moral courage. In the context of the history of the Chrysanthemum Throne and the opposition of his supporters, it took some courage to surrender to the Allied forces and to renounce his 'divine origins'. MacArthur tries to make it seem as though Hirohito will gain something personally by renouncing divinity: 'If you betray your country, I won't make you do anything. I won't insist on anything'. But is it really a 'betrayal' or is it not Japan's salvation? Hirohito takes the daring step of making the announcement himself, in the name of peace, in a radio address to his people.[32]

The 'problem' with this film as 'objective' history lies not so much in Hirohito's characterisation, although it is generally accepted that he *did* know about Pearl Harbor and actively approved it. Nor does it lie in

Still from *The Sun*: Hirohito during the dinner with MacArthur. Courtesy of Artificial Eye.

the representation of MacArthur, who at least *thought* he was being polite to the emperor. As in *Taurus*, Sokurov compresses and distorts the time frame; the importance of time is again signalled by loudly ticking clocks.

The compression of time and reordering of events is so extreme that it goes well beyond artistic license.[33] Like *Moloch* and *Taurus*, *The Sun* seems to take place in a day. It moves from morning to night, more or less according to the daily schedule that was announced to Hirohito at the beginning of the film, with several unexpected interventions, notably the meetings with MacArthur and the arrival of the empress. Sokurov gives us two clues that this is *not* in fact one day. The first signpost is that the emperor delivered his radio address ending the war in the Pacific on 15 August 1945;[34] his renunciation of his divinity was in a different radio broadcast on 1 January 1946. Furthermore, he did not meet MacArthur until six weeks after the end of the war, on 27 September 1945.[35] As already noted, altering the order of events is not a minor issue in historiography because of the impact on cause and effect relationships. In this case, for the first time, Sokurov strongly implies causation: MacArthur suggests to Hirohito that he 'betray' his country, and Hirohito does so (although he does not consider it a betrayal). This scene is entirely imagined. Hirohito surrendered and renounced his divinity on his own volition.[36] Obviously, it is more dramatic this way. I also want to argue, as I have above, that through this chronological disjuncture, Sokurov is questioning modern history's foundations, especially the insistence on chronology and process. Why do history's stories have to be told 'in order'? Why cannot time—days, weeks, even years – be compressed? What can be learned when they are told out of order and distilled to their very essence? *Ostranenie* (to make something 'strange') in historical representation allows the audience to query previously held assumptions about history as a construct and to become an active participant in the 'making' of history.

This *ostranenie* extends beyond the way Sokurov manipulates time to the film's sets. As in *Taurus*, the sets are oddly empty, not only Hirohito's rooms, but also the ornate reception room at the American Embassy. The film's hyper-realism in showing the actions that are almost never shown in history or film – the extreme close-ups of a sweaty brow, the emperor's fingers tracing a pattern on a tablecloth, the slight trembling of a retainer's hand – is disrupted by the abstraction of the set design and set decorations. Of course, there are limits to historical imagination in a re-creation. Unless there are photographs documenting a space, who knows what fills that space? Sokurov could imagine it, of course, just as he imagined the actions of Hirohito and the individuals surrounding him, but he chose not to. As was the case with his manipulation of time, this choice indicates his interrogation of historical convention. The sharp contrast between hyper-realistic action and underdressed sets compel the audience to think about the role of imagination in filling in the inevitable blank spaces of history.

Moving from the sets to the geography of the film is another exercise in frustration. As in *Taurus*, Sokurov eschews establishing shots; often we have no idea of the geography of a room, where the doors are, who is situated relative to whom. This becomes especially important when considering the role of 'witnesses' in this film. Like Lenin in *Taurus*, the emperor is always being watched, whether by his staff, MacArthur, the interpreter, or the photographers. Without observers there is no history; if there is no one to hear the tree fall in the forest, the historian must say it did *not* make a sound. There are plenty of observers in this film, but what is their perspective on the action? Historians are trained to analyze point of view, but what is the 'view' when the 'point' is unclear? In short, all eleven of Rosenstone's characteristics of the postmodern historical film emphatically appear in *The Sun*.

In the spirit of the postmodern, I should refuse, in Rosenstone's words, 'to focus or sum up' about the role of historical representation in these three films. Therefore I shall offer a few observations in place of a conclusion. In this essay, I have shown how each film functions as postmodern according to the Rosenstone/White model and articulated the questions the films pose, deliberately eschewing answers. I hope that I have also demonstrated that Sokurov needs to be considered a 'real' historian as evidenced by the way these three films engage in a serious historical discourse.[37]

By telling the stories of three men who 'made history' in *Moloch*, *Taurus*, and *The Sun*, Sokurov has taken the most traditional kind of history, the biography of the 'great man', and turned it on its head. By deconstructing and reorganizing a traditional genre, he has subverted its certainties and offered a provocative view on 'history making' – which is, after all, what *historians*, not great men, do. Sokurov has also offered a very distinctive view on power in the twentieth century that can only be understood by considering the three films as a unit.

Moloch and *Taurus* take two of the most important dictators of the century and undermine their greatness (in a Hegelian sense), by showing them as weak and vulnerable (more so for Lenin than Hitler) and out of touch with reality (Lenin tries to keep abreast of affairs but cannot). By situating these anti-narratives in 'ordinary' settings, Sokurov questions not only Hitler's and Lenin's 'greatness', but also their power *and* their reputations for evil. We see only indirect manifestations of their power in the way that other people react to them. (Goebbels, Bormann, and even Stalin to a degree are certainly sycophantic.) But there is nothing in *Moloch* or *Taurus* to indicate that these men are 'evil'. Hitler is depicted as an unpleasantly eccentric individual, given to rages, but that is all; he supposedly knows nothing about Auschwitz. Lenin is positively sympathetic; we can empathise with his rage against the 'dying of the light'. Viewers have to bring their own, probably highly imperfect knowledge of Hitler and Lenin to the theatre in order to interpret them as 'evil' – or even as 'dictators'. Indeed, if one did not know in advance who these individuals represented, one would not understand their world historical importance from these films. We learn nothing of their crimes. This is not an accident.

Hirohito is altogether different from Hitler and Lenin. They actually *had* absolute (or close to absolute) power at one point in their lives; Hirohito only *represented* absolute power ('divinity'). Like the filmic Hirohito, after the war the real Hirohito was disingenuous about his stance on the war, but he also understood where the real power lay, with General Hideki Tōjō for most of the war, and then with the Supreme Commander MacArthur after the war. As Julian Graffy puts it: 'Sokurov's Hirohito has learned, in a way that his Hitler and Lenin never did, that power and imperial ambition are a murderous trap'.[38] However, even if we suspect that their personalities would not allow it, Hitler and Lenin *could not* learn this lesson because they did not live long enough to see the full extent of the destruction and misery that their ambitions had wrought.

Notes

1. Only later do we see a bust of Lincoln. These three busts, which were on his 'real-life' desk, indicate his love of science and history. Stephen Large, *Emperor Hirohito and Shōwa Japan: A Political Biography*, London and New York: Routledge, 1992, p. 19.
2. 'Arguably' only because I omit *Russian Ark* from the list.
3. Also known as 'the tetralogy of the dictators or leaders'. I have chosen 'power' because Sokurov has explicitly rejected the notion that his theme is dictatorship; see 'Sun' on *Island of Sokurov*, http://sokurov.spb.ru/island_en/feature_films/sun/mnp_sun.html (accessed 8 August 2010). The final part of the tetralogy is based on Goethe's *Faust*, Part I, and in post-production at the time this volume goes to print.
4. Fredric Jameson has focused on historical time in *Moloch* and *Taurus* in 'History and Elegy in Sokurov', *Critical Inquiry* 33.1 (2006), pp. 1–12. Jeremi Szaniawski has discussed the issue of 'historic space' in the tetralogy from filmic and cultural studies perspectives, rather than from a 'true' historical perspective (that is to say, the historian's perspective) in 'Historical Space in Sokurov's *Moloch*, *Taurus*, and *The Sun*', *Studies in Russian and Soviet Cinema* 1.2 (2007), pp. 147–62.
5. Hayden White, 'The Modernist Event', in Vivian Sobchack (ed.), *The Persistence of History: Cinema, Television, and the Modern Event*, London and New York: Routledge, 1996, pp. 17–38 (p. 17).
6. Hayden White, 'Historiography and Historiophoty', *American Historical Review* 93.5 (1988), pp. 1193–99 (p. 1193).
7. White, 'The Modernist Event', p. 21. White here uses modernist and postmodernist almost interchangeably, considering the postmodern a subset of the modern. I have chosen to use 'postmodern' consistently in this essay as the term most often used to describe this type of history.
8. White, 'The Modernist Event', p. 32.
9. Robert Rosenstone, 'History in Images/History in Words: Reflections on the Possibility of Really Putting History onto Film', *American Historical Review* 93.5 (1988), pp. 1173–1185; Rosenstone (ed.), *Revisioning History: Film and the Construction of a New Past*, Princeton: Princeton University Press, 1995; Rosenstone, *Visions of the Past: The Challenge of Film to Our Idea of History*, Cambridge, MA: Harvard University Press, 1995; Rosenstone, *History on Film/Film on History*, Harlow and New York: Pearson Longman, 2006.
10. Robert Rosenstone, 'The Future of the Past: Film and the Beginnings of Postmodern History,' in Vivian Sobchack (ed.), *The Persistence of History: Cinema, Television, and the Modern Event*, New York and London: Routledge, 1996, pp. 201–18 (p. 215).
11. Rosenstone 'The Future of the Past...', p. 206.
12. In an essay on Sokurov's website on *Island of Sokurov*, Alexandra Tuchinskaya places the action at the Kehlsteinhaus.http://sokurov.spb.ru/island_en/

feature_films/moloch/mnp_mol.html (accessed 8 August 2010), even though the Berghof was Eva Braun's home for most of the war. See Angela Lambert, *The Lost Life of Eva Braun*, New York, St Martin's Press, 2007, which includes a number of photographs of the Berghof, which was destroyed after the war.
13 Hitler believed that the difficulty of taking Voronezh fatally delayed the Germany army's progress to Stalingrad, hence ensuring a Soviet victory there.
14 Alan Bullock, *Hitler: A Study in Tyranny*, New York: Harper & Row, 1962; Ian Kershaw, *Hitler*, London and New York: Longman, 1991.
15 Kershaw, *passim*.
16 Mikhail Iampolskii, 'Sokurov, Aleksandr', in Arkus, L. (ed.), *Noveishaia istoriia otechestvennogo kino, 1986–2000: Kinoslovar'*, vol. 3, St Petersburg: Seans, 2001, pp. 114–117 (p. 115).
17 In fact, Hitler abhorred dancing: Bullock, p. 395.
18 Hitler is puzzled by the word 'Auschwitz', suggesting that he is unaware of the full extent of the Holocaust.
19 Szaniawski, 'Historical Space', p. 161. He also notes the importance of multiple perspectives to Sokurov.
20 Lenin was born 22 April 1870 (N.S.), hence his astrological sign is Taurus. In Greek mythology, Taurus, a beautiful white bull, was the form Zeus assumed in order to abduct and rape Europa. The bull was also important in the cult of Moloch, thus tying Hitler and Lenin together.
21 Robert Service, *Lenin: A Biography*, Cambridge MA: Harvard University Press, 2000, p. 369.
22 Lenin's condition was unusually unstable for a stroke victim; he would seem to be getting better, then have a severe relapse. As a result, there is still controversy about what he was able to do when. See Dmitri Volkogonov, *Lenin: A New Biography*, New York and London: The Free Press, 1991, pp. 409–20.
23 Jameson (p. 5) also discusses this issue.
24 Julian Graffy, '*The Sun*', *Sight & Sound* 9 (2005), pp. 82–83 (p. 82).
25 Hirohito was a serious naturalist, with discoveries to his name: see Large, *Emperor Hirohito*, p. 19. He was also known to be very fond of haiku.
26 The real Hirohito never smiled in official portraits, which would be seen unbecoming to a god. Herbert P. Bix, *Hirohito and the Making of Modern Japan*, New York: HarperCollins, 2000, p. 550.
27 Hirohito enjoyed dressing in Western clothes and in differentiating himself from other Japanese elite by adopting Western pastimes: see Large, p. 23. Sokurov's representation of MacArthur is at odds with American historiography.
28 A figurative palace. The real palace had been bombed by the Americans and the emperor was living in his bunker and at his laboratory on the palace grounds.
29 Bix, p. 548.
30 MacArthur actually had a great deal of respect for the emperor; based on his own recollections, the meeting went well; Bix, pp. 548–49.
31 The reason that Hirohito gives for the alliance between Germany and Japan is: 'Germany's chances in the war were 100/100. Japan's were 50/100'.
32 The scene at the very end of the film, however, undermines this point. When Hirohito hears that the sound engineer who taped the recording has committed hara-kiri, his face registers shock, but he quickly takes the empress's hand, and they scamper off to find their children, hardly the sign of a 'daring' individual. I have been unable to confirm whether the sound engineer did indeed commit suicide.

33 Writing from a different perspective, Julian Graffy (p. 82) sees in the film an 'entirely persuasive sense of time and place'.
34 This was the first time that the Japanese people heard 'the voice of the crane'; see http://www.pbs.org/wgbh/amex/macarthur/peopleevents/pandaAMEX97.html (accessed 7 January 2009). Sokurov marks this by having a crane figure prominently in the scene with the photographers, before Hirohito makes his appearance.
35 Stephen Large (chapter 5) provides a standard historical account of the Hirohito era that details the order of these events.
36 In the film, it is also unclear that the war is over. We hear the sounds of planes roaring overhead, and an air raid alarm sounds. Hirohito is shuttled off to the bunker. He has a marvelously bizarre dream about the war in which planes and bombs are imaged as fish.
37 Sokurov has, of course, demonstrated his interest in history in other films and we should not forget that he is a historian by training.
38 Graffy, p. 83.

CHAPTER 9

HISTORY, ALIENATION AND THE (FAILED) CINEMA OF EMBODIMENT: SOKUROV'S TETRALOGY

Stephen Hutchings

Introduction

Alexander Sokurov's films provoke a mixture of idolatry and contempt, consternation and controversy. He is portrayed variously as bearer of the legacy of the post-Tarkovskian Russian avant-garde, a pretentious mystic, a polemical nationalist, a profound metaphysical auteur, and a sublime innovator.[1] Sokurov is nonetheless one of the few post-Soviet Russian directors to have established a serious reputation in the West, attracting praise from not only Susan Sontag, but also the *éminence grise* of American postmodernist theory, Fredric Jameson, who describes the Russian director's indifference to commercial pressures as an indication that he is one of the last great modernists,[2] hailing him as harbinger of a new 'aesthetic of marginality'.

One of the reasons for the puzzlement that Sokurov's oeuvre evokes is the apparently disparate nature of the works that constitute it. It has seemingly veered from films of a deeply intimate nature in which the camera never deviates from an intense focus on the human subject in its intimate relationship with the Other, to epic sweeps across Russian history, to political biopics of twentieth-century dictators. It is in the latter category that the tension between the historical and the personal would appear to have been resolved; the tetralogy of films treat their historical subjects (Hitler, Lenin and Emperor Hirohito – and in the final instalment, Faust) quite literally *in camera*, as vulnerable, childlike individuals cocooned from the harsh political/military realities for which they themselves are responsible.

But the individualising gesture has been criticised as absolving the tyrants from the guilt they bear.[3] In the biographical films, Sokurov, the argument goes, indulges in the ideological bad faith of a humanist universalism as reprehensible as the nationalist mysticism traversing a film like *Russian Ark*. And running throughout the oeuvre is the common thread of the uncompromising Sokurovian aesthetic with its interminable *longeurs*, its plotlessness, its claustrophobic interiors, its lugubrious colours and its extraneous details. Such an aesthetic is particularly difficult to reconcile with the historical subjects to which Sokurov often turns. Yet few fail to acknowledge the strangely compelling experience of watching a Sokurov film, the sense, when the director is at his hypnotic best, that one is in presence of a cinematic genius who knows not only something that we cannot name, but something that he struggles to understand himself.

It is the purpose of this chapter to attempt, in unravelling some of the contradictions, to name the unnameable. It will be my contention that, far from representing a detour from his central aesthetic concerns, Sokurov's tetralogy is key to understanding what motivates them. I shall argue that the concerns with history on one hand, and the intimate mutuality of human bodies on the other, are not at odds. Rather, both concerns reflect an attempt to overcome the alienation which provides Sokurov's oeuvre with its unifying core. Our estrangement from historical narrative is at one with our estrangement from human intimacy and this, in Sokurov's scheme, is in turn bound up with film's own relationship with alienation. I will suggest that, through the tetralogy in particular (but also elsewhere), Sokurov struggles to articulate a radically new embodied cinema in which the different modes of alienation are overcome at once.

The paradox that Sokurov must confront is that he is working from within a form that is itself alienated. The paradox is reflected in some of the key tensions, figures and aesthetic quirks that characterise the director's oeuvre, and the tetralogy in particular. These will provide my point of entry into the films. The tensions are principally those pitting the private and intimate against the public and impersonal (and expressed in a peculiar Sokurovian take on the motif of voyeurism), fiction against truth, representing present against represented past, viewer against viewed, and, ultimately, body against spirit.

The tensions account, in turn, for the subjects of the tetralogy – all-powerful, semi-mythic twentieth-century personas whose names coincide with the period or the historical phenomenon that they dominated – and the manner in which they are portrayed: not as architects of the tyrannies with which they are historically associated, but as vulnerable human bodies in transition to death (Lenin, Hitler, both played by Leonid Mozgovoy) or mortal status (Hirohito, played by Issei Ogata), and as adults on the point of reverting to a new infancy. Finally, all three films are replete with the aesthetic tics that are responsible for the unique texture of Sokurov's cinema and that act to prevent his films gelling into factual narratives.

Alienation

In its standard philosophical meaning, the term alienation derives from Hegel, who used it to refer to the process by which 'finite Spirit', the human self, 'doubles' and externalises itself, then confronts its own other being as something separate, distinct and opposed to it.[4] Whilst I do not necessarily endorse the idealist assumptions underlying Hegel's philosophical system, my usage of 'alienation' is closer to his broad-based, metaphysical definition and does not carry the precise political connotations later ascribed to it by Marx (though Sokurov's films can be situated in the materialist tradition to which Marx belongs). The further Hegelian implications of man's alienation include the separation of subjective experience from the objective world, the situation of the self within a reified nature, and the subsequent reification of the other, and of time. Under the conditions of alienation, history becomes detached from its perceivers in two ways: the rupture between the subject and his past being, and the de-personalisation of the public realm in which historical events occur. Finally, aesthetic form is sundered from its original connection to the sensual body (and thus from its etymological roots in *aesthos*) and instrumentalised in support of a 'content' intended for an anonymous mass audience.

The implied theory of alienation in the sense outlined bears affinities with a prominent strand in Russian philosophy which can be traced from its origins in Eastern Orthodox theology, through Pavel Florensky, Mikhail Bakhtin, Alexei Losev and others.[5] Thus, Florensky's critique of linear perspective as entailing the solipsistic viewpoint of a self isolated from the world he describes rather than engaged in bodily communion with it is essentially a critique of alienation,[6] as is Bakhtin's assault on abstract 'theoretism'.[7] Whilst they assiduously avoid religious subject matter, Sokurov's films represent an effort to create an 'embodied' cinema that heals the wounds of alienation and restores Russian art to its iconic roots, an association that, crucially, the director has himself made.[8]

The Tetralogy: Shared Attributes

Apart from the common interest in delving behind the scenes of the lives of prominent twentieth-century dictators, the three films share themes, settings, and aesthetic qualities. The settings, for example, are all enclosed, semi-private spaces to which, nonetheless, public figures of importance have access (a mist-laden Kehlsteinhaus to which Hitler has retreated with his closest wartime associates, Bormann and Goebbels, and female friends; the Gorki mansion in which the dying Lenin spent his last days; Hirohito's sealed palace beyond which he ventures only to meet with MacArthur to discuss the terms of the Japanese surrender). In each film, the leader is at the point of losing the awesome power he has acquired (and in the case of Hitler and Lenin, this is bound up for the viewer with knowledge of their imminent demise), and in each of them he reverts to a form of strained, but comic, infantilism. As Jameson puts it

> [In] this peculiar space—neither public nor private nor their synthesis [...] there seems to reign an utterly different conception of private life, one of a kind of schizophrenic dissociation, in which the great and powerful lapse back into senility or second childhood.[9]

Still from *Moloch*: Hitler in the car.

The action always occurs in 'real time' and is contained within the course of a single day. It is, in each case, made up of a combination of historical fact (the Japanese surrender and Hirohito's meeting with MacArthur; Hitler's relationship with Eva Braun; Lenin's long final illness and meeting with Stalin) and minute apocryphal detail, amongst which the leaders' various bodily ablutions and idiosyncrasies feature prominently. As noted, an internal voyeurism, linked specifically to the act of cinematic viewing, is foregrounded to varying degrees. This, in turn, is connected to the aura of power that the leaders retain, and the ridicule to which they must submit (from characters and viewer alike).

Finally, the films are all unmistakably Sokurovian in the inverted relationship between significance and insignificance that their temporal structure perversely favours; in other words, 'important' moments in the familiar histories of the three leaders (Lenin's encounter with Stalin; Hirohito's war crisis meeting with his ministers) account for considerably less viewing time than transient minutiae (Lenin's physical tribulations during a picnic with Krupskaya; Hirohito's extended marine biology session). Moreover, these inversions do not readily submit to psychological recuperation (the claim that they generate insights about the leaders' deep-seated motivations for their actions is barely sustainable).

Moloch

Of the three films, the first, released in 1999, is the most explicit in foregrounding voyeurism as a figure for the objectification entailed in the cinematic experience. It brings Sokurov ostensibly close to the kind of avant-garde self-awareness more commonly associated with the political cinema of Godard, and with Mulvey's feminist theory of film. It opens with a long, silent sequence in which Eva Braun is performing morning exercises atop the mist-laden castle, clad only in a revealing body stocking. As she struts narcissistically across the ramparts, the camera reveals that she is being watched through binoculars by a male observer. Staring out into the mist, she gives the impression of knowing of, and enjoying, being the object of this voyeurism. Part One of the film ends with Eva again being watched, this time through a rifle sight, as if to reinforce the connection between voyeurism and male fantasy. Moreover, when Eva flirts lasciviously with Bormann at the meal, he tells her that he 'could eat her alive'. Part Two concludes with a recapitulation of the opening scene, but this time without any inner mirroring of the act of observation, as though to close the circle linking the voyeurism of the characters with that of the viewer.

That Sokurov is not indulging in text-book Mulveyan critiques of the male gaze, however, is evident from the fact that Hitler, too, is the object of the voyeuristic gaze, most strikingly when a soldier spies him defecating in the snow during a trip out into the winter surroundings of the Obersalzberg. This is preceded by Eva bursting into the bathroom, unaware that Hitler is relieving himself. The body is, thus, also an object of disgust and the scenes in which Eva displays her athletic beauty are paralleled by those featuring Hitler's flabby, white body.

Revulsion at the body is not restricted to Hitler; Bormann is shown smelling his hands, contorting his face in disgust. But revulsion at the dead matter excreted by the body is accompanied by a fascination with the dead body itself. Hitler makes several bizarre, related jokes at the dinner party, first inviting his fellow diners to partake of 'corpse tea', and then, in reference to the crab that they are served, suggesting that the corpses of dead old women are used to catch crabs. In a complex chain of associations, the camera itself is drawn into the game of desire for, and disgust at, lifeless matter; the extreme and prolonged focus on the green liquid soup that the diners are eating is swiftly followed by Bormann's suggestion to Eva that he would like to 'eat her'. Thus, sexual desire for the female body is linked to desire for food, connected in turn with lifeless matter and death itself.

The morbid obsession is more than merely corporeal. Hitler expresses anger and anxiety in a conversation with a priest about his own death, and his consequent lack of faith. When the priest has departed, Hitler rants to an invisible figure behind the camera, complaining that he cannot believe in the afterlife as 'you don't exist'. Ostensibly berating God, Hitler effectively addresses the viewer as the ultimate, yet unattainable, arbiter of his (fictional) life and death. Solitude in a Godless universe in which all that remains is lifeless matter doubles the separation between cinematic character and a viewer, in turn desirous of, and revolted by, the (likewise unattainable) material representations before him. The ultimate sexual (and political) power wielded by twentieth-century dictators is worthless in the face of the return to lifeless matter to which all are subject and the solipsistic hell which ensues. By inverting that power and subjecting the despots to objectification and ridicule, by other characters, and by the viewer, Sokurov reinforces the disjunction between them.

Still from *Moloch*: Eva Braun and Hitler *en plein air*.

The mutual alienation of viewer and viewed, powerful and powerless, is highlighted in a curious scene towards the end of the film when Goebbels shows a propaganda film celebrating Nazi successes.[10] Hitler cuts a pathetic, lone figure standing in front of the screen, 'commanding' the troops with the gestures of a conductor. His acolytes lamely humour him as the on-screen troops march by, as oblivious of Hitler's presence as he is oblivious of that of Eva and her female friends, mocking him behind the scenes, and likewise unaware that they are themselves being 'observed' by the viewers of Sokurov's film.

Moloch is no mere dark, metaphysical rumination on human solitude. Braun's relationship with Hitler is a tense combination of mutual affection and contempt, expressed in the childish games of corporeal repulsion and attraction in which they indulge (Eva pokes Hitler's protruding belly with a mixture of intimacy and disgust; Hitler pursues Eva around a table in half-playful, half-aggressive manner). At times the merriment has an air of infantile physicality about it in keeping with carnival's tendency to erase the boundaries between participant and observer, viewer and viewed, powerful and powerless, and its emphasis on death, sex, bodily excrescence and joyful rebirth. That the viewer is not party to this excess accounts for the surreally distanced impression that they make. The connection between the superfluity of dead, corporeal matter and the emergence of a joyfully embodied spectacle of rebirth is, perhaps, what Mikhail Iampolskii invokes in his characterisation of Sokurov's films as depicting 'a transition from the bodily to the visual [...] the emergence of an aesthetic illusion out of the dying process'.[11]

The oddest element is the role of Goebbels and Bormann. Within the historical narrative they are Hitler's sinister henchmen. In Sokurov's film, they are curious, clown-like figures, Goebbels, diminutive and quirky,

Bormann clumsy and sullen, yet lascivious and disloyal. Like its two successors, *Moloch* is structured around the viewer's fleeting penetration into the intimate space of the everyday life of mythic figures. The fact that Sokurov's portrayals jar significantly with the myths undermines the reified time in which they are located.

Sokurov is working within an established cinematic genre: the historical biopic in which fictional license with respect to the hero's private life supports a recasting of our understanding of the facts behind the public image. But the intimate detail that Sokurov highlights (bodily functions; tics, such as Hitler's constant itching under his arms and Eva's obsession with exercising; lingering close-ups of the food they consume) have little psychological purchase, subverting the relationship between fact and fiction, historical past and present reality by installing an aesthetic regime based on a highly corporeal present.

This is not to say that there is no sense of history in *Moloch*. One of the film's most hypnotic aspects is the sensual texture of the historical sounds and images that form the backdrop to the bizarre rituals of the Nazi entourage: the crackling of Eva's gramophone as it plays war-era music; the trinket box embossed with a swastika which she raises to her lips. But they are divorced from the epic historical events with which they are associated; mention of wartime events is sporadic and off-beam: Hitler's bizarre ideas about Ukrainian food; his grandiose claims of a thousand-year Reich (*tsarstvo*) advanced in the context of his fear of death.

The apotheosis of Sokurov's assault on the historical biopic arrives in the closing sequences in which Hitler again rails insanely to camera (with Eva, present, but inattentive) about the Hitler family's physical frailty; his performance clearly recalls the (in)famous footage of the Führer's impassioned political speeches on Aryan superiority, arms wildly gesticulating, face tense with anger. The Führer's public myth is emptied of its familiar content and filled with a set of meanings inconsequential if read according to the rules of the biopic genre and its assumptions about time, history and cinema, but deeply significant in the context of Sokurov's radical non-representational aesthetic. The closing shots of a naked Eva stalking the castle ramparts in full view of the voyeuristic camera, confirms Sokurov's awareness that this aesthetic exists only *in potentia*, condemned to express itself within the confines of representational cinema, as Iampolski argues in this volume.

Taurus

The second film in Sokurov's tetralogy, released in 2000, shows continuities with *Moloch*, but also anticipates the concerns of *The Sun*. *Taurus* begins with a shot almost identical to that with which its predecessor opens: the secluded, mist-laden retreat in which the ailing subject is housed with his 'supporting' entourage. *Taurus* and *Moloch* share other features confirming their common concern with the human body in its relationship with the Other, and with brute matter. Already prone to feverish mumblings, and barely able to walk, the ailing Lenin is at a point further along the path to his final demise than Hitler. Like Hitler, however, his flabby body is exposed to humiliation. He is shown being washed naked, pushed roughly around by his entourage, and, later, hoisted unceremoniously onto the shoulders of an official sent to rescue him after he has fallen in a field whilst on a country picnic. His carers express disgust at having to empty his bedpan, recapitulating the earlier film's obsession with human matter.

The fact that the humiliating ridicule to which Lenin is subjected is public in nature (rather than being poked and teased in an intimate setting, he is mocked and manhandled in full view of his household) intensifies his estrangement from his surroundings. Likewise more public in nature are the acts of voyeurism to which Lenin is subject. Peripheral characters peer constantly through half open doors to gawp. Correlated with this is the group photograph that Lenin is made to sit for; again, the act of visual scrutiny that doubles that of the film itself takes place in public view, rather than in secret; the objectifying function of the cinematic gaze does not require sexual desire, nor is it always a solipsistic act in which the power of the gazer lies in his invisibility to the gazed at. In Jameson's view, for Sokurov, 'the screen becomes an experimental laboratory, an isolation chamber in which we follow processes that are neither public nor private in any traditional sense'.[12]

Lenin resembles Sokurov's Hitler, too, in that an awareness of the frailty of his failing body leads to a concern about what lies after his death. He questions Krupskaya continually about her plans when he dies, and expresses anxiety that his achievements will be promptly forgotten by those around him. Unlike *Moloch*, however, *Taurus* appears not to shy away from linking such existential problems with their historical context. Lenin is equally concerned about the way that he has been abandoned by the Party's Central Committee and, in the encounter with Stalin, the issue of his legacy, and the roles of Trotsky, Kamenev and Molotov in the succession, are all broached.

Ostensibly, then, *Taurus* is a rather more conventional biopic than *Moloch*. But there is something deeply puzzling about the way in which, whilst skirting briefly over political questions such as Lenin's awareness of the mismatch between Bolshevik philosophy and the bourgeois lifestyle of his household, the camera dwells for so long on inconsequential minutiae (the flight of a bee as it buzzes around the field in which Lenin and Krupskaya sit; the close-up view of Lenin's toes as they are clipped by a servant; the prolonged sight and sound of feet as they walk to and fro). For struggling to break free from the constraints of the historical biopic is an alternative film mode in which the subordination of cinematic time (the real time of viewing) to historical time (the public time in which the political events took place) is subverted. As José Alaniz puts it:

> [T]hrough a marshalling of chance, peculiarity and error normally confined to the realm of filmic excess (and thus usually discarded from the final work as 'spoiled footage'), Sokurov enacts an ecstatic deconstruction of the diegesis itself.[13]

The counter-narrative dimension explains other aspects of Sokurov's aesthetic. Notable for example is the assiduous avoidance of the name of Stalin (and, indeed, the surname of Lenin) throughout *Taurus*. Lenin himself

Still from *Taurus*: Lenin.

seems confused over whether the figure who visits him is a Georgian or a Jew (a cause of mirth amongst his entourage). But instead of motivating the film's own 'confusion' over Stalin's identity by reference to Lenin's psychological frailties, we would do better to view it in the context of Sokurov's later film, *Russian Ark*, in which the director refuses to confirm that the central character touring the Hermitage is the Marquis de Custine on whom he is clearly modelled. Here, too, Sokurov rejects the notion of the historical film as an unproblematic 'embodiment' of the time and events that it claims to represent. The eschewal of familiar historical names is a rejection of the alienated time in which conventional history unfolds.

Similarly important is the classical musical soundtrack that provides the auditory correlative to the visual indulgence in transient detail and prevents the familiar historical narrative, with its alienated time, from dominating the film. It points to an, as yet vague and unspecific narrative, pitched in a parallel key, and attune to the everyday, embodied time of the cinematic moment of viewing. It illustrates Kristin Thompson's notion of a 'cinema of excess' entailing 'a whole "film" existing...alongside the narrative film we think of ourselves as watching'.[14]

The fact that the alternative narrative is submerged beneath the 'biopic' structure reflects the alienated mode to which it must give way. Alienation – of the individual from bodily existence, of the self from the other, of the human being from the world of matter –provides the interpretative key to the tetralogy. In *Taurus*, it is thematised overtly and shapes the words, behaviour, and interactions of the characters. It explains why Lenin is fated incoherently to rail about his predicament without response (even from his wife). It accounts for the verbal motif 'I can do it myself' (*Ia sam*) with which Lenin rebuffs every attempt to offer him physical assistance, and for his autistic obsession with the mechanical task of multiplying 17 by 22.

The full horror of the atrocities with which all the leaders are bound up is not lessened through the emphasis on alienation; together with its connection to the dynamics of power, the concept highlights the inevitability of violence as its inevitable conclusion, without diminishing the responsibility of the individuals concerned.

If in *Moloch* the theme of bodily intimacy degenerates into a mix of barely contained lust on one hand, and semi-contemptuous prodding on the other, then in *Taurus*, it more or less disappears; there is a measure of affection between Lenin and Krupskaya, but little intimacy. Nor are there the same moments of visual indulgence in corporeal beauty. Rather, the action is punctuated by close-ups of Lenin's unkempt toes, or of disembodied feet echoing along hard wooden floors. Here the tetralogy bears comparison with *Mother and Son* (1997) and *Father and Son* (2003) in which bodily intimacy between a man and a woman is likewise de-eroticised and keyed to Sokurov's radical aesthetic with its emphasis on the sensuality of the real time of viewing, but this time via the familial nature of their relationship. The disjunction of viewing time and represented time is a hallmark of the alienated cinema which Sokurov seeks to transcend.

The audience is always deeply implicated in Sokurov's cinematic system. The objectification of the central figure, his estrangement from his surroundings and his fellow human beings, is foregrounded as part of the viewing experience. The inclusion of voyeurism and cameras within the diegesis, clearly designed to achieve this effect, is, in *Taurus* supplemented by the semi-metaphorisation of the hero as a part of the animal world. Throughout the film, Lenin emits animal-like sounds of pain expressing his frustration at his condition. In the closing frames he is depicted, abandoned, in a park-like setting, apparently sleeping. Suddenly, he raises himself from his wheelchair and utters a bestial bellow. This shot is succeeded by a long shot of a horned bull in a misty field. The sequence is reminiscent of Eisensteinian montage, establishing the metaphoric comparison between Lenin and the bull. With no point of viewer identification available other than that of the camera, the viewer is compelled to take stock of his/her own role in articulating the metaphor, and, thus, in assimilating Lenin to the impassive world of nature.

But the very availability (and directorial signalling) of the metaphoric reading simultaneously accommodates nature to the realm of human intellect, guaranteeing its ambiguous status securely inside and irretrievably outside the viewing subject. In Alaniz's words, Sokurov 'makes nature consolingly homelike and disconcertingly foreign at the same time'.[15] Like the characters of his films, Sokurov's viewers are 'caught in some limbo between body and spirit, half in and half out of nature, literally contorting [themselves] to reconcile that contradiction'.[16] This in between-ness underpins Sokurov's assault on a cinematic referentiality predicated on single, authoritative vantage points from which reality might be fixed. It is the reason for the disorienting multiplicity of viewpoints that Jeremi Szaniawski has noted in Sokurov's historical films,[17] and echoes Pavel Florensky's critique of post-renaissance perspectivism that removes man from the plurality of encounters with real, embodied others, reducing them to the function of a single, perspectival point in abstract, geometric space.[18]

Taurus closes with Lenin mumbling incoherently before a final shot of the sky – a symbol of an unattainable plane of meaning reconciling the external, corporeal matter of the animal world with the inner life of the spirit, and corrupted human history with the eternal time of Bergson's 'privileged moment'.

The Sun

Fittingly, the metaphysical plane towards which Sokurov gestures throughout the tetralogy receives its most overt treatment in the third film. In one of the opening scenes of *The Sun*, the emperor assures the nervous servant assigned to help him dress that he has a body like any other human being (a reference to the Japanese emperor's descent from the 'sun goddess'). Much of the film is taken up with demonstrating just how unlike other human beings Hirohito's deferential, ritual-bound entourage treat him, reinforcing the emperor's sense that 'only his wife and son love him'.

Hirohito's bodily distance from his awe-struck fellows conflicts with our experience of Hirohito's frail, diminutive frame and disconcerting bodily tics; the defining feature of his physical demeanour is the uncontrollable contortion of his lips into a fish-like pout indirectly presaging the sequence in which he indulges his passion for marine biology and examines a rare crab under a microscope. The disconcerting facial tic, like Lenin's bestial groans, estrange the viewer from the body of the central character, reifying it as a metaphoric object of curiosity. The reification process is doubled within *The Sun* as the camera gazes down in extreme close up from Hirohito's viewpoint on the shining, bald pate of the servant who assists him.

Hirohito is, then, like Hitler and Lenin, disjoined from his fellow humans, but also from the shell of his own body over which he cannot exert full control. In *The Sun*, the distancing process is most closely integrated with the historical subject matter. The action is restricted primarily, as in the two preceding films, to an enclosed setting: that of the Emperor's embattled palace as the Americans close on Tokyo. The viewer is never allowed to forget the context; the narrative is punctuated by sequences in which Hirohito meets with his senior commanders to receive updates on the US incursion. The fulcrum of the narrative is the defeated Hirohito's meeting with MacArthur. Throughout the hum of circling warplanes is audible: the counterpoint to Hirohito's increasing solipsism and a reminder of the fatal consequences of the way in which he has cocooned himself from the catastrophe of impending defeat.

In *The Sun* the connection between alienation and the misuse of power is most vividly revealed. In a striking sequence, Hirohito falls into a restless sleep following his marine biology session. He is immediately beset by a surreal nightmare in which images of the bombs descending upon Japan mutate into fish-like creatures swimming through walls of flames. The emperor's subjective indulgences – a function of his estrangement– are bound up with the terrifying consequences of the inability to take account of the effect of his actions.

Hirohito compensates for his loneliness through other idiosyncratic intellectual pursuits: the contemplation of old photographs of film stars and the writing of Japanese *haiku* poetry. In a hypnotic scene depicting the latter, the emperor labours as lovingly over drawing the symbols of the haiku as the camera dwells on each movement of the brush, and the viewer is made privy to the soporific mutter of the emperor's words as he intones the poem aloud. The scene's soothing intimacy counters on the level of viewer-character relations the ritualised formalism of the interactions between the characters.

Hirohito, however, is brought face to face with the outside world when Japan finally capitulates and he is forced to meet with General MacArthur. As he emerges from his headquarters he is met by a posse of American soldiers who surround him and attempt to photograph him, initially disappointed at his unimposing demeanour, but then amused by his resemblance to Charlie Chaplin; here, then, rather than tool of intimate communion with the other, the camera serves as instrument of that other's public humiliation.

The two encounters with MacArthur are awkward, but compelling, affairs, shot with characteristic Sokurovian deliberation and attention to 'inconsequential' detail. Hirohito's pride in adhering to ritual is conveyed in lingering close-ups of his belaboured attempts to pull his formal white gloves over his hands, his bows and his stiff manner of sitting. In one arresting shot, however, as MacArthur offers him a light for his extinguished cigar, the two leaders stare briefly into one another's eyes, formalities shattered, as self and other are brought into unmediated contact.

Through MacArthur Sokurov engages with the key historical questions one would expect in a biopic of Hirohito: why did he order the assault on Pearl Harbor? (the emperor claims that this was done without his knowledge); why did he enter an alliance with Hitler? (Hirohito denies that he ever met the Führer personally). But, here too, there is always the sense of a parallel narrative, with its own peaks, lulls and peripetiae, centring on the leading character's struggle to come to terms with his estrangement from his body, and from the Other, and played out on the level of viewer-screen interactions in the pauses, contradictions and peripetiae in the camera's engagement with its subject.

All three planes (historical, 'alternative', audience) converge at the moments of visual self-reflexion. For example, during the meeting with MacArthur, the general leaves the room and, thinking himself free from the gaze of the outside world, Hirohito practices dance steps across the floor of the room. MacArthur, however, is peering in amusement from the half-open

Still from *The Sun*: Hirohito and MacArthur. Courtesy of Artificial Eye.

door, finding confirmation of his previous assertion that the emperor is 'like a child'. This adds to the sense of irresponsibility associated with Hirohito's evasion of true interaction with the world. But it also bolsters the implicit critique of voyeuristic objectification to which the emperor is subjected.

It is in keeping with the notion of a network of intersecting narrative planes that, on his return to his headquarters, Hirohito is informed of the arrival of his wife. In the film's final sequence, the emperor finally sheds the shell of formal ritual and enjoys moments of true affection with his wife (stroking her hair, allowing her to rest her head on his shoulders) as he informs her that he has resolved to abandon his divinity.[19] Divine status has imposed upon him the burden of ritual and alienation from his fellow humans. It is the 'freedom' from that burden that finally enables him to reconcile his bodily existence with the world of others, and with the eternal realm of the spirit.

But, before the camera repeats the now familiar gesture, panning skywards, Sokurov ensures that the viewer is left in a state of ambiguity. As the emperor's wife leads her husband away, he barely hears the answer to the question he posed to an official about the fate of the soldier who brought news of Japan's defeat: he committed *hara-kiri*. Hirohito's final act is, then, to evade responsibility for the historical tragedy that his country has suffered. In critiquing the reified history within which we situate Hirohito, *The Sun* is not exonerating the emperor. Rather it portrays the reification of history as part of the same process that decoupled Hirohito from the consequences of his actions.

Conclusion

Sokurov can never articulate the pure cinema of embodiment to which his tetralogy implicitly aspires. The time unfolding before us remains, despite the impediments to free-flowing plot, the disorientated spaces and multiply shifting viewpoints, a time of representation, the history that of an objectified narrative. Nor, revelations of our voyeuristic stance notwithstanding, can we enter bodily communion with the fictional characters before us (they are precisely fictional, as Sokurov's refusal to accord them their full historical names testifies).[20]

Sokurov is, through his experimentation with the visual eavesdropping device, and his rejection of the fact/fiction distinction, gesturing towards an entirely new history. Szaniawski suggests that, in the tetralogy: 'We glimpse the dark ocean of history which both swallows and spits back these figures like a wrecked ship on its shores, where we dwell before being swallowed ourselves'.[21] But, with its own spaces and its own temporality, Sokurov's history, I would argue, is neither this dark ocean, nor what Szaniawski then posits as 'a matter of perspective, converging towards and then moving abruptly away from these "central" figures, forcibly monstrous and forcibly human',[22] but rather one freed of the burden of alienation and open to true, embodied communion between present and past, observing self and observed other. The morose tones in which it is rendered reflect less qualities inherent within it, than the inevitability that it will forever elude the grasp of those who would seek to capture it.[23]

Notes

1 P. McGavin, 'Movie Review: Moscow Elegy', *Courant.Com*, http://xml.courant.com/topic/mmx-17813_lgcy,0,1172452.story (accessed 7 January 2009); C. Ravetto-Biagioli, 'Floating on the Borders of Europe: Sokurov's Russian Ark', *Film Quarterly*, 59.1 (2005), pp. 18–25; David Gillespie and Elena Smirnova, 'Alexander Sokurov and the Russian Soul', *Studies in European Cinema*, 1.1 (2004), pp. 57–65; Mikhail Iampol'skii, *O blizkom*, Moscow: Novoe Literaturnoe Obozrenie, 2001; Susan Sontag, 'A Century of Cinema', http://southerncross-review.org/43/sontagcinema.htm (accessed 8 January 2009).
2 Jameson, 'History and Elegy in Sokurov', p. 10.
3 Stefan Steinberg writes scathingly: 'Sokurov elevates the formal aspects of film-making...to daub the walls of mankind's prison cell in interesting shades (and sanitise his jailors). His work [is] artistically and intellectually bankrupt'. See Steinberg, 'Aesthetic Choices: Sokurov's *The Sun*', World Socialist Website, http://

www.wsws.org/articles/2005/mar2005/ber4-m11.shtml (accessed 5 January 2009).
4   See Georg Friedrich Hegel, *Phenomenology of Spirit*, Oxford: Clarendon Press, 1977.
5   For an analysis of embodiment in Florensky and Losev, see Stephen Hutchings, 'Gender Theory and the Metaphysics of Losev and Florenskii: Flashpoint as Fleshpoint', in Peter Barta (ed.), *Gender and Sexuality in Russian Civilisation*, London: Routledge, 2001, pp. 141–63.
6   Pavel Florenskii, 'Obratnaia perspektiva', in *Sobranie sochinenii* (4 vols), vol. 1, Paris: YMCA, 1985.
7   Mikhail Bakhtin, *Toward a Philosophy of the Act*, Austin: Texas UP, 1993.
8   See the following exchange in an interview: AS: Since camera lenses are generally designed specifically to create the impression of volume, we have had two developed in Russia especially for our films. They reverse traditional illusionistic volume and emphasise the illusion of a plane. – LS: Pavel Florenskii's 1919 text *Inverted Perspective* extrapolates the alternatives to linear perspective from the study of icons. Is the icon the paradigm? – AS: In Russian artistic practice, the most brilliant examples are Kuzma Petrov-Vodkin [and certainly the Russian icon as such, of the Yaroslavl and the Novgorod schools and, to a lesser extent, the Pskov school]. See Sedofsky, 'Plane Songs'.
9   Jameson, 'History and Elegy...', p. 5; p.4.
10 Benjamin Halligan comments on Sokurov's awareness of the complicity of the cinematic medium in the fascistic abuse of power which his own film critiques: 'To implicate fascism is to implicate aesthetics; to implicate Hitler is to implicate cinema (made explicit in the scene of Goebbels watching propaganda films)'. See Benjamin Halligan, 'The Elusive Hitler: A Dialogue on *Moloch*', *Central Europe Review*, 2.3 (2002), http://www.ce-review.org/00/3/kinoeye3_halligan.html (accessed 7 January 2009).
11 Iampol'skii, *O blizkom*, p. 136.
12 Jameson, 'History and Elegy...', p. 6.
13 Alaniz, ' "Nature", illusion and excess...', p. 186.
14 Kristin Thompson, 'The Concept of Cinematic Excess', in Philip Rosen (ed.), *Narrative, Apparatus, Ideology*, New York: Columbia University Press, 1986, pp. 130–42 (p. 132).
15 Alaniz, ' "Nature", illusion and excess...', p. 189.
16 Alaniz, ' "Nature", illusion and excess...', p. 192.
17 Szaniawski, 'Historic Space...', p. 153.
18 Florenskii, 'Obratnaia perspektiva'.
19 In Sokurov's own words: 'The body is a blessed reality, because it is only through this sensory feeling of the human body, its warmth, that one gets an idea of the soul's location or an answer from it' (Sedofsky 'Plane Songs...').
20 Sokurov's impossible mission can be compared with Dziga Vertov's utopian desire to merge human perception with cinematic vision, and body with camera, by creating what Malcolm Turvey terms 'a physical relation of kinship' between the two. See Malcolm Turvey, 'Can the Camera See? Mimesis in Man with a Movie Camera', *October* 89 (1999), pp. 25–50 (p. 29).
21 Szaniawski, 'Historic Space...', p. 160.
22 Szaniawski, 'Historic Space...', p. 161.
23 Aware that the cinematic form within which he works must inevitably distance itself from the history that it aims to represent, Sokurov expresses the contradiction through overt use of filmic indices of that distancing process: sepia toning, crackling sound, foregrounded artistic frames, etc.

PART IV

REMAPPING THE EMPIRE

CHAPTER 10

CROWD CONTROL: ANXIETY OF EFFLUENCE IN SOKUROV'S *RUSSIAN ARK*

José Alaniz

A work of cinema is not shot – it is composed.

Alexander Sokurov[1]

Although the masses give rise to the ornament, they are not involved in thinking it through.

Siegfried Kracauer[2]

Alexander Sokurov, Russian romantic cine-poet par excellence, has long enjoyed a reputation as *the* auteur of morose, anguished solitude. To cite one of innumerable such characterisations, Louis Menashe notes, 'The mood of Sokurov cinema, including the many documentaries, "Elegies" and features, is usually dreamy, vaporous, deeply spiritual; the look of his films matches their opaque storylines and the quiet characterizations – spare, gloomy, contemplative'.[3]

Yet in late 2001, Sokurov deviated sharply from his long-established filmic practice of intimate set pieces with tiny casts to manage a crew of over 4,700 for *Russian Ark*, a 90-minute one-take feature shot on location at St Petersburg's Hermitage Museum, on digital video.[4] Leading his collaborators to an unprecedented artistic goal, the director would work with a German cinematographer through a translator; foresee and defuse countless technical issues; keep himself and a half-dozen other staff carefully out of frame for the entire single take; and most importantly, herd hundreds of actors, extras and technicians through complicated, clockwork-like movements that had to be precise down to the second and centimetre, with any visible error spelling disaster. On 23 December 2001, after four years of preparation, eight months of rehearsals (though no full rehearsal at the Hermitage itself), Sokurov and crew had four hours and no more to take their 'cinema in one breath' – or else have the entire project collapse into an embarrassing, costly boondoggle. As one reviewer put it, this was 'a cinema high-wire act'.[5]

Crucially, the nerve-wracking shoot of *Russian Ark* would ultimately succeed or fail based on one predominant factor: Sokurov's talent for crowd control – his capacity to direct, police and contain the effluence of his assembled masses. This chapter examines the phenomenon of Sokurov as traffic cop, at the centre of a remarkable, real-time filmic event, and its resonance with issues of aesthetic authority; nationalist ideology; cinematic excess; and the fraught meaning of 'the masses' in post-Soviet Russian culture.

The Crowd

As celebrated by Edgar Allan Poe, Charles Baudelaire, Thomas de Quincey and others, and as argued by such social scientists as Gustave LeBon in his *Psychologie des foules* (1895), Georg Simmel, and later commentators including Walter Benjamin and Siegfried Kracauer, the advent of modernity came about concurrently with the rise of the crowd as *locus classicus* of the urban experience. As LeBon noted, modernity is 'the era of crowds'.[6] The many fluctuating meanings of the crowd often associated it with mindlessness, or with having a mind of its own; with ineffectively dispersed energies or with supremely frightening power when mobilised; with cowed docility and with the sublime: a threat of chaos, loss of control, overspillage and breaching of all restraints. This presumed, frighteningly destructive inclination of assembled masses is foregrounded in, for example, Elias Canetti's influential 1962 study:

> The Crowd, suddenly there where there was nothing before, is a mysterious and universal phenomenon. A few people may have been standing together – five, ten or 12, not more; nothing has been announced, nothing is expected. Suddenly everywhere is black with people and more come streaming from all sides though streets had only one direction. Most of them do not know what has happened and, if questioned, have no answer; but they hurry to be there where most other people are. There is a determination in their movement which is quite different from the expression of ordinary curiosity. It seems as though the movement of some of them transmits itself to others. But that is not all; they have a goal which is there before they can find words for it. The goal is the blackest spot where most people are gathered.[7]

As evident from Canetti's at times hysterical account, the crowd's supreme threat calls for strategies – political, aesthetic – to contain and direct its power. Jeffrey Schnapp, in fact, describes the masses as the 'literal specter of the Enlightenment [...] the revolutionary crowd, hovering between reason and hallucination, between the emancipatory dreams of 1789 and the terror of 1792'.[8] Schnapp identifies two dominant overlapping iconographies of the crowd in Western visual representation, dating to the early modern period: the emblematic and the oceanic/multitudinous.

The former organises the body politic into a unified, disciplined whole, originally for the end of paying reverence to the divine. The emblematic mode (as seen in the ordered ranks of saints, angels and martyrs of such diverse masters as Fra Angelico, Giotto, Perugino, Pieter Breughel the Elder and some Russian icons dating back to the fifteenth century) presented a structured manifestation of the masses, both shaped by and reflecting God's reverence. The emblematic, Schnapp argues, denotes a static ideological order; its later, more secular iterations depict the multitudes comprising the body of the sovereign, evidenced in the well-known Abraham Bosse frontispiece to Thomas Hobbes's 1651 political tract *Leviathan*. Political rallies and the impeccably ordered German masses in Leni Riefenstahl's *Triumph of the Will* [Triumph des Willens, 1935] exemplify the modern version of the emblematic mode.

The second technique for rendering the crowd, the oceanic/multitudinous, emphasises its association with the forces of nature, instability, energy, chaos and the threat of losing control. In this scheme, according to Schnapp, the divine or sovereign power is dispersed throughout the mass rather than serving as its focus; the crowd appears as sublime, appallingly on the verge of revolution. Unsurprisingly, this representational strategy often arises in revolutionary works: the heterogeneous unconstrained masses in Walter Ruttman's documentary *Berlin, Symphony of a Great City* [Berlin. Die Sinfonie der Großstadt, 1927], or indeed the many unruly crowds in early Soviet films, such as Sergei Eisenstein's 1928 *October*. In the latter, the machine-gunning scene and the episode featuring Lenin's address at the Finland station both depict highly energised crowds, either out of control or inspired to struggle on by the great leader.

For all their seeming differences, however, Schnapp emphasises that the two modes, emblematic and oceanic, overlap and interpenetrate each other:[9] the crowd holds potential for both leading and being led, revolt and obeisance; in modernity, the ruler who can seize the reigns of the masses and 'take' it where it already thinks it wants to go, wields enormous power. Indeed, the aforementioned unruly crowds in early Soviet cinema may be depicted as oceanic or 'out of control', but they are simultaneously unified – rendered 'emblematic' through montage and dialectical *mise-en-scène*.

In this light, the Odessa Steps sequence from Eisenstein's *The Battleship Potemkin* [Bronenosets Potemkin, 1925], as discussed by Michael Tratner, evinces elements of both modes (the terror and disorganisation of the victims; the serried ranks of inhuman Tsarist troops) to construct an allegorical vision of abstract social forces:

> The movie goes to great lengths, in fact, to deny that the revolution is a conflict between humans; it is rather a conflict of institutions. Thus, when the guards face the women, the guards have been transformed into repeated straight lines, which, besides suggesting

masculinity, also suggest utter uniformity and unnaturalness; the guards are not humans attacking humans, but pistons and rods being pumped by the machine of the state. The women resisting the guards are not individuals, either, but simply 'humanity' as curved flesh and questioning eyes.¹⁰

Both modes, then, Schnapp claims, serve an ideological purpose; the represented crowd is both 'anonymous' and 'nationalised': 'For all their formal divergences and differences in use, procedure and location, for all the seeming absence of emblematic artifice in oceanic crowd scenes, both the emblematic and the oceanic are reducible, in the end, to allegories of crowd control'.¹¹

In Russia too (as further elaborated in the conclusion of this chapter), the representation of the crowd remains a fraught issue for post-Soviet culture. 'March of the Enthusiasts,' a 2007 exhibit on crowds in art at Moscow's Kovcheg Gallery, elicited both sarcastic guffaws and an ironic nostalgia from critics. Writing on the Soviet era, Anna Tolstova noted, 'In a word, to walk in formation was ideologically loyal, while to walk on your own was a manifestation of bourgeois individualism'.¹²

Containing the Crowd: Sokurov's 'Evening Sacrifice'

The foregoing discussion of the emblematic and oceanic modes informs my reading of Sokurov's 1984/87 documentary *Evening Sacrifice,* a Soviet-era attempt by the director to 'capture the essence of a crowd'. In this 17-minute film, the tension between recording and interpreting the profilmic masses is made palpable.

Evening Sacrifice depicts an ostensibly happy subject: a May Day celebration on the streets of Leningrad in 1984. To document the event, Sokurov places his mostly static cameras at various points along Nevsky Prospekt at different times of day, as partygoers stream by in their multitudes. Most of the film consists of ground-level and overhead shots depicting the revellers, some of whom greet the camera, holler and wave. Others appear oblivious as they stroll by, in their hundreds upon hundreds.

The film opens with a long shot of the Leningrad skyline at midday, the firmament dominating the image, as if pressing down on the city below. An artillery unit, guns pointing at this overpowering sky, sets off several loud blasts. The soldiers are still, standing to attention, moving only to follow orders to load, fire, release. The spent shells, spewing smoke, gather in a growing pile – abjected, fallen. Sokurov presents the first of only two close-ups in the film: the smoking pile of spent shells. The shot lasts about a minute, obviously far more than needed to read the mere fact of the shells as an image. The shot, furthermore, is in slow motion; wisps of smoke slowly waft into the air from the dead ordnance.

Immediately following, long shots of the enormous crowds fill the screen as the light begins to die. The sky, once so dominant, diminishes as the city's buildings, filmed from the streets, push it out of frame. Like some vast herd of cattle, the people shuffle along in their countless numbers and daunting variety. The image often breaks down into patches

Still from *Evening Sacrifice*: The crowd.

of darker and brighter shades; the hosts of humanity go from distinct to anonymous, with gender, age, facial features impossible to make out; in one tight telephoto shot, the raucous crowd goes hazily in and out of focus.

Sokurov here invokes the nameless (predominantly oceanic) crowds of Hieronymus Bosch and Breughel: the viewer comes to understand the heterogeneity of the people as well as their equivalence. The latter comes to predominate, however, as, by the end of the film, they are all (emblematically) moving as one huge body; a dissolve from one long shot to another underscores the endlessness (and uniformity) of the masses: the first shot shows them approaching, the second receding like rolling waves.

The steady visual 'emblematisation' and containment of the masses for a larger ideological purpose over the course of the film is repeated in the cacophonous multi-layered soundtrack. These images, despite the celebration they represent, are melancholic, not least due to the sound collage Sokurov provides as accompaniment: radio broadcasts, sirens, the people's own hoots and hollers, and Pavel Chesnakov's vespers music, *Evening Sacrifice*, with its haunting baritone. The latter, crucially, rises to drown out all the other sounds precisely when the emblematic masses are shown in long shot, walking together in the same direction. The film is revealed as a modern *memento mori*. The medium of photography contributes to its saddening mood: Sokurov captures the crowd's 'hereness', its reassuring aliveness, but also signals that all these people will die (resembling Roland Barthes' reading of the photograph in *Camera Lucida*). The more living human beings appear on the screen, strolling and laughing and mugging for the camera, the more one feels that they are in a sense already lost, that they will someday all exist only on film. They are like those smoking shells, cooling off in the dying light.

Sokurov makes this linkage explicit in the closing shot of the film. As night falls, the crowds begin to scatter, and the camera enters a packed public bus. Inside, a seated woman, perhaps one of the revellers, perhaps only an observer – like the viewer – stares wearily out the bus window at the blackened street. The final shot, the movie's second close-up, shows the woman's face, *in slow motion*. Not a very young woman (she is perhaps in her mid-30s), her haggard features contain the trace of their own eventual dissolution. She is here, like the crowd; also like it, she already carries the seeds of decay. The close-up and the slow motion of course invite us to make an equivalence between this woman and the spent, cooling artillery shells. (Notably, the Chesnakov piece continues to play over the woman's image.) This poetic montage recalls the painful lesson of Freud's essay 'On Transience', that 'all this loveliness of Nature and Art, of the world of our sensations and of the world outside, will really fade away to nothing'.[13]

The nameless woman, in other words, *stands in* for the now-vanished crowd; like the sovereign of past representations, she is comprised of them – and she is mortal. As if to underscore this, her reflection is visible in the darkened window, like a willowy ghost, an afterimage of life.

Despite its real-life subject matter, *Evening Sacrifice* clearly manipulates crowd imagery for what was, at the time, a politically incorrect message (the film was held up due to its unorthodox depiction of the masses). Precisely these issues of containment, aestheticisation and cinematic excess (for at times individual members of the crowd seem to be having too good a time for such a sombre theme) would come up again in Sokurov's much better-known filmic oddity of 2002, *Russian Ark*.

Russian Ark

A great deal has been written on *Russian Ark* since its release and wide distribution throughout Europe and the US, so that here I need hardly rehearse the ideological, historiographic and aesthetic debates it launched.[14] Suffice it to say that, while many Westerners and contemporary Russians were left cold (or befuddled) by the film's politics,[15] scores of viewers and critics lauded its technical achievement (what Benjamin Halligan called 'a Bazinian utopian text'). Indeed, technique formed the main thrust of the movie's international marketing campaign (to Sokurov's chagrin).

Accounts of the film, furthermore, are often rendered in breathless lists: 867 costumed actors; 35 rooms of the Hermitage involved; 33 rooms lit and traversed; more than 1.5 kilometres covered; 77 pounds of camera equipment borne by cinematographer Tillman Büttner; four years of preparation; only 36 hours to set up the lights and set; 4,700 cast and crew coordinated; only four hours of December light; only two days to work in the Hermitage itself; eight months of off-site rehearsals; zero full on-site rehearsals; −23 degrees Celsius outdoor temperature; no more than four minutes exposure to the cold or else the camera lens would fog up once back indoors; 50 electricians; 10 buses for transporting extras; 22 assistant directors; Mariinsky Symphony conductor Valeri Gerghiev in town from New York for only four hours, after which he had a plane to catch; no more grant money after 2001; 30 seconds: how much at a time Büttner could rest

Still from *Russian Ark*: Gerghiev conducting the orchestra.

on a specially-designed bar-stool; three false starts. And, of course, the most important statistic, the one for the record books: one single, uncut, 90-minute shot.[16]

Despite Sokurov's protestations that the one-shot device was not the point,[17] it of course was.[18] To an admirable degree, any discussion of *Russian Ark* had to take in the unique circumstances of its production. Stuart Klawans's account for the *Nation* may stand in for countless such reviews:

> Considered just as a stunt, this single, feature-length shot is superlative, if not utterly mad. Think of the months of planning and rehearsal it required. Then picture the anxiety-racked day of the shoot: the assistants whispering frantically into their headsets, the grips trying to duck unseen past the camera (there were almost as many grips as credited performers), the heroic Steadicam operator Tilman Büttner carrying on long after his thighs must have turned to lead. Had anything gone visibly wrong in those ninety minutes, the whole movie would have been ruined.[19]

In terms of theme, *Russian Ark* deals with the Hermitage museum as a repository or 'ark' for European culture; it embodies the most cherished high-culture values of (aristocratic) pre-revolutionary Russia. Wandering its hallways and galleries, the Marquis (Sergei Dreiden), a ghostly visitor from the West, pontificates on Western superiority and Russian backwardness, as the unseen Narrator (voiced by Sokurov) defends Russia with patriotic fervour. In the course of the unbroken journey, we see Peter the Great; Nicholas II and his family; Catherine the Great; Alexander Pushkin and other luminaries and restaged events from Russia's past, but largely missing is the Soviet era; i.e., most of the twentieth century. (When it does appear, it is primarily in foreboding tones: a conversation about KGB surveillance; the Second World War–era siege of Leningrad; Red Army soldiers marching by.)

As Nancy Condee writes about such a conspicuous absence, which clearly denotes Sokurov's Russophile stance: 'This directorial decision performs a curious inversion: history is subject to montage, but the film is not'.[20] Rising to its defence, Arkadi Ippolitov argues that *'Russian Ark* is a film precisely about memory, not history. History is constructed and logical, while memory is sensual and indistinct. [...] Memory is inseparable from imagination'.[21]

Regardless of where one stands in such debates (which have dominated scholarly discussion of the film), it can hardly be argued that *Russian Ark* is first and foremost a film about absolute auteurism; everything about it is in fact predicated on complete control of two things: the camera's gaze and the crowd. To unfailingly guide the camera through all its manoeuvres; to contain the 'oceanic spillage' of its hundreds of actors, 'emblematise' them in set piece after set piece, room after room; to maintain thorough command of the entire enterprise without a single visible mistake for an hour and a half [...] like no film before it, Sokurov's work is a monument to megalomaniacal control – indeed utter recreation after one's own image – of the object.

Such vaulting ambition, such domination of the aesthetic over the real cannot but lead to a countervailing, subconscious force: in short, an 'anxiety of effluence'. No wonder Jean Oppenheimer compared Sokurov's undertaking to 'a game of Russian Roulette' (90); nerves of steel would be required to impose one's vision over blind circumstance.

Indeed, Sokurov himself promoted this image of auteur as high-wire tyrant. In 2001, before the actual filming, he told an interviewer:

> It is not, of course, the customary way of making a film, but how tempting it is, like leaping off a twenty-metre tower as an act of faith. You just take a deep breath and step into space, believing, but not really knowing if you are going to survive.
> On the whole, this is a project for experienced and dedicated professionals. Everything will have to be calculated down to the last second and the least detail.... What we are going to attempt is the cinematic equivalent of climbing at high altitude, of using a small window of opportunity, in the face of adverse conditions and limitations of time, to enter a highly rarefied atmosphere, and we need first-class equipment to attain our cinematic peak.[22]

As with *Evening Sacrifice,* that peak would be reached – but not without bumps and stumbles, a certain resistance of the object (and the filmic apparatus): i.e., effluence. Effluence is directly related to (and is in fact, a subset of) cinematic excess, what Kristin Thompson and others have argued as 'the [material] aspects of the [cinematic] work not contained by its unifying forces' (130).[23] As I have argued elsewhere,[24] Sokurov's films deploy excess (which we can liken to Roland Barthes' Third Meaning),[25] misdirection and chance – a 'Sokurovian unconscious' – to counterpose and subvert the 'surface' content of the auteur's work. Effluence is what I want to term the particular form of cinematic excess inherent in the very unusual (singular!) production circumstances of *Russian Ark*. And in this film, the anxiety of effluence – the shadowy twin to the directors' megalomania for control – manifests itself, first and foremost, as the film flub.

Film Flubs

Over the last several years, with the rise of the VCR, DVD player and internet technology, there has emerged a growing body of discourse – most of it produced by non-film specialists – which takes as its object the so-called 'film flub', blooper, goof, error, or 'movie mistake'. In websites with names like Nitpickers.com, Moviemistakes.com and Moviebloopers.com, filmgoers, fans and industry professionals routinely send in shot-by-shot critiques of feature films, pointing out continuity errors, anachronisms, production flaws, etc., often in meticulous detail.

The widely-used Internet Movie Data Base has its own 'Film Flub' section, which encourages submissions by eagle-eyed movie viewers, and several 'movie error' book collections have been published. As one can gather from titles like *Oops!: Movie Mistakes That Made the Cut*, this material is written and consumed for purposes of diversion and the slight sense of empowerment that comes from mocking the flaws in a slick, multi-million-dollar corporate product.

While drawing attention to a peasant with a wrist-watch in a gladiator film may seem anodyne, this sort of critical analysis bears more than passing resemblance to interpretive strategies outlined by Barthes, particularly his concept of the punctum, the 'accidental' detail in the photograph which disrupts its culturally-coded signifying scheme or 'intended meaning' (what he calls the *studium*).[26] Barthes' highly subjective, affective and unstable definition of the punctum in *Camera Lucida* renders it somewhat problematic, though Jennifer Friedlander identifies its salient points in her description:

> Although unintentional, unplanned, unpredictable and uncoded, the punctum...de-naturalizes the image, making what seemed ordinary appear suddenly strange or uncanny, *unheimlich* in the Freudian sense....The punctum points beyond both nature and culture and signals their limitations. In short, the punctum, which cannot be expressed in language, embodies the failure of the symbolic... (100).[27]

For its resistance to a pre-determined representational scheme, Friedlander and critics such as Slavoj Žižek link Barthes's punctum with Jacques Lacan's domain of the 'Real', that which falls outside the realm of the Symbolic and Imaginary orders. For my purposes, the punctum here refers to that 'uncontainable' beyond the director's control, that sliver of the object that cannot be finalisably organised, re-made or smoothed over in representation (unlike, for example, in Sokurov's beloved Hermitage paintings).

In the case of *Russian Ark*, with its imperative to exert maximum directorial control (and concomitant anxiety) over an unruly 'oceanic' crowd moving in real time, with no opportunity for cut-aways or re-takes, the punctum expresses itself repeatedly as the film flub – constantly threatening to shatter Sokurov's elaborate and fragile signifying scheme of 'cinema in one breath'.

And indeed, *Russian Ark* contains innumerable flubs (more, one could argue, than in a film where cutting away would be an option). This despite the fact that, according to the film's German producer Jens Meurer, over 30,000 digital effects were utilised on the film image in post-production,[28] in part to 'erase' mistakes.

I will limit myself to only a small portion of *Russian Ark's* vast film flub 'catalogue', each instance a part of the unavoidable 'effluence' in even the most emblematic of filmic crowd scenes.

Reflections/Shadows
- Just after the title sequence, mere seconds into the film's opening (at 2:14), the crew's reflection is clearly visible in the carriage window out of which the nineteenth-century party exits.
- At 6:48, Büttner's camera makes an appearance, reflected in the lower left of the window through which we gaze into Peter I's private quarters.
- At 11:12, the camera and crew's shadows appear on the set and cast of Catherine's play (unavoidable, as the light source seems to emanate from directly behind the camera).
- As Tamara, the blind woman, and the Marquis leave the Van Dyck room (at 28:51), the camera's shadow again appears, on the wall.

Mysterious figures/Things out of place
- A figure in modern dress appears on the balcony more than once during the Persian ambassadors scene.[29]
- Several guards (just before the Persian ambassadors scene, and during the Sèvres porcelain scene), stand by and order the Marquis to wait or stand aside; according to Sokurov, these were actual Hermitage security men in period dress ensuring the integrity of the art objects or else holding up the action while the set and cast were still setting up.
- During the final ball scene, a cellist's bow comes dangerously close to the camera, and another musician's head pops up unexpectedly into the frame at the end of the music.
- Dreiden's face was apparently itching in some scenes; he incorporated this discomfort into the Marquis' odd mannerisms.[30]

The Problematic Crowd
- Try as they might, several actors and extras look directly into the camera, often to avoid running into it. This is particularly evident in the Persian ambassadors scene (several soldiers in formation, as the camera swoops very close) and the final ball scene. In the latter, one older gentleman in particular looks several times, smiling sheepishly (at, for example, 1:16:32, when he says, 'Wouldn't it be nice to jump about like that?'). Another badaud is a musician in Gerghiev's orchestra (at frame right), who at music's end looks about the room anxiously, as if uncertain where the camera is. He turns (at 1:24:14) and gawks straight at the viewer.
- In the ball scene, the dancers' movements grow awkward whenever the camera approaches for a medium shot; they constrain their limbs unnaturally to avoid hitting it.[31]

- Despite such precautions, a major bump occurs as the camera descends the crowded Jordan staircase at the film's finale. This occurs at 1:29:23 (someone is saying: 'I think we should invite your nephew Varenka. Let him see.'), when the image noticeably jolts; the culprit appears to be a rather ample older lady who enters the frame from below and gazes at the camera, smiling guiltily.
- Once the camera reaches the bottom of the staircase and tracks back, the crowd closes the gap in its wake; the effect is mannered and unnatural.

'The spiritual side ... was not really his field': Control and the Nation

– You understood Sokurov's conception? [Laughter] Or did you?
– I'm not sure. I tried to understand, but I don't know if he understood me, and what I could do for him.
(Menashe in conversation with Büttner)³²

Clearly, the aforementioned aspects of *Russian Ark* (stemming directly from its highly unusual production) make it a fascinating and unique film: a hybrid of cinema, theatre, stunt performance, travelogue and farce. It restores to the movies a sense of live-action, high-wire suspense: Will they pull it off? Will it contain its own effluence? What traces of its mad conception will it betray, and how will these compromise its monomaniacal director's vision? Will the puncta prevail?[33]

As it happened, the film succeeded on its own terms (the film flub peanut gallery notwithstanding); its achievement entered the annals of cinema. Yet an international controversy that erupted after principal photography underscores the depths of Sokurov's nationalist project with *Russian Ark,* and how the issue of control (of the crowd, of the apparatus, even of how to interpret his technical accomplishment) and anxiety over ideological effluence remained at the core of the director's patriotic project.

Still from *Russian Ark*: The Ball.

In 2002, the European Film Academy nominated Sokurov (for Director) and Büttner (for Cinematographer) in its European Film Award competition. However, Sokurov, in a letter dated 19 November 2002, objected to Büttner's nomination, citing his improper designation as cinematographer and called for a reconsideration of the film as a wholly and indivisibly collaborative effort:

> *Russian Ark* is the fruit of the work of a large group of Russian and German filmmakers. As the author of the idea, co-author of the screenplay, director, and creator of the image design of this film, I understand very well the great significance of our production for the history and practice of professional cinema. Therefore the moral aspect of the estimation of such a film is of special importance.
>
> I care a lot about the group of my collaborators and cannot accept any attempt to praise the efforts of some of them without admitting the role of the others. THE FILM SHOULD BE TAKEN AS A WHOLE – only thus the contributions to this unique project of all members of the group and each of them in person could be judged. By the way, *Russian Ark* producers [sic] have known for a long time that the author-director maintains such an attitude to the estimation of the film.[34]

The EFA's non-committal response to Sokurov's objection (they refused to withdraw either nomination) seems to have incensed the director. In a follow-up letter dated 29 November, he and his Russian producer Andrei Deriabin elaborated on the original request:

> As a result of the development of new technologies, it's often impossible to see the borderline at which the technical provisions of the project end and the creative act of forming the image of the film as a whole begins. The realization of this unexpected and complex conception demonstrated that the absolute author of the images of *Russian Ark* is, of course, the director, rather than the steadicam operator. To a large extent, this relates to the complexity of the task that had been set, on one side, and, on the other, to the large number of professional errors that Tilman Büttner committed during the shoot.[35]
>
> The complexity of the task that was set, no doubt, was beyond the professional ability of the steadicam operator because, suddenly, he was confronted by the distant outer horizons of his profession.[36]

Sokurov went on to accuse his German partners of promoting *Russian Ark* solely as a 'phenomenon of German cinematography' and emphasised its status as a 'national Russian project – a project that could only be realized in Russia'. In 'artificially divid[ing] up the film through its nomination for "German 'technological direction"' the director lamented, the EFA was supporting 'destructive processes'.[37] In a second letter Sokurov – apparently again feeling rebuffed – further escalated his rhetoric:

> Your phrasing, to be frank, we have no desire to withdraw the two nominations [...] is a magnificent specimen. And this you write to

a famous director, to the auteur of the film *Russian Ark*, the auteur of more than 50 films. Did I ask whether or not you have a desire? And in general, what does someone's desire have to do with the resolution of problems like this? Only respect, only the unconditional adherence to the requests of an auteur [matter], for an auteur is the primary figure in art. Even if 100 other people stand opposed to this opinion.
IT IS PRECISELY IN THE ACADEMY THAT SUCH A PRINCIPLE SHOULD HOLD SWAY. IF NOT IN THE ACADEMY, THEN WHERE?[38]

Sokurov followed up this angry missive with his resignation from the EFA (European Film Academy), on 9 December.[39] (As it happened, at the 2002 EFA the cinematography award went to Pawel Edelman for Roman Polanski's *The Pianist*, while the director prize went to Pedro Almodóvar for *Talk to Her* [Hable con ella, 2002].)

Several things stand out about this episode: Sokurov's insistence on the collective nature of the project, while paradoxically promoting himself as the undisputed leader to whom one owes 'unconditional adherence'; his diminution of Büttner's role to steadicam operator rather than cinematographer, despite the German's extensive creative work in lighting all 33 rooms featured in the Hermitage[40]; the director's exaggeratedly territorial claims for this German co-production as an exclusively Russian national project; his binary opposition between a 'primary' lone auteur figure and 100 others (a crowd?) whose views should always remain subordinate.

Sokurov's declarations on what he considered Büttner's shortcomings did not end with the EFA episode. As he back-handedly elaborated to an interviewer:

> First of all, we had a problem with the image. The cameraman with whom I collaborated on this film had been suggested (due to various circumstances, first of all economical) by the German co-producers, and for me this was a chance encounter. For him, I suspect, I was also an alien problem as a director. The artistic tasks I was giving him were too unusual for him. Tilman Büttner is a strong and hardy man. He was diligently preparing himself for physical work, which was hard indeed: he had to carry on his waist more than 30 kilos. But the spiritual side of this film – the most significant for its artistic result – was not really his field. Perhaps, if we had been shooting the Olympic Games, he would have been in the right place.[41]

For his part, Büttner noted his collaboration with Sokurov on matters both technical and aesthetic – though he admitted the relationship had soured. As he told Menashe:

> We really didn't have any conflicts as such, but by the end I felt there was a loss of trust. I did my best, but I think Sokurov wasn't satisfied. He didn't show or express that, but I felt it. I think he would have liked to run the camera himself, so in a way it was natural for him

> to be dissatisfied. But he isn't familiar with new camera technology; he thinks in terms of 35mm film. Exposure works differently with video, its reaction to light is different.... He wanted to shoot without light. Impossible, I told him; you would have no picture on the monitor if you use no lighting with this camera.⁴²

What emerges here – apart from notions of the 'right' to Russian primacy in European auteur cinema co-productions – is a (nationalistically-charged) confrontation to determine the creative vision of the film, i.e. the director's highly personal vision of Russia, and, given its odd production requirements, an argument over the best means to achieve it – with Sokurov on one side, Büttner on the other. Strikingly, several commentators and critics, in addressing *Russian Ark* and its production, likewise tended to split along national lines. Svetlana Proskurina, who witnessed the principal photography on 21 December 2001 and later observed the post-production work, defended Sokurov's selective history of Russia, calling it a very personal artistic vision. She moreover reiterated Sokurov's characterization of the shoot as a group effort, indeed a 'brotherhood' in which 'professional boundaries don't matter, you don't feel the need to figure out who is the cinematographer, who the auteur, who wrote the dialogues – you don't want to know any of that, nothing except the common, collective task'.⁴³ Though she makes no mention of Büttner, Proskurina does note Sokurov's steady hand guiding the camera, speeding it up, slowing it down, and marvels at the technical capacities of high definition video that make the unique shoot possible. Yet mark her curious elision:

> I believe that such technology gives the director a new, unprecedented level of freedom. Not so much that one can get by without a cinematographer. But then, later, *without his participation*, one can correct a great number of mistakes, one's own as well as the operator's, to delete, let's say, some spot of inappropriate colour, to define an angle more precisely.⁴⁴

For his part, in his postmodernist critique of the film Dragan Kujundzic interprets the Sokurov-Büttner incident as a symptom of the director's totalizing, chauvinist, grand-narrative impulse:

> It is as if the director has to extract precisely the otherness of the technical mastery from the very achievement of the movie in the name of the purity of ethnic origin. That anxiety, needless to say, which in the movie is energized and turned into the creative impetus of the film, here appears as the blind spot, and incapacity to see the ideological implications of this protest against the very genealogy of the movie. Sokurov appears as the jealous twin of his European (br)other.⁴⁵

Similarly, Isabelle de Keghel reads the row as stemming from an age-old insecurity over, as Kachurin and Zitser put it, 'Russia's perennial indebtedness to Western models'.⁴⁶ In this view, Sokurov's mastery over the project is stymied by the 'soulless' technocratic German cinematographer who – like all the rest of the crowd's effluence – must be contained and disciplined, symbolically if not in actuality:

> [Sokurov's] viewpoint is identical with the camera view and this defines the visual experience of the film,[47] providing a clear hierarchy within its intercultural value system. This is even evident on the production level where the architecture of cooperation was constructed to correspond to Sokurov's understanding of the German and Russian national characters: the German side was entrusted with the technical side of the project, whereas the Russian side maintained control of the artistic work. Thus, despite its intercultural ambience, Sokurov ultimately deploys the notion of a dialogue between Russian [sic] and Europe in order to claim *Russian Ark* as a decidedly 'native' project, one, moreover, which presents a culturally hegemonic view of Russian identity.[48]

In this, de Keghel continues, Sokurov's marginalization of Büttner echoes the film's tussle between the Narrator (voiced by Sokurov) and the Marquis (based in large part on the Marquis de Custine, a noted Russia-basher). And in that engagement, as seen in the film's conclusion, Sokurov holds all the cards.[49]

Conclusion: Death by Crowd?

> Sokurov is concerned with a collectivity held together by linkages of cultural value and political power for which the figure of the empire [...] serves as a recurrent interpretive frame. [...] Sokurov's universe is chaotically diverse, inhabited by an internally stratified cultural elite and a distant, even Orientalized mass.[50]

Sokurov's digital magic trick is a bravura piece of cinema, made by a director at the height of his powers, at the dawn of a new century poised for Russia's resurgence under the young Putin administration. Not unlike launching the first man into space, vanquishing fascism or achieving superpowerhood, it is an act of determination, drive, imagination, and breath-taking courage; its achievement is ideological, national, no less than aesthetic.

> Indeed, *Russian Ark* may be seen as [Sokurov's] assertion that a contemporary Russian artist can rely on Western models (for example, such single-shot films as Alfred Hitchcock's *Rope*) and technology (high-definition video camera and the foreign expert to operate it) and still produce a work of striking originality.[51]

Russian Ark's culminating staircase scene (with its hundreds of cast members in pre-revolutionary dress languidly descending the steps) incarnates Sokurov's most overt evocation of *sobornost'*, allying his beloved European high culture with traditional Russian religious-nationalist sentiment. A mobile version of Ilya Glazunov's *Eternal Russia*,[52] as well as a restaging of his own *Evening Sacrifice* (only now with a 'trained' crowd), the procession calls for solemn contemplation of the 'Russia that we lost'. It functions too as a repudiation of Soviet cinema, since it 'de-montages' and inverts the ending of Vsevolod Pudovkin's *The End of St. Petersburg* [Konets Sankt-Peterburga, 1927].[53] Critics rightly point out this scene as among Sokurov's most ideologically loaded and backward-gazing.

Indeed, Schnapp's discussion of the nostalgic venues that served as the locations for Italian Fascist rallies find a disconcerting resonance with the marble staircase scene (to say nothing of Putin-era 'great power' nostalgia):

> Architectural settings – Roman ruins, Renaissance and Baroque palaces, squares from the Risorgimento period – remind the viewer that the crowd is not the timeless, placeless, faceless socialist crowd rallying around abstract principles, but rather a *national* crowd, shaped by a national sense of place and tradition, and rallying around principles delimited by time and space.[54]

And yet, Sokurov's pure nationalist vision of Russia's immortals descending the staircase is 'marred', as discussed, first by the obvious wide berth given the cameraman by the streaming throng, with many of them all too blatantly trying not to look at the device (and often failing); second, the crowd closing the gap once the camera has passed, like the fast-sealing wake of a boat – which only announces its ghostly presence all the more; and third, the perceptible bump as Büttner turns on the landing (followed by the stout woman's entry into the frame, uncomfortable, guilty-looking). For the careful viewer, such 'effluent' slip-ups, if not disastrous, constantly threaten to turn Sokurov's traditionalist posturings into the stuff of farce.

For all that, *Russian Ark*'s atmosphere of high-wire anxiety contributes enormously to its audiences' spectatorial pleasure, as does the palpable sense that the huge burden for this ludicrous artistic venture is, in the end,

Still from *Russian Ark*: The Guests leaving the Ball.

borne by one man, the director. This auteur, who would ordinarily wield absolute control on the set – the power to yell, 'Cut! Do it again!' – has willingly neutered himself, and now hangs on the mercy of a nameless mass (cast, crew), which any second could destroy his picture with a stumble, a missed cue, a fatal flub. Far from the absolutist, monomaniacal tyrant, then, Sokurov stands revealed as a slave to contingency – to over 4,700 contingencies, in fact.

No coincidence, then, that *Russian Ark*'s grandest, most impressive set-piece after the 1913 ball depicts Nicholas I welcoming a Persian delegation. They have come to apologise for the poet/statesman Alexander Griboedov's 1829 murder at the hands of a Tehran mob. The scene, nearly an hour into Sokurov's daredevil act, recalls and recoups the director's worst fear: symbolic death by crowd.[55]

As I have argued, we can trace Sokurov's unseemly, xenophobic derogation of Büttner to his 'anxiety of effluence'; the German is after all the first of 4,700 whom the director must discipline – the main, most recalcitrant 'oceanic' obstacle (as much as implement) to the purity of his 'emblematic' vision. Like the Marquis, Büttner has the capacity to stray, disappear, decide his own way (recall that in end, the Marquis elects to stay put); like the Narrator, Sokurov has the power (the patriotic duty) to put him in his place.

What we see on screen, then – despite years of preparation, despite whatever digital correctives get introduced in post-production – is the spectral auteur at his most helpless, lost in the labyrinth of the Hermitage for 90 minutes of Bazinian *real time*. Unmoored, knifeless, with a stranger at the wheel, Sokurov wanders the dark corridors; around every corner: the oceanic masses, threatening to capsize his visionary ark – not with swells or tsunamis, but the mere prickly puncta of faces, grinning dumbly, at sea.

Notes

1. Alexandra Tuchinskaya, 'Interview with Alexander Sokurov' (2002), *Island of Sokurov* http://www.sokurov.spb.ru/island_en/feature_films/russkyi_kovcheg/mnp_ark.html (accessed 30 July 2009).
2. Siegfried Kracauer, *The Mass Ornament: Weimar Essays*, Cambridge: Harvard UP, 1995, p. 77.
3. Louis Menashe, 'Filming Sokurov's "Russian Ark": An Interview with Tilman Büttner', *Cineaste*, 28.3 (2003), pp. 21–23 (p.21).
4. Condee deems *Russian Ark* neither typical nor representative of Sokurov's work (*The Imperial Trace*, p.160) – though this has not prevented it from becoming by far the director's best-known work in the West. For his part, Menashe calls the film 'an anti-Sokurov carnival' (Menashe, p. 21).
5. Menashe, p. 21. For technically-driven reports on the film and its daring one-shot technique, see Jean Oppenheimer, 'Tour de Force', *American Cinematographer*, January 2003, pp. 84–95 and Natal'ia Sirivlia, 'Svetlana Proskurina: glazami ochevidtsa', *Iskusstvo kino* 7 (2002), http://www.kinoart.ru/magazine/07–2002/now/proskurina (accessed 30 July 2009).
6. Gustave LeBon, *The Crowd: A Study of the Popular Mind*, New York: Viking, 1960, p. 14.
7. Elias Canetti, *Crowds and Power*, New York: Macmillan, 1984, p. 16.

8   Jeffrey Schnapp, 'Mob Porn', in Jeffrey Schnapp and Matthew Tiews (eds), *Crowds*, Stanford: Stanford UP, 2006, pp. 1–46 (p.2).
9   Schnapp, p.12.
10 Michael Tratner, *Crowd Scenes: Movies and Mass Politics*, New York: Fordham University Press, 2008, pp. 81–82.
11 Schnapp, p. 12. My too-brief foray into Schnapp's thesis has hopefully not diluted it. Suffice it to say that his examples – taking in ancient Greek accounts, Renaissance painting, photographs of Italian Fascist mass rallies and Soviet photomontage, among other things – build a compelling case. The tension between the emblematic/oceanic crowds also appears in propaganda meant to critique the modern-day sovereign; see the anti-George Bush photomontage *The War President*, which constructs a portrait of the former US leader from pictures of Iraq war victims, originally posted to the blog *American Leftist* on 7 April 2004.
12 Anna Tolstova, "'Marsh entuziastov" v galeree "Kovcheg"', *Kommersant*, 23 November 2007, http://www.kommersant.ru/doc.aspx?DocsID=827202 (accessed 30 July 2009). The exhibit was devoted to twentieth-century, primarily Soviet, art. Apart from rallies, protests, soldiers in formation, etc., the show also featured depictions of ordinary citizens standing in line for consumer goods, bathhouses, and the like. As noted by Maksim Krekotnev: 'The ongoing "March of the Enthusiasts" displays mainly provincial works devoted to a wide-ranging phenomenon, momentous for Russia, in which a mythical collectivism and *sobornost'* smoothly flow into the collectivity of frenzied rallies and other state machines formed from human bodies. To this we can also add the surprising level of unanimity in the pre-electoral upsurge of propaganda observed today, which the show's organisers themselves do nothing to hide'. Maksim Krekotnev, 'Marsh posle orgazma', *Gazeta.ru*, 28 November 2007, http://www.gazeta.ru/culture/2007/11/28/a_2355794.shtml (accessed 30 July 2009).
13 Sigmund Freud, 'On Transience' [1915], in James Strachey (ed.), *Standard Edition of the Complete Psychological Works of Sigmund Freud*, vol. 14, London: Hogarth Press, 1957, pp. 305–08 (p. 305).
14 Postmodernist critique: Dragan Kujundzic, 'After "After": The "Arkive" Fever of Alexander Sokurov', *ArtMargins*, 5 May 2003, http://www.artmargins.com/content/cineview/kujundzic.html (accessed 30 July 2009); conceptualist: Oleg Kovalov, 'Russkii kontekst', *Iskusstvo kino* 7 (2003), http://www.kinoart.ru/magazine/07-2003/repertoire/kovcheg/ (accessed 30 July 2009); post-postmodernist: Raoul Eshelman, 'Sokurov's "Russian Ark" and the End of Postmodernism', *ArtMargins*, 30 July 2003, http://www.artmargins.com/content/cineview/eshelman.html (accessed 30 July 2009); historiographic: Pamela Kachurin and Ernest A. Zitser, 'After the Deluge: "Russian Ark" and the Abuses of History', *NewsNet* 43.4 (2003), pp. 17–22 (also at http://www.bu.edu/historic/hs/julyaugust06.html#kachurin_zitser (accessed 12 September 2010); aesthetic: Tim Harte, 'A Visit to the Museum: Aleksandr Sokurov's *Russian Ark* and the Framing of the Eternal', *Slavic Review* 64.1 (2005), pp. 41–58.
15 For some skeptical reviews, see Mikhail Brashinskii, 'Russkii kovcheg', *Afisha* 15 April 2003, http://www.afisha.ru/movie/171260/review/147590/ (accessed 30 July 2009); and Dmitrii Komm, 'Kovcheg bez potopa', *Neprikosnovennyi zapas*, 3/29 (2003), http://magazines.russ.ru/nz/2003/29/komm.html (accessed 30 July 2009).
16 Though this is, to be precise, misleading: the film has no edits, but it actually contains two shots; the second comes at the end, when an image of the frozen Baltic Sea digitally replaces the Neva River.

17 '...the continuous shot is only a medium – not the aim, nor the artistic task' (Tuchinskaya, 'Interview').
18 As noted by the critic Roger Ebert, 'Every review of *Russian Ark* begins by discussing its method' (Ebert, 'Russian Ark', *Chicago Sun Times*, 31 January 2003). http://rogerebert.suntimes.com/apps/pbcs.dll/article?AID=/20030131/REVIEWS/301310304/1023 (accessed 30 July 2009). For an informative discussion of the film in relation to other movies that utilise long takes, see Alan Bacchus, 'The Long Take', *Daily Film Dose*, 4 May 2007, http://www.dailyfilmdose.com/2007/05/long-take.html (accessed 30 July 2009).
19 Stuart Klawans, 'Haunted Hermitage', *The Nation*, 14 October 2002, http://www.thenation.com/doc/20021014/klawans (accessed 30 July 2009).
20 Condee, p. 177.
21 Arkadii Ippolitov, 'Mir-Rossiia-Petersburg-Ermitazh', in *Sokurov 2*, pp. 282–91 (p. 282).
22 Interview with Alexander Sokurov, 9 April 2001 at http://www.russianark.spb.ru/eng/film_socurov.html (link no longer active).
23 Kristin Thompson, 'The Concept of Cinematic Excess', in Philip Rosen (ed.), *Narrative, Apparatus, Ideology*, New York: Columbia UP, 1986, pp. 130–142.
24 Alaniz, '"Nature", Illusion and Excess ...'.
25 Although Thompson identifies some differences between excess and the third or obtuse meaning, Barthes notes a similar anti-narratival quality in cinematic representation which, among other things, escapes the intent of the film-maker (he cites Eisenstein's *Ivan the Terrible I and II*): 'It is clear that the obtuse meaning is the epitome of a counter-narrative; disseminated, reversible, set to its own temporality, it inevitably determines (if one follows it) a quite different analytical segmentation to that in shots, sequences, syntagms (technical or narrative): counterlogical and yet "true." Imagine "following" not Euphrosyne's schemings, nor even, again, the face of the Wicked Mother, but merely, in this face, this attitude, this black veil, the heavy, ugly flatness – you will then have a different time-scale, neither diegetic nor oneiric, a different film' (Roland Barthes, *Image, Music, Text*, New York: MacMillan, 1988, p. 63).
26 Barthes, *Camera Lucida*. Barthes' arguments in *Camera Lucida* were anticipated in, among other works, the Third Meaning essay.
27 Jennifer Friedlander, 'How Should a Woman Look?: Scopic Strategies for Sexuated Subjects', *Journal for the Psychoanalysis of Culture & Society* 8.1 (2003), pp. 99–108.
28 He mentions this on the producer's commentary track of the *Russian Ark* DVD. On post-production digital corrections, see Oppenheimer, p. 94.
29 Peter Bradshaw may be referring to this man when he writes: '... at one stage a bewigged gentleman, bent double, is seen scampering out of shot. But this only heightens the sense of witnessing an extraordinary, one-off event: a ballet in which the camera itself is the principal dancer, never off stage'; see Bradshaw, 'Breathtaking History of Russia', *The Guardian*, 10 April 2003; http://www.cdi.org/russia/252-18.cfm (accessed 30 July 2009).
30 Also, one of the three false starts was caused by Dreiden flubbing a line. The crew pulled off the shoot in the fourth (and last possible) take.
31 Büttner told an interviewer: 'Sometimes the actors and extras had to improvise their movements and positions during the shooting because of mistakes we made'; Menashe, p. 23.
32 Menashe, p. 22.
33 As Halligan puts it: 'through the use of what is effectively a single set-up, the film achieves a freshness and a sense of the unexpected just around the corner, making for a frisson of reality in this real-time timelessness'; Benjamin

Halligan, 'The Remaining Second World: Sokurov and "Russian Ark"', *Senses of Cinema*, February 2003, http://archive.sensesofcinema.com/contents/03/25/russian_ark.html (accessed 30 July 2009).

34 Alexander Sokurov, 'To the European Film Awards 2002', *Island of Sokurov*, 19 November 2002, http://www.sokurov.spb.ru/island_en/ans_1.html (accessed 30 July 2009); emphasis in original.

35 Among these 'errors', presumably, Sokurov counts the innumerable film flubs – which, as discussed, were in any case all but unavoidable given the nature of the shoot (and, I would add, the nature of cinema in general).

36 Alexander Sokurov and Andrei Deriabin, 'Refusal to take part in the ceremony for the awarding of prizes by the EFA in December, 2002', *Island of Sokurov* 29 November 2002. http://www.sokurov.spb.ru/island_en/ans_2.html (accessed 30 July 2009).

37 Sokurov and Deriabin, 29 November 2002.

38 Alexander Sokurov, 'Letter from A.N. Sokurov of November 29, 2002', *Island of Sokurov* 29 November 2002, http://www.sokurov.spb.ru/promo/russian_ark/ru/ark_fin2.html (accessed 30 July 2009); emphasis in original.

39 Alexander Sokurov, 'Letter from A. N. Sokurov of December 9, 2002', http://www.sokurov.spb.ru/promo/russian_ark/ru/ark_fin4.html (accessed 30 July 2009).

40 Büttner, in fact, played a significant role in crafting the look of *Russian Ark*, having worked with Sokurov on pre-production for 18 months, ultimately convincing the director that the Sony HDW-F900 24p High Definition camera was the best equipped to handle the innumerable lighting challenges posed by the film. Büttner was familiar with the camera, since his Berlin company had been the first in Germany to acquire one. As he told an interviewer: 'The story was Sokurov's alone, but it was possible for me to point out how certain positions and movements would help the story' (Menashe, p. 22). He elaborated to Jeremiah Kipp: 'It would have been much too complicated to divide the responsibilities among three people: steadicam operator, director of photography, and lighting designer. And I wanted to prove that I was not just a steadicam operator, but a full photographer as well' ('The March of Time: Jeremiah Kipp Interviews "Russian Ark" Director of Photography Tilman Büttner', *Filmmaker*, 4 December 2002, http://www.filmmakermagazine.com/archives/online_features/march_of_time.php (accessed 30 July 2009). Finally, Büttner is listed in all sources (the film's credits, production records, even Sokurov's own website, not as steadicam operator but as director of photography (*operator*).

41 Tuchinskaya, 'Interview'. Büttner's most notable work before *Russian Ark* was as steadicam operator for the celebrated action sequences in Tom Tykwer's *Run Lola Run* [Lola rennt, 1998]. Sokurov seems to be taking a swipe at that old job.

42 See Menashe. Sokurov had previously served as his own director of photography on *Taurus* and *Sun*.

43 Sirivlia, 'Svetlana Proskurina: glazami ochevidtsa'.

44 Sirivlia, my emphasis. The critic Raoul Eshelman is one of the few Westerners to side with the Russians, despite his acknowledgement of Büttner's 'self-mortification' for the sake of the film: 'Sokurov's protest regarding the prize awarded [sic] to his German cameraman, though disconcerting in terms of its nationalist conceit, is at least understandable from an aesthetic point of view: the long camera shot and the director's *mise-en-scène* are not meant to be cut apart anywhere, at any time'. (Though one wonders how a prize nomination cuts apart anything.)

45 Kujundzic, 'After "After"...', *ArtMargins* 5 May 2003
46 Kachurin and Zitser, 'After the Deluge...', pp. 17–22.
47 Or at least he wishes it so; but can we not argue that the viewpoint is in fact identical with *Büttner's*, who as the person physically guiding the camera, whose actions cannot be corrected or repurposed through montage in this edit-less film, functions as the implacable intermediary between Sokurov and his cherished vision?
48 Isabelle de Keghel, 'Sokurov's "Russian Ark": Reflections on the Russia/Europe Theme' in Stephen Hutchings (ed.), *Russia and Its Other(s) on Film*, New York and Basingstoke: Palgrave Macmillan, 2008, pp.77–94 (p. 91).
49 'The Russian narrator's full knowledge of Russian and Soviet history gives him an advantage over his European guest. This enables him to distance himself from the European's statements by changing his intonation as he repeats them, portraying the guest as an observer who, as a result of his preconceived views, misunderstands things'; de Keghel, p. 88.
50 Condee, p. 160.
51 Kachurin and Zitser.
52 The Slavophile artist Ilya Glazunov's mammoth canvas *Eternal Russia* (1988), commemorating a thousand years of Christianity, depicts a procession of Russian martyrs, saints, and historical figures, grouped very similarly to the crowd in Sokurov's final set-piece.
53 On this, see de Keghel, p. 78 and Kujundzic. It also refutes Eisenstein's *October* and Sergei Bondarchuk's *War and Peace* [Voina i mir, 1967], which both made use of the Jordan staircase and, as in Pudovkin's film, showed the figures walking in the opposite direction to Sokurov's vision.
54 Schnapp, p. 20, my emphasis.
55 And this scene, too, as we have shown, is flub-heavy, puncta-plagued: soldiers eyeing the camera, the figure that scampers away on the balcony.

CHAPTER 11

AND THE ARK SAILS ON ...
Birgit Beumers

The filming of Sokurov's *Russian Ark* took place on 23 December 2001, the shortest day in the year, in the Hermitage Museum in St Petersburg, leaving just four hours of daylight during the polar nights for the 90-minute-long tracking shot filmed by the director of photography Tilman Büttner and recorded directly in HD digital onto hard disk, with sound and images mastered in post-production. There is not a single cut in this film. Yet when it reached distribution, *Russian Ark* was generally screened from 35mm prints, which come on separate reels to the projectionist who mounts the entire film onto a large reel, sticking the individual film strips together with tape.

Thus, the technical feat – the take in one breath – that so many reviewers have commented upon, is fragmented during the projection. The aim for perfection during the shooting – with the crowd management and the flubs only partly corrected in post-production, as José Alaniz has shown – leaves us wondering then about the purpose of this high-tech exercise. Sokurov has outdone Tarkovsky in the length of shot; he has opposed Vertov's and Eisenstein's montage, even if only on a technical level, because his distortion of historical space and time is just as manipulative as that of the great masters in *October* or *The Battleship Potemkin*.

I want to explore here the motivation for the long take by examining the artistic images viewed and the scenes enacted on the historical journey in the space of a museum in order to define Sokurov's view of the art of cinema, less so in its place in the hierarchy of art forms, as in the use of the camera to capture images – still and moving, on canvas and live action. Much has been written about frames and thresholds, delineating the ephemeral from the eternal, that place *Russian Ark* firmly into the thematic scope of Sokurov's oeuvre, preoccupied with morbidity and death;[1] about the entrapment of history in a museum space;[2] or about the archivisation of artefacts.[3] Likewise, the dilemma of Sokurov's view on Russia's national and cultural identity has been discussed at length, as a 'creative appropriation of the Western cultural tradition',[4] or as imitative: 'The dramatic tension of the movie as it pertains to the question of identification (and the Russian national identity, for example), lies in the fact that the space of commemoration relies also on artifacts that have nothing to do with Russia, but are entirely imported from the West...'.[5] However, in the light of the film's (and film-maker's) preoccupation with the Hermitage's space, which is used both to gaze at the museum's art objects and to re-enact historical events in the former imperial palace, the film oscillates between a representation of history through performance and through visual art. The camera captures both theatrical enactment (in motion) and painting (fixed image), (self)-reflecting on the optical and technical device that records both movement and stasis, that plays the role of director-choreographer and of the painter, here a predecessor of still photography. The oscillation between fixed image and moving image is further intensified by two discursive lines: a Narrator who has no face, and no memory of the past, but who seems to know the future/destiny of Russia; and a Visitor who remembers a past that becomes the present (through the enactment), but who has no knowledge of the future as he remains inside the museum space at the end of the journey. In this context, the rejection of filmic cuts in order to create the illusion of a temporal flow leads to another kind of montage that juxtaposes the content in the frame (the canvas) with the theatre performances in the architectural space, synthesised, as it were, by the ultimate tool of the film camera. Sokurov assembles two parallel discourses, of representation and performance, breaking the chronology of the enacted scenes through the histories told on canvas, within the (pictorial) frame. That frame (of the painting) is as selective as the lens of the camera which singles out scenes, tilts and turns, as it follows the gaze of the Visitor.

I suggest that Sokurov uses the camera to elevate cinematic art as capable not of creating and remaking the past, but of erasing it: between the painted and performed scenes lie the 'real stories', the gaps that are blanked out. Kujundzic has spoken of the 'vigilant erasure of the entire Soviet period',[6] but I would go further than that: Sokurov's long take of the galleries, loggias, gardens, halls and staircases of the Hermitage is a funeral procession, leading to the burial of the once glorious past in the murky waters of the Neva: what remains are the paintings, which are but a pale reflection of that which is no longer, and which therefore cannot be captured on celluloid (rather, HD). Sokurov rejects film as a medium to capture, record or (re-)create history: images are only façades (performative and framed), with the camera wavering between (performance) stages and frames. In this reading, the excursion into the room with the empty frames (of paintings evacuated during the siege) draws attention to the (relative) absence of visual records of the siege – intensified and elaborated in the static image vs. acoustic/aural 'animation' of the siege memoirs in Sokurov's *We Read the Book of the Blockade* (2009). Sokurov may rank visual art over cinema; he may assert that art captures the eternal, while the camera's lens sees the transient; however, his camera creates the ultimate content (the void) at the film's end.

A Virtual Journey

The journey through the museum space is a journey through time performed by the invisible Narrator, who speaks with Sokurov's voice, and Astolphe, Marquis de Custine, who visited Russia in 1839 (played by Sergei Dreiden [Dontsov]). History unfolds chronologically, from Peter the Great and ending with Nicholas II, and yet Custine's status in this chronological unfolding shifts. In the Hermitage's state apartments, he passes through unnoticed; meanwhile, in the rooms with collections of European art – populated by contemporary visitors and people from different centuries – Custine is visible and converses with the visitors. To compound this intricacy, not all the paintings he sees were actually in the possession of the museum at the time of Custine's visit to Russia.

In compressing 300 years into 90 minutes Sokurov collapses time in curious ways. On the one hand, there are enacted, performed scenes from the life of the Russian tsars: Peter the Great bashes his general; Catherine the Great attends a rehearsal in the theatre; Nicholas I receives the Persian ambassador to accept an apology for the murder of Russian diplomats, among them the poet Alexander Griboedov, in Tehran; and Nicholas II has breakfast with his wife Alexandra and his children. This sequence of historical events ends with the finale, the last ball in the Winter Palace in 1913, on the eve of the Great War, celebrating the tercentenary of the Romanov dynasty. On the other hand, there are characters of different epochs, rupturing the neat chronology of the Romanov dynasty: Valeri Gerghiev conduct's the Mariinsky Theatre's orchestra, playing the mazurka from Glinka's *Life of a Tsar* (*Ivan Susanin*, 1836). Two past and the current directors of the Hermitage Museum – all Orientalists – discuss problems of conservation and worry about the authorities' lack of understanding of cultural heritage: the Armenian-born Hovsep (Iosif) Orbeli (1887–1961),

Still from *Russian Ark*: Custine enters the Raphael Loggias.

director of the Hermitage from 1934 to 1951; and Boris Piotrovsky (1908–90), director of the museum since 1964, and his son, the current director, Mikhail Piotrovsky. Contemporary visitors (students and sailors) and public figures (the dancer Alla Osipenko, the blind artist Tamara Kurenkova, the pathologist Oleg Khmelnitsky and the actor Lev Yeliseev) stand next to historical characters in the museum. The Marquis twice comments on the smell of oil paint and formaldehyde, a collapse of past (the fresh paint) and present (the preserved art object). Moreover, time passes at the speed of breath: the Empress Catherine is a young woman during the rehearsal at the Hermitage Theatre; a few rooms later she is an old woman, running off into the Hanging Gardens to get some fresh air. Similarly, the guests who arrive for the ball along with the Marquis and the Narrator at the film's beginning reappear 85 minutes – and 300 years – later for the ball. Some rooms contain future history, from the perspective of the oblivious Marquis: a room with empty hoar-frosted frames remind us of the Leningrad siege, when canvasses were evacuated to Sverdlovsk (Ekaterinburg). The journey through the space of the past is a journey through time, but the two never intersect. History flows chronologically, yet it co-exists simultaneously with the present (the visitors in the museum) and other epochs (represented on canvas).

Custine is a figure beyond space and beyond time. The historical Custine visited the Hermitage in 1839 after a fire had destroyed large sections of the actual building in 1837. However, in *Russian Ark* he moves essentially through rooms designed by Leo von Klenze in 1851. Of the original building, only the rooms of the imperial apartments had been restored in 1837 by Vasili Stasov, largely drawing on the original designs by Auguste de Montferrand and Giacomo Quarenghi. While the spaces filled by historical figures were actually visited by Custine, his visit to the Hermitage's art collection takes him to a virtual space, to rooms that he could not have visited in 1839. It is also curious to note here that the Russian art collection contained in rooms that had been restored by Karl Briullov in 1837 are removed from Custine's path. Sokurov thus grants Custine a view into the 'ark', into the space of an art collection that he was unable to see in its full glory in 1839. Therefore Custine's comments on these paintings are crucial for an understanding of the assessment that Sokurov gives to his main character, whose historical and political observations we know full well from his memoirs. Custine gazes at a number of pictures that were not in the Hermitage in 1839, notably Stanzione, Canova, Tenerani, and El Greco. However, he does not differentiate in his commentary on paintings by way of indicating whether he is seeing a painting for the first time on his present tour with Sokurov, or whether he has seen a work before.

The Museum's Guide: Custine

Sokurov guides his viewer on the journey through the Hermitage not with an authorial narrative, but through the character of Astolphe, Marquis de Custine, the French aristocrat who visited Russia in 1839 in an attempt to find there a justification for an absolute monarchy. He returned to France a convinced republican. The choice of Custine as a guide deserves a short excursion into the Marquis's life. Custine was born in 1790 into a French aristocratic family, but his father and grandfather fell victim to the terror after the Revolution and were guillotined in 1792. His mother, Delphine, overwhelmed her only child with love, and it was through her protectionism that he was assigned posts as a military commissioner and later as aide to Talleyrand during the Congress of Vienna. Delphine also arranged a marriage for him, hushing up his homosexual orientation. Custine was no diplomat; his vocation lay in travel and literature, and after several personal tragedies he gained recognition for his travel account of a journey to Spain in 1838. His success, together with the publication of Alexis de Tocqueville's *Democracy in America* (1835), led him to venture on a trip to Russia as a country that, like Spain, only partly belonged to European traditions while offering a possible 'cure' from French republicanism.[7] Custine's account of his visit to Russia brought him success as a writer, while his harsh and cynical account of Russian despotism was banned in Russia. Custine finds Russia a terrifying police state, a country where people lie bluntly to the foreign visitor and erect a façade of splendour and entertainment to hide chaos; where the ruling despot is adored by his slaves, who live in their misery only to be rewarded with salvation in death; where neither the church has any moral authority nor the nobility any duties. Russia is a country that lacks a national identity, imitating Europe instead:

> I do not blame the Russians for being what they are; I blame them for pretending to be what we are. They are still uneducated – this condition, at least, leaves the field open for hope. But I see them endlessly possessed with a mania for imitating other nations, and they imitate them in the manner of monkeys, making what they copy ridiculous. [...] Wavering for four centuries between Europe and Asia, Russia has not yet succeeded through its own efforts in making its mark in the history of the human spirit because its national character has been effaced by borrowings.[8]

The use of Custine as a guide through Russian history is thus an ambivalent gesture on the part of the Russian film-maker. He is, above all, a character out of time and out of space. Custine actually confuses the Hermitage with Chambord at one point, and the film never refers to the year of his actual visit, 1839. He is almost ghost-like, remaining invisible to some and being chased away by others. Custine's comments are aggressive and cynical. He has no esteem for Russian culture or history, as is clear from his *Russia in 1839*, yet he enjoys the splendour.

During his walk through the Museum and Russia's past Custine is engaged in a conversation with an invisible character reminiscent of the men Custine suspected of following him during his 1839 visit ('They refuse you nothing, but they accompany you everywhere: courtesy becomes a means of surveillance here').[9] The Narrator himself is lost, though: he is not sure what happened. Some catastrophe eclipsed the past, making the Narrator uncertain about his own identity and role, and suspecting that the spectacle he is about to witness has been staged for him rather than expecting to take a part in the performance: the film-maker sways between the role of spectator and actor, between guide and visitor. Sokurov's own approach to the film's staging of history finds justification and legitimisation in Custine's criticism of the theatricalisation of Russian court life:

> The more one sees what court life is, the more one sympathizes with the lot of the man who is obliged to direct it – especially the court of Russia. It produces the effect of a theatre where the actors spend their lives in dress rehearsals. No one knows his role and the day of the presentation never arrives as the director is never satisfied with the performance of his subjects. Actors and directors thus waste their lives preparing, correcting, endlessly perfecting their interminable comedy of society...[10]

The Narrator remains vague and passive in his defence of Russia from Custine's attacks; he guards Custine from intruding into the past if there is a danger of his presence being inappropriate; he hurries him on and tries to prevent him from seeing the future (Revolution, Second World War). Often he repeats Custine's words with an ironic tone in his voice, yet he never contradicts, argues, or offers an alternative view to Custine's assessment of Russia. His assessment of Russia as a country without national identity stands uncontradicted, as the Narrator's voice accompanies and counterpoints Custine's intonations, but never engages him in a dialogue, thus confirming Custine's judgement that Russia has no ideas and no opinions: 'Russia is a nation of mutes [...] Nothing is lacking in Russia... except liberty, that is to say life'.[11]

The Marquis de Custine abhors Russia's despotism. He begins by commenting on Peter the Great, comparing him to the despots Alexander the Great and Timur in discussing that he had his own son Alexis killed. At this point the Narrator tries to contradict, pointing out that Peter taught Russia how to have fun. Yet Custine is not impressed by the Russian fêtes, poor imitations of European balls. He dislikes Petersburg, the 'chimera' on the swamp. Custine believes only in European culture: the orchestra in the Hermitage Theatre must be European, and Glinka must be a German composer. He clearly invests no confidence in Russia as a country with its own culture. And quite rightly so: what he sees during his tour of the Hermitage is exclusively Western art. Like Custine, Sokurov denies Russia the right of its own culture, its own voice and its indigenous tradition. Russia is a ship that is never going to dock, neither on Europe nor on Asia. 'One has to come to Russia to see the result of this terrible combination of the intelligence and the science of Europe with the genius of Asia'.[12] Even Custine's obsession that Petersburg will be destroyed or perish is adopted by Sokurov in the final images of the film: 'The Baltic Sea with its sombre shades and its little travelled waters proclaims the proximity of a continent deprived of inhabitants by the rigours of the climate. There the barren shores harmonize with the cold and empty sea. The dreariness of the earth, of the sky, and the cold tinge of the waters, chill the heart of a traveller'.[13]

Russia has seen its glory under European influence. Only thanks to Europe has Russia made an impact on world culture and history. The use of Custine's comment as a non-contradicted, 'authorial' voice (the author's voice of the invisible Narrator has no authority) defines 'Russian cultural heritage' as the European collections in the Hermitage, and 'Russian history' as the history from 1689 to 1913.

The Hermitage functions as the ark of Russian cultural heritage, containing one of the largest collections of paintings and the treasures of the Romanov Empire. Sokurov draws, however, exclusively on that period of Russian history when the country was most exposed to European influences. He excludes the period before Peter the Great (the tsar who opened Russia to the West and founded the city of Petersburg as the 'window onto Europe') and ends his account with the last tsar, Nicholas II, erasing eighty years of Soviet rule and ten years of post-Soviet Russia. Sokurov refuses to see continuity from the Russian Empire to Soviet rule, as well as from the Kievan to the Russian Empire; moreover, he is not at all concerned with the politics of the time. Sokurov thus renounces the twentieth century as unworthy of depiction and lacking cultural value; its only task lies in preservation. As one critic argues: 'In the absence of historical parallels with the social cataclysms of the following century, the audience is left to conclude that the Empire produced everything beautiful in Russian culture and the only task left now is to preserve it intact for posterity'.[14]

During his walk through the Hermitage Custine dismisses the temperas in the Raphael Loggias as cheap copies of the originals of the Vatican Palace. Russia is a country without ideas, without authority; this explains also the Narrator's lack of authority in his voice. Russia imitates out of laziness and lack of initiative. Even the Winter Palace, part of the Hermitage, was built by the Italian architect Francesco Rastrelli. The Hermitage's collection of paintings was acquired from the European collections of Johann Gotzkowski, Pierre Crozat, Heinrich von Brühl, Sir Robert Walpole, Count

Still from *Russian Ark*: **Custine with Khmelnitsky and Yeliseev before the Tintoretto painting.**

Baudouin, and John Lyde-Brown, in an attempt to bring Russia to the same level of cultural heritage as European monarchies and to satisfy the cultural aspirations of the largely foreign-born emperors and their spouses from the houses of Brunswick-Holstein, Anhalt, Hesse, and the courts of Denmark and Prussia. If Russia cannot produce a cultural heritage itself, neither can it master its space or form a national identity: 'Space is always too vast for them to form. That is the advantage of a country where there is no nation'.[15] This is Custine's view of Russia before he visits the art collection of the Hermitage.

Custine proceeds to the Small Italian Skylight Room, crowded with contemporary visitors to the Museum. He offends the Narrator with his comments on a vase in 'Empire' style and the chandeliers by Andrei Voronikhin (1759–1814, architect of the Kazan Cathedral in St Petersburg), objects which are, in Custine's assessment, but a pale reflection of the 'Empire' under Napoleon that he detests. He is introduced to the Narrator's contemporaries, the doctor Oleg Konstantinovich Khmelnitsky and the actor Lev Mikhailovich Yeliseev. They draw his attention to the details in Tintoretto's *Birth of John the Baptist*, noting the tranquillity emanating from the scene of baptism that reconcile even the chicken and the cat in the foreground – natural enemies and symbols for greed and cruelty respectively. Custine is uninterested in this, turning his back on the painting with a comment on its acquisition: it was acquired from the Crozat collection under Catherine the Great. Turning to the opposite wall, the Marquis remembers the acquisition history, while also criticising the hanging arrangement of the paintings. Massimo Stanzione's *The Death of Cleopatra* (1630–40) – in fact not acquired until 1968 –, is displayed along with Lodovico Cardi's (Cigoli) *The Circumcision of Christ* (1590), Carlo Dolci's *Saint Cecilia* (1640s) and Francesco Maltese's *Still Life with Eastern Rug* (1650s). The array of paintings represents a motley range of art exhibits, dealing with themes of antiquity and Christianity alongside muses and still lives. Custine comments on Russia's useless copying and borrowing from Europe, without penetrating the meaning of the paintings, as his Russian companions do. Indeed, he fails to pay any attention to the references to miracles that so interest Khmelnitsky and Yeliseev in Tintoretto (the effect of John's birth on animals; the miracle of Zachary gaining his speech after naming the child as ordained by God; Cleopatra's sacrifice of life to avoid suffering; the Jewish beginning of Christ's life as demonstrated by the ritual of his circumcision). Custine's comment on the paintings is as superficial as the vague movement of the camera that does not focus on any of the paintings on the wall and almost fails entirely to capture *The Circumcision*. Custine leaves the room and enters the Gallery of the History of Ancient Painting with its statues. The pictorial frames open the view onto other cultures. While Custine crosses the thresholds of rooms that contain time in their performance, he never enters the pictorial frame – the window into another world, another culture. He fails to see the content of the paintings, in fact his own culture, and thus echoes the strategy of the Narrator to see Russian culture with his own eyes, using instead those of Custine. The Narrator looks at Russia as the Other, rather than the Self.

Custine is excited about the pure, neo-classical sculptures of Canova, in particular *The Three Graces* (1813–16), a work created during the Marquis' lifetime, but not acquired by the Hermitage until 1901. Custine fails to recognise Pushkin, who ascends the Main Staircase before he strikes up a conversation with a blind woman, Tamara Kurenkova. Kurenkova was a frequent visitor to the museum, and when she learnt she would lose her sight she spent her entire time in the Hermitage trying to memorise the art work. Here she is touching a sculpture that resembles Tenerani's *Psyche* (but her arms are raised), admiring its grace and beauty. Custine asks her to accompany him into the Van Dyck Room.

Kurenkova leads Custine to one of her favourite paintings, Van Dyck's *Madonna with Partridges* (*Rest on the Flight to Egypt*) – a painting re-hung to locate it on their path. Then Custine misleads her by claiming that Rubens' *Feast in the House of Simon the Pharisee* is not in the Rubens Room and has never been part of the Hermitage collection. A few steps on he realises he is wrong, and places Kurenkova with her back to the painting that he claims is now in front of her. In the Rubens painting Custine pays no attention to the opposition between the dogmatism of Simon the Pharisee and Christ's benevolence. He avoids the connection between the theme of the painting and his own situation, misleading an angelic person with his arrogance. Kurenkova's face lights up as she tells the story of Christ's benevolence, indicating the blind person's deeper understanding of the painting's spiritual meaning than Custine's understanding of art. Custine knows the historical facts and he can see, but this does not grant him the insight into European art of which Russians are capable.

Custine pauses at Frans Mieris' *Lady at her Toilet* (1659), for the first time now discerning the details of the painting and uttering his boredom with the themes of 'rags, dogs and eternal people'. In the Cabinet of Spanish Painting he corners a boy scrutinising El Greco's *Peter and Paul* (1590s), quizzing him about the scriptures and their significance for the painting. Custine alludes to the superiority of the Roman over the Orthodox Church and implies a lack of religious education in the Russian people. In a meek and vague tone, the Narrator tries to hustle Custine on. In the next room Custine finds the dancer Alla Osipenko talking to Rembrandt's *Danae* (1636). Danae, the virgin who was seduced by Zeus and gave birth to Perseus, is a painting with double significance. On the one hand, Danae is a victim of her own beauty (Zeus's rape of Danae and Russia's rape of Europe or vice versa); and on the other, the painting is a special treasure of the Hermitage since its restoration after an attack with a razor and acid in 1985. Sokurov seems to suggest once again, that Russians relate to paintings in an emotional way – Osipenko speaks to the canvas and feels such elevation that she dances through the room. Custine strolls through the Rembrandt Room, viewing its exhibits. The camera lingers on *Abraham and the Three Angels*, before it finds Custine transfixed by *The Return of the Prodigal Son*. The theme of redemption through repentance that Rembrandt portrayed in this work would seem to be a concept alien to Custine – and it leaves him speechless.

Custine leaves the exhibition rooms and finds himself on the Council Staircase, chased out of the Museum by the guards. Having lost his sense of direction, he enters a room with empty, frost-covered frames: the room represents the Hermitage during the blockade, when paintings were evacuated to the Urals. Custine knows nothing of the catastrophes of twentieth-century Russian history and the narrator makes no attempt to tell him. From here on Custine returns to the historical part of his journey.

In the Pavilion Hall he meets an aged Catherine II, who runs into the Hanging Garden of the Small Hermitage. After his visit to the painting collection Custine turns to life at the court: in the Winter Palace a masked ball is in preparation; in St George's Hall Tsar Nicholas I receives the Persian Ambassador, apologising for the murder of Russian diplomats: the ceremony reflects the harmonious meeting of two cultures. Custine leaves the Hall and enters the banquet room, admiring the Sèvres porcelain. In the Memorial Hall of Peter the Great, Orbeli and the two Piotrovskys discuss the conservation of Peter's throne. In the Romanov Dynasty Gallery Anastasia plays with her friends; together with her mother Alexandra she joins the family at the breakfast table. Finally, in the Great Hall the ball is under way as guests dance the mazurka, played by an orchestra conducted by Gerghiev. After the ball they exit via the main (Jordan) Staircase.

Custine remains behind, in the past, refusing to leave the Great Hall after the ball; the Narrator exits with the other guests. Custine is a piece from another time, but an astute observer and cynical commentator on the events. He at once glorifies the imperial splendour of the monarchical past, while condemning Russia as a country incapable of creating her own history and culture. Sokurov's voice does not contradict, but merely queries his view occasionally from the perspective of somebody with the knowledge of recent history of which Custine is oblivious.

Using Custine as a prism for a view on Russian history and culture, we are invited to acknowledge in that history only those elements that are pale imitations of European culture and history, while detaching Russia's history of the twentieth century from a continuous temporaneity: the Narrator warns Custine not to look into the room with the empty frames from paintings taken out of the city during the siege, symbolising the removal of visual representations of the past from a period that left no visual historical record, as one scholar suggests of Sokurov's film *We Read the Book of the Blockade*: the siege experience cannot be depicted, but only verbalised.[16] Its performance by those who have not experiences it turns into a farcical performance – not unlike the acting performances (as opposed to real figures) during the journey of *Russian Ark*. At the end of the twentieth century nothing of value remains of Russia. Russia without its European connection is void. Russia is neither part of Asia nor its master, as Sokurov stresses: 'The bent for Asia, for the Caucasus, the desire to subjugate them, is in my view a global mistake on Russia's part'.[17]

The final image of the film leads from the 'ark' (Hermitage) to the sea (the Neva) – a murky, foggy, grey patch of marshland rises outside the entrance to the Hermitage, as Hoberman argues:

> Pondering the imperial capital's tenuous relation with the sea, the marquis had a vision of flooded St Petersburg sinking back into

marshland. The digital fog that rolls around the Hermitage ghost ship shrouds Sokurov's ambiguous declaration: 'We are destined to sail forever, to love forever'...[18]

Sokurov bids farewell to Europe and thus annihilates Russia's history that ensues. What remains in the ark is the splendid past, eclipsing the horrors of the Soviet regime, but also the Russian art movements of the nineteenth and early twentieth century. Having severed its links with Europe, the ship – à la Fellini, whose film *And the Ship Sails on* [E la nave va, 1983] was supervised by Sokurov when dubbed into Russian – is destined to sail forever in the limbo between Europe and Asia, in the same manner as his German-Russian co-production falls into a 'void' in the light of Sokurov's conflict with the European Film Academy, as suggested by Alaniz.

Sokurov's obsession with aesthetics, with the photographic and poetic composition of frames and the filming of paintings to capture both content and texture – for example in *Robert, A Fortunate Life* –[19] is, I would argue, what matters for *Russian Ark*. The film loads content – however European and 'unoriginal' – into the space of the Hermitage: yet this content belongs to the past, and is resuscitated through the gaze (the paintings), the touch (the artwork), the smell (oil paint) and movement (the enacted historical events). It is buried again when the doors close behind the camera. Russia had its glory in the past, but that past is dead, and 'preserved' only in the museum, while the present is void, empty, non-existent. The present is an empty frame that signals the helplessness of the film-maker at the secondariness of cinema, about which Sokurov has talked at length.[20] The painter or architect may create spaces (historical), the painter captures the essence of life (beauty, grace, benevolence, redemption, faith) on canvas, the actors may perform historical events – they can bring to life what is dead. Sokurov's camera can do nothing but capture these primary art forms. When

Still from *Russian Ark*: The view onto the Neva at the film's end.

history's doors close for the last time, the frame remains empty, reflecting the murky grey waters of the Neva (in a digitally mastered image, not a nature shot).

This is Sokurov's own empty frame, in which the images of the past can be re-hung and reinstated: they can be returned to the frames from which they were removed during the war. As Iampolski has argued elsewhere in this volume, the camera never captures reality: here it focuses on surfaces and performances in a hermeneutically sealed space, drawing attention to itself camera as a 'framing' device. Sokurov needed that long take to disallow the editor or cutter from juxtaposing points of view.

Notes
1   Harte, 'A Visit to the Museum'.
2   Jameson, 'History and Elegy in Sokurov'.
3   Dragan Kujundzic, 'After "After": The *Ark*ive Fever of Alexander Sokurov, *Quarterly Review of Film and Video* 21.3 (2004), pp. 219–239.
4   de Keghel, 'Sokurov's *Russian Ark*', p. 91.
5   Kujundzic, p. 222.
6   Kujundzic, p. 227.
7   For details of Custine's life, see George F. Kennan, *The Marquis de Custine and his 'Russia in 1839'*, London: Hutchinson & Co., 1972.
8   Astolphe, Marquis de Custine, *Journey for Our Time: The Journals of the Marquis de Custine*, ed. and trans. by Phyllis P. Kohler, London: Prior, 1980; entry for 12 July 1839, p. 69, p. 229.
9   *Journey for Our Time*, entry for 1 August 1839, p. 138.
10 *Journey for Our Time*, entry for 15 July 1839, p. 81.
11 *Journey for Our Time*, entry for 29 July 1839, p. 118.
12 *Journey for Our Time*, entry for 21 July 1839, p. 95.
13 *Journey for Our Time*, entry for 10 July 1839, p. 40.
14 Elena Razlogova, 'Grave Consequences', *Popmatters*, 31 October 2002, http://www.popmatters.com/pm/review/russian-ark/ (accessed 29 November 2002).
15 *Journey for Our Time*, entry for 14 July 1839, p. 78.
16 Polina Barskova, 'A Loud Reading', *KinoKultura* 28 (2010), http://www.kinokultura.com/2010/28r-blockadebook.shtml (accessed 20 July 2010)
17 Sokurov, interview with Anton Ivanov, 'Nash chelovek v Kanne', *Itogi* 17–18 (2002), http://www.itogi.ru/archive/2002/17/96445.html, (accessed 20 July 2010).
18 J. Hoberman, 'Russian Ark', *Film Comment Magazine*, 2002 http://www.filmlinc.com/fcm/9-10-2002/sokurov.htm (accessed 29 November 2002).
19 Mikhail Iampolski, 'Representation – Mimicry – Death', in Birgit Beumers (ed.), *Russia on Reels*, London: I.B.Tauris, 1999, pp. 127–43.
20 See Condee, *Imperial Trace*, pp. 180–83.

CHAPTER 12

ENDSTATE AND ALLEGORY

Nancy Condee

Endstate

The final scene is of the greatest importance. It has to be clear.
— Alexander Sokurov, *Moloch*

What does it mean: 'to be clear'? In *Moloch* (Sokurov's focus in the epigraph above), Hitler and Eva close the film with a brief exchange about death. In *Taurus*, a debilitated Lenin lows at the sky. In *The Sun*, Hirohito reacts mutely to news of the radio dispatcher's ritual suicide. In *Alexandra*, the elderly heroine is allotted the final lines ('Go with God...'), as she boards the train.

Much can be said about these examples but, most obviously, the endings share some glimpse – direct or oblique – at mortality. This fact is hardly a surprise: the director is Sokurov and not someone else. In Sokurov's world, all days are last days. The elegy, after all, emerges from 1978 onward as the director's most enduring form to which he repeatedly returns, producing at least ten explicitly titled works over thirty years.[1] It is only a slight exaggeration to claim that Sokurov's work is always about the endstate, and the potential for that endstate to transform itself into something else: death as initiation; the sublation of mundane habits to a higher power; stasis as incipient rapture.

An example of this paradoxical state is *Russian Ark*, where the final scene – 'Farewell, Europe!' – is a lament for the ties severed from European high culture in the early twentieth century. At the same time, this film artefact is nothing if not a reinvigoration of European cultural ties, evident in the collaborative initiatives of the film's production. Balanced between verbal assertion ('Farewell, Europe!') and physical embodiment – between the discursive ruptures of 1917 and technological linkages of 2002 (its release year) – the film savours this threshold status: are we parting forever or are we re-uniting? In the present volume, Julian Graffy has cogently elaborated the liminal or threshold state as a recurrent condition in Sokurov's work.[2] Indeed, it would seem at times that Sokurov's account of both his production practices and his ideal spectatorship casts them as liminal elements in a ritualism of the kind traced by Arnold Van Gennep (*Les Rites de Passage*, 1909) and Victor Turner (*The Forest of Symbols*; 1967 and elsewhere).

This threshold status in *Russian Ark* is signalled precisely in the film's final shot: the Winter Palace windowsill, opening out into the flood space of ocean. More ambitiously, in the realm of spectatorship, an analogous threshold is offered at this same moment, when the viewers' experience in the specific exhibition space reaches its end. As if the act of viewing were a rehearsal for sacred uptake, the spectators are prepared to embark on a potential second life, imperceptibly different from the quotidian in external features, but anticipating eternal life to which they now strive in a more conscious state.

Is this extrapolation too attenuated from the logic of the film? If so, let us bracket it for now. In the pause, I will register some preemptory scepticism. Surely, Sokurov's final scene is of no more importance than those of his other art-house colleagues – say, Kira Muratova or Alexei German Sr. They too, after all, must treasure the final scene. In fact – if the reader will permit a small digression – the very ostentation with which these two *auteurs* tend to ironise the final scene suggests, if somewhat perversely, their endings' saturated significance. Recall, for example, the interminable hiccups in the closing shot of Muratova's *Melody for Barrel Organ* [Melodiia dlia sharmanki, 2009] or the final dismissive expletive ('Khrena-nakhrena!') that closes German's *Khrustalev, the Car!* [Khrustalev, mashinu!, 1998].

But these perverse dismissals, in fact, mark a key contrast to Sokurov's work. Where Muratova or German might insist on a trivialising fillip, one ensured to undercut closure's conventional gravitas, Sokurov is committed unequivocally to its weight, to the freighted nature of a film's ending. It is one of several ways in which Sokurov, at least stylistically, remains a firmly neo-conservative director: the work must never be relieved of this burden of meaning, which is, above all, a spiritual burden.

This insistent gravitas is certainly a central thing that may be said about Sokurov's final scene. Not all creatures in Sokurov's system, however, may access eternity. Let us return to the final scene of *Taurus*: Lenin rises up; his bovine sounds are echoed by the surrounding cattle. 'The difference between animals and humans', Sokurov has insisted elsewhere, 'is that dogs don't realize they are mortal. After death, a human starts his second life in the remembrance of those who have lost him'.[3] Lenin – one might extrapolate – starts his second life in Sokurov's remembrance, a film in which the materialist thinker – like the cattle – has no conceptual access to the coordinates of his own immortality. Caught in that liminal state between human and beast, at the approaching threshold between life and death, Sokurov's atheist is subjected to one of film-maker's cruellest 'clarities'.

The portrait of Hitler in *Moloch* displays with a similar tension between human and beast on the threshold between life and death. Here the narrative frame is a litter of puppies, newly born when Hitler arrives. At his departure, Hitler learns that the newborns have died 'from the plague'.

This animal-death triggers the couple's final exchange (Hitler: 'we will beat death'; Eva: 'death is death'). Together, Lenin and Hitler stand in for two related errors: one leader would insist that death is the final horizon; the other would conquer death. Sokurov's third political leader – the emperor-God of *The Sun* – displays a third error in his hypertrophic understanding of his personal immortality. Finally, having renounced his status as deity and passed into the realm of mortal, Hirohito is mute at the news of the dispatcher's ritual suicide. On either side of life and death, the two men are mortals with immortal souls. At this moment, Hirohito is Sokurov's most sympathetic leader: renouncing his divinity, he voluntarily descends to that state of mortal being that he, like the radio dispatcher (and implicitly, the film director), had in fact never left.

This pattern in Sokurov's final scenes – I will call it 'the remedial encounter with mortality' – is a concern familiar to film scholarship.[4] My interest, however, lies in an aspect less explored in the critical literature: the process by which this encounter with mortality sublates to an ideological register.

At the end of *Alexandra*, the heroine is accompanied to the military train by three Chechen women. It is to these women that Alexandra utters the film's final lines cited above. The scene is cinema's customary train-station closure, informed by conventional codes, except that – under the social circumstances of Sokurov's topic (ethnic separatism, military occupation, potential combat) – the farewells take on a hyper-saturated weight, enhanced by the generational display: a young Chechen woman, a middle-aged Chechen woman, and the elderly Malika. The studied self-consciousness of a *tableau* dominates this generational diorama; any hint of incipient irony, as we have mentioned, is absolutely excluded.

Still from *Alexandra*: Alexandra Nikolaevna. Courtesy of ProLine Production.

Instead, three ages of Chechen womanhood embrace the Russian grandmother. They accept Alexandra's invitation to visit her at home, just as Alexandra had visited Malika – her structural equivalent – in a brief stay that (mandatorily, within this symbolic universe) involved both sustenance and sleep. The Russian grandmother then returns northward to 'put her home in order', as she herself had earlier described it, after the death of her overbearing husband, the tyrant of the family.

We need not bleed this scene dry of meaning. Suffice it to say here that the otherwise conventional parting scene comes to bear a heavy ideological load as the film's ending is transformed into dense geopolitical allegory: the impending Ordered Home, the Russian Woman's newly independent state, the anticipated Reciprocal Hospitality. It is no particular interpretive stretch to suggest that the film invests much of its hope in a newly autonomous Russia, recovering from irreparable loss, comparable in scope to the loss of a spouse. If the old imperial habits would redeem their troubled legacy, then the best of the 'shared' culture – what others might call colonial culture – must recuperate its spiritual value. Those with shared memories must find new, common re-enchantment. The oldest Chechen woman, Malika is, after all, not just a random contemporary to her Russian counterpart; she is a Chechen teacher of Russian. Their 'common language' – we will call it that without comment – is offered to us as a natural, empirically inevitable state of historical belonging.

Indeed, it is with reference to *Alexandra* that a passage on Sokurov's website, *Island of Sokurov* [Ostrov Sokurova], elaborates the logic of how this cultural cohesion is enacted:

> When an intonation of trust emerges, all else remains insignificant, all the more so if everyone speaks in a single language – in Russian. [...] Therefore, a great deal of attention [in the film] is devoted to the unifying significance of the Russian language. [...] [A]bove all else, it is the language of unification.

This 'language of unification' strengthens geography's logic of belonging. It translates relations of spatial dominance into a natural, intergenerational order of distant members, sustained by a common tongue, as if somehow Alexandra and Malika were second-grandmothers-once-removed. In this respect, it might be said that *Alexandra* belongs to the same cluster as *Mother and Son* and *Father and Son* not because its content concerns kinship, but because kinship is the instrument through which the allegorical structure of belonging is lent visual credibility.

Allegory

Allegories are, in the realm of thoughts, what ruins are in the realm of things.
– Walter Benjamin[5]

It is reasonable to argue that allegory is at the heart of all artistic narrative – and all commentary for that matter, Frye would remind us.[6] Were this exclusively true, however, it would be meaningless to say that some texts were more intensely allegorical than others, or that allegoresis is a more fruitful mode of critical engagement with this artistic text rather than that. In Sokurov's work, his fluctuating reliance on allegory is a useful measure to highlight differences in his work, where the allegorical operations of the text may be intensified or reduced.

Here I take allegory loosely to mean – as the etymology suggests[7] – the act of speaking otherwise than one seems to speak. Allegory typically contains both a realistic ('literal') and a symbolic ('abstract') register. It offers a second set of latent meanings that lie distinct from the manifest content of the narrative itself. In this respect, its *dramatis personae* often functions as a placeholder for moral or political positions.[8] Joel Fineman, viewing 'allegory' from the vantage of its rhetorical structure (and relying on Jakobson's foundational 'Linguistics and Poetics'), has suggested that at the heart of allegorical operations is the projection of the metaphoric axis across the metonymic axis.[9] In simpler terms, one could speak of the image (in a static or synchronic mode) spooled out across the plot (in a dynamic, diachronic mode). Similarly, one could speak of a vertical structure, advancing across horizontal sequence (for our purposes, across the continuum of narrative). Condensing this operation to a single act, Fineman describes allegory as the transformation of the temple into the labyrinth, architectural choices curiously suited to Sokurov's universe.[10]

This line of argument, whose antecedents recede to Quintilian, has multiple value for Sokurov's films – in particular those that tend toward plotlessness – because here the deeper investments of Sokurov's plotlessness may be glimpsed. To borrow Fineman's terms, the stasis of the temple retains more sacred value than the complex dynamism of the labyrinth. Consistent with this speculation are the film-maker's comments on the lowered status of narrative itself. 'If [a given] film is based on the principle of the story, the narrative', he insists, 'then it is not art'.[11] His periodic scriptwriter Yuri Arabov confirms this preference. 'A large part of the films of world cinema are anchored in the plot', Arabov explains. 'Alexander Nikolaevich goes against this flood'.[12]

However much plotlessness may be Sokurov's working ideal, he is – to his own dismay, perhaps – a film-maker, and not a painter, a still photographer, or other artist dealing in static media. Sokurov's elegiac work may manifestly mourn such figures as Fedor Chaliapin (*Elegy, Petersburg Elegy*), Andrei Tarkovsky (*Moscow Elegy*), Boris Yeltsin (*Soviet Elegy*), or Vytautas Landsbergis (*Simple Elegy*), but it may also be said to lament its status in the fallen world of film-making, in the labyrinth instead of the temple. In the labyrinth, the film-maker is condemned to struggle with the production of structure through time – the metaphor spun out along the narrative line – or what Craig Owens, in discussing allegory, has described as 'structure as sequence'.[13]

In dialogue with Owens, Fineman has suggested an interpretive range inadvertently useful in situating these features of Sokurov's work:

> [T]here are allegories that are primarily perpendicular, concerned more with structure than with temporal extension, as, say,

illustrations of Fortune's wheel, or Fludd's famous diagram of the great chain of being. On the other hand, there is allegory that is primarily horizontal, such as picaresque or quest narrative where figurative structure is only casually and allusively appended to the circuit of adventures through time.[14]

In Fineman's terms, Sokurov's family cluster (and, arguably, the Japanese cluster) could be described as bearing a strong 'perpendicular' (that is to say, vertical) axis: the metaphor moving through time *only to the minimal extent* necessary for cinema. In contrast to such restless films as *Mournful Unconcern* or *Save and Protect*, Sokurov's later films have tended to avoid the dynamic, eventful narrative in favour of a segmented, stationery gaze with deep affinities to painting or allegorical performance, that eighteenth-century imperial *tableau vivant* of silence and motionlessness.

Retarding the movement of structure through time, Sokurov's later films often make extensive use of the photograph as a kind of motionless, commemorative object. Photographs populate most of Sokurov's films – recall, for example, the picture album in *The Sun* – but they exhibit a particular intensity in the elegies, where long takes show figures contemplating photographs. Sokurov's lengthy takes seem at times to seek a rapprochement between cinema and photography, reconciling their differences in a fashion similar to the reconciliations of cinema with painting in such films as *Hubert Robert*, *Mother and Son*, *Elegy of a Voyage*, as well as the Japanese cluster (*Oriental Elegy*, *A Humble Life* and *dolce...*).

The goal of this alignment between the moving picture and the still image, I would argue, is the suspension of time, a reprieve from the secular regime of historical narration, that profane linear flow of time that constitutes plot. Sokurov's cinematic system, often resistant to historical linearity in favour of an idealised, continual simultaneity, becomes

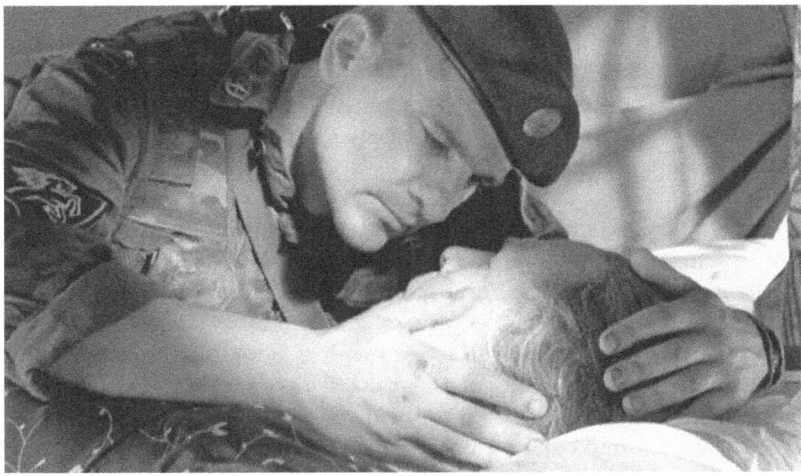

Still from *Alexandra*: Alexandra Nikolaevna and Denis. Courtesy of ProLine Production.

sensitive instead to texture and surface, the palpability of its subject, operating in a realm of textuality that Frow has linked to a co-presence of all time:

> The time of textuality is not the linear, cause-and-effect time, embedded in the logic of the archive, but the time of a continuous analeptic and proleptic shaping. [...] [A]ll moments of the system are co-present, and the end is given at the same time as the beginning.[15]

But it must be added that the visual arts (broadly conceived) are not Sokurov's only potential ally. A kinship with music, in particular symphonic music, might be understood as a deeply compatible practice of structure-through-time that coheres in the very substance of its craft. Indirect confirmation might be found in the film-maker's comments: 'for me, the strongest sensations in the arts are always produced by painting and symphonic music';[16] 'I can live without cinema, but I cannot live without music'.[17]

Sokurov's preference for stasis and co-presence helps to illuminate a feature of his film-making practice that would otherwise appear as a series of perpetual loose ends. His insistence that many of the individual films are integral parts of a larger project, indifferent to production schedules and deadlines, seems to promise that each film is merely an instance, an embodiment or incarnation of an extra-temporal whole. The ongoing elegy cycle, the power tetralogy, and the open-ended family cluster are the most familiar examples.[18] This open-ended tendency transforms any individual film – however much it may appear to be finished – into an element of a larger contemplative system in which each work has a perpetual afterlife as the recapitulation of the leitmotif.

And so let us return to *Alexandra*, which may now reveal more starkly its allegorical commitments – that is to say (more dryly), the projection of the metaphoric axis across the metonymic axis. At the risk of simplification, I propose the following account – quaint, perhaps, in its structuralist inclinations – of the film's story. Two parallel columns of potential equivalency organise the film's vertical axis (with metaphor's strong potential for substitution): on the one side, an elderly Russian woman and her grandson; on the other, they include an elderly Chechen woman and her young neighbour.

As for the horizontal axis (the practice of combination, of syntactical or diachronic linkage), the film restricts itself to a short span of time, with the narrowest range of human functions – sleeping, eating, procuring food – carried out in both the military and the domestic settings. Behind this humdrum syntagm, however, are two less evident dramas: on the one hand, the fractious geo-political macrocosm; on the other, the Russian family's contentious microcosm. Each drama is kept relatively muted until the end of the film, when each is finally broached in an episode of mild rebuke directed at the heroine. The Chechen boy's remark to Alexandra (concerning the right to political sovereignty) and the Russian grandson's remark to Alexandra (concerning the right to individuated privacy) confirm that the allegory is structured so as to crosscut these parallel columns of statehood and family. It is through this cross-cutting – a wilful violation of the parallel structure – that the allegorical investments of these largely off-stage dramas are thereby revealed: on the one side, the perils of geo-political independence; on the other, the perils of youthful independence.

It is a matter of argument which of these two dramas is the allegory's traditional 'literal' register and which is the 'symbolic'. I am indifferent to

Still from *Alexandra*: Malika. Courtesy of ProLine Production.

the resolution of this debate. The very substitutability of these two registers allows us to read the film's lesson in either direction, recognizing (for example) sovereign self-determination as an adolescent maturation tale. We know, of course, that Chechnya's aspirations to sovereignty are hardly adolescent; they have in fact extended over centuries (certainly as long, one might argue, as the 1783 Treaty of Georgievsk). But Sokurov's film offers us the classic fetishistic split – 'je sais bien, mais quand-même...'.[19] In accepting its logic, we engage in a moment of willed amnesia about historical fact in order to accept the film's re-scripting of history as a maturation tale. Unconcerned with secular ambitions of history *wie es eigentlich gewesen* [sic],[20] the film ushers us into a memory theatre of family, ritual, and piety. Confirming these ties, the film invites us to participate in a spiritual practice with its deepest roots in ancestor worship.

It is in this way that *Alexandra* and the allegorical structure support each other in a system of mutually sustaining significance; the family as a powerful instrument for the logic of occupation. As its parallel columns move through diegetic time, we can understand Sokurov's narrative minimalism, forged from the utter necessity for the simplest possible plot line, so as to bear the heavy burden of this grand, imperial metaphor.

Indeed, the weight of the metaphor, one could argue, is in direct relation to the hypertrophy of its intended appropriation. As Owens suggests:

> The allegorist does not invent images but confiscates them. He lays claim to the culturally significant, poses as its interpreter. [...] He does not restore an original meaning that may have been lost or obscured; allegory is not hermeneutics. Rather, he adds another meaning to the image. If he adds, however, he does so only to replace...[21]

Here we might suggest an intense compatibility of allegory (as an act of confiscation and imposition of meaning) with Sokurov's 'unifying significance of the Russian language', as contingent practices of empire. I do not suggest that these are practices of empire under any circumstances whatsoever. Nor do I suggest that they are exclusively practices of empire. Moreover – if the reader can tolerate a third caution – I advance this line of argument with no interest in political censure. Instead, my interest is the apparent happenstance: Sokurov has elaborated an immensely delicate structure to support a logic of natural appropriation, ethno-linguistic on the one hand, rhetorical on the other.

Postscript: Dead Organs of the State

> *An appreciation of the transience of things, and the concern to rescue them for eternity, is one of the strongest impulses in allegory.*
> – Walter Benjamin[22]

I will not pursue this speculation with regard to the other family films, other than to note a major difference. Their allegorical drive is, of course, concerned less with geo-politics, and more with a modelling of ideal structural relations, condemned though they may still be to move through the profane diachronic world.[23] Beyond the family cluster, however, several other films lend themselves readily to an intense allegorical logic. Most evident among them are *Days of Eclipse*, about which Jameson has written at length,[24] and *Second Circle*, with its grotesque, even horrific project of getting the dead father's corpse out of the apartment.

That the corpse in *Second Circle* operates simultaneously as dead father (at the 'literal' level – that is to say, biological and diegetic) and dead state (at the symbolic level) has been argued elsewhere.[25] Sokurov himself encourages such an allegorical reading in his comments about the film's son: 'The main character represents the modern Russian people, wilting under the stress of the current climate, who turn apathetic and just sit and stare'.[26] Sokurov's film advances those features of allegory through what Howard Caygill has described as the 'spectacle of ruin, [...] the contemplation of bones, an anatomical art form that does not bring life, [...] "mortuary art" '.[27]

It is clear from the film's opening scene of Sokurov's mortuary art that the hero's father was not a beloved, but rather an unfamiliar and unwelcome object. All the same, in Sokurov's oneiric space, the obligation for the proper disposal of the father's residue must not be sloughed off. The corpse is not merely the unwanted prop; it carries the entire weight of the hero's history in its dead organs, the history that produced the hero. The very social obstacles that prevent an efficient burial, themselves produced by the conditions of socialism, are moreover intimately tied to the conditions retarding the professional completion of Sokurov's film project itself.

In this respect, *Second Circle* (as film artefact) might be seen as a ritual object of perpetual, reluctant mourning, reluctant not out of grief for the beloved object, but the opposite – out of an extreme ambivalence toward the traumatic object itself, with its death grip on the hero. The director's struggle to complete the film, the protagonist's struggle to bury the father, the spectators' struggle to extrude themselves from Soviet power become analogical projects, enriched rather than harmed by their perpetual failure to overcome stagnation and motionlessness. This retardation and potential failure – to complete the film, to bury the father, to leave the debased conditions of Soviet society – usher along, rather than impede the thaumaturgic operation.

Finally, however, overcoming all resistance, the film is completed; the father is disposed of; the spectator passes out of Soviet dominion. But, more than this, thanks to these protractions and near-failures, the core goal of Sokurov's allegory – to 'rescue things for eternity', as Benjamin puts it – is accomplished. In its own fashion, *Second Circle* might be seen as a precursor to the more clearly articulated geo-politics of *Alexandra*, not in the sense that they share a common ideology, but in the sense that their common imaginative geography, extending from the northern, icy limits of *Second Circle* to the southern, dusty limits of *Alexandra*, make visible the dominion of Sokurov's allegorical logic.

Notes

1. See the filmography at the end. After several elegies were completed, Sokurov had considered uniting them all under a single title. He intended to produce a total of twenty-five, the age at which, in the director's view, one begins to live consciously (Sokurov, 'The Solitary Voice', p. 75).
2. Other scholars who have mentioned this preoccupation in passing include Harte, Kujundzic, and Levine (see bibliography for details).
3. Sokurov, 'The Solitary Voice', 75.
4. On the theme of death in Sokurov's work, see (among others) Viktoriia Belopol'skaia, *'Mariia'*, in *Sokurov 1*, pp. 143–46; Condee; Harte; Iampolski, 'Representation'; Mikhail Iampol'skii, 'Smert'' v kino', in *Sokurov 1*, pp. 273–78; Jameson, 'History'; Sokurov, 'Death'.
5. Walter Benjamin, *The Origin of German Tragic Drama*, London: New Left, 1977, p. 187.
6. Northrop Frye, *Anatomy of Criticism: Four Essays*, Princeton: Princeton University Press, 1971, p. 89.
7. allos = other + agoreuei = to speak.
8. The literature is vast, but texts that have informed this larger effort include Erich Auerbach, 'Figura', in his *Scenes from the Drama of European Literature: Six Essays*, Minneapolis: University of Minnesota Press, 1984, pp. 11–76; Paul Bove, 'Misprisions of Utopia: Messianism, Apocalypse, and Allegory', *Field Day Review* 6 (2010), pp. 71–94; Howard Caygill, 'Walter Benjamin's Concept of Cultural History', in David S. Ferris, ed., *The Cambridge Companion to Walter Benjamin*, Cambridge: Cambridge UP, 2004, pp. 73–96; Stephen J. Greenblatt, *Allegory and Representation*, Baltimore: Johns Hopkins University, 1981; C. S. Lewis, *The Allegory of Love: A Study in Medieval Tradition*, Oxford: Oxford University Press, 1985; A. D. Nuttall, *Two Concepts of Allegory*, New York: Barnes and Noble, 1967; and of course Quintilian, *Institute of Oratory*, Book 8, Chapter 6, Nos. 14, 44, 53–54, at http://www2.iastate.edu/~honeyl/quintilian/8/chapter6.html.
9. Joel Fineman, 'The Structure of Allegorical Desire', *October* 12 (1980), pp. 46–66; p. 50.
10. Fineman, p. 46.
11. Jeremi Szaniawski, 'An Interview with Aleksandr Sokurov', *Critical Quarterly* 33.1 (2006), pp. 13–27; p. 18.
12. Irina Liubarskaia, 'Stsenarist – eto naemnik', Interview with Yuri Arabov, *Iskusstvo kino* 4 (2005), pp. 105–11; p. 110.
13. Craig Owens, 'The Allegorical Impulse: Toward a Theory of Postmodernism, *October* 12 (1980): pp. 67–86; p. 72.
14. Fineman, p. 50.
15. John Frow, '*Toute la mémoire du monde*: Repetition and Forgetting', *Time and Commodity Culture: Essays in Cultural Theory and Postmodernity*, Oxford: Oxford University Press, 1997, pp. 218–46; p. 229.
16. Szaniawski, 'An Interview with Aleksandr Sokurov', p. 14.
17. Aleksandr Sokurov, 'Tvorcheskii al'favit', *Kinograf* 3 (1997), pp. 72–94; p. 84.
18. Sokurov's unfinished tetralogy (*Moloch, Taurus, The Sun*) includes a planned fourth film on Mephistopheles. His unfinished family cluster currently includes *Mother and Son* and *Father and Son*, while *Two Brothers and a Sister* [Dva brata i sestra] has not yet been shot; plans have extended over a decade or more. Another cluster, sometimes described as Sokurov's trilogy, is marked by its absence of internal coherence: *Days of Eclipse* (a quasi-science fiction film, set in Turkmenistan); *Second Circle* (a naturalistic film, set in the provincial North); and *Stone* (an ectoplasmic biopic set in Chekhov's former house).

19 Octave Mannoni, 'Je sais bien, mais quand-même..', *Clefs pour l'imaginaire ou l'autre scène*, Paris: Editions du Seuil, 1969, pp. 9–33; p. 10.
20 Leopold von Ranke, 'Vorrede', *Geschichten der romanischen und germanischen Völker von 1494 bis 1514. Sämtliche Werke*, 54 vols., vol. 43, Leipzig: Duncker & Humblot, 1867–90, pp. vii.
21 Owens, p. 69.
22 Benjamin, p. 223.
23 The best work on geopolitics in Sokurov's cinema remains Jameson, 'On Soviet Magic Realism'.
24 Jameson, 'On Soviet Magical Realism'.
25 Iampol'skii, 'Smert' v kino', in *Sokurov 1*, p. 273.
26 Edwin Carels, 'The Solitary Voice: An Interview with Aleksandr Sokurov', *Film Studies* 1 (1999), pp. 73–77; p. 76.
27 Caygill, p. 87.

Part V

RUSSIAN RESPONSES

SCRIPT-SOUND-EDITING

1. Yuri Arabov: The Director Becomes the Author

It so happens that, from *The Lonely Voice of Man* onwards, I was not present at the shooting of the films that I made with Sokurov. The exception was *Mournful Unconcern* and there I was not required on location at all. I was involved in the work only at the preliminary and sound-montage stages. But my relations with Sasha – those of a scriptwriter and director – went through two phases. In the earlier phase I had a completely free hand and wrote whatever came into my head. This went on right up to and including *Save and Protect*. Sasha and I fixed the general features of the concept of the film-to-be in advance – the idea, the plot [*siuzhet*], the aesthetics. Sasha accepted the script straight away and shot it on the wing without any serious changes. If the original concept was modified during the process of shooting and ready-made material was introduced that was inconsistent with it, I was called in at the sound-montage stage. For example, in *Days of Eclipse* I had to re-write the whole of the hero's dialogue from beginning to end, while he kept his mouth closed on the screen: the filmed material displayed quite different impulses than those envisaged in our initial concept. The Asiatic material was so powerful and so metaphorical that it did not need a 'fantastic' prop in the dramatic structure. For this reason, all the monologues and dialogues had to be corrected accordingly – simplified, made more down-to-earth [*bytovoi*], perhaps. Then, once the film had been shot, we had once again to re-write the entire text completely. Later, in *The Second Circle* and *The Stone* I also completely re-wrote the text to include some ready-made material. But it was with *The Second Circle* that a new phase in my collaboration with Sasha really began.

I wrote the script about the death of a woman who had been close to me and whom I had outlived. This was my own personal situation. However, for a long time Sasha and I had been discussing a film on a similar subject and it was as if it was this subject that was being made: somebody close to the hero dies but he cannot bury them – because a Soviet person does not know how to do this. I wrote the script and sent it off to Sasha. A week later he returned my script to me – a good half of it had been crossed out. That is, he had consistently and resolutely crossed out everything that bore the imprint of the grotesque and that exceeded the limits of the hermetic situation – the scenes on the street, the scenes with other characters, and so on. In our earlier phase he had also crossed things out but never with such ruthlessness. It was an aesthetic turning point. Sokurov had begun to graduate towards confined space [*zamknutoe prostranstvo*]. His mindset had altered and a completely new phase in his work in cinema had begun. It might be defined as the phase of minimalism, if we may express ourselves in the coarse language of the common man. He shot the film from the second version of the script, which I had written to take account of his every wish. Whereas the first version was the usual sixty pages long, the second was quite short – no more than about a dozen pages. All the action unfolded in confined space. Nonetheless it seems to me that *Days of Eclipse* and *The Second Circle* are the best works to emerge from my collaboration with Sokurov. In any case, these are the two films that I love more than the others.

After *The Second Circle* Sasha began giving me ever more precisely defined minimalist tasks. I wrote the script for *The Exterminating Angel* – but he rejected it and the film was made by another director. I suggested a script for *Presence* but he did not accept that either.[1] Then he suddenly told me that he wanted to make a film in which Chekhov comes back to life and returns after his death to his own house. 'Let's do it,' I said, 'But what exactly do you want?'

I wrote *The Stone*, on the whole setting his ideas aside. Sasha simply told me, 'There should be this, that and the other.' But these ideas had a more atmospheric character and therefore it was very difficult to write the script. All the same Sokurov had previously been interested in both the plot lines of a film and the various aesthetic resolutions, and even certain comic elements (it is of course difficult to talk of comic elements as applied to Sokurov's films but they were there at script level). I must confess that,

Still from *Second Circle*.

in principle, all this found its deepest embodiment so far in *Mournful Unconcern*. But Sasha went off in a different direction and, in what he does now, my role is reduced in practice to nothing.

His world is becoming ever more confined and, as a consequence, ever more unique. I already find it difficult to enter into it. When a director develops his own aesthetic, which does not in fact presuppose the existence of any paths or windows from outside, it is impossible to work together. Sasha and I are very similar people in some ways, but quite different in others. When, working on *The Stone*, I was faced with the task of submitting completely and entirely to an aesthetic that had been presented to me, I was not equal to the task. I was unable to submit, however hard I tried, because it was not mine. Nonetheless I am very fond of *The Stone*.

In *Whispering Pages* all this became completely clear. To all intents and purposes Sasha did not accept any of my suggestions. The first version of the script did not suit him. He rang me and I re-wrote the words from start to finish. The same thing happened with the second version and I know that another scriptwriter was re-writing all the dialogue. When everything is taken into consideration Sasha shot this film from his own script – or, more precisely, with no script at all. Perhaps we really had worked together long enough? All the same we had seven films behind us. Nowadays our paths cross only if I accept his aesthetic. It goes without saying that I think it is interesting. Everything that Sasha does is very important to me, but I find it difficult to participate in it myself. We both understand this. It is not a question of technology but of a way of thinking at the deepest levels of our conscious and subconscious.

We can no longer get together and start working as simply as, say, the early Lennon and McCartney: 'What are we doing today?' – 'Let's make a Bentley today!' – 'A Bentley? Great! And tomorrow?' – 'Tomorrow – a swimming pool!'

That happened only when we were young.

But it was never really like that with Sasha and me. With the possible exception of *Mournful Unconcern* – that was something like the 'swimming pool'. But now, just talking about it is amusing.

The greatest drama does not, of course, lie in our aesthetic divergences – these problems are not, in the final analysis, all that important. I am afraid that a break in our creative links could serve as the cause of a breach between us, because everything is too closely interconnected. That would be very difficult to bear. We have after all known one another far too long for that and we have together experienced the despair of *The Lonely Voice* and the dreadful blow of *Mournful Unconcern*, which involved a search warrant against Sasha and threats from the KGB... God alone knows what we have been through together. It is better not to recall it, as they say.

I do not know how the situation will develop in future. The fact is that my interest in cinema as a whole has been reduced to nothing. At some time in the past I began to get involved in scriptwriting for cinema solely because I had no chance of becoming a legitimate writer of prose or poetry. But I was interested only in *auteur* cinema, and in this cinema the scriptwriter starts from a subordinate position. The director is the author. I understood this and knew what I was doing, but now I am no longer the right age for it. Previously, when I sat down to write a script, my poetic ambitions were always suppressed. In my view that dramaturgy should be quite simple so that a complex film can be made from it. But for Sasha in recent years the most important aspect of the script has been the atmosphere. To all intents and purposes he is asking me to write atmospheric scripts, which did not happen before. But I can create an atmosphere in my poems while I cannot understand or accept it in dramaturgy.

The last two films[2] are indisputably Sasha's solos. He is the author through and through. Perhaps a little bit of me survives in them, but basically I think he can manage without me. I have told him several times that he needs to write his own scripts.

Now he has suggested that we work together on a new project, apparently along the same lines. But, whereas previously I regarded my work as collaboration, now I view it solely as assistance.

Translated by Richard Taylor

Source: Dmitrii Savel'ev, 'Iurii Arabov: Avtorom iavliaetsia rezhisser', in *Sokurov 1*, pp. 313–315.

2. Vladimir Persov: This is a Process

Olga Shervud: Vladimir Markovich, your first collaborative work with Alexander Sokurov was on *Mournful Unconcern*...

Vladimir Persov: It has to be said that he was the first director to invite me to work as a sound editor. Before that I'd worked as an assistant. We agreed straight away that we would try and make a directly recorded speech soundtrack [*chistovaia rechevaia fonogramma*]. At that time the technology for this kind of work hadn't yet been completely lost,[3] although I realised that, with our technical equipment, it wouldn't be quite that simple to do it. It was important to find the sole means that would express the director's intention. The work progressed rapidly, almost nobody let us down and we left the shooting schedule far behind. The subsequent history of the trials that befell this film is well known...[4] I just want to say that it was precisely this directly recorded soundtrack that came to our aid – among the powers-that-be who were examining the case for resuming the film it gave the impression that it had already been completed.

OS: An interesting side effect. But what were the creative reasons that prompted such a rare directly recorded soundtrack?

VP: On the whole they were the traditional ones: working in sound with an actor on set is always something that can't be repeated. The shooting conditions, the mood of the actors, their relations with one another and with the group, the immediate proximity of the rehearsal and the filming – there are very many factors here, including some central bits that would be omitted later, even in the most successful speech recording. This was especially so because a lot of non-professional actors were appearing in the film.

But I think the main factor was something else – the attitude of Sokurov himself to the culture of the directly recorded soundtrack, a culture instilled in him by radio programmes at a time when television was not yet as widespread. Before we started filming we watched some old movies, where the culture was one of natural sounds, of immediacy, of vocal uniqueness that originated solely on the set. In a word, Sokurov was right in the way that he set the task. But how could we realise it? There were lots of problems. Among them was one that arose later: matching the directly recorded soundtrack to the sound scenes (because they hadn't given us the appropriate technical equipment when the film had been stopped, so we had to add sound to some scenes in the sound studio): it was impossible to make the inevitable difference imperceptible...

OS: The soundtrack of *Mournful Unconcern* is totally saturated with sounds and music... The pattern is extremely intricate. How was it made?

VP: The very general principles were, of course, agreed in advance... But a mere two months after we started shooting and after our discussions on even the abstract subjects I realised that what I'd proposed was dependent on what Sokurov had proposed. For me the key to the film was the romance 'The Bell Rings Monotonously',[5] performed in Russian by a foreign singer in a very old recording, in the scene of Randall's suicide. I must confess that even to me this very idea seemed paradoxical. But the director supported it and it was precisely this romance that 'explained', defined for me (I repeat, for me) all the counterpoints and surprises in this film... As for the actual music in it... it's as if we hadn't separated it off from the sounds or the dialogue. There was only one score and that included very different musical fragments (I note Sokurov's propriety in his treatment of musical texts: for instance, playing the finale of a work at the beginning, followed by its opening is impossible). Sokurov has very definite and serious musical predilections and his knowledge of this field is extremely extensive. Furthermore, it goes without saying that an individual's personality is important to him – in this case the composer's. At that moment we were avoiding the intrusion of a new character into the general structure of the film and music was used that would, as it were, itself convey what had to be conveyed in this film, in this way, in this context. But, as early as our work on *Save and Protect*, our experience with the same composer [Yuri Khanin] was less successful. The composer wrote a lot of interesting music but almost none of it found its way into the film. This meant that for Sokurov something did not work. 'The director knows what he wants' is a popular phrase, but true. Sokurov feels straight away whether something is 'right' or 'wrong', 'yes' or 'no', and what can be altered, or not altered, for example, in the montage if music makes an appearance.

OS: Let us return to *Days of Eclipse*.

VP: There the question of a directly recorded soundtrack was not even addressed. I think this was because the actual structure of the film, the way it was put together, seemed to require constant interpretation. That meant that it was quite difficult for the director (and all of us) to imagine how the film would turn out in the context of its Turkmen location (even though Sokurov was very familiar with it) and in those hot conditions. Or even what kind of text there would be. I think that was why we had consciously to keep enough freedom in the sound...As a matter of fact it turned out that almost the entire text was altered.

OS: I don't think anyone noticed.

VP: Well, specialists may judge whether this was done with sufficient precision...And the sound atmosphere – complex, multinational, multilayered – of Krasnovodsk, the city where we were filming, determined the sound structure of the film. It was like an 'artificial' place, inhabited by Turkmens and Russians, Azerbaijanis, Armenians and Kazakhs... There had been some attempts to preserve the culture, like that real singing competition that fitted organically into the film. But something had been violated within the structure of each nationality and in their life in common: so I found out that nobody on the competition jury understood what they were singing about. In the city itself a kind of light music [*estradnaia muzyka*] was playing endlessly from countless recording booths, the radio was playing, and you could hear people speaking different languages...All this was incorporated into the film, both as 'overheard' sound and as something consciously fashioned later in the studio. I showed the film at a seminar for sound engineers and our Armenian colleagues complained: what a pity it was that so many people wouldn't understand what was being said in the film in Armenian (in the dialogue between the daughter and her dying father), and how important this was for the film. Yet, as far as we were concerned, the literal meaning was not an end in itself, but the sound was essentially that of some sort of painful note in this scene...There was a similar problem in the scene with the deserter: a shot rang out – a child started crying but nobody else reacted, apart, I hope, from the sensitive viewer...This film is extremely viscous and the music in it is contemplative; it doesn't illustrate the situation but is simply contemplative, and this brings an independent entity into the make-up of the film – this replay in *Days of Eclipse* of the ending to *Mournful Unconcern*: in both cases Schumann's 'Romance'... In the farewell scene between the heroes on the jetty there is the soundtrack from *Mournful Unconcern* with the song of *The Three Little Pigs*. Generally speaking, the sound compositions of this director's films are a rich field of activity for serious students of film.

OS: And, in my view, not just the sound...Parallel with your example you could cite the many repetitions in the imagery.

VP: I think this can be explained: his films are like links in a single chain...But I wanted to say more about one principle of working with music. It's very important that, even in the presence of good original music, you retain the freedom to use a musical classic and include it in the film when necessary, as, for instance, with the 'Barcarolle' from Offenbach's *Tales of Hoffman*...

OS: And you used fragments from a classic, which inevitably provoked in the audience a chain of general cultural associations (from which 'new' music is free) in exactly the same way as, for instance, a fragment from a Brezhnev speech, which is also a classic but of a different kind?

VP: Yes. There's one more important moment: we've been increasingly daring in dividing the music between, as it were, the principal and the subsidiary, not simply by masking the latter with the former, but by discarding the subsidiary altogether. One extremely primitive example: people are walking around within the shot but no steps are audible. There are no realistic sounds, but suddenly – there are... The viewer, schooled in tame verisimilitude, protests, forgetting that cinema always represents a situation modelled in accordance with the laws of art, rather than a fragment of life...

But a clean soundtrack like this, free from attendant noise, make the thoughtful viewer start to think...

OS: It concentrates his attention and provokes a fantasy...

VP: Of course.

OS: It is in this sense that we can compare the process of perceiving Sokurov's films to reading. When we read, put crudely, we see only the letters. But we all know that this limitation (no sound, image or smell) is a convention of literature and not an obstacle but a spur to the work of perception, and we feel and experience the whole of the picture described. However, *Save and Protect* seems to me in this sense to represent absolute music...

VP: It was conceived as a musical (in the usual application of this term) film. It was our plan that, in a three-hour film, more than two hours would have music. We even thought of using Bach's 'Well-Tempered Clavier'. The idea was that any life – whatever form it took: comic, tragic, unthinkable, whatever – is a correctly composed life, written, as it were, like a score. The motifs of Fate, Destiny, are refracted in precisely this particular way: for a particular life this is quite correct. But Cécile Zervudacki, who was playing the principal role, exceeded all our expectations. She gave the film a rhythm, communicated her tonality, took so much upon herself that the sounds, the music – all seemed superfluous.

I realised how difficult it would be to arrange the soundtrack. The concept of 'isolating the principal sound' applied here absolutely: synchronised sounds appear only where they are necessary, while at the same time non-synchronised sounds are actively at work. Khanin's music is barely audible... While Cherubini's 'Requiem' furnishes the general tone for the opening and also leads the film towards its ending...

Adding a soundtrack for the principal heroine was particularly complicated.

When Cécile began to speak in Russian, she lost the whole flavour and musicality of her own speech, in terms of both timbre and tone. Then we resolved: let her speak French and the meaning should be clear from the responses of her fellow actors. However, we had to do this in a way that ensured that her speaking a foreign language was not perceived as the cause of the tragedy of a heroine in an alien setting.

Luckily, the organic behaviour of her fellow actors allowed us to avoid this... In all the actress speaks two languages – and this created the quite particular musical and vocal subject of her voice.

Unfortunately this aspect of a sound engineer's work – on poor-quality materials, on slender resources – is made very much more complicated by our primitive technical equipment. On an optical soundtrack much of what has been recorded on a magnetic track is lost, and in the transfer process it's very difficult to envisage the end result.

OS: In the titles to the film we read, 'This film is based on motifs from the novel *Madame Bovary*'. What did this formulation mean for you?

VP: Of course, that you shouldn't re-create the sound atmosphere of the beginning of the last century as is done in the usual screen adaptation. There's no indication in the film of any specific period, and place of action, there are not even any names – Emma, Rodolphe, Léon... The characters wear the costumes of both the nineteenth and twentieth centuries, the architecture is of no explicit style – suddenly a Jeep appears... This is natural in a Sokurov film. That is why in the sound too equal value is given to locomotive whistles, the 'voice' of the radio, including the tuning of the receiver, the rumble of an aircraft, and the noise of a 'motor carriage'... All this, obviously, required careful selection and had to be justified in terms of the dramaturgy, the imagery and the acting. I repeat: sound in film, like everything else, is constructed according to the rules of the film itself.

OS: Why do you use only real sounds and noises in your own work?

VP: Now, despite the fact that we are so far behind foreign cinema, we do still have a lot of equipment to process sound. I think that this technology is unavoidable and has to be used, but sensibly, so that the means does not become an end in itself. So it turned out that I never once needed to use it according to a plan. As for music, I quite simply feel closer to the normal sound of a good symphony orchestra...

The secret lies, not in how to capture sound by character, but in how to do it and precisely why. Quite often this cannot be explained...

OS: It seems to me that it is real, rather than transformed, sound that Sokurov once again, perhaps even subconsciously, adheres to as his principle and he has spoken about it on more than one occasion: a film grows alongside real life, it depends on it, after all cinema is a played world...

VP: I would say it was even more complicated: it sometimes happens that real sound in this world of 'artifice' produces an additional unpredictable emotional effect on a scene or on the film as a whole.

One instance: all that Armenian dialogue in *Days of Eclipse*...

OS: Tell me, is there any difference in a sound editor's work between played and documentary film?

VP: In Sokurov's case, of course, none. I've already said that I think of his films as an unbroken chain. Each link in it is special but the whole is inevitable. As a professional I was, in this sense, quite simply lucky: I have the opportunity not just to work the whole time but also constantly to resolve ever newer problems. It is only because of Sokurov that I can see my work as some kind of sequence. For the time being it transpires that we seem to be moving from formal, outer complexity towards ever greater outward simplicity...

OS: But at the same time the movement in the content and emotions is towards ever greater depth... the 'asceticism' of form in *Soviet Elegy* is simply staggering...

VP: That was an incredibly complex task for me – for two whole weeks I simply couldn't go into the sound library [*fonoteka*]. I didn't know what to do. The film is very simple in all its component parts – specialists can comprehend this. But on the inexperienced viewer it produces the impression of very painstaking labour. At the same time, as always everything derives from the sound transfer and emerges from the generally brisk movement of the film. The process itself passed quite quickly – at least once I'd understood how to realise this 'emptiness' on the soundtrack... It's interesting that the scene with the leaders' portraits could, in principle, have been resolved in sound quite differently. We could have accompanied it with a composition of music and noise (and the music had already been chosen), conveying the entire history of our state, and moreover conveying it in a detached and 'abstract' way. We could have accompanied the scene with a multi-layered soundtrack that would have reflected our assessment, and in an extremely categorical manner. We could also have accompanied the scene using a single, sufficiently complex work of classical music, for instance by Shostakovich, and that would have provoked its own associations... But all these approaches would've imbued the scene with a sense of tragedy and would have politicised it. In the end we came to a resolution: the gallery of faces could be shown in almost complete silence, the viewer himself would create for them the background that appeared to be true for him, the viewer. This programmed non-violence against the viewer led to varying reactions to the film... The noises that are there, from the general structure of the film, concern the life of insects, a cemetery, urban sounds, some conversations, something indistinct, some ringing, a cuckoo... Something is taken away, something added, but it's all one and the same thing. There is some concrete text but on the whole no music. Once again nothing is dictated: here you see this, there you understand that... For me the film demonstrated once again the intelligence of Sokurov's approach to sound in film. I have to say that several times my colleagues (even when, I must admit, they were censuring the quality of the execution in places), admitted to me that they envied me for working with a director whose creative attitude to sound in cinema was obvious.

It seems to me that I work with him alone, even though formally that's not the case, and there are no films that I wouldn't take responsibility for. The fact is that he makes quite unbelievable creative demands (in the general sense of the term) that require constant intensive research to resolve.

I've already said that the form in which a project is realised is very much a movable feast – and every day something changes inside me... What's important is that for Sokurov nothing's impossible, there's no immature 'you can't do it like that', but 'you can' – everything is permissible if it's been justified. In this there is obviously a revolutionary quality to his work with sound. The most important thing is that there's not a single film we approached where we might have said: it's all worked out, this'll be an easy job. With every film we started again from scratch.

But, to tell you the truth, Alexander Nikolaevich and I have already discussed this: we've already got ourselves into some sort of blind alley – we have to find new ways of working with sound, and basically with speech. What has been done will not satisfy him as director, nor me as sound editor. The fact is that today our artistic ideas are much more sophisticated than our technical capabilities.

Translated by Richard Taylor

Source: 'Vladimir Persov: Eto – protsess...,' Interview with Olga Shervud, in *Sokurov 1*, pp. 327–330; full version first published in *Tekhnika kino i televidenie* 1 (1990).

3. Leda Semenova: Montage is the Final Approximation to the Idea

I would prefer not to talk about my work in concrete technical terms. Everyone who has anything to do with our profession knows what an editor [*montazher*] does. But I really do want to say that from our very first collaboration – *Mournful Unconcern* – fate has granted me the good fortune to work with wonderful people – Alexander Sokurov, Vladimir Persov[6] [...].

Our working life has developed so that we have almost no time to reflect on and analyse the idea. Probably not everybody needs this... An understanding of Sokurov's personality helps me, I'd say, to understand it. He is a man whose honesty is crystal clear. Honest and pure. That's why it's easy to understand him, even without penetrating the full philosophical depth of his films. I think that, in turn, this realisation gives me the right idea of how to edit Sokurov's films. Each specific shot in each specific picture dictates the conditions: how long we should look at this take in order to understand a person's condition. How far should we scrutinise nature and what should we see in this nature, whether luxuriant or faded – and how far should we realise that man and nature are one, and shouldn't be separated...

It's precisely this that defines my work and the work of the sound editor...

Undoubtedly the director expresses some wishes, but they are not set in concrete. They are in a form that helps to reveal... or does not get in the way of revealing what should not be there. Work goes on at such a level (using the language, appropriately, of literature rather than technology) that at any particular moment it is the presence or absence of something that is significant. How long should a piece of music be audible, or inaudible? Or everything has to be built on silence, on listening attentively, or wanting to hear what we don't hear... It's only then that you can achieve the right perception of the action... It's precisely for this reason that we have those stupendously long takes. They give us the opportunity to interact in silence with another person and with what is happening on the screen... Our last film was *Whispering Pages*. The idea was interesting and very complex: Mahler and Dostoevsky. *Kindertotenlieder* and terribly young heroes, essentially children too...[7]

The circumstances of the production (which drove the director – and not just Sokurov – into a corner) meant that a lot wasn't filmed. When we viewed the material we realised that the original idea, which appeared to consist of the 'monolithic quality' of the background in the unity of space – in which we were not supposed to notice that a character moved from a room on to the street – seemed to have been destroyed. There was no unity. The monolith had been broken up. The material led in a different direction, at another angle. This was all the more so since nothing is trivial for Sokurov. Everything has its significance: the way the cameraman moves the camera, the way the lighting engineer uses light – these change the dramaturgy and the sense... The director suffered terribly at this particular moment: I understand how he intended one thing, but got something completely different. He had to relinquish the original dramaturgy. Construct a new one. You have simply 'somehow' to link the scenes together, 'forgetting' that for various reasons this did not happen.

For instance, we had filmed the murder of the old woman. There was nothing physiological, of course: but it was nonetheless a 'murder'. In none of the versions, however, did the scene appear essential to the film. So we took it out altogether. This was a joint decision. The search was a joint effort. When we took out the scene of the old woman's murder, I suggested a single take: she lies there, filmed through the legs of a chair... It is as if she is lying there because she has been 'spirited away'... The hero (he is not called Raskolnikov in the film) returns home after his conversation with Porfiri Petrovich, looks and sees – her. This is like an apparition – of what was, or wasn't, or might have been, of what haunts him: is it possible that he only imagined this murder? He had wanted to do it, and it is from this single thought that all his torture and suffering derives: he might take upon himself a sin like this...

Sokurov and I probably already work like deaf-mutes. We look at one another and I understand: I don't know what but now I'm supposed to do something... An emergency arose when we were filming *Save and Protect*. For various reasons no copy of the scene of Emma in the quarry in its entirety was made. The director had to re-think the scene completely, and very quickly, so that he could film some additional material before the actress departed. I started editing those bits that we had. Where it could be joined together by montage, it was simply glued. Where it couldn't be joined like that we decided to use a dissolve. This produced a startling artistic effect. How did we make this decision? It's impossible to say. Was it intuitive? Partly... I find it easier to sit and do something than to formulate it for myself.

There is another example from our last film *Whispering Pages*, which has a subtitle, 'Based on motifs from nineteenth-century Russian literature'. A young man approaches a girl. It was incredibly complicated to edit this scene. 'Sonia' was played not by an actress but by a schoolgirl. There was no understudy. We filmed with two cameras. We joined together the material they'd shot (which in itself was understandably difficult) according to the girl's mood: despair, depression, hands by her side... The scene was constructed on the most emotional and expressive levels, but not on the level of dialogue, which was the only thing that perhaps rested on the prose: she killed, she didn't kill – repent... The dialogues were eliminated, omitted. I chose fragments from the material – I was viewing endlessly... Hence the long shot: the girl rushes around the small room, clasping her hands to her body, stooped, a child but with the face of an old woman... Hence, her astonishing eyes... Putting the scene together thematically, in the absence of the director, I tried to use these fragments because the girl expressed everything she could of her personality...

Sokurov trusts my work; he knows that I shan't distort things. Of course he'll then introduce some amendments, mainly he makes up for my excesses. That is also our work. We construct one scene, then a second, then a third... Not infrequently what comes first begins to be condensed, compressed, shortened. The scenes influence one another's size.

Montage is the re-interpretation of material. Re-interpretation. That means that in the first place there has to be an actual interpretation. Starting with the original story [*literaturnyi stsenarii*]. When I read it, I don't think about how I'd make it, but about how Sokurov would. What happens during the filming can turn everything upside-down. I also read the accompanying literature and keep an eye out for markings for the cameraman and the sound recordist in the director's script [*rezhisserskii stsenarii*]... If I don't do that, I'm morally and psychologically unprepared for the montage. Then I'd have to ask the director endless questions and he'd be forced to say all the time: do this, that or the other. I prefer the director to be relieved, as far as is possible, from unwelcome questions and unnecessary work. So very much falls to the director: the finances, the accounting [...]. Now he's dictating which scene is to be filmed and which isn't. That's why the creative idea disintegrates.

But I know him. This means that during the montage we have to use all available resources to get as close as possible to the original idea. The result, more often than not, is something different from what we envisaged. But we have to preserve what is most important. Given that every Sokurov project is unusually profound and rich, it is important to avoid trivialisation and simplification. No simplification come what may. No loss of the original idea is allowed.

It has to be said that Sokurov doesn't spare himself. If something doesn't work out, if something doesn't turn out right, he suffers a great deal but, summoning all his energy, he tries to find a way out of the situation.

Sometimes the losses are so critical that we should describe it as a different, 'new' film. Perhaps *Days of Eclipse* and *Save and Protect* are closer to their original intention. But *Elegy from Russia* and *Whispering Pages* changed a great deal...Judge for yourselves whether in this last film the 'Svidrigailov line', which was so interesting in the script, has survived. Whether the line of the mother and sister – that means the theme of roots, origins, genealogy – has completely disappeared...

We've already talked about our penchant for long shots. There are certainly no hurried or hasty shots in Sokurov. But are there that many long shots? You can go a whole reel. You can go fifty metres. Everything's strictly subordinated to the idea. That's the chief principle of his montage. It's not an end in itself. Even if there are some 'tricks', some experiments, they are imperceptible, they don't strike the eye, they are dissolved in the general task. This means that something that's an end in itself is impossible. Everything else is possible because as a director Sokurov is very progressive and agile.

And there's more. The later a film was made, the less it relies on dialogue, on 'literature'. Imagination is more important in it. Everything becomes a 'character' – chronicle, landscape, personality...Nothing's left to chance. Everything has a purpose. To what end? So that the viewer manages to see, compare and analyse – that's what montage is for.

What is more, Sokurov's later films are much more laconic and sparing in their expressive resources. Remember *Mournful Unconcern*: it's much more of a staccato film in terms of its montage, more musical, more densely rich in its effects...The later films are manifestly stronger. I'd put it like this: in these films there's less explanation and elucidation, here the viewer is drawn more deeply into what's happening, he becomes a kind of accomplice, so that he himself has to look, see, decide and take over. The authorial conception is constructed precisely on drawing the viewer in and 'forcing' him to do the work. This involves an absolute trust in him. There's none of this 'I know what the viewer wants.' He himself takes from the film what he needs and finds interesting. Trust – and the conviction that what is being shown is accessible and intelligible to everyone. Equality of rights – 'I am not doing the thinking for you': you have sovereignty. The absence of any *diktat*. We are offered a subject for our consideration – and we either go with the film, or we don't. Otherwise, what kind of art would this be?...

Translated by Richard Taylor

Source: Olga Shervud, 'Leda Semenova: Montazh – poslednee priblizhenie k zamyslu', in *Sokurov 1*, pp. 331–333.

FILM REVIEWS

4. Oleg Kovalov: We in *The Lonely Voice*

A landmark work seems at first to be not merely something that is 'incorrect' but something that disturbs the peace and there is a reason for this. What is seditious about the subject matter of 'Olympia' or 'Les Demoiselles d'Avignon'?[8] But the philistines who poked their umbrellas into the image of the slender body of a street girl were in their own way sensitive to art: Olympia's regal gaze heralded times where they would have no place. A new aesthetic is the signal for a break between epochs and the aggressive rejection of it represents an unconscious desire desperately to protect an island of personal space [*obustroennost'*].

Landmark films also involve landslides of social scandals – the aura that surrounds them is permeated with cataclysmic currents. The echo of distant passions seems with time to form part of the screen's flesh and blood. *The Birth of a Nation* [USA, 1915] would not have existed without the explosion of racial struggles; or *Potemkin* without the naval mutinies that those passions provoked; or *L'Avventura* [Italy, 1960] without the legendary barracking arranged by the audience of glitterati at the Cannes Festival...

In 1978 a landmark film emerged in our country where nobody had been expecting a prophetic word. In the practice studio at VGIK [All-Union State Cinema Institute, Moscow] one of the students in the popular-science film workshop, Alexander Sokurov, was making a film assignment based on motifs from Andrei Platonov – a full-length acted film, *The Lonely Voice of Man*. The propagandists for perestroika portrayed the VGIK of the 1970s as a sinister cesspool of reaction. The conservatives were too obtuse to play the obvious trump card in their own defence: even in the darkest period VGIK had sketched out the perspective for cinema's development for the years ahead. I myself recall how in 1982 Lenfilm was astonished at the acuteness of the work of the students [Vasili] Pichul, [Vladimir] Tumaev, [Evgeni] Shermergor and [Alexander] Baranov – where would the official cinema of that time have been heading without them?! But none of these films frightened the governing body of VGIK as much as *Lonely Voice*. Even Vasili Pichul's dissident film, based on a story that was highly rated by the Party General Secretary Yuri Andropov, was given top marks in the examination – but there was no talk of examining Sokurov's *Lonely Voice*. This disgraced film was mentioned only in whispers and the wall newspaper in which it was reviewed was surreptitiously torn down.

The apparently chamber history of the love between Red Army soldier Nikita and the girl Liuba particularly infuriated the authorities at VGIK because, given its evident ideological inadmissibility, it was difficult to eradicate the obvious political sedition from it: the two 'dubious' dialogues about fallen enemies and the radiant future did nothing to alter the transcendentally detached meditative tone of the film.

But even its sincere proponents were unable to grasp the real essence of the film's novelty – and by force of habit all those very same 'ideological inconsistencies' worked in the director's favour. No wonder – it was not only the works of Solzhenitsyn that were circulating round the floors of the student hostel [*obshchaga*] but even leaflets by Trotskyites and the Polish 'Solidarity'. Imperial Moscow seemed to any thinking VGIK student like a Surrealist city, in whose labyrinthine depths lurked the keys to the enigmas of history. Reality was swarming with what seemed to be winking signs and signals. These might be: an archival film shot, a fragment from an old newspaper, an announcer's slip of the tongue, a portrait that someone forgot to tear out of an encyclopaedia or to hack off the façade of a building. The most unexpected activities became unwitting pieces of political information, such as the Eastern European film weeks of the Moscow/Paris exhibition. To the poorly politicised student the film *The Lonely Voice of Man* must have seemed insufficiently radical. Nevertheless it was in precisely this student milieu that it was recklessly accepted as something that belonged to them intimately, by a blood relationship.

Sokurov's diaries from the time he was making *Lonely Voice* seem to be filled with the atmosphere of midnight intrigue in the VGIK hostel. Any one of us VGIK students at that time would find in them, affectionately like old friends, quotations from Thomas Mann taken from the lectures of our universal favourite, Bakhmutsky, and references to Mamardashvili, a visitor at the semi-underground seminars.[9] The director's fantasies on themes from Platonov's text, depicting the chilling world of a Russia laid waste by fratricide, with the ruins of churches and the ordinary rites of poverty-stricken funerals against the melancholy whistles of distant locomotives – are a clear reaction against the sharply drawn propaganda of the 'heroism of the Civil War'. From the diary entries it is obvious that with time the naive student discoveries and the litter of topical polemics are cleansed by the energy of artistic intuition and are smelted into the ingot of the project, shorn of their socio-publicistic [*sotsio-fel'etonnyi*] characteristics. *Lonely Voice* astounded people as the embodiment of their own unformulated dreams of an ideal film that liberates consciousness from the tedious secrets of our popular history. They are comprehensible in art, not through some brainy schema, but through the poetic image, which is always both obvious with a brilliant clarity and bottomless to unfathomable depths.

One official art historian thundered that Sokurov's film was born of the malevolent influence of *Mirror*.[10] That might have been the case, had it not been for several apparently local differences, which is why *Lonely Voice* remained on the shelf, while Tarkovsky's film went into very limited distribution. Sokurov's film, despite its pronounced subjectivity, is defiantly anti-lyrical – it is a poetic film shorn of the characteristics of lyric poetry, reflecting the internal world of the man who made it. From the films *8½* [Italy/France, 1963] or *Mirror* it is easy to envisage not only the spiritual make-up but also the physicality of their makers. *Lonely Voice*, however, is absolutely closed: this is unusual for a first-timer, who is usually bursting to amaze people with his originality. In this respect Sokurov's film corresponds through and through to the most astonishing feature of Platonov's artistic universe. We know what pejorative connotations the innocent pronoun 'We' acquired at the hands of post-Revolutionary writers and it was the title of a novel about an invasion by a uniform ant-like multitude. In Zamiatin, Bulgakov and Olesha the 'private' individual shuddered at the tramping of steel cohorts. Platonov was the only writer who brilliantly expressed from within, not the convulsions of this frightened individual, but the opposite. His world is scarcely divisible into individual units of human plasma from this simultaneously enigmatic, frightening and magnificent 'we': essentially all his works are written as if from the first person plural's point of view. That is why, for political researchers, the figure of the writer is so unsettling: in the perestroika years *The Foundation Pit*[11] became the emblem of denunciation literature but the publication of the far more significant novel *Happy Moscow*,[12] in which the hymning of the Soviet thirties reached the heights of idiocy, provoked silent bewilderment. Nonetheless Platonov is of one piece – the inner life of the popular 'corpus' that he depicts both blinds our sight with its sacred urge to sacrifice and bewitches us with its troubled and frightening depths, while the search for the ideal is inseparable from masochistic ecstasy through personal suffering, which has manifestly been mixed up in a metaphysically abnormal attraction to non-existence. That is why Hell on Earth is made by the heroes of *Chevengur*[13] and *The Foundation Pit* themselves and in this instance is not something foisted on the 'good' people by 'bad' leaders.

The film is called *The Lonely Voice of Man* apparently because the director himself was not fully aware at the time of the meaning of his own work – essentially the film represents the voice of the collective unconscious. The 'chamber' history of Nikita – who is unable to realise in this world the full harmony of love and who can only be revived through voluntarily submitting to unimaginable religious torments for a union with somebody close to him – outgrows the specific historical details and becomes the archetype of the tragic Russian mentality and the embodiment of the social complexes of the unique Platonov hero whose name is – 'we'.

That is why *Lonely Voice* is a landmark film for us: it is shot as if from the first person plural point of view. Is this the first time that the collective unconscious has been expressed on the Soviet screen? The history of our cinema is too rich for there to be no precedents. One of these attempts has been pointed out by Sokurov himself, who has consistently noted the influence on his own work of Eisenstein's film *The Strike* [Stachka,

1925]. Another attempt dates from 1932, when Pudovkin made his very strange film *A Simple Case* [Prostoi sluchai], which was lambasted for 'formalism': its key is absolutely that of Platonov. But *Lonely Voice* really does stand alone: even in recent cinema, where there is no organic sense of self as 'we'. That is why the scorching presence on screen of alarming images of the collective unconscious so frightened the VGIK governing body. However strange it might seem, an 'individualistic', lyrically personal basis might have saved the film from a ban from on high, transforming it into an author's caprice bearing no relation to unclouded images of reality. A little later something similar was the condition for the release of Alexei German's *My Friend Ivan Lapshin* [Moi drug Ivan Lapshin, 1984], which was another landmark film for us. The images, imbued with evident Flaubertian impassiveness, of Russian provincial life in 1935 had to be enclosed somehow within the framework of a retrospective view. German's cinema does not exist outside everyday life, outside the rugged realities of the period. In his work the path to historical 'Heaven' runs through a rubbish-filled kitchen and the bowels of a communal passageway. Sokurov however enters a historical world as if bypassing everyday life. Within the shot there are of course some – carefully selected – objects, but everyday life as an element is absent. The director turns to history's subconscious, stripping off its outer layers, like skin. He does not seem to move from the individual to the general, but immediately takes the bubbling burning magma of historical everyday day life in the palms of his hands. In a recently published study Ilia Alekseev compares the Catholic cultural tradition, founded on the omnipotence of image, with the Russian, where His Majesty the Word reigns supreme. In this sense the absence of everyday life [*bezbytnost'*] in Sokurov's film represents the plastic analogue of the dominant tradition in our national art – like icon painting, the prose of Dostoevsky and Platonov, the film *The Lonely Voice of Man* represents the incarnation, the embodiment of the non-material basis for reverie, prayers and hallucinations.

This characteristic of the film gives a certain higher meaning to the film's fate, which at first seems unenviable. In fact it was scandal, a decade of silence, an inconspicuous limited release... But the history of landmark works is always like this, and that is how it should be. Let us recall the rumours among film buffs a long time ago: one section of the public was convinced that the film had been wiped on the orders of the authorities; another had heard something about underground screenings, while a third forced their way into them. The only copy of the film surfaced here and there, like an untraceable solar flare, doing the rounds of the film clubs... For ten years *Lonely Voice* was an invisible film, a ghost film, a film legend, a film rumour – it seemed to exist by word of mouth, as if itself determining its own fate, defined in good time by its aesthetic essence.

Translated by Richard Taylor

Source: Oleg Kovalov, 'My v odinokom golose cheloveka', in *Sokurov*, St Petersburg, 1994, pp. 39–41; reprinted in *Sokurov 2*, pp. 7–13.

5. Maya Turovskaya: 'How is it with me when every noise appals me? What hands are here?'[14]

> *'Out damned spot! out, I say!... What need we fear who knows it, when none can call our power to account?'*[15]

I have the most subjective attitudes towards *Sonata for Hitler*, because the lion's share of the documentary shots used in it was also used in *Ordinary Fascism*, which I made with Mikhail Romm, so that I know them all off by heart but in a different sequence and a different context. This obviously complicates – and possibly also facilitates – my attitudes towards Sokurov's film. Here's a little information for historians of cinema: in the mid-60s we spent eighteen months viewing almost the entire corpus of Nazi newsreels and selected 60,000 metres of material, from which we used around 4,000. This material could have been an inexhaustible source for all time for all film and television programme makers. We begged for our 'selection' to be kept for precisely this purpose but in the interest of economy the material was wiped at Mosfilm and as a consequence for me almost all the reminiscences of Nazism on the large and small screen in our country are neither novel nor informative.

But the fact is that Sokurov is not offering novelty at all. It is as if the material is run and measured on the editing table – but the viewer appears on the screen at the beginning and end of the imaginary screening, a young man of Jewish appearance. It is as if he is looking beyond the frame into the past. Hitler plays the principal part in this sonata from the recent, and already almost complete, past. It is as if the flute solo signifies this temporal distance. The accompanying part belongs to the 'common man' – sometimes these are invalids, women or simply an undifferentiated crowd – the human mass.

It is certainly possible to take different views of this visual 'sonata', so full of contrasts and sorrow. I repeat: I view it from the perspective of my own experience. Once our literary version of the screenplay began as a suite of human hands: how much they own and what they sometimes do. Then the visual material brought quite different solutions, and the theme of hands moved to the deepest layers of the film, giving way to another semantic alphabet.

It may be that this is an aberration in my vision, but it seems to me that the leitmotif of *Sonata for Hitler* has become precisely those hands and the leitmotif shot, reproduced and repeated many times, is of Hitler rubbing his hands. It is as if this shot itself stitches the whole film together, but is read differently according to the different montage and historical sequence. At the beginning it is an anticipation. Hitler rubs his hands, the hands of invalids blinded in the First World War working on an assembly line, the heavy hands of the unemployed hanging around with nothing to do. Hitler speaks from the podium – all this seems to be a prelude to fascism. But the shots of the blind invalids are repeated, as are the shots of Hitler. A man is blinded, he works for the system, which

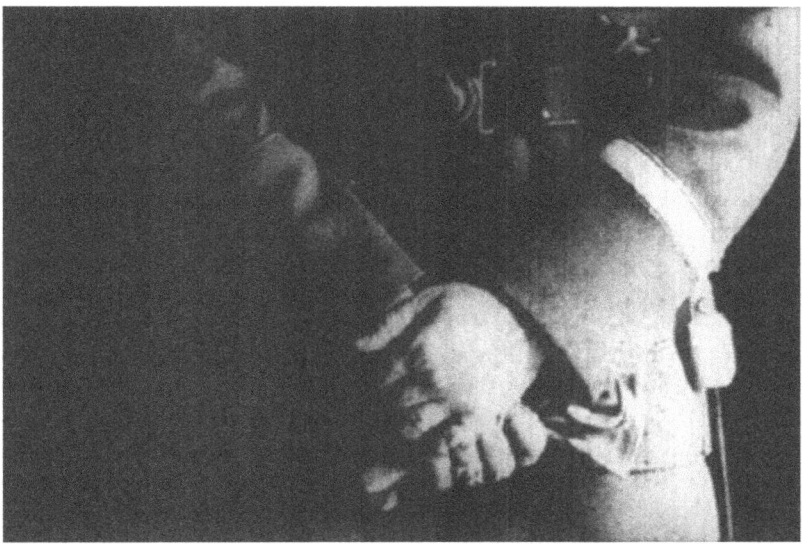

Still from *Sonata for Hitler*.

soon abandons him as waste. Then we see the hands of Hitler the agitator, Hitler the exorcist: the well-known gesture on the podium as he apparently vows to make Germany great. And the hands of the masses: applause, a forest of hands raised in a general greeting, even paralysed invalids who have been brought in wheelchairs assiduously raise their own unbowed extremities in this ritual gesture. Women stretch their hands out ecstatically towards their Führer. Meanwhile Hitler is rubbing his hands – the deed has been done. The long, and also infamous procession of the Führer through the countless throng, the mass, the people compressed into a mass: he soars above them, his hand raised in the Nazi salute, soars above his conquered nation. Hitler's peaked cap, turning briskly here and there, seems to mark the moment of realisation of the principal idea – military expansion. Hands twirl a rifle round, give out and receive decorations, soldiers grope old women in occupied countries while playing their accordions.

Do you think to live by war – you will have to pay for it: an enormous dead hand sticks up out of the mud like a terrible memento.

After the realisation of the ideal comes its collapse and ruin. The notorious cadres of 'total war'. Hitler reviews a unit of boys. People still extend their hands in the Nazi salute, but Berlin is in ruins; a coffin with a woman's corpse cumbersomely partitions off the frame, as in the old picture by Chagall; the former bosses, as if sheltering from the blows of fate, bashfully enclose their private parts in the palms of their hands. Germany, like a wild boar, pierced with arrows in a toy hunt, swiftly goes under. An old woman on a ruined street painstakingly uses her finger to take some remnants of food from an open barrel and licks her finger. The ritual hanging of a war criminal – in the shot on this occasion the legs dangle.

The same young man of Jewish appearance stares intently into the frame.

Once again, Hitler rubs his hands over and over again, and this time the technically multiplied subject for some reason brings to mind mad Lady Macbeth, who was quite unable to wash the blood off her white hands.

The flute. The rough outline of the film, its thematic development, looks like this, or approximately like this. A shot, especially a documentary shot, always carries a whole supply of latent meanings, which are by no means programmed. Using old film, a 'montage film', such as *Sonata for Hitler* appears to be, has to do with these meanings and their selection depends on the director's intention. Here is a very simple example: a blind man working on an assembly line seems to lead the second part of the film – the part of the 'people'. Sometimes the shots that we used in *Ordinary Fascism* in their straightforward, informative or ironic sense, reveal in Sokurov's hands a capacity to provide a metaphorical allegorical meaning. For instance, the stuffed wild boar from the episode 'Göring Going to the People'.[16] Or the bigwig [*Bonze*] covering his private parts with his hands. We collected an entire suite of similar shots, beginning with Hitler himself and, as we accumulated them (the accumulation or multiplication of shots is one of the 'laws' of montage cinema), they became irrationally funny, ironic in every possible way, while in Sokurov the same gesture acquires a different tonality – of fear or self-defence. The capacity of an old shot for transformation, for the revelation – through montage – of latent meaning, the possibility of a different treatment of the shot, will always attract artists of an intellectual artistic bent, amongst whom Sokurov belongs. But the

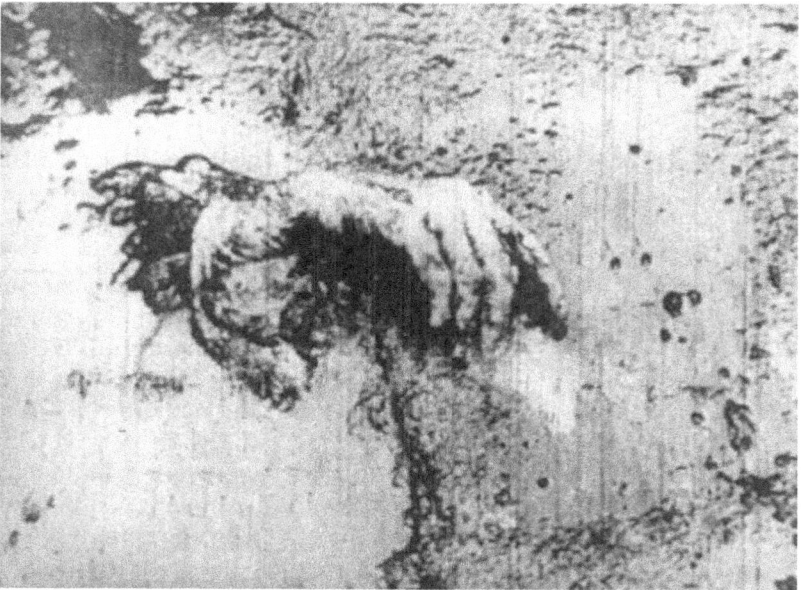

Still from *Sonata for Hitler*.

motif of a charismatic leader and the people is one of the leitmotifs of our era. This is what *Sonata for Hitler* is concerned with.

Translated by Richard Taylor

Source: Maiia Turovskaia, ' "Mne strashen vsiakii zvuk. Ch'i eto ruki?" ', in *Sokurov 2*, pp. 33–35.

6. Petr Bagrov: On Music – However Strange

Sonata for Viola. Dmitri Shostakovich is a film by two directors who are utterly different. You can work out which part is by Aranovich and which by Sokurov. But by most accounts this is not important; historians will clarify things when a quarter of a century passes and the dust has settled. It is something else that is interesting: how the film was viewed in 1986 and how it is perceived twenty years later.

We are looking at an evolution. During the perestroika years of the 1980s, whether the directors liked it or not, politics and history were at the forefront. The 'canonical' Shostakovich – winner of five Stalin Prizes, Hero of Socialist Labour, composer of programmatic symphonies, of a 'Cantata on the Homeland'[17] and so on – appeared on the screen as 'a tragic and contradictory figure' (I am quoting the text closely), 'an artist condemned to create within the paralysing confines of Stalinist ideology', 'a creative artist imprisoned in his own epoch'. A 'screaming contradiction between the pompous parades and the tragic music of a great artist' was revealed. A few metaphors worked in favour of this conception, for instance the then popular attraction of a furiously rotating disc, people trying to stand firm on it but inevitably flying off to the edges under the pull of centrifugal force. Newsreel of the aforementioned parades also worked in its favour – not just because of the familiar 'Song of the Counterplan' but also because of the sinister music of the Eleventh Symphony.[18] In recent years, however, so many revelatory materials about Shostakovich have been published that nowadays the viewer may be surprised not so much by the tragic fate of the composer but, on the contrary, by the five Stalin Prizes.

It would seem that the film was destined to become hopelessly old-fashioned. But this has not happened. This is because it was not a film about politics but about music. Music is in principle apolitical. As is the figure of Shostakovich.

How does music come into being? This is precisely what *Sonata for Viola* is about. There are some shots from silent films, which illustrate the start of Shostakovich's career 'tickling the ivories'. It is worth noting that these excerpts are taken, not from the avant-garde films of the 1920s, but from crude early melodramas. At first the music appears to come from the standard repertoire of the 'film accompanist'. Then suddenly – to shots of Moskvin as Polikushka[19] being hanged, the eerie wedding chorus from *Lady Macbeth of the Mtsensk District*.[20] What is this doing here? It is inexplicable. But it works.

While the chorus sounds, the melodrama gives way to a newsreel devoted entirely to daily life: the countryside of the 1920s, peasants, then a town with children riding bicycles. And it all works. Now the opposite happens: the cyclists go on riding but the chorus from Lady Macbeth is replaced by the life-affirming first movement of the Concerto for Trumpet and Piano.[21] Once again it works.

The film is like a kaleidoscope. The newsreel footage is, for the most part, unfamiliar to the viewer. There is no effect of recognition and you have to look intently at this fleeting glimpse [mel'teshenie]. In actual fact there is no fleeting glimpse: it is simply that the music contrasts rather painfully with the music. The selected film materials and biographical information appear optional. Therein lies the principle. Here is a distressing discussion of the opera The Nose[22] in one of Leningrad's workers' clubs, there a very detailed re-telling of the intricate libretto for The Golden Age. The libretto that, so people think, caused the ballet's failure.[23] Shostakovich's music is not about that at all.

Or the 'wartime' part. The great actor, Ivan Mikhailovich Moskvin, delivers a patriotic speech in front of a microphone, gesticulating earnestly and with commitment. Olga Fedorina, the heroine of the agitational film Girls, to the Front!, lets it rip with a frenzied entreaty to Soviet young women.[24] Suddenly, there is Shostakovich, quiet, shy and bespectacled, like a schoolboy. He reads out a speech in an expressionless voice – actually reads it from a sheet of paper. He hurries, loses his place and, clearing his throat, reads it to the end. The text is standard, official. You do not associate these shots with the war and they do not move you at all. But, if you think about it, neither the appeal by Fedorina the volunteer nor the speech by People's Artist Moskvin move you either. What does move you is the Seventh Symphony, which you heard several minutes earlier. It is about war. No question.[25]

In the film there is almost none of Shostakovich's lyrical or satirical music. This reflects a certain preconception on the authors' part. We are left with the tragic Shostakovich – which matches the time but, as becomes clear, runs counter to the underlying content of the film. Tragic music accompanies the shots depicting various events in Shostakovich's life. The award of the Lenin Prizes, the death of the composer Shebalin, Shostakovich's illness, his life at the dacha, his last meeting with Akhmatova, her death.[26] The young Aranovich filmed Akhmatova's funeral. He was very fond of this footage and it is not surprising that he included them in the film. Aranovich and Sokurov show us the context for creativity. There is so much context that it is transformed from context proper to background. Background for the music. Just as it was in Shostakovich's lifetime. But the visual and musical lines do not combine together: the music here stands on its own.

For me the most powerful and dramatic scene in the film comes when the two finales to the Fifth Symphony are placed one after the other.[27] The haughty and majestic Yevgeni Mravinsky,[28] in medium shot so that we cannot see the orchestra, as if he were playing alone and only miming playing, only rarely looking to either side and clenching his teeth at the moments of greatest tension. Then Leonard Bernstein, impulsive, drained, living every beat to the last breath. The result is two different symphonies. This is a real conflict; it is emotionally, rhythmically, visually – whatever you will – more powerful than any political newsreel in the film. There, somewhere close to one another, are the attack for formalism, and the death of his wife... But the music is immeasurably more significant than all this.

If you think about it, the overall structure of the film is built like this. Scenes from Shostakovich's life alternate with newsreel footage of his last days and it seems as though the whole thing should be permeated with a sense of death. But it does not turn out like that at all. At the very beginning of the film there is a scene of a rehearsal for *The Nose* – of the scene in which the unfortunate Major Kovalev discovers the loss. Just before the actual end of the film there is the final scene from the opera: the nose has been found, to the inexpressible delight of Major Kovalev and Ivan. This is also the closure of the plot. The concluding credits roll to the last chords of the third and final movement of that same Piano Concerto no. 1 – almost the only cheerful work by Shostakovich. The Concerto that the composer so liked to play. The Concerto, whose opening movement was heard at the beginning of the film, the second in the middle, while the third brings the film to an end. And so the Concerto is completed. Brilliantly. Unlike the Fifth Symphony, the First Concerto does not permit of interpretations – such is the structure of this work.

The last thing that we see before the closing credits is a long shot of Shostakovich's grave. Off-screen there is a telephone conversation between the composer and the violinist, David Oistrakh.[29] The conversation is not about politics, time, or even about art. The conversation is about musical technique, about how one of the passages in the Violin Concerto should be played, what changes need to be made to the score. Two great musicians talk about music. Music in the pure sense. I do not know what the film-makers wanted to say in 1981. But for the present day this is a film about music. Because music does not age – unlike politics and cinema.

Translated by Richard Taylor

Source: Petr Bagrov, 'Kak ni stranno – o muzyke', *Sokurov 2*, pp. 45–49. The Russian title echoes an article by Sergei Eisenstein on the acting style of Aleksandra Khokhlova, entitled 'Kak ni stranno – O Khokhlovoi' (1926).

THE OEUVRE

7. Sergei Dobrotvorsky: The City and the House[30]

In the middle of *Moscow Elegy* there is a striking visual effect. A photograph of Andrei Tarkovsky, which occupies the whole frame, shudders, tilts and slips downwards and to one side, revealing behind it a snow-covered graveyard.

Moscow Elegy is at the same time both a requiem and a posthumous retrospective. A genius flees from the Fatherland that has rejected him, from his House, and from the graves of his nearest and dearest. The genius trots around the globe, wandering from one film to another, in the end finding eternal peace in a foreign land. Having thus done his duty by the real biographical canvas and corroborated its social causality, Alexander Sokurov, the director of *Moscow Elegy*, also gives us his own version of fate. According to this version, the true aim of the restless artist, the object of his constant nostalgia and his not always explicit sense of *déjà vu*, is death. For Sokurov Tarkovsky is living two lives away from home. He is drawn from comfortable, humane Italy towards his uncomfortable, snowbound and repellent homeland. The metaphor is clear: foreign walls are no substitute for one's own waste land. Although it is mainly interiors that are shown in the shots of exile, while the country that has been left behind appears as an open space, hostile to man, the artist, who has found the outward appearance of peace, looks through the window and sees the same fields, waste lands and neglected country churchyards. The echo of an obituary announcement bursts through the window, confirming with insincere regret the death of the head of state... The window closed, the voice falls silent, but all the same the artist makes a film about homelessness, in which the final transfer of fire across water, thanks to Sokurov, corresponds rhythmically with the movement of a crowd walking towards the grave.

The Sacrifice, filmed in Sweden, ended with a house being set on fire. Sokurov intercuts the video footage of the set, destined for the fire, with Tarkovsky's Moscow apartment. Immediately we see the derelict rooms where the director spent his youth, and then the country house that he bought and furnished in a last attempt to sort out his daily life in his homeland. This composition closes. A corner of a Paris cemetery and the interior of his last house, where, according to Sokurov's own off-screen

Still from *Moscow Elegy*.

admission, the camera crew could not even get warm, crown this second, and last, life. A fire blazes in the hearth but neither it nor its sacrificial screen double can drive out the sepulchral cold. We appreciate that the creative artist did not set out from here towards ideological exile, but merely abandoned the latest shelter on the path to the one and only dwelling-place for which he alone was destined.

For Sokurov, death crowns the path of our earthly wandering, our worldly exposure [*nepriutnost'*] (*Moscow Elegy* and *Petersburg Elegy*); it presupposes illumination, breakthrough, a moment of truth (*Soviet Elegy*) or man's participation in his own un-alienated nature. Plunging Vytautas Landsbergis into the stream of the lethal present day and, on the other hand, into the element of his first and main profession, *A Simple Elegy* conveys the image of a statesman who has not returned 'home' for long. Although the Lithuanian prime minister does not leave the confines of his official suite, the real time of the playing of music by Čiurlionis[31] seems to liberate him from the burden of historical immortality and return him to his natural capacity, doomed to an end. Music – a synonym for eternity – addresses death as an indivisible substance that is understood and determined here and now, in the certainty of seconds and sounds.

Sokurov's *House* mediates between the illusion of life and the certainty of death to the same extent that a coffin endows the deceased with a last resemblance to the living, while simultaneously promising physical decomposition beyond the grave, and sees the deceased off from earthly life, while not guaranteeing eternal life. The heroine of *Save and Protect* was buried in three coffins – a sign that in the hereafter she would have to break through the material shells, against which the soul of the demon of passion was smashed to bloody pieces.

In *Soviet Elegy* a low camera angle organises the spatial perspective so that a gravestone and a high-rise construction look like neighbouring buildings. In the next scene, a typical Brezhnev-era district seems like an extension of a cramped and characterless Soviet-style cemetery-'hostel' [*obshchaga*]. Against this background the image of Yeltsin – at that time the leader of the populist opposition – is conveyed in the unity of the themes of the 'Prodigal Son' and the almost Fedorovian 'resurrection of the ancestors'.[32] Giving substance to the title of the 'son of the Party and the people', Sokurov illustrates the hero's inner vision with a portrait gallery of the deceased: photographs of his own father and a ceremonial iconostasis of political patriarchs. Static images (in *Lonely Voice*, death first summons Nikita through a photograph album) are associated with a cemetery and the dynamic procession through the corridors of government gives way to the quiet of a private residence, a public figure appears in the fluctuation of mechanical time (I have already shown the meaning of this device, which is central to Sokurov's work through the example of *A Simple Elegy*) ... The literal and figurative 'homecoming' and the ensuing reflections take place on territory that borders on death. It is all the more important that this meditation concerns the strategy of life, putting up the walls of the new communal House. Everything that has been said might appear to be an exaggeration, both on the part of the director and on that of the critic who is interpreting his intention, unless you are aware that for Sokurov the truth lies on the plane of physical existence, that which is susceptible to death. Thus, in the frequently described duel between Yeltsin and Gorbachev, the latter loses precisely because, although he expresses himself with agility, he appears on the ethereal dimension of the television screen, in the embraces of the new Golem, in the spectral flickering of electronically transmitted broadcasting. By contrast, his silent opponent, in his own home (I don't think the scene would have worked if it had been filmed in, let us say, Yeltsin's office), is visible, tangible, and consequently susceptible to death and to the passing of time, which, in Platonov's words, is the 'uniform taut force of a spring'.

Platonov's world, with its naïve machinations, is without doubt close to Sokurov. However, while he shares Platonov's views on the 'power of the global laws of matter', Sokurov, in his only direct address to the writer's prose, executed an instructive about-turn. In 'The Origin of a Master'[33] the hero wanted 'to live in death', threw himself into the river, drowned and was buried by the fence in a country churchyard. The character in *The Lonely Voice of Man*, seduced by the same 'intellectual curiosity', surfaces in the finale. The bodies of Nikita and Liuba, separated in life, find one another in the zone of death. A house with the grass from a graveyard growing through its floorboards becomes their refuge.

In Platonov Home is deprived of its sacral value, but appears as an object in a series of other objects. Its layout becomes clear mechanically, through decay or demolition. A barbaric analysis triumphs in the ruins, just as a peasant triumphs at his hearth once he has decided to establish the nature of fire and invite it into his own cottage.

In Sokurov the semantic weighting is more tangible. In *Lonely Voice* there are two homes and each of them is authenticated by the global symbolism of Life and Death. In the first frames Nikita, cast into the uninhabited landscape of the Earth 'before the Creation' (that is how the secular scenes in Pasolini's *The Gospel According to St Matthew* [Il Vangelo secondo Matteo, Italy, 1964] were filmed, in the visible absence of Heaven), returns to the place where he was born and finds his father asleep. I shall not start to overload this scene with a broad interpretation, but it is most probable that for Sokurov paternity entails some sort of basic demiurge for life (the plot of *The Second Circle*, which finally asserted abandonment by God, develops from the death and funeral of the father). It is all the more important to remember that at one time Nikita dreamed that his father would marry Liuba's mother, whose presence in the film is linked to the theme of death. We shall see something similar in *Days of Eclipse* – a half-mad history teacher will first show Malianov a strange hinged photo album and then go out in pursuit of a young Asian girl, either a Madonna or an exterminating angel. The heretical rationale for this misalliance is clear: Nikita is the first in a line of Sokurov Dukhobors[34] to crave a blood relationship between life and death, the Kingdom of Heaven and life beyond the grave. At first the father rejects this: 'They have high Moscow armchairs... What shall I talk about?' (it is interesting that, years later when he was filming *Moscow Elegy*, the director will find exactly the same armchairs in Tarkovsky's apartment on Mosfilmovskii pereulok), but, seeing his son's departure, he wants to follow. From the House of Life to the House where Death resides.

Apropos of Sokurov's next work *Mournful Unconcern*, the ironic critic Alexander Timofeevsky has remarked: since Rubens spoke not of the downfall of the cosmos but merely of the collapse of Giorgione's myth, it has become at the very least comic to assert the sacral identity of the House and the Cosmos. Without wishing to engage in polemics, I shall observe that Sokurov's metaphor of the Home glimmers in precisely this broader sphere of meanings, in that universal space where first principles are objectified and objects appear as high principles. The architectural project of the Shaw play is erected on the local basis of the European crisis at the turn of the century, while Sokurov's House stands on the edge of the Apocalypse. In Shaw, the ark driven by Captain Shotover, sailed away from the historical maelstrom, while in Sokurov the home, which seems to have been built by a Russianised Gaudí, moves through the stagnant waters of the end of history.[35]

First and foremost we must now consider the relationship between the director and literature (in the final analysis, six of the eight feature films he has made so far are in one way or another screen adaptations). This must also include a consideration of the cultural sources for Sokurov's poetics. Adapting the same Platonov motifs as Sokurov but to an American setting,

Mikhalkov-Konchalovsky, in his *Maria's Lovers* [USA, 1984], by no means brought the image of Home to the surface. An easily readable mythologeme was concealed beneath a coating of everyday life in elements of the narrative discourse: the drinking bout with the father, the local dance, the chair turned towards sunset over the steppe. Eternal opposites were buried deep: in biology, in the psyche, in the depths of the subconscious, but they were not objectified on the outside, in the global joint presence of the creation of the world. In Mikhalkov-Konchalovsky's *Uncle Vanya* [Diadia Vania, 1970] the intelligentsia gatherings were made strange only twice – at the beginning and the end, when mortal life was knocking at the gate, reminding us of itself through terrible documentary shots. In *Mournful Unconcern* the crumpled flattened film witness of death sneaks from shot to shot, marks time, grimaces, winks... In a word, it lives in the house on an equal footing. There is no doubt that Sokurov's barbaric metaphysics grows out of Soviet cultural history. Where the barbarian lives, we find idols and demons co-existing, cultic attributes and funeral accoutrements, indistinct snatches of ethnicity and dishearteningly simple shots of the cosmos, a Bible that has not yet been written and a *Pravda* that is no longer read, the quick and the dead, the angels and the Politburo... Everything that fills the frame so substantially in *Days of Eclipse* and that is gradually driven from the House at the approach of its real owner – Death.

In *Days of Eclipse* the composition is obvious. I do not claim that it is a sequence of shots, but confirm its subjective sense – the objective milieu lurks, becomes clear, and goes away. The interiors become more sparing, barer, more severe. From the panning shot across Malianov's table (there is time to examine both the printed headlines and a page of manuscript) to the pock-marked wall in Vecherovsky's incomprehensibly furnished apartment. Objects peel off and die – in the unbearably long scene of the search of Snegovoy's room a counter records the mechanical time that Sokurov is so enamoured of, shadowy figures move among the carcasses of objects. In the end the town also disappears: for the first time in one of Sokurov's acted films it is portrayed as a cemetery, and even more accurately as a crush of incidental graves which excludes the very idea of the noble geometry of eternity.

Malianov remains in the dark hole of the place that was once a town. Sasha Vecherovsky leaves here – nominally and externally he lays claim to being a self-portrait by the director (let us compare this screen double with the trying on of Tarkovsky's death mask and determine the spectre of Sokurov's self-reflections). In cinema a final departure usually signifies the start of a new life. In Sokurov it hastens the next spiral of death.

'Crossing the boundary of a circle, you lose forever what lies within its circumference... There is no way back...' warned the talking corpse in *Days of Eclipse*. The fear of non-return was borne out: beyond the first circle the next, even more cramped and uncomfortable opened out. Schematically, *The Second Circle* is a repetition of *The Lonely Voice of Man*, but the formal rhythm is as relative as the apocryphal similarity between a nocturnal dream and eternal oblivion. In *Lonely Voice* an inquisitive savage, having returned home, woke the Creator in order to betroth him to death for the sake of a customary and true life. In *The Second Circle* God the Father is hopelessly dead and demands the return of everything only as an onerous ritual service.

Not yet having crossed his family threshold, Nikita jumped off the precipice against the all-embracing background of an empty land (a conceptual similarity to Breughel's *Fall of Icarus*[36] is too obvious here for me to comment in detail). Malianov-2 turns up at his father's house out of a mirage, a white-out, some kind of flat blizzard in which there is no longer any top or bottom, volume or depth. There is also no house as such: the passage across the dark staircase leads straight to the doors of the apartment. There is no cemetery either: that is the reserve of death. It is replaced by movements along the streets of a regional centre in the polar region where the stone barracks look like gravestones.

Noting the traces of the earthly existence of death, the earlier Sokurov filmed houses like graves and cemeteries like cities. The Sokurov of *The Second Circle* no longer sees any difference between life here and now and life on the other side. In victory death has abolished not only the third dimension – of depth – in which it had been concealed, since it is the alleged antithesis of life, but also any comparison, however illusory. The part of speech 'how' escapes from the structure of the posthumous dwelling-place – leaving the bare steps of a sarcophagus, a refuge for the intermediate life, a coaching-inn for wanderers between adjacent worlds.

The same composition roams from one Sokurov film to another: a man, 'cropped' at the shoulders by the bottom border of the frame, raises his head and looks up and back. I think that this is the most 'subjective'

Still from *Save and Protect*.

of Sokurov's camera angles. Everyone sees this in his own way: Nikita always sees the same archaic landscape; Malianov in *Days of Eclipse* a cloud-capped summit; the heroine of *Save and Protect* the warm golden light and the fluttering of down. However, in the final analysis, everyone sees the same thing: the reality beyond daily life on which our inner vision is focused. Malianov in *The Second Circle* appears in this canonical camera angle against the background of a solid wall. A cold dead light streams in, on one side a crack of indeterminate origin steals in, the surface seems to force the hero, abandoned by God, into a two-dimensional projection of despair. In the House, to which death has returned, there are no longer any windows. Windows, and especially the spaces beyond windows, have in Sokurov always furnished a 'significant boundary' (using Mikhail Iampolski's formulation) between worlds. In *Lonely Voice* streams of light flooded through the glass; the jump from the window in *Mournful Unconcern* implied a height guarded on the outside. In *Days of Eclipse* the giant lizard Iosif looked at Malianov through the grille of a small window and that same grille cut off from the outside Malianov's conversation with the angel. A metal transom preserved the junction between the galaxies, as if cast off by a slap in the face from the Fear of God, Malianov performed a reverse somersault off the windowsill and landed up on the trestle-bed in his own room. Up above, in the darkness of universal night, a balcony loomed – the place where Malianov and Snegovoy had last met. In *Save and Protect* the horizontal ordinariness of the interiors clashed with the extended contour of the window. On the outside another – vertical – life was going on, the road ran uphill, the architectural lines went upwards and the vaulted end of the window embrasure made a clear allusion to the life of a saint [*zhitie*].

In *The Second Circle* a window appears only once. Pitch blackness gives way to a blood-stained square. Non-existence was grounded on both sides of the optical boundary; it is impossible to go on contemplating non-existence from the sidelines; you have to live in it and move around blindly – that is why there are no windows in the father's house, but only doors and zones of light, conventionally marking the current state of human substance. Nikita and Liuba went to the House of Death through the gate, tinkered with the keys and picked the lock. Nikita suddenly woke up at the foot of the gates – entry into another reality involved violence and then a hypnotic trance. The doorways of *Second Circle* do not conceal anything, but merely build the tunnels within death – so somebody deprived of sight takes the doors off their hinges in order to facilitate movement around a residence familiar to the touch. In *Stone* the door posts serve as frames for blank mirrors. These are not the exemplary poetic mirrors of Jean Cocteau, capable of being both a screen of indirect reflection and a pool filled with the waters of the Styx – but clots of darkness, the dummy corridors of a non-existent labyrinth. In the final analysis they are blotches on the substance of the film, which vainly call out to the heroes visiting it. 'Through the looking glass', there is nothing: touching the cold surface means only feeling your own palm, which has iced over in the hard frost of the grave. Doing the round of its possessions, Death has removed the walls and curtained the windows. The scale of the interiors was hidden in the mortal shadow, spreading round the blind socket of the camera lens. Outside, quite the contrary: the house has grown larger, magnified, become inflated... Peering at life, which mutates before the shamanic call of the ending, the earlier Sokurov depicted people larger than buildings, and even entire cities. The deceptively habitable crypts of *The Second Circle* and *Stone* overwhelm with their temple-like super-humanity. Moreover, the graveyard landscapes in them are organised, not horizontally but vertically – in a premonition of a new macabre gothic in the structural symmetry that ascends towards death. God is dead and there is a vacancy for a Creator – in the ending of *Whispering Pages* a stone idol, a hybrid of the pagan lion and the Roman wolf, the Trojan Horse and the Bronze Horseman, emerges with the promise of a new Temple... Thus the second circle is closed. Parallel figures come together in the wilderness of the surmounted world beyond the mirror – is impossible to live in it, but you must not die there either. The only thing left is to build. However, the screen often forces the director to be an architect: the history of film architecture has left us with Lang's subterranean *Metropolis* and the disjointed streets of *Caligari*, Greenaway's capricious palaces and Medvedkin's *New Moscow*, Griffith's Babylonian squares and Wenders' city mirages. In this history Alexander Sokurov also deserves a place.

Translated by Richard Taylor

Source: Sergei Dobrotvorskii, 'Gorod i dom', in *Sokurov*, St Petersburg, 1994, pp. 305–308; reprinted in *Sokurov 2*, pp. 328–337.

8. Mikhail Trofimenkov: Sokurov in the Struggle with Reality

The line between 'played' and 'documentary' in [Sokurov's] work has always been fundamentally unstable and in the course of time it has disappeared altogether.

At the basis of Sokurov's cinema there lies a single *Weltanschauung*, a single philosophy of seeing. In his cinema documentary and played representation live by the same rules. If we turn to history we can see that the masters of the first French cinema avant-garde possessed the same cohesive unity of seeing. Buñuel's strictly documentary naturalistic film *Las Hurdes, tierra sin pan* [Land without Bread, Spain, 1933] had far more in common with the hallucinations in *Un Chien andalou* [1929] than with social cinema. Jean Vigo treated scenes of everyday life in Nice in the same way as the syllables in an avant-garde poem. So it does not make sense to write about the 'documentary' Sokurov after making a proviso like this. Because on Earth there is the Great Book of Ecclesiastes, and the whole of the Petersburg director's work is consonant with it. Every one of his formal devices (and he can shock as well as exasperate) is based on a particular philosophy of life, which is both ancient and tragic. There are many examples: I shall limit myself to a few.

One constant device – and it is not so much a device as a real passion for Sokurov – is old photographs. The faces of the parents, brothers, sisters, children of his characters. The commentaries are circumstantial: names, patronymics, dates of birth. Sometimes the text, as if remembering something, loops the loop, turns back, paying attention to one forgotten face. As a rule, however, we do not learn any more about the fate (the profession, the particular gifts) of the people depicted in the photographs. In *Petersburg Elegy* the director is so enamoured of Chaliapin's family (enumerating his children) that (and this is a unique instance in 'biographical' film) he makes no mention of the singer's art and practically omits any shots relevant to his creative work. Instead he includes a minute scene from Fellini's *Roma* (Italy/France, 1972) showing Chaliapin as a young man. The change in generations, the natural cycles are more important than the trace they have left on the land. Even the scene depicting the shooting of *The Maid of Pskov*[37] is only necessary to attract our attention – there, over Chaliapin's shoulder, stands his future wife. In *Moscow Elegy* Sokurov includes a large amount of materials on Tarkovsky filmed by others, [and he does this] apparently unwillingly, apparently submitting to the traditional genre of the obituary. It was after all probably necessary in 1987 to say something significant about the recently deceased director in order to rectify the shameful conspiracy of silence. It seems, however, that Sokurov was more willing to confine himself, as in his other 'elegies', to the story of his hero's father and mother.

In *Soviet Elegy*, the film about Yeltsin, there is not a single word or shot about the political situation in the country. And that was in 1989, when the democrats brought millions of people on to the streets and when the 'object of filming' was transforming himself from a Party outcast [*izgoi*] into the leader of a mass movement. There is nothing about this: instead, as always, there is circumstantial material about Yeltsin's father, mother and wife. Photographs, more photographs, dates and names. But it does not follow at all from this that Sokurov is indifferent to 'Russia's fate'. On the contrary, *Soviet Elegy* is a preview of the future Russia that is unique in its simplicity and its intensity. That is not the point.

The viewers are, of course, well informed about Chaliapin's art or the upheavals in Yeltsin's fortunes. More precisely, these names appear to them to be indisputable symbols of the Singer and the People's Defender. But Sokurov makes no distinction between the great singer and the peasant woman Maria Voinova [in *Maria (Peasant Elegy)*], in the sense that her family drama is no less significant than the drama of Chaliapin. Everybody – both the priests and the collective farm-workers – is equal in the face of eternity, precisely because they are included in the endless cycle of birth and death:

> Abraham begat Isaac; and Isaac begat Jacob; and Jacob begat Judas and his brethren; And Judas begat Phares and Zara of Thamar; and Phares begat Esrom; and Esrom begat Aram; And Aram begat Aminadab; and Aminadab begat Naasson; and Naasson begat Salmon... (Matthew I, 2–4)

The character of the hero is formed from the traits of his ancestors and, just as they have disappeared, so too will he disappear in the course of time. For Sokurov any hero is a son of the human race. No more and no less.

> Vanity of vanities, sayeth the Preacher, vanity of vanities; all is vanity. What profit hath a man of all his labour, which he taketh under the sun? One generation passeth away, and another generation cometh; but the earth abideth for ever. (Ecclesiastes I, 2–4)

In *Soviet Elegy* insects drone above the dead foliage in the cemetery, and the camera moves slowly along the gravestones, new and old, while the disgraced Yeltsin remains silent in his office and portrait upon portrait of the members of the Politburo alternate unhurriedly. Dozens of faces (a device the like of which would not be permissible in documentary cinema) pass across the screen. The contemporary viewer still recognises Lenin, Trotsky, Dzerzhinsky and the Stalinist guard. Then there is slight confusion, and not just because, among the twin brothers, the official retouched portraits that were yesterday so frightening, you cannot distinguish a single one from any other. Did they really exist, or is the director pulling our leg? Who were: Korotchenko, Aristov, Mikhailov, and Puzanov? Perhaps they ruled long ago over one sixth of the globe, instilling fear and loathing into their subjects, but have now dispersed. Like a hallucination, one more empire has collapsed, just as Babylon and Rome collapsed, but, just as the sun set, so it rose again. Looking at history as if from above, Sokurov performs an act of political foresight: he closes the portrait gallery with the same photograph of Lenin with which it began. The circle breaks with Yeltsin, the future destroyer of the Soviet Union, who for the time being is looking out at night through his window, feeling for the first shifts in the power that will come to him. But vanity is not merely a change in the timeservers who are in power. Vanity is also 'high art' but the director of *Petersburg Elegy* does not have time to discuss this. Chekhov's posthumous return in *The Stone* is an admission of the impotence of the classical tradition, of which the neglected museum is a remnant. Even earlier, in *Mournful Unconcern*, the dancing characters in the burning house joyfully bury Bernard Shaw. In *Petersburg Elegy* Sokurov quotes the correspondence between Chaliapin and Gorky about the curious crowd at Chekhov's funeral: 'Is this the scum he wrote for?' Is it worth writing? Is it worth making films?

Vanity is the palace intrigues at Yalta and the Second World War battles in *The Allies* [working title for *And Nothing More* – RT], one of Sokurov's most traditional films. The neutral elements of reality, the innocent rural landscapes that penetrate the wartime newsreels turn the hatred of previous years to ashes, like a nameless 'walrus' crawling out of the melting Petersburg ice, indifferent to Chaliapin's family history.

Vanity is any collective human endeavour in general. One of Sokurov's favourite camera angles is the view from a stationary camera on a swaying crowd, rumbling inarticulately like an ant-hill. It seems to be time for the camera to follow someone, but this impression quickly dissipates, yielding to a distressing sense of depersonalisation. The shots of the holiday demonstration on Nevsky Prospekt in *The Evening Sacrifice* are not a cause for political reflection but an attempt to show the tragic dark side of the holiday. The onlookers [*zevaki*] are not intimidating; they are not frightening, but doomed, meaningless and deserving of our mournful contempt. One of the least accidental titles in his filmography is *Mournful Unconcern*. Without noticing it themselves, people have already turned to ashes, like the smoking cases of artillery shells, like the dead foliage in a cemetery, like the mud in country lanes, like the steam rising above the roadway from the manholes of the sewers, or cigarette smoke rising above our heads. It is no accident that Sokurov begins *Moscow Elegy* with a scene of mass panic, of a collective loss of reason in the face of unavoidable mass destruction.

We might observe that the swaying of the crowd involuntarily repeats Sokurov's favourite natural rhythm of movement. Its rhythm corresponds to the rhythm of the water spotted by specks of light in *Petersburg Elegy* or the quiet way the shadows slip across the snow in *An Example of Intonation*. Man and the crowd return to nature and turn out to have no more sense than the shadows on the snow.

Man's static states are close to him: the hero at his writing desk, at the piano, even better – in a photograph. His favourite device is an endlessly long static camera stare into the face, a device that provokes a sense of awkwardness and tires the viewer out. This device achieves an effect that is diametrically opposed to European cinema thought, which is grounded in theory. It is not the discovery of the innermost mystical essence of man, but the dissolution of the face in the surrounding atmosphere, in the specks of light, the mortification, the transformation of the film image into the photographic – and then its complete disappearance.

The peace of an immobile countenance, the peace of a photograph – and eternal peace. The motif of death, the motif of the cemetery, are always present in Sokurov's films, whether it be Tarkovsky's last refuge in Paris, the transfer of Chaliapin's ashes or the scenes of Maria's funeral taken by a naïve rural photographer.

Nature – in Sokurov's films that is also doomed to crumble to dust just as men's bodies do. An almost physical sense of gravity is achieved by the fact that the audience seems to make its exhausting way alongside the director towards the 'object of filming'. The time of monotonous shots through a car windscreen in *Maria (Peasant Elegy)* or *An Example of Intonation* scarcely comes close to the real. The long path to Yeltsin's house becomes meaningless when the crunch of the snow under foot drowns out the dialogue between the director and the president. The sense of the exceptional value of the 'object' is devalued by the efforts that have it be made to reach him and get away: the 'object's is lost in the surrounding space, which is silent and boundless.

It is possible that this endurance test for the audience – which is a kind of antidote to traditional documentary cinema – has no significance as an ideological token. That cinema masked an indifference to people through colourful depictions of flourishing nature and smiling peasants, haymaking and dining-tables, it was a cinema without any onerous path to the hero, with no reflection on the world or mankind, but it made up for this with a deceptively clear structure.

Sokurov trod the path of 'normal' Soviet documentary film in *And Nothing More*. He examined the ornamental and voluptuous accumulation of elements of reality in the film *Patience. Labour*. Playing with representation, he endowed an official holiday newsreel with a sinister retrospective sense in *Sonata for Viola. Dmitri Shostakovich* and made a preparation of documentary materials from the beginning of the century in *Mournful Unconcern*. But it is precisely *Maria (Peasant Elegy)*, work on which stretched over more than a decade, that is the film that marked a turning point in Sokurov's documentary series, in its own way a manifesto. It is a turning point not just because the director, without taking pity on himself, demystified the work of his earlier years, revealing behind the sunny façade of the Brezhnev 'cinema village' melancholy and death. The melancholy behind the façade had an existential, rather than a socio-political character. Sacrificing his first film, Sokurov has devoted himself to the 'cinema of melancholy'. He promises to return in nine years' time to the same village and to film the subsequent course of events, although what could have happened, apart from new deaths and births, weddings and partings?

In its way, *Maria (Peasant Elegy)* is an anthology of the visual and sound effects and motifs that are present in all Sokurov's films: static shots of faces, numerous photographs, a visit to a cemetery, a panning shot across meaningless snow-covered plains and decrepit roads with a mellifluous Italian aria encroaching on the muddy soundtrack.

Sokurov does not fight against the generally accepted understanding of documentary cinema. In the final analysis, to fight against the prevailing style is senseless, insofar as the predominant style is always right, unassailable. It simply looks at the world with a strained and bitter view. There is no life left in it: obviously in the vanity of vanities there is a self-sufficient and unknowable meaning.

Translated by Richard Taylor

Source: Mikhail Trofimenkov, 'Sokurov v bor'be s real'nost'iu', in *Sokurov 1*, pp. 161–163.

9. Andrei Plakhov: Rulers and Tyrants

The title and the anxiously intimate subject matter of *The Lonely Voice of Man* have secured for Sokurov the image of an artist who is remote from worldly vanity – and even more from politics – and immersed in his own secret inner world. Nonetheless even this film – and it is no accident that it is based on Platonov's prose – is permeated with an, albeit very subjective, sense of history. It is above all the newsreel shots, which refer to Eisenstein's *The Strike*, that introduce this sense into the structure of the film. However, the support that Andrei Tarkovsky rendered for the film helped to promote the legend that Sokurov was the heir precisely to the cinema of Tarkovsky with its triumphant lyricism and extreme degree of subjectivity.

From the very outset it seemed to me that this was mistaken. Tarkovsky was a poet and lyricist and remains both in his only 'historical' (the quotation marks are self-evident) film *Andrei Rublev*. Sokurov, who was originally trained as a historian, is an artist with a more overtly social temperament in a rather epic mould. For this reason I am not disavowing the pieces I wrote at the end of the 1980s in which I represented Sokurov, whose works had only just been legalised in the heat of perestroika, as 'the voice of a generation'. This does not mean that he was the leader of a movement, but his lonely voice nevertheless sounded from nothing remotely like an ivory tower and did not present itself as a Messianic 'n-th degree of self-assertion' (as the critic Alexander Timofeevsky entitles his article on *Mournful Unconcern*). In making and defending his films and his right to work, Sokurov fought against the VGIK authorities, the governing body of Lenfilm, wrote letters to Lev Kulidzhanov and Armen Medvedev and generally behaved in a way that was nothing like an 'accursed poet', an arrogant and at the same time an ephemeral being who is not of this world. By defending himself against the authorities with all his energy, he was in actual fact fighting for the creative freedom of all the film-makers of his generation.

Furthermore, let us not forget that in parallel with *The Lonely Voice of Man* Sokurov was filming *Sonata for Hitler*, which was the first documentary treatment of the theme of the tyrannical leader and the exultant, and then suffering people. Moreover, in this ten-minute montage film it was already clear that Sokurov was not just – or rather not so much – interested in the charismatic manipulation of mass consciousness. It was not 'ordinary fascism' (the fashionable sociological subject of the 1960s) or the infernal sexual pathology of Nazism (in the spirit of the interpretations of the 1970s), but the sombre and self-destructive metaphysics of power. Any power – not just in the Third Reich.

This subject matter is developed at greater length in Sokurov's second montage film, *And Nothing More*. Filmed at the height of the period of out-and-out stagnation and the decay of the Soviet system, this shows the democracies who were once our allies in the struggle against our common enemy – Hitlerism. However, the author's attitude (which is expressed in the selection of shots that are not merely emblematic but also appear to be fortuitous, showing the historical extras in slow motion with a fixed gaze) creates a particular retrospective view in which there is no place for that pathos of victory, but there is a new and cruel re-distribution of the world between governments which emerges after the mass deaths and the total destruction. Three of the documentary heroes of this film appear later in Sokurov's feature films: Hitler in *Moloch*, Hirohito in *The Sun* and Stalin in *Taurus*, but even Roosevelt and Churchill, the leaders of the democracies he is promoting, might well appear as heroes in Sokurov's 'tyrannology'.

In the course of the 1980s and the very beginning of the 1990s Sokurov released a number of films that dealt directly with current affairs/contemporary politics: *Soviet Elegy* and *An Example of Intonation* (about Yeltsin), *A Simple Elegy* (about Landsbergis), and *On the Events in Transcaucasia* (about one of the first manifestations of inter-ethnic tension). *Mournful Unconcern* (with its liberal sprinkling of documentary footage of the First World War) was unshelved and released, as was *Days of Eclipse*, which was permeated by a cosmic view from above. But even in the most intimate of the works from this time, *Save and Protect*, the latent subject of power is nevertheless present – fascinating and seductive, corrupting and elusive. Even if, as in the case of Madame Bovary, it is the power of love alone.

The two films about Yeltsin are startling: made before he became President, they actually predict both his triumph and his fall, and his special mission to liberate the country against its wishes. For Sokurov, Yeltsin is the same as Madame Bovary, moved by the obscure impulses of Fate, but he is presented against the background of the merry-go-round of politics rather than love. His silence in front of the camera is so eloquent that it is as if, in the words of the German critic Peter Jansen, 'there was nothing more to be said about Russia, especially at that time'. When the faces of 'the political champions of the century' – the faces of the Carbonari and the Messiahs, the *vydvizhentsy* and the criminals – pass one after another across the screen the camera views them in the same impassive and concentrated was as in erotic play. Most of them lie in the same fraternal historical grave by the Kremlin wall, but the funeral ritual, as throughout their entire lives, follows a religion without God. The principal hero of the film follows it too, although he is still capable of an indistinct whisper like the Greek Frenchwoman who whispers in Russian 'save and protect'.

Even here you can sense the wholeness of Sokurov's approach to social and private life: both disintegrate if there is no basis in God, if politics and love become objects of worship, if they become drugs, they exercise power over the rulers themselves. However, there then follows a long period of 'intimisation': throughout the major part of the 1990s Sokurov produces a hermetically esoteric cinema, which culminates in the masterpiece of this cycle, the film *Mother and Son*. During this period, on the other hand, social and historical subjects (such as confrontation on the Afghan-Tajik frontier in *Spiritual Voices*) are resolved as if they were intimate matters. In Sokurov's work there has been an accumulation of mysticism (partly brings him closer to Tarkovsky), the hypnosis of death, asceticism (provoking in observant critics a suspicion of erotic phobias), hypertrophied spirituality and introversion. This was the route to a dangerous frontier, beyond which communication even with the viewer who was well disposed towards the director threatened to come to an end. Then on the very threshold of the new century Sokurov films *Moloch*, the first part of his 'tyrant-breaking trilogy' [tiranoborcheskaia trilogii]. Now he almost comes into the mainstream, to a key theme of history at large, while in no way sacrificing in the process his individual view and spiritual priorities. Once more the director decisively translates a 'provocative' political subject on to the level of intimate existence. The moustached dictator Adolf Hitler, with the unaesthetic rolls of fat, suffers from a fistula in his throat and is manic about tumours. He rehearses his paranoid speeches in front of his girlfriend Eva Braun, and she arouses his failing sense of a stab in the back. One day in 1942 our two leading heroes (along with Goebbels and Bormann) in a secret residence in the German sticks are both filled with hysterics, loneliness and a fear of unavoidable death.

At the same time Sokurov broadens the historical subject matter, extrapolating it into a mythological past and future. Adolf and Eva are simultaneously Adam and Eve: the first sinners who have not yet reflected on their sins. They are also the children of the end of the twentieth century who have lost contact with reality, living in a virtual world, which manipulates them more than they do it. Eva admits that to love a genius is the same as loving the sun or the moon, and that she is not even clearly aware of who is fighting whom in Europe. The war newsreel showing in the auditorium might give an answer to the inhabitants of the ivory tower, or rather the one made of human bones. But Eva does not see it and, pressing the revolver to her chest, she hides behind the screen to conceal herself.

This film contains reflections of Wagner's operas, Visconti's 'German trilogy' and the films of Fassbinder – the sound codes of European cultural consciousness. But it has nothing in common with István Szábo: Sokurov is not worried about the theme of conformity, but about the particular conformity of the artist. In his work you can rather suspect solidarity with Coppola, who maintains that the film director is also in a sense a 'Moloch', the last dictator in the contemporary world. We cannot exclude the possibility that Tarkovsky too would willingly have put his name to this statement.

The connection between power and art (or culture in the broad sense of the word) is revealed in *Taurus*, the second film in Sokurov's trilogy. In the director's interpretation Lenin (who did not understand modernism and despised it) is the product of the ideology, morality and psychology of the modern; he emerged as a result of a tectonic shift in the cultural ground, which occurred at the turn of the century (Sokurov once made *Mournful Unconcern* about this shift). The director declines to view either Hitler or Lenin as 'leaders', dependent on emotions, sicknesses and manias – in the final analysis, on fate; they hover helplessly between life and death, like the other 'nameless' people in the world. They only imagine these demiurges and this helps, rather than hinders, their capacity for evil on a universal scale.

Death – a substance that has previously attracted Sokurov – hovers over the heroes of *Taurus*, and it is a death that is not brightened by religious humility or human compassion. Atheistic Messianism and melancholy expediency provide no comfort. They cannot be saved even by the devotion of a loyal companion. Lenin wrote to Krupskaya, 'Perhaps you will be my successor? What would be the best thing for the cause?' Even the death of Marx was commented on with lugubrious Communist humour: he is not dead yet, but Engels is already in the doorway. It is not Stalin, not the boorish retinue at Gorki, nor the doctor-murderers, who appear to the Patient (as the film's hero is officially called) as an image of approaching death, but the yawning void, the inescapable hole that forms when the conceit of rational matter disintegrates. Lenin was one of those leaders who cultivated this material and believed in its all-conquering primacy. For him this was an experiment, an act, a *démarche*, a rejection of the 'Philistine traditions' of his own family. For the man who succeeded him traditions in general did not exist. When the Guest (Stalin) appears in Gorki he does not say or do anything that is obviously terrible, but clearly maintains that Lenin's fate is pre-determined and that ideological mutants – the revolutionaries – are being replaced by physical and moral freaks, cold-blooded professional bandits. After this scene with the sick monster you start to feel pity. After all, he worries about the fact that birds freeze to death in winter, people are dying from starvation, and Politburo members make mistakes when they write. After all, he is ashamed to 'die in luxury' in a state-owned house, surrounded by expropriated (stolen) goods. After all, he is determined to ask the Party for poison, but will these people with stern names – Kamenev, Molotov, Rykov – agree? Suddenly Trotsky will abstain against him?

In *Moloch* Sokurov had something to lean on – or something to react against. The Wagner-Visconti mythology, the opera- or operetta-like ornamentalism of Nazi rituals. Early Bolshevism had only just begun to create its own aesthetic and iconography. In *Taurus* the director is far from stylisation. He creates a portrait likeness of his heroes, preserves the museum appearance of objects and in the process almost entirely rejects anything remaining that is characteristic of the 'epoch', even cinematographic materials. The smooth movement of the camera (for the first time Sokurov also acts as cameraman), the soft resolution of the lighting, the delicacy of the montage joins and the equally unobtrusive musical interjections – fantasies on a theme by Rachmaninov. The almost disappearing subject of image and reflection. Minimalism, which prepares the way to the maximalism of the artistic task. The subject is: a historical and physical person facing death and eternity. The task is: whether to burden the viewer with thoughts that to him are unpleasant and undesirable. You don't want to think about death? Don't: that is what Ilyich, who has become wise in his madness, says – from the metaphysical point of view death is an unproven fact. Nature lives and breathes in the name of eternity, scudding clouds and fully grown grass into which you can fall and forget yourself, are accessible even to a stooping tyrant. Sokurov's sombre film is in its own way an optimistic tragedy: to use an old expression, it contains catharsis. Man is weak and mortal, history is cruel and unjust, but there is a higher sense and a higher beauty and sometimes we can recognise their reflections.

To external appearances Sokurov is moving from the intimate to the epic, but this trajectory is always deceptive. In fact the reverse is happening: the historical layer of the plot/subject matter is filmed like a shaving, leaving the smooth, pure surface of intimate existence – the loneliness of man, the most celebrated of them all, in the face of his physical and spiritual impotence. This theme undergoes an unexpected turn in the last film in the 'trilogy of power', *The Sun*. Unlike *Russian Ark* and *Father and Son*, which are suffused with light, this film is immersed in semi-darkness: not once does the director succumb to the temptation to provide a visually literal equivalent of the image of the Sun. Nonetheless there is less darkness in *The Sun* than in *Moloch* and *Taurus*; there are more shafts of light and it is particularly noticeable that there is humour present – yes, indeed, humour, which allowed French critics to compare the final film in Sokurov's tyrants' trilogy with Chaplin's *The Great Dictator* [USA, 1940].

Humour in Sokurov? This very juxtaposition might make some people laugh. Nonetheless as early as *Mournful Unconcern* we can detect a link with the tradition of early twentieth-century clowning [*ekstsentrika*], which fed not only on popular humorous culture but also on intellectual humour. The montage effects in *The Strike* are tragic in content but their mechanics are akin to comic clowning. The classic figures of montage cinema, headed by Griffith, owed a great deal to English literature, and not just to Dickens, so that Sokurov's choice of Shaw (rather than Brecht, which might have seemed more appropriate to his ends) as a literary model is fully justified.

In *The Sun* Sokurov operates at a far higher level of mastery and deploys irony with much more refinement. This is irony as alienation (from a 'foreign' culture, although German is close to us, isn't it?), irony as a mirror reflecting two 'island' traditions (the British and the Japanese) to one another, the irony of a man who has become ruler by birth, rather than calling, and who has done everything to cast off the shackles of Power. What Lenin and Hitler strove for with all their might was given to Emperor Hirohito by dint of his birth, and he starts from the point that others approach in their own uncompromisingly hardened way. But, feeling that he is responsible for numerous misfortunes and deaths, he willingly renounces the divine office of the 'Sun' (which would itself bring further victims) and is born again as a man who is gifted in his own particular profession (ichthyology) and personal life.

Translated by Richard Taylor

Source: Andrei Plakhov, 'Vlastiteli i tirany', in *Sokurov 2*, St Petersburg, 2006, pp. 340–350.

Notes

1 *The Exterminating Angel* was instead directed as *The Initiated* [Posviashchennyi] by Oleg Teptsov in 1989 while *Presence* [Prisutstvie] was directed by Andrei Dobrovolsky in 1992.
2 Arabov is referring here to *Elegy from Russia* and *Whispering Pages*, both made in 1993.
3 Each source of sound, voice, and noise has to be recorded onto a different track.
4 Completed in 1983, *Mournful Unconcern* was released only in 1987 during Gorbachev's glasnost campaign.
5 A mid-nineteenth-century romance composed by A. Gurilov with lyrics by I. Makarov.
6 Sokurov's sound editor. For his involvement in Sokurov's films, see filmography. See also his interview in this section.
7 *Whispering Pages* draws on themes from Dostoevsky's works; in the following she refers to the character and plotlines borrowed from *Crime and Punishment*: Raskolnikov, the prosecutor Porfiri Petrovich, Sonia Marmeladova and Svidrigailov.
8 These two paintings both caused a sensation when exhibited in Paris: 'Olympia' depicted a full-frontal naked courtesan and was painted by Edouard Manet in

1863 and exhibited two years later; 'Les Demoiselles...' was painted by Pablo Picasso in 1907 and depicted five naked prostitutes in a brothel in Barcelona.
9   Vladimir Bakhmutsky (1919–2004) was a member of the VGIK teaching staff, specialising on foreign literature. Merab Mamardashvili (1930–90) was a Georgian philosopher. In 1978 he was a professor at Moscow State University and deputy editor of *Voprosy filosofii* [Problems of Philosophy].
10 For a discussion of the parallels between these two films, see chapter 4 of the present volume.
11 *The Foundation Pit* [Kotlovan] was written by Andrei Platonov in 1929–30 and first published in an English translation in London in 1969. The *povest'* was not published in Russian until 1987, with a fuller critical edition following in 2000.
12 *Happy Moscow* [Schastlivaia Moskva] was written by Platonov in the early 1930s and left unfinished. It was first published in a scholarly edition in 1999. One early reviewer called it, 'Platonov's most terrifying novel'.
13 *Chevengur* is the name of a village in Platonov's novel of the same name, written in the late 1920s.
14 Macbeth in William Shakespeare, *Macbeth*, Act 2, Scene 2.
15 Lady Macbeth in *ibid.*, Act 5, Scene 1.
16 The Russian for this, *Khozhdenie Geringa v narod* has an echo of the failed Populist 'Going to the People' [*Khozhdenie v narod*] movement of the 1870s.
17 The full title is 'The Sun Shines on Our Homeland' [Nad Rodinoi nashei solntse siiaet], op. 90, written in 1952.
18 The 'Song of the Counterplan' was written for the film *Counterplan* [Vstrechnyi, 1932], directed by Fridrikh Ermler and Sergei Yutkevich.

The Eleventh Symphony, subtitled 'The Year 1905', written and performed in 1957, led to the composer's rehabilitation and the award of the Lenin Prize in 1958.
19 *Polikushka* was directed by Alexander Sanin in 1922 and starred Ivan Moskvin (1874–1946), later director of the Moscow Art Theatre.
20 *Lady Macbeth of the Mtsensk District* [Ledi Makbet Mtsenskogo uezda] was Shostakovich's op. 29, based on a story by the nineteenth-century writer, Nikolai Leskov and first performed in 1934. Despite its popularity, the opera was used as an excuse to denounce Shostakovich in a notorious article entitled 'Muddle instead of Music' [Sumbur vmesto muzyki], allegedly inspired, if not actually written, by Stalin and published in *Pravda* on 28 January 1936. The composer later re-worked the opera as *Katerina Izmailova*, op. 114, and this version was first performed in 1963.
21 This reference is to the Concerto for Piano, Trumpet and String Orchestra in C minor, op. 35, written and first performed in 1933 and which contains a significant part for trumpet.
22 *The Nose* [Nos], was a satirical opera based on a story by Nikolai Gogol, written in 1928 and denounced for formalism after its Leningrad premiere in 1929. It was not performed again until 1974.
23 *The Golden Age* [Zolotoi vek], op. 22, was written in 1929–30.
24 *Girls, to the Front!* [Podrugi, na front!] was an eight-minute agitational short produced by Lenfilm in 1941 and directed by Viktor Eisymont.
25 Symphony no. 7 in C Major, op. 60, was composed in besieged Leningrad in 1941 and dedicated to the city.
26 Vissarion Shebalin (1902–63) was a close friend of Shostakovich, who dedicated his second string quartet, op. 68, composed in 1944, to Shebalin.

Anna Akhmatova (1889–1966) was a distinguished Russian poet who, like Shostakovich, survived the 900-day siege of Leningrad.
27 The Fifth Symphony in D minor, op. 47, written and premiered n 1937, was one of the composer's most popular works and was styled as 'a Soviet artist's creative response to justified criticism'.
28 Yevgeni Mravinsky (1903–88) was the conductor of the Leningrad Philharmonic Orchestra for fifty years and conducted the premieres of six of Shostakovich's symphonies.
29 David Oistrakh (1908–74) was the USSR's leading violin virtuoso.
30 The Russian word *dom* means both 'house' and 'home' and the reader needs to bear in mind both connotations in this piece since English requires the translator to choose between them.
31 Landsbergis led Lithuania to independence from the USSR in 1990. He had previously been Professor of Music at the Lithuanian Conservatory and author of a study of Mikalojus Konstantinas Čiurlionis (1875–1911), the Lithuanian artist and composer associated with Symbolism and art nouveau.
32 Nikolai Fedorov (1829–1903) was a Russian religious philosopher, known as 'the Moscow Socrates' who did not accept the existence of a straightforward distinction between the living and the dead.
33 Platonov's 'The Origin of a Master' first appeared in 1929 and later constituted the first chapter of his novel *Chevengur*.
34 The Dukhobors were a Russian Christian Spiritualist sect who rejected secular government and believed in pacifism.
35 The reference is to Shaw's play *Heartbreak House*, written during the First World War, which the film is based on. Antoni Gaudí (1852–1926) was a Catalan architect whose most famous Modernist building is the as yet unfinished Cathedral of the Holy Family [*Sagrada Familia*] in Barcelona.
36 The reference is to the painting 'Landscape with the Fall of Icarus' in the Musée des Beaux-Arts in Brussels, which has also been the subject of poems by both William Carlos Williams and W.H. Auden.
37 *The Maid of Pskov* (Pskovitianka) was an opera by Nikolai Rimsky-Korsakov, first performed in 1873.

FILMOGRAPHY

Alexander Nikolaevich Sokurov

b. 14 June 1951, Podorvikha (Irkutsk Region)

Graduated from the History Department of Gorki (now Nizhny Novgorod) State University (1974), and the director's department of the Film Institute VGIK (1979, workshop of Alexander Zguridi); from 1969–75 assistant director at Gorki Television. Since 1980 he has lived and worked in Leningrad/St Petersburg at the studio Lenfilm. In 1998–99 presenter of the television programme 'The Island of Sokurov', for Channel Kultura. State Prize of the Russian Federation (1996, 2001); Merited Artist of the Russian Federation (1997); Triumph Award (2002); People's Artist of the Russian Federation (2004).

Feature Films
The Lonely Voice of Man (Odinokii golos cheloveka), 1978, rel. 1987
76 minutes
Script: Yuri Arabov
DoP: Sergei Yurizditsky
Production Design: Vladimir Lebedev, Liutsia Lochmele
Music by Krzysztof Penderecki, Otmar Nussio, Alexander Burdov
Editing: A. Bespalova (1978), Leda Semenova (1987)
Sound: Irina Zhuravleva (1978), Vladimir Persov (1987)
Cast: Andrei Gradov (Nikita), Tatiana Goriacheva (Liuba), Vladimir Degtarev (Nikita's father), Liudmila Yakovleva (Liuba's mother), Nikolai Kochegarov, Sergei Shukailo, Vladimir Gladyshev, Ivan Neganov, Yevgenia Volkova, Irina Zhuravleva
Production: Lenfilm (USSR); restored at Lenfilm in 1987
Festivals & Awards:
- Locarno IFF 1987, Bronze Leopard

The Degraded (Razzhalovannyi), 1980
Short, 31 minutes
Script: Alexander Sokurov
DoP: Sergei Yurizditsky
Production Design: Yuri Kulikov
Costume Design: Elena Amshinskaya
Composer: Alexander Mikhailov
Editing: Giulsium Subaeva

Sound: Igor Vigdorchik
Cast: Ilya Rivan, Viktoria Yurizditskaya, Elena Mishchenko, Anatoli Petrov, Sergei Koshonin, Stanislav Sokolov, Alexander Suliaev, Irina Sokolova
Producer: Debiut (Mosfilm)

Mournful Unconcern also translated as *Painful Indifference* (Anaesthesia Psychica Dolorosa) (Skorbnoe beschuvstvie), 1983, rel. 1987
92 minutes
Script: Yuri Arabov
DoP: Sergei Yurizditsky
Production Design: Yelena Amshinskaya
Costume Design: Yelena Amshinskaya, Galina Subbotina
Music by Krzysztof Penderecki, Oleg Karavaichuk, Alfred Schnittke, Georges Bizet, Peter Tchaikovsky, Dmitri Shostakovich, Felix Mendelssohn
Editing: Leda Semenova
Sound: Vladimir Persov
Cast: Ramaz Chkhikvadze (Shotover), Alla Osipenko (Ariadne), Tatiana Egorova (Hesione), Dmitri Briantsev (Hector), Vladimir Zamansky (Madzini), Viktoria Amitova (Ellie), Irina Sokolova (Nanny Guinness), Vadim Zhuk, Andrei Reshetin, Ilya Rivin
Producer: Lenfilm

Empire Style (Ampir), 1987
Short, 32 minutes
Script: Lucille Fletcher, Alexander Sokurov
DoP: Sergei Sidorov
Production Design: Sergei Brzhestovsky (Bolmant)
Editing: Leda Semenova
Sound: Vladimir Persov
Cast: Alla Osipenko
Producer: Lenfilm

Days of Eclipse (Dni zatmeniia), 1988
125 minutes
Script: Yuri Arabov, Boris and Arkadi Strugatsky, Petr Kadochnikov
DoP: Sergei Yurizditsky
Production Design: Elena Amshinskaya
Costume Design: Lidia Kriukova
Music by Robert Schumann, Alfred Schnittke, Jacques Offenbach, Mikhail Glinka
Composer: Yuri Khanin
Editing: Leda Semenova
Sound: Vladimir Persov
Cast: Alexei Ananishnov (Dmitri Malianov), Eskender Umarov (Vecherovsky), Irina Sokolova (Malianov's sister), Vladimir Zamansky (Snegovoy), Kirill Dudkin (Glukhov), Alexei Yankovsky (driver), Viktor Belovolsky (Gubar), Sergei Krylov, Ilya Rivin
Producer: Lenfilm, Troitsky Most
Festivals & Awards:
- Felix 1988, special prize for Best Music (Yuri Khanin)
- NIKA 1988, Best Sound (Vladimir Persov)
- IFF Toronto 1988; IFF Ontario 1988

Save and Protect [*Madame Bovary*], (Spasi i sokhrani), 1989
165 minutes
Script: Yuri Arabov
DoP: Sergei Yurizditsky
Production Design: Yelena Amshinskaya
Composer: Yuri Khanin
Editing: Leda Semenova
Sound: Vladimir Persov
Cast: Cécile Zervudacki, Robert Vaap, Alexander Cherednik, Viacheslav Rogovoy, Darya Shpalikova
Producer: Lenfilm, Troitsky Most
Festivals & Awards:
- FIPRESCI award at IFF Montreal 1989

The Second Circle (Krug vtoroi), 1990
93 minutes
Script: Yuri Arabov
DoP: Alexander Burov
Production Design: Vladimir Soloviev
Costume Design: Natalia Zamakhina
Music: Otmar Nussio
Editing: Raisa Lisova
Sound: Vladimir Persov
Cast: Petr Alexandrov, Nadezhda Rodnova, Tamara Timofeeva, Alexander Bystriakov, Sergei Krylov
Producer: Troitsky Most, Centre for Creative Initiatives
Festivals & Awards:
- FIPRESCI award and Dutch Film Critics' Award at IFF Rotterdam 1990

The Stone (Kamen'), 1992
88 minutes
Script: Yuri Arabov
DoP: Alexander Burov
Production Design: Vladimir Soloviev
Music by Peter Tchaikovsky, W.A. Mozart, Gustav Mahler
Editing: Leda Semenova
Sound: Vladimir Persov
Cast: Leonid Mozgovoy (Chekhov), Petr Aleksandrov, Vadim Semenov
Production: Perm Studio, Lenfilm
Festivals & Awards:
- Volk Award for Best Sound (Vladimir Persov), Lenfilm 1993
- IFF Toronto 1992

Whispering Pages (Tikhie stranitsy), 1993
Russia, Germany. 80 minutes
Script: Alexander Sokurov, Yuri Arabov, Andrei Chernykh
DoP: Alexander Burov
Production Design: Vera Zelinskaya
Music by Gustav Mahler
Editing: Leda Semenova
Sound: Vladimir Persov
Cast: Alexander Cherednik, Sergei Barkovskii, Yelizaveta Koroleva, Galina Nikulina

Producer: Martin Hagemann, Thomas Kufus, Vladimir Fotiev
Production: Zero Film, Esko Film, Severny Fond
Festivals & Awards:
- IFF Berlin 1994; IFF Karlovy Vary 1994; IFF Chicago 1994

Mother and Son (Mat' i syn), 1997
Russia, Germany. 70 minutes
Script: Yuri Arabov
DoP: Alexei Fedorov
Production Design: Vera Zelinskaya, Esther Rittersbusch
Music by Otmar Nussio, Mikhail Glinka, Tomaso Albinoni, Giuseppe Verdi
Editing: Leda Semenova
Sound: Vladimir Persov
Cast: Gudrun Geyer, Alexei Ananishnov
Producer: Thomas Kufus; executive producers: Alexander Golutva, Martin Hagemann, Katrin Schloesser
Production: Lenfilm, Roskomkino, Zero Film
Festivals & Awards:
- Ecumenical Jury Prize, CICAE Jury Prize at IFF Berlin 1997
- FIPRESCI Prize, Guild of Film Critics Prize, Kinotavr 1997
- Special Jury Prize, Tarkovsky Prize, Guild of Film Critics Prize at IFF Moscow 1997
- IFF Toronto 1997; Sao Paolo 1997; Rotterdam 1998

The Moloch (Molokh), 1999
Russia, Germany, Japan, Switzerland, Italy. 107 minutes
Script: Yuri Arabov
DoP: Alexei Fedorov, Anatoli Rodionov
Production Design: Sergei Kokovkin
Costume Design: Lidia Kriukova
Music by Wagner, Beethoven, Mahler
Editing: Leda Semenova
Sound: Vladimir Persov
Cast: Yelena Rufanova (Eva Braun), Leonid Mozgovoy (Hitler)
Producer: Viktor Sergeev
Lenfilm, Goskino, Fusion, Zero Film
Festivals & Awards:
- IFF Cannes 1999: Best Script (Arabov)
- Grand Prix (rejected by producer Viktor Sergeev) and Best Actress (Rufanova) at Kinotavr 1999
- EFA nomination for Best Cinematography (Fedorov)
- Nominated by Russia for the Academy Award for Best Foreign Film 1999
- IFF Chicago 1999; IFF Toronto 1999; IFF Karlovy Vary 1999. IFF Rotterdam 2000

Taurus (Telets), 2000
Russia. 101 minutes
Script: Yuri Arabov
DoP: Alexander Sokurov
Production Design: Natalia Kochergina
Costume Design: Lidia Kriukova
Composer: Andrei Sigle
Editing: Leda Semenova

Sound: Vladimir Persov
Cast: Leonid Mozgovoy (Lenin), Maria Kuznetsova (Krupskaya), Sergei Razhuk (Stalin), Lev Yeliseev (doctor)
Producer: Viktor Sergeev
Production: Lenfilm, Bereg, Ministry of Culture (Russia)
Festivals & Awards:
- State Prize of RF 2001 (Sokurov, Arabov)
- NIKA 2001 for Best Film, Best Director, Best Script, Best Cinematography, Best Production Design, Best Actor, Best Actress
- Special Jury Prize, Festival of Russian Cinema Honfleur (France), 2001
- IFF Pusan 2001; IFF London 2001; IFF Stockholm 2001; IFF Rotterdam 2002

Russian Ark (Russkii kovcheg), 2002
Russia/Germany. 96 minutes
Script: Alexander Sokurov, with Boris Khaimsky and Anatoli Nikoforov
DoP: Tilman Büttner
Production Design: Yelena Zhukova, with Natalia Kochergina
Costume Design: Lidia Kriukova, Tamara Seferian, Maria Grishanova
Music by Mikhail Glinka
Editing: Sergei Ivanov
Sound: Vladimir Persov
Cast: Sergei Dreiden (Custine), Sokurov (Narrator)
Producer: Andrei Deriabin, Jens Meurer, Karsten Stoeter
Production: Ermitazhnyi Most, Hermitage, Ministry of Culture, Egoli Tossell, Koppfilm
Festivals & Awards:
- IFF Toronto 2002, Visions Award
- EFA nomination for Best Director, Best Cinematography
- Critics' Prize at OFF San Francisco, 2003
- NIKA 2003 for Best Production Design, Best Costume Design
- Ranking among the ten best films of 2002 in *Time* magazine
- IFF Cannes 2002; IFF Karlovy Vary 2002; IFF Chicago 2002; IFF London 2002; IFF Pusan 2002

Father and Son (Otets i syn), 2003
Germany, France, Netherlands, Italy, Russia. 84 minutes
Script: Sergei Potepalov
DoP: Alexander Burov
Production Design: Natalia Kochergina
Costume Design: Bernadette Corstens, Maria Grishanova
Composer: Andrei Sigle
Editing: Sergei Ivanov
Sound: Vladimir Persov
Cast: Andrei Shchetinin (father), Alexei Neimyshev (son)
Producers: Thomas Kufus, Igor' Kalenov, Hengameh Panahi, Ineke van Wierst, Roberto Cicutto, Luigi Musini, Els Vandevorst
Zero Films, Nikola Film, Mikado Films, Lumen Films, Isabella Film
Festivals & Awards:
- FIPRESCI award at IFF Cannes 2003
- FF Kinotavr 2003; IFF London 2003; IFF Rotterdam 2004

The Sun (Solntse), 2005
Russia, France, Italy, Switzerland. 110 minutes
Script: Yuri Arabov
DoP: Alexander Sokurov
Production Design: Yelena Zhukova, Yuri Kuper
Costume Design: Lidia Kriukova
Composer: Andrei Sigle
Editing: Sergei Ivanov
Sound: Vladimir Persov
Cast: Issei Ogata (Hirohito), Robert Dawson (Douglas MacArthur), Kaori Momoi (Empress)
Producer: Andrei Sigle, Igor Kalenov, Marco Mueller
Production: Nikola Film, ProLine, Downtown, Mact, Riforma
Festivals & Awards:
- Golden Apricot, Erevan IFF 2005
- IFF Eurasia 2005, Almaty: Best Director
- NIKA for Best Script (2005)
- IFF Berlin 2005 (competition); Kinotavr 2005

Alexandra (Aleksandra), 2007
Russia. 90 minutes
Script: Alexander Sokurov
DoP: Alexander Burov
Production Design: Dmitri Malich
Costume Design: Lidia Kriukova
Composer: Andrei Sigle
Editing: Sergei Ivanov
Sound: Vladimir Persov
Cast: Galina Vishnevskaya (Alexandra Nikolaevna), Vasili Shevtsov (Denis Kazakov), Raisa Gichaeva (Malika)
Producer: Andrei Sigle, Laurent Danielou
Production: ProLine, Rezo Film
Festivals & Awards:
- Special Jury Prize at IFF of European Cinema in Seville, 2007
- Best Director at Tallinn IFF Black Nights, 2007
- IFF Cannes 2007 (competition); Kinotavr 2007 (special event)

Faust, 2011
Russia
Script: Yuri Arabov
DoP: Bruno Delbonnel
Production Design: Yelena Zhukova
Costume Design: Lidia Kriukova
Composer: Andrei Sigle
Editing: Jörg Hauschild
Cast: Anton Adasinsky, Johannes Zeiler, Isolde Dychauk, Gerog Friedrich, Hanna Schygulla
Producer: Andrei Sigle

Documentaries
Call Sign R1NN (Pozyvnye R1NN), Gorki TV, 25 min., 1975.

The Earthliest of Concerns (Samye zemnye zaboty), Gorki TV, 30 min., 1975.
The Summer of Maria Voinova (Leto Marii Voinovoi), Gorki TV 1975.
The Automobile Gains Reliability (Avtomobil' nabiraet nadezhnost'), Gorki TV, 1977.
The Last Day of a Rainy Summer (Poslednii den' nenastnogo leta), 1978.
Maria. Peasant Elegy (Mariia: Krest'ianskaia elegiia), LSDF [Leningrad Studio of Documentary Films], 40 min., 1978, rel. 1988. DoP: Alexander Burov; Production Design: Sergei Debizhev; Sound: Mikhail Podtakui; Editing: Leda Semenova; Composer: Alfred Schnittke.
Sonata for Hitler (Sonata dlia Gitlera), LSDF, 11 min, 1979, rel. 1989. Composer: Krsysztof Penderecki.
Sonata for Viola. Dmitri Shostakovich (Dmitri Shostakovich: Al'tovaia sonata), with Semen Aranovich, LSDF, 90 min., 1981, rel. 1986. Script: Boris Dobrodeev; DoP: Yuri Lebedev, Yuri Alexandrov.
And Nothing More (I nichego bol'she), LSDF, 70 min., 1982, rel. 1987. Script: A. Nikiforov, DoP: Alexander Burov, Lev Rozhin, Liudmila Krasnova; Production Design: Sergei Debizhev; Sound: Mikhail Podtakui.
The Evening Sacrifice (Zhertva vecherniaia), LSDF, 20 min., 1984, rel. 1987. DoP: Alexander Burov, Sergei Yurizditsky, Lev Rozhin, Alexander Yakubovsky, Alexander Degtiarev, Liudmila Krasnova, Sergei Sidorov; Sound: Mikhail Podtakui.
Patience. Labour (Terpenie. Trud), LSDF, 10 min., 1985, rel. 1987. Script: I. Efremova; DoP: Alexander Burov; Sound: S. Litviakov.
Elegy (Elegiia), LSDF, 30 min., 1985, rel. 1986. DoP: Alexander Burov, Lev Rozhin, Liudmila Krasnova; Sound: N. Vinogradskaya.
Moscow Elegy (Moskovskaia elegiia), LSDF, 88 min., 1986, rel. 1988. DoP: Alexander Burov, Andrei Naidenov; Sound: A. Pugachev, Vladimir Persov.
Petersburg Elegy (Peterburgskaia elegiia), LSDF, 40 min., 1989. Script: Alexander Sokurov with T. Smorodinskaya; DoP: Alexander Burov; Sound: Vladimir Persov; Editing: Leda Semenova.
Soviet Elegy (Sovetskaia elegiia), LSDF, 37 min., 1989. DoP: Alexander Burov; Sound: Vladimir Persov; Editing: Leda Semenova.
On the Events in Transcaucasia (K sobytiiam v Zakavkaz'e), LSDF, Leningradskaia kinokhronika, 10 min., 1990. DoP: M. Shnurikov, Alexander Burov; Sound: Vladimir Persov; Editing: Leda Semenova.
A Simple Elegy (Prostaia elegiia), LSDF, 20 min, 1990. DoP: Alexander Burov; Sound: Vladimir Persov; Editing: R. Lisova.
A Leningrad Retrospective (1957–1990) (Leningradskaia retrospektiva), LSDF, 788 min., 1990.
An Example of Intonation (Primer intonatsii), Perm Studio, 57 min., 1991. DoP: Alexander Burov; Sound: Vladimir Persov; Editing: Leda Semenova, I. Kiseleva.
Elegy from Russia (Elegiia iz Rossii), Russian Government's Committee for Cinematography, 69 min., 1992. DoP: Alexander Burov; Sound: Vladimir Persov; Editing: Leda Semenova.
Spiritual Voices (Dukhovnye golosa), TV: Eskomfilm, Lenfilm, North Foundation, Pandora Japan, 327 min., 1995. DoP: Alexei Fedorov, Alexander Burov; Sound: Sergei Moshkov, Editing: Leda Semenova.
Soldier's Dream (Soldatskii son), North Foundation, 12 min., (excerpt of *Spiritual Voices*), 1995.
Oriental Elegy (Vostochnaia elegiia), North Foundation, Lenfilm, SONY, 44 min., 1996. DoP: Alexei Fedorov; Production Design: Vera Zelinskaya; Sound: Yoshinori Kawabata, Sergei Moshkov.

Hubert Robert. A Fortunate Life (Rober. Schastlivaia zhizn'), Hermitage Bridge Studio, 26 min., 1996. DoP: Alexei Fedorov, Sound: Vladimir Persov; Editing: Leda Semenova. Producer: Andrei Deriabin.

Alexander Sokurov: Calendar of a Generation (Aleksandr Sokurov: Kalendar' odnogo pokoleniia), TV, 5 series, 1997.

The St. Petersburg Diary: Inauguration of a Monument to Dostoevsky (Peterburgskii dnevnik: Otkrytie pamiatnika Dostoevskomu), TV: Studio Nadezhda, 45 min, 1997. Texts: Alexandra Tuchinskaya; DoP: Alexei Fedorov; Sound: Sergei Moshkov, Editing: Leda Semenova.

A Humble Life (Smirennaia zhizn'), Japan Foundation, North Foundation, Pandora Japan, 75 min., 1997.

Confession (Povinnost'), Studio Nadezhda, Lenfilm; TV mini series, 260 min., 1997. DoP: Alexei Fedorov; Sound: Sergei Moshkov; Editing: Leda Semenova.

The St. Petersburg Diary: Kozintsev's Apartment (Peterburgskii dnevnik: Kvartira Kozintseva), TV: Studio Nadezhda, 45 min., 1998. DoP: Alexei Fedorov; Sound: Sergei Moshkov; Editing: Leda Semenova.

The Knot: Dialogues with Solzhenitsyn (Uzel: Besedy s Solzhenitsynym), Studio Nadezhda, 89 min., 1999. DoP: Alexander Degtiarev and Alexei Fedorov; Sound: Sergei Moshkov and Vladimir Persov; Editing: Konstantin Stafeev, Vladimir Vasiliev.

dolce... (nezhno...), Studio Bereg, Quest (Japan), 61 min., 1999. DoP: Koshiro Otsu, Sound: Sergei Moshkov; Editing: Alexei Yankovsky, Sergei Ivanov.

Elegy of a Voyage (Elegiia dorogi), Ideal Audience (France), Studio Bereg, Kassander Film, 47 min., 2001. Sound: Sergei Moshkov; Editing: Sergei Ivanov.

The St. Petersburg Diary: Mozart. Requiem (Peterburgskii dnevnik: Motsart. Rekviem), Studio Bereg, Sterkh Film, RAI 3, 70 min., 2004.

Elegy of Life. Rostropovich. Vishnevskaya (Elegiia zhizni. Rostropovich. Vishnevskaia), Studio Bereg, Sterkh Film, Svarog Film, 110 min., 2007. DoP: Mikhail Golubkov, Kirill Moshkovich, Egor Zherdin; Sound: Vladimir Persov; Editing: Sergei Ivanov.

We Read the Book of the Blockade (Chitaem blokadnuiu knigu), Telekanal 100, 96 min., 2009. DoP: Alexander Tarin; Sound: Nikolai Almaev, Viacheslav Arkhipov; Editing: Tatiana Orlova.

Intonation (Intonatsiia), Telekanal 100, 251 min., 2009.

BIBLIOGRAPHY

Key Publications in Russian
Arkus, Liubov', (ed.), *Sokurov*, St Petersburg: Seans, 1994 (referred to in the text as **Sokurov 1**).
Arkus, Liubov', (ed.), *Sokurov. Chasti rechi. Kniga 2*, St Petersburg: Seans, 2006 (referred to in the text as **Sokurov 2**)
Tuchinskaia, Aleksandra, (ed.), *The Island of Sokurov*: Official Website, http://sokurov.spb.ru/index.html (accessed 28 August 2010)

Interviews (in English)
Carels, Edwin, 'The Solitary Voice: An Interview with Aleksandr Sokurov', *Film Studies* 1 (1999), pp. 73–77; p. 76.
Menashe, Louis, 'Filming Sokurov's "Russian Ark": An Interview with Tilman Büttner', *Cineaste* 28.3 (2003), pp. 21–23.
Schrader, Paul, 'The history of an artist's soul is a very sad history', Interview with Alexander Sokurov, *Film Comment* 33.6 (November-December) 1997, pp. 20–25. http://www.paulschrader.org/writings.html and http://sokurov.info/?id=1225965602
Sedofsky, Lauren, 'Plane Songs: Lauren Sedofsky talks with Alexander Sokurov', *ArtForum* 40.3 (November 2001), p. 124; available online at http://www.thefreelibrary.com/Plane+songs%3a+Lauren+Sedofsky+talks+with+Alexander+Sokurov.-a081258061
Szaniawski, Jeremi, 'An Interview with Aleksandr Sokurov', *Critical Quarterly* 33.1 (2006), pp. 13–27.

Select Bibliography: On Sokurov
Alaniz, José, ' "Nature", Illusion and Excess in Sokurov's "Mother and Son" ', *Studies in Russian and Soviet Cinema* 2.2 (2008), pp. 183–204.
Arnaud, Diane, *Le Cinéma de Sokourov. Figures d'enfermement*, Paris: L'Harmattan, 2005.
Aronson, Oleg, 'Giperdokument, ili svidetel'stvo o zhizni. Lenin po Aleksandru Sokurovu', *Metakino*, Moscow: Ad Marginem, 2003, pp. 173–83.
Bohn, Anna, 'Pinsel und Leinwand. Aleksandr Sokurovs gemalte Landschaften in *Mutter und Sohn*', *Schnitt* 3 (1997), p. 16.
Christie, Ian, 'Returning to zero', *Sight and Sound* 4 (1998), pp. 14–17.
Christie, Ian, '*Russkii kovcheg / Russian Ark*', in Birgit Beumers, ed., *24 Frames: The Cinema of Russia and the Former Soviet Union*, London: Wallflower Press, 2007, pp. 242–51.

Condee, Nancy, *The Imperial Trace. Recent Russian Cinema*, New York: Oxford University Press, 2009.
de Keghel, Isabelle, 'Sokurov's "Russian Ark": Reflections on the Russia/Europe Theme' in Stephen Hutchings (ed.), *Russia and Its Other(s) on Film*, Basingstoke and New York: Palgrave Macmillan, 2008, pp. 77–94.
Drubek-Meyer, Natascha. 'An Ark for a Pair of Media: Sokurov's *Russian Ark*', *ArtMargins* 5 May 2003, http://www.artmargins.com/content/cineview/meyer.html
Eshelman, Raoul, 'Sokurov's "Russian Ark" and the End of Postmodernism', *ArtMargins*, 30 July 2003, http://www.artmargins.com/content/cineview/eshelman.html
Gillespie, David and Elena Smirnova, 'Alexander Sokurov and the Russian Soul', *Studies in European Cinema*, 1.1 (2004), pp. 57–65.
Graffy, Julian, '*The Sun*', *Sight & Sound* 9 (2005), pp. 82–83.
Halligan, Benjamin, 'The Elusive Hitler: A Dialogue on *Moloch*', *Central Europe Review*, 2.3 (2002), http://www.ce-review.org/00/3/kinoeye3_halligan.html.
Halligan, Benjamin, 'The Remaining Second World: Sokurov and "Russian Ark"', *Senses of Cinema*, February 2003, http://archive.sensesofcinema.com/contents/03/25/russian_ark.html
Hänsgen, Sabine, 'Stille Bilder. Zur Minimierung des Filmischen bei Aleksandr Sokurov (Film > Photo > Malerei)', in Mirjam Goller, Georg Witte (eds), *Minimalismus. Zwischen Leere und Exzeß*, special issue of *Wiener Slawistischer Almanach* 51 (2001), pp. 375–390.
Harte, Tim, 'A Visit to the Museum: Aleksandr Sokurov's *Russian Ark* and the Framing of the Eternal', *Slavic Review* 64.1 (2005), pp. 41–58.
Hoberman, J., 'Russian Ark', *Film Comment Magazine*, 2002 http://www.filmlinc.com/fcm/9-10-2002/sokurov.htm
Iampolski, Mikhail, 'Representation – Mimicry – Death: The Latest Films of Alexander Sokurov', in Birgit Beumers (ed.), *Russia on Reels. The Russian Idea in Post-Soviet Cinema*, London: I.B.Tauris, 1999, pp. 127–143.
Iampolski, Mikhail, 'Truth in the Flesh', *Film Studies* 1 (1999), pp. 70–72.
Iampolski, Mikhail (as Jampolski, Michail), 'Sokurows Regiearbeit', *Kunst und Literatur* 3 (1990), pp. 309–315.
Iampol'skii, Mikhail, 'Sokurov, Aleksandr', in Arkus, L. (ed.), *Noveishaia istoriia otechestvennogo kino, 1986–2000: Kinoslovar'*, vol. 3, St Petersburg: Seans, 2001, pp. 114–117.
Jameson, Fredric, 'History and Elegy in Sokurov', *Critical Inquiry* 33.1 (2006), pp. 1–12.
Jameson, Fredric, 'On Soviet magical realism' in his *The Geopolitical Aesthetic: Cinema and Space in the World System*, Bloomington and Indianapolis: Indiana University Press; London: BFI, 1992, pp. 87–113.
Kachurin, Pamela and Ernest A. Zitser, 'After the Deluge: "Russian Ark" and the Abuses of History', *NewsNet* 43.4 (2003), pp. 17–22.
Komm, Dmitrii, 'Kovcheg bez potopa', *Neprikosnovennyi zapas*, 3 [29] (2003) http://magazines.russ.ru/nz/2003/29/komm.html
Kovalov, Oleg, 'Dokumental'noe kino v SSSR', *Noveishaia istoriia otechestvennogo kino. 1986–2000. Kino i kontekst*, vol. 4, St Petersburg: Seans, 2002. http://www.russiancinema.ru/template.php?dept_id=15&e_dept_id=6&text_element_id=35.
Kujundic, Dragan, 'After "After": The *Ark*ive Fever of Alexander Sokurov', *Art Margins* 5 May 2003, http://www.artmargins.com/content/cineview/kujundzic.html; as 'After "After": The *Ark*ive Fever of Alexander Sokurov, *Quarterly Review of Film and Video* 21.3 (2004), pp. 219–239.

Levine, Amy, 'Sokurov and Lacan, Painting's Luminous Archive and Anamorphic Imaginaries', http://www.ias.umn.edu/pdf/Amy%20Levine.pdf

Listov, Viktor, 'Dokumental'nyi Sokurov', *Iskusstvo kino* 9 (1991), pp. 66–74.

McNab, Geoffrey, 'Aleksandr Sokurov's new film is an upbeat character study of the Japanese emperor Hirohito', *Sight and Sound* 9 (2005), pp. 12–14.

Petrovskaja, Katja, 'And He Saw: It Was Good', Roundtable on Alexander Sokurov's film *Russian Ark*, ArtMargins 30 July 2003, http://www.artmargins.com/content/cineview/roundtable.html

Rancière, Jacques, 'Le cinéma comme la peinture?' *Cahiers du cinéma* 531 (January 1999), pp. 30–32.

Ravetto-Biagioli, C., 'Floating on the Borders of Europe: Sokurov's Russian Ark', *Film Quarterly* 59.1 (2005), pp. 18–25.

Schlegel, Hans-Joachim 'Transtsendentnost' autentichnogo: O dokumental'nom u Andreia Tarkovskogo i Aleksandra Sokurova', *Kinovedcheskie zapiski* 49 (2000), pp. 180–84.

Schmid, Ulrich, 'The Empire Strikes Back: Sukorov takes Revenge on de Custine', *ArtMargins*, 30 July 2003, http://www.artmargins.com/content/cineview/roundtable.html

Sokurov, Aleksandr, '"Glavnym iskusstvom po-prezhnemu ostaetsia literatura..." Obsuzhdenie fil'ma "Kamen'", organizovannoe redaktsiei zhurnala "Seans" (25 iiunia 1991 goda, Sankt-Peterburg),' *Kinovedcheskie zapiski* 23 (1994), pp. 65–75.

Sokurov, Aleksandr, 'Death, the Banal Leveller (on Tarkovsky)', *Film Studies* 1 (1999), pp. 64–69.

Sokurov, Aleksandr, 'Izobrazhenie i montazh. Besedu vedet Dmitrii Savel'ev', *Iskusstvo kino* 12 (1997), pp. 110–123.

Sokurov, Aleksandr, 'Pogranichnaia zona', *Seans* 32 (2007), p. 118.

Sokurov, Aleksandr, 'Tvorcheskii al'favit', *Kinograf* 3 (1997), pp. 72–94.

Szaniawski, Jeremi, 'Historical Space in Sokurov's *Moloch*, *Taurus*, and *The Sun*', *Studies in Russian and Soviet Cinema* 1.2 (2007), pp. 147–62.

Totaro, Donato, 'Staring into the Soul: Aleksandr Sokurov's *Povinnost*'', *Central European Review* 2.3 (24 January 2000), http://www.ce-review.org/00/3/kinoeye3_totaro.html

Ustiugova, E. (ed.), *Aleksandr Sokurov na filosofskom fakul'tete*, St Petersburg: Izdatel'stvo Sankt-Peterburgskogo filosofskogo obshchestva, 2001.

INDEX

Bold page numbers for images of the relevant film. Russian film titles in brackets. References in endnotes are marked with 'n' and follow the Library of Congress system.

Abbado, Claudio 101, 102
Agamben, Giorgio 111, 121n
Akhmatova, Anna 224, 244n
Alexandra (Aleksandra) 2, 5, 6, 7, 74, 87, 89n, 105, 109, **110**, 111, 119, **190**, 191, **193**, 194, **195**, 197
Almodovar, Pedro; *Talk to Her* 167
Ananishnov, Alexei 4
And Nothing More (I nichego bol'she) 21, 111, 235, 237, 238
Andropov, Yuri 16, 98, 216
Anninsky, Lev 95
Antonioni, Michelangelo, *L'Avventura* 216
Arabov, Yuri 4, 7, 10, 60, 71n, 76, 83, 88n, 89n, 93, 119, 192, 203–06
Aranovich, Semen 223, 224
Aristotle 117
Arnaud, Diane 10n, 25, 27n
Aronson, Oleg 18, 26n
Auschwitz 6, 19, 126, 134
Avant-garde 36, 43, 53, 54, 138, 141, 223, 233

Bach, Johann Sebastian 19, 209
Bakhtin, Mikhail 140, 152n
Balabanov, Alexei, *Cargo 200* 80
Baranov, Alexander 216
Barthes, Roland 38, 42n, 159, 162, 163, 173n
Baudelaire, Charles 156
Baudouin, Count 183
Bazin, André 18, 44, 54n, 55n, 160, 171
Beatles 16; John Lennon and Paul MacCartney 205
Beethoven, Ludwig 45

Benjamin, Walter 3, 10n, 44, 54n, 123, 156, 191, 196, 197, 198n, 199n
Bergson, Henri 72n, 148
Bernstein, Leonard 224
Bolshoi Theatre 102, 106n
Bondarchuk, Sergei 102, 175n
Bormann, Martin 124–26, 134, 140, 142–44, 239
Bosch, Hieronymus 159
Braun, Eva 111, 124–26, 129, 131, 136n, 141–44, 188, 190, 239, 240
Brecht, Bertolt 242
Breughel, Pieter 95, 157, 159, 231
Brezhnev, Leonid 16, 35, 80, 98, 209, 228, 237
Briullov, Karl 179
Bulgakov, Mikhail 218
Buñuel, Luis, *Land Without Bread* 9, 233
Burimsky, Alexander, *Thoughts about the Hero* 98
Büttner, Tilman 160, 161, 164–68, 170, 171, 173n, 174n, 176

Call Sign R1NN (Pozyvnye R1NN) 15
Canetti, Elias 156, 171n
Canova, Antonio 179, 183
Cardi, Lodovico 183
Caspian Sea 77, 84
Central Committee (CC) 127, 145
Chagall, Marc 221
Chaliapin, Fedor 20, 29, 37, 40, 42n, 90, 192, 234, 235, 236
Chaplin, Charlie 111, 131, 149; *The Great Dictator* 241
Chechnya (Chechen) 74, 110, 190, 191, 194

Chekhov, Anton 112, 204, 235
Cherubini, Luigi 209
Chesnakov, Pavel 159, 160
Chkheidze, Rezo, *Father of a Soldier* 110
Churchill, Winston 238
Čiurlionis, Mikalojus 36, 55n, 227, 244n
Civil War 96, 217
Cocteau, Jean 232
Cold War 102
Communist Party (CPSU) 16
Confession (Povinnost') [Service] 21, 22, 24, 27n, 42n, 74
Coppola, Francis Ford 240
Custine, Astolphe Marquis de 6, 34, 146, 161, 169, 171, 178–85, 187n

Dante, *Divine Comedy* 61; *Inferno* 69
Darwin, Charles 122
Days of Eclipse (Dni zatmeniia) 2, **4**, 74–83, **84**, 85–89, 117, 197, 198n, 203, 204, 207, 208, 210, 214, 229, 230, 232, 239
De Quincey, Thomas 156
Degraded, The (Razzhalovannyi) 75
Deleuze, Gilles 49, 54n, 55n, 65, 66, 72n
Dickens, Charles 242
Dobrotvorsky, Sergei 9, 226–33
dolce... (nezhno...) 42n, 193
Dolci, Carlo 183
Dostoevsky, Fedor 42n, 91, 213, 219, 242n
Double vision 2, 16, 17, 21
Dreiden, Sergei 6, 161, 178
Dürer, Albrecht 48
Dzerzhinsky, Felix 235

Earthliest of Concerns, The (Samye zemnye zaboty) 14, 15
EFA (European Film Academy) 166, 167, 174n, 186
Eisenstein, Sergei 44, 49, 55n, 147, 176, 242; *Strike* 71n, 218, 237; *October* 157, 175n, 176; *Potemkin* 80, 157, 176, 216; *Ivan the Terrible* 173n
El Greco 179, 184
Elegy 2, 3, 29–32, 35, 40, 41, 90, 155, 194
Elegy (Elegiia) 29, 37, 192
Elegy from Russia (Elegiia iz Rossii) 42n, 214, 242n
Elegy of a Voyage (Elegiia dorogi) 193

Elegy of Life. Rostropovich. Vishnevskaya (Elegiia zhizni. Rostropovich. Vishnevskaia) 29, 39, 40, 41, 55n
Eliade, Mircea 70, 73n
Engels, Friedrich 240
Evening Sacrifice, The (Zhertva vecherniaia) 15, 16, 46, **47**, 158, **159**, 160, 162, 170, 236
Example of Intonation, An (Primer intonatsii) 42n, 236, 238

Fassbinder, Rainer Werner 240
Father and Son (Otets i syn) 2, 5, 75, 105, 109, 110, 111, 114, 116, **118**, 120, 147, 191, 198n, 241
Fellini, Federico 42n, 186, 218, 234
Filmmakers' Union 76
First World War 75, 220, 239
Flaubert, Gustave 1, 74, 114
Florensky, Pavel 140, 148, 152n
Freud, Sigmund 117, 160, 172n
Friedrich, Caspar David 51, 115, 121n

Gaudí, Antoni 229, 244n
Gerghiev, Valeri 160, **161**, 164, 178, 185
German, Alexei 90, 189, 219
Glasnost 79, 99, 242n
Glazunov, Ilya 169, 175n
Glinka, Mikhail 31, 178, 181
Godard, Jean-Luc 142
Goebbels, Joseph 124–26, 134, 140, 143, 239
Gorbachev, Mikhail 35, 36, 48, 80, 228, 242n
Gorky, Maxim 235
Goskino 76
Gotzkowski, Johann 182
Greenaway, Peter 233
Griboedov, Alexander 171, 178
Griffith, D. W., 242; *Birth of a Nation* 216
Guerra, Tonino 41
GULag 24

Hegel, Georg Friedrich 139, 140, 148, 152n
Heraclitian (metaphor) 60–2, 65
Hermitage 6, 42n, 52, 53, 146, 155, 156, 160, 161, 163, 164, 167, 173n, 176–85

Hirohito, Emperor 1, 5, 6, 74, 75, 111, 122, 130–35, 136n, 137n, 138–41, 148–51, 188, 190, 238, 242
Hitchcock, Alfred, *Rope* 169
Hitler, Adolf 1, 5, 8, 19, 20, 74, 111, 116, 122, 124, 125–27, 129–45, 148, 188–90, 220, 221, 238, 239, 240, 242
Hobbes, Thomas 157
Hollywood 46, 54
Horace 82, 89n
Hubert Robert. A Fortunate Life (Rober. Schastlivaia zhizn') 42n, 52, 186, 193
Humble Life, A (Smirennaia zhizn') 29, **38**, 39, 40, 193

Jakobson, Roman 192
Jameson, Fredric 26n, 75, 78, 88n, 89n, 135n, 138, 140, 145, 151n, 152n, 187n, 199n

Kalatozishvili, Mikhail, *Wild Field* 87
Kamenev, Lev 145, 241
Kaplevich, Pavel 104
Khanin, Yuri 75, 207, 209
Khaniutin, Yuri 8
Khmelnitsky, Oleg 179, 183
Khutsiev, Marlen; *Ilyich Gates* 98
Kierkegard, Søren 117, 121n
Knot, The: Dialogues with Solzhenitsyn (Uzel: Besedy s Solzhenitsynym) 42n, 98
Kovalov, Oleg 8, 27n, 55n, 92, 96, 105n, 106n, 172n, 216–19
Kracauer, Siegfried 155, 156, 171n
Krasnovodsk 76, 77, 208
Kristeva, Julia 99, 106n
Krupskaya, Nadezhda 127, 129, 141, 145, 147, 240
Kuleshov, Lev 44
Kulidzhanov, Lev 238
Kuper, Yuri 103, 104
Kurenkova, Tamara 179, 184

Lacan, Jacques 114, 116, 117, 118, 163
Landsbergis, Vytautas 1, 29, 36, 41n, 55n, 192, 227, 238, 244n
Lang, Fritz; *Metropolis* 9, 233
Last Day of a Rainy Summer, The (Poslednii den' nenastnogo leta) 15
LeBon, Gustave 156, 171n
Lenfilm 93, 216, 238

Lenin, Vladimir 1, 5, 16, 35, 48, 50, 74, 80, 85, 111, 112, 122, 126, 127, 129, 130, 134, 135, 136n, 138–41, 144–48, 157, 188–90, 234, 240, 242; Leninism 46
Lenin Prize 224, 243n
Leningrad Siege 40, 75, 179
Leviathan 112, 157
Lévi-Bruhl, Lucien 120, 121n
Listov, Viktor 2, 16, 17, 26n, 55n
Little man 10
Lonely Voice of Man, The (Odinokii golos cheloveka) 2, 4, 9, 25, 27n, 59–62, **63**, 64–66, **67**, **69**, 70, 71, 92, 92, 96, 97, 203, 205, 216–19, 228–30, 237, 238
Losev, Alexei 140, 152n
Lumière (Brothers) 47
Lutsik, Petr 87
Lyde-Brown, John 183

MacArthur, Douglas 130–36, 140, 141, 148, 149
Mahler, Gustav 213
Majdanek 19
Maltese, Francesco 183
Mamardashvili, Merab 217, 243n
Mann, Thomas 217
Marey, Etienne-Jules 2
Maria. Peasant Elegy (Mariia: Krest'ianskaia elegiia) 9, 15, **17**, 18, 21, **29**, 30–2, 75, 93, 234, 236, 237
Mariinsky (Kirov) Theatre 101, 102, 160, 178
Marker, Chris 42n, 98, 101, 106n
Marx, Karl 97, 140, 240; Marxism 46
May Day 15, 16, 46, 158
Medvedev, Armen 238
Medvedkin, Alexander *New Moscow* 9, 233
Messiaen, Olivier 21, 45
Mieris, Frans 184
Mikhalkov-Konchalovsky, Andrei 230
Minimalism 3, 7, 10, 35, 36, 43, 44, 46, 50, 54, 241
Modernism 53, 124, 240,
Moloch, The (Molokh) 2, 7, 74, 91, 111, 116, 121n, 122, 123, **124**, 126, 1277, 29, 133, 134, 135n, **141**, **143**, 144, 145, 147, 188, 189, 198n, 238, 239, 241
Molotov, Viacheslav 145, 241
Montferrand, Auguste de 179

Moscow Elegy (Moskovskaia elegiia) 16, 20, 29, 40, 92, 97–100, 192, 226, 227, 234, 236
Moskvin, Ivan 223, 224, 243n
Moskvina, Tatiana 80, 88n, 89n
Mother and Son (Mat' i syn) 2, 5, 10, 50, **51**, 52, 56n, 75, 91, 109, 110, 114–6, 147, 191, 193, 198n, 239
Mournful Unconcern (Skorbnoe beschuvstvie) 7, 9, 75, 193, 203, 205, 207, 208, 212, 215, 223, 230, 235–38, 240, 242
Mozart, Wolfgang Amadeus 21, 22, 45
Mozgovoy, Leonid 139
Mravitsky, Yevgeni 224, 244n
Mulvey, Laura 142
Mussorsky, Modest 101–3; *Boris Godunov* 92
Muybridge, Eadweard 2

Nazism, Nazi 19, 143, 144, 220, 221, 238, 241
Niyazov, Saparmurat 77
Nostalgia 81, 84, 90, 91, 97, 100, 101, 158, 170, 226

Obersalzberg 74; Kehlsteinhaus 124, 140; Berghof 125
Oedipal 5, 109, 110, 116, 117, 121n
Offenbach, Jean Jacques 75, 208
Ogata, Issei 130, 139
Oistrakh, David 225, 244n
Olesha, Yuri 218
On the Events in Transcaucasia (K sobytiiam v Zakavkaz'e) 99, 238
Orbeli, Hovsep 178, 185
Oriental Elegy (Vostochnaia elegiia) 39, 193
Orthodoxy 16, 95, 117, 140
Osipenko, Alla 179, 184
Ostranenie 133
Ovchinnikov, Viacheslav 98

Pabst, G.W. *Don Quichotte* 37, 42n
Pasolini, Pier-Paolo 229
Pasternak, Boris 91, 105
Patience. Labour (Terpenie. Trud) 15, 237
Pearl Harbor 6, 132, 149
Penderecki, Krzysztof 20
Perestroika 21, 79, 223
Persov, Vladimir 7, 206–12

Petersburg Elegy (Peterburgskaia elegiia) 20, 29, 37, 42n, 192, 227, 234, 235, 236
Petrov-Vodkin, Kuzma 95, 106n, 152n
Pichul, Vasili 216
Piotrovsky, Boris 179, 185
Piotrovsky, Mikhail 179, 185
Plakhov, Andrei 9, 10, 237–42
Platonov, Andrei 1, 4, 8, 59–63, 66–8, 70, 71, 92, 93, 95–7, 105n, 216–19, 228, 229, 237, 243n, 244n
Poe, Edgar Allen 156
Polanski, Roman, *The Pianist* 167
Politburo 35, 230, 235
Potudan 4, 59–68, 70, 92
Proskurina, Svetlana 168
Proust, Marcel 66
Pudovkin, Vsevolod 175n, 219; *End of St. Petersburg* 170; *Simple Case* 219
Pushkin, Alexander 161
Putin, Vladimir 169, 170

Quarenghi, Giacomo 179
Quintilian 192

Rancière, Jacques 91, 105n
Rastrelli, Franscesco 182
Red Army 18, 161
Rembrandt, Harmenszoon van Rijn 184
Resnais, Alain, *Hiroshima mon amour* 65
Riefenstahl, Leni, *Triumph des Willens* 157
Riffaterre, Michael 59, 71n
Robert. Hubert 52, 53, 104
Romanov (dynasty) 178, 182, 185
Romm, Mikhail 8, 19, 220; *Ordinary Fascism* 8, 19, 220, 221
Roosevelt, Franklin D. 238
Rosenstone, Robert 5, 10n, 123, 134, 135n
Rostropovich, Mstislav 1, 20, 29, 39, 41
Rubens, Peter Paul 184, 229
Russian Ark (Russkii kovcheg) 1, 2, 6, 7, 10, 20, 25, 34, 75, 87, 90, 98, 120, 135n, 139, 146, 155–75 [**161, 165, 170**], 176–87 [**178, 182, 186**], 188, 189, 241
Ruttman, Walter, *Berlin, Symphony of a Great City* 157
Rykov, Nikolai 241

Samoriadov, Alexei 87
Save and Protect [*Madame Bovary*], (Spasi i sokhrani) 3, 74, 114, **115**, 193, 203, 207, 209, 210, 213, 214, 228, 232, 239
Schnittke, Alfred 31, 75
Schumann, Robert 75, 208
Second Circle, The (Krug vtoroi) 5, 7, 75, 91, 109, 112, **113**, 114, 197, 198n, 203, 204, 229, 230, 231, 232, 233
Second World War 3, 43, 65, 75, 161, 235
Semenova, Leda 7, 10, 212–15
Shakespeare, William 8, 243n
Shaw, George Bernard 1, 9, 75, 229, 242, 244n
Shemiakin, Andrei 86, 89n
Shepitko, Larisa 95
Shermergor, Evgeni 216
Shevardnadze, Eduard 35
Shostakovich, Dmitri 8, 20, 98, 211, 223–5, 243n, 244n
Sigle, Andrei
Simmel, Georg 156
Simple Elegy, A (Prostaia elegiia) 29, 36, 55n, 192, 227, 228, 238
Sivash Lake 65, 66
Snow, Michael, *Wave Length* 53
Socialist Realism 46
Solzhenitsyn, Alexander 1, 217
Sonata 3, 20, 220
Sonata for Hitler (Sonata dlia Gitlera) 8, 15, 18, 19, 20, 21, 220, **221**, **222**, 223, 238
Sonata for Viola. Dmitri Shostakovich (Dmitrii Shostakovich: Al'tovaia sonata) 8, 20, 21, 42n, 98, 223, 237
Sontag, Susan 138, 151n
Soviet Elegy (Sovetskaia elegiia) 9, 20, 29, 33, **34**, 35, 36, 40, 42n, 47, 49, 50, 74, 114, 192, 211, 227, 228, 234, 235
Spiritual Voices (Dukhovnye golosa) 21, **22**, 23, 42n, 45, 74, 87, 111, 239
St. Petersburg Diary: Inauguration of a Monument to Dostoevsky (Peterburgskii dnevnik: Otkrytie pamiatnika Dostoevskomu) 42n
St. Petersburg Diary: Kozintsev's Apartment (Peterburgskii dnevnik: Kvartira Kozintseva) 42n
St. Petersburg Diary: Mozart. Requiem (Peterburgskii dnevnik: Motsart. Rekviem) 42n

Stalin Prize 8, 223
Stalin, Iosif 48, 84, 126, 127, 134, 141, 145, 146, 238, 240
Stalingrad (Battle of) 19, 126
Stanzione, Massimo 179, 183
Stasov, Vasili 179
Stone, The (Kamen') 114, 115, 198n, 203, 204, 205, 232, 233, 235
Strugatsky, Boris and Arkadi 1, 75, 76, 88
Styx 62
Sun, The (Solntse) 2, **7**, 74, 75, 103, 111, 122–24, 126, 128, 129, **130**, **132**, 133–135, 144, 148, 149, **150**, 151, 174n, 188, 190, 193, 198n, 238, 241, 242
Suslov, Mikhail 35

Tarkovsky, Andrei 4, 8, 9, 16, 18, 29, 32–34, 40, 41, 42n, 44, 54, 59, 60, 64, 65, 69, 70, 71, 72n, 88, 90, 92, 93, 95–105, 106n, 138, 176, 192, 218, 226, 229, 234, 236–38, 239, 240; *Andrei Rublev* 95, 238; *Boris Godunov* 5, 101–4; *Ivan's Childhood* 98; *Mirror* 8, 42n, 59, 60, 64–66, 69, 70, 72n, 92, 93, 95, 96, 97, 98, 217, 218; *Nostalgia* 42n, 98, 100, 102; *Sacrifice* 42n, 98, 99, 100, 101, 102, 226; *Solaris* 95, 99; *Stalker* 88, 99; *Tempo di Viaggio* 98, 100, 105
Tarkovsky, Arseni 33, 61, 65
Taurus (Telets) 2, 7, 74, 75, 87, 111, 122–24, 126, **128**, 129–35, 144–45, **146**, 147–48, 174n, 188, 189, 198n, 238, 240, 241
Tenerani, Pietro 179, 184
Third Reich 19, 238
Thompson, Kristin 146, 152n, 162, 173n
Tintoretto 183
Tolstoy, Lev 102
Toqueville, Alexis de 180
Trofimenkov, Mikhail 9, 78, 79, 88n, 89n, 233–37
Trotsky, Leon 145, 217, 235, 241
Tumaev, Vladimir 216
Turovskaya, Maya 8, 19, 26n, 42n, 55n, 78, 80, 88n, 89n, 220–23
Tykwer, Tom, *Run Lola Run* 174n

Van Dyck, Anthony 184
Vertov, Dziga 16, 44, 176
VGIK (Film Institute) 8, 92, 93, 216, 217, 219, 238

Vigo, Jean 233
Visconti, Luchino 240, 241
Vishnevskaya, Galina 1, 20, 29, 39, 40, 41
Von Brühl, Heinrich 182
Von Klenze, Leo 179
Voronikhin, Andrei 183

Wagner, Richard 111, 240, 241
Walpole, Robert 182
Warhol, Andy 8, 21, 53; *Empire* 53
We Read the Book of the Blockade (Chitaem blokadnuiu knigu) 75, 177, 185

Whispering Pages (Tikhie stranitsy) 2, 91, 114, 205, 213, 214, 233, 242n
White, Hayden 5, 123, 134, 135n

Yeliseev, Lev 179, 183
Yeltsin, Boris 1, 9, 29, 33–36, 40, 42n, 47–9, 74, 90, 114, 192, 228, 234, 235, 238, 239
Yurizditsky, Sergei 93, 106n

Zamiatin, Yevgeni 218
Zervuducki, Cécile 3, 209
Žižek, Slavoj 72–3n, 163

www.ingramcontent.com/pod-product-compliance
Ingram Content Group UK Ltd.
Pitfield, Milton Keynes, MK11 3LW, UK
UKHW021905220326
469204UK00008B/198